The Modern World

TONY LANCASTER & DEREK PEAPLE

CPL

CAUSEWAY PRESS LTD

Dedication   *Tony Lancaster:*   To Jane, Stephen, Sarah, Lisa, Ruth and Maisie.
                    Derek Peaple: To Jackie, Dorothy and Len.

Acknowledgements

Cover design: Caroline Waring-Collins (Waring Collins Partnership)

Cover photo: Celebrations at the Brandenburg Gate in Berlin on 3 October 1990 to mark the reunification of Germany.
                         Reproduced by kind permission of Topham Picturepoint.

Page design: Caroline Waring-Collins (Waring Collins Partnership)

Original graphics: Elaine Sumner (Waring Collins Partnership)

Cartoons: Brick

Original photograph: James Pass (p.235b)

Reader: Mary Walton

Thanks to George Fabry for his help on p.204.

Thanks to the pupils of Oxted County School for testing material in this book.

Picture credits

Advertising Archives 91b, 93, 95b; Associated Press 197, 207t; Bayerische Staatsbibliothek 73b; BFI Stills, Posters and Designs 97b, 183; Brick 180, 188; Mary Evans Picture Library 21br, 50b; Sally & Richard Greenhill 228, 231, 233m, 234t, 234b; Hulton Getty 2tl, 6, 10, 14b, 50t, 52t, 53t, 92l, 95t, 96tr, 96b, 97t, 106t, 116bl, 132b, 153t, 159tl, 211t, 222t, 232t; Imperial War Museum 2bl, 7bl, 13t, 18t, 19, 20b, 22bl, 25, 45b, 158, 159tr, 160t; David King Collection 16, 26tr, 26b, 28tr, 29t, 29b, 33b, 34, 35m, 35b, 36t, 37, 39tl, 40, 41m, 119l, 120t, 124b, 125r, 127b, 130, 131tr, 131l, 133tl, 201tl; Moro Roma 64br; Peter Newark's Historical Pictures 14t, 23b, 44, 53b, 159b, 190, 191t, 218tr, 221, 229, 230, 233b; Peter Newark's Military Pictures 2br, 2tr, 8b, 11, 13b, 17, 18b, 20t, 22ml, 61t, 64bl, 69tl, 154b, 189; Peter Newark's American Pictures 86tl, 86ml, 86tr, 86bl, 88, 91tl, 94t, 96tl, 98, 102tr, 103b, 104tr, 105t, 105b, 164, 182tr, 185t; Novosti (London) 26tl, 31, 199tl; James Pass p.235b; Popperfoto 2bl, 7br, 8tr, 12, 99, 100, 109r, 137, 141t, 142t, 173l, 184t, 184b, 192, 202, 204, 205t, 207b, 219t, 219b, 232b, 233t, 235t; Punch 9, 46, 48, 73, 170, 173r; Rex Features 23t; SCR Photo Library 30t, 33t, 41t, 41b, 125tl, 125bl, 199tr, 209b, 213b; Topham Picturepoint 4, 8tl, 15, 24b, 91tr, 102tl, 111, 117b, 151br, 155t, 165t, 225; Ullstein Bilderdienst 49t, 61b, 63b, 67r, 69b, 75t, 81b, 82; Weimar Archive 60, 62b, 64t, 68, 69tr, 70, 71t, 72t, 72b, 75b, 76b, 84l, 84r; Wiener Library 51, 62t, 76, 79t, 83.

Every effort has been made to locate the copyright owners of material used in this book. Any omissions brought to our attention are regretted and will be credited in subsequent printings.

Causeway Press Ltd
PO Box 13, Ormskirk, Lancashire, L39 5HP

© Tony Lancaster and Derek Peaple 1996

1st impression 1996

British Library Cataloguing in Publication Data - a catalogue record for this book is available from the British Library.

ISBN 1 873929 05 6

Origination and layout by Caroline Waring-Collins (Waring Collins Partnership), Ormskirk, Lancashire L39 2YT

Printed and bound by Jarrold Book Printing Ltd, Thetford, Norfolk

CONTENTS

Themes

The First World War was not like previous wars. It was different for four main reasons. First, it involved more countries than previous wars. Although it began as a conflict between European countries, these countries drew support from their allies and colonies overseas. By 1918, troops from the Middle East, Africa, Asia, North America and Australasia had fought in the war. Second, new technology ensured that the war was fought in a new way. On the Western Front, for example, defence proved easier than attack and, after a short war of movement, troops became bogged down in trenches. This stalemate lasted for three years and resulted in huge casualties as each side tried to make a decisive breakthrough. Third, the war was fought on land, sea and air (air warfare was new). And fourth, the First World War affected the lives of civilians more

than had been the case in previous wars (civilians worked hard to keep the war effort going and some fell victim to bombing raids and enemy bombardment). This chapter examines the nature of the First World War both on the battleground and at home in Britain. It examines the following questions.

* Why did war break out in 1914?
* Why was the war not over by Christmas 1914?
* What were the effects of the military deadlock on the Western Front?
* How important was the war in the air and the war at sea?
* What was the significance of the war on other fronts?
* How was the military deadlock on the Western Front broken?
* How did World War I change life in Britain?
* How was propaganda used by the British government?

Key Events

1914 |———**War of movement**➤|——**1915**——**Deadlock**————➤

28 June 1914 Archduke Franz Ferdinand (above) is assassinated in Sarajevo. First step on the road to war in August.

4 August 1914 Outbreak of the war. The German army sweeps into France via Belgium, following the Schlieffen plan.

5-10 Sept 1914 Battle of the Marne. British and French troops stop the advance of the German army.

Sept-Nov 1914 Race to the Sea. By November 1914 both sides had established positions opposite each other. For the next four years, these positions hardly changed.

Allied troops landing in Gallipoli in April 1915 (left). The Gallipoli campaign began in February 1915.

1916 Deadlock continues on Western Front 1917————➤ **1918**

May 1916 Battle of Jutland. The only major naval battle in the war. Result indecisive.

1 July 1916 The Battle of the Somme. On that day the British suffered 57,000 casualties, about 20,000 fatal. The battle lasted until November. Result indecisive.

April 1917 The USA agrees to join the war on the side of the Allies.

November 1917 Bolsheviks seize power in Russia. Russia withdraws from war in March 1918, allowing the Germans to concentrate on a single front.

21 March 1918 The Germans begin an offensive in the west. After some successes, offensive loses its momentum.

8 August 1918 The Allies begin to counter-attack. German resistance is weak and the Allies push the Germans slowly back until the armstice is signed.

11 Nov 1918 The Germans agree to an armistice. The war is over.

The war to end all wars?

1   The costs of war

(i) Casualties and participants

NORWAY

SWEDEN

DENMARK

9,500,000

BRITISH EMPIRE 13,250,000

1,000,000

London HOLLAND

Berlin

GERMANY

Prague

13,000,000 ○ Moscow

RUSSIAN EMPIRE

eastern front

9,000,000

1,700,000

UNITED STATES 1917 3,800,000

116,000

JAPAN 800,000

2,000

AUSTRALIA & NEW ZEALAND 710,000

105,000

100,000

7,222   SPAIN

PORTUGAL

380,000   41,000

BELGIUM

LUX.

western front

8,200,000

Paris ○

FRANCE

1,500,000

1,950,000

Vienna

Budapest

AUSTRIA- HUNGARY

SWITZ.

5,600,000

ITALY 533,000

Sarajevo

1,000,000

50,000

3,000

MONTENEGRO ALBANIA

1,050,000

1,000,000

322,000

SERBIA

GREECE

200,000

5,000

ROMANIA

158,000

950,000

49,000

BULGARIA

Constantinople

TURKEY

Gallipoli

2,850,000

325,000

Central Powers   total armed forces

Allied Powers

neutral states   killed and died as a result of war 1914-1918 (estimated figures)

(ii) The financial cost of the war (all figures in 1000 million German goldmarks)

German Empire	194	
Great Britain and Empire	268	
France	134	
USA	129	
Russia	106	
Austria - Hungary	99	
Italy	63	
Remaining countries	23	
TOTAL:	**956**	

(iii) British weapon production, 1915 and 1917

1915	1917	
369 million	619 million	Bullets
2 million	23 million	Artillery shells
2 million	8 million	Grenades
173,000	325,000	Rifles
1,700	19,000	Machine guns
1,200	2,100	Heavy guns

2   A historian's assessment of the impact of the First World War

The world before war broke out in 1914 was so different from that which emerged at the end of the war that many people refused to see any continuity with the past. 'Peace' meant 'before 1914'. After that came something that no longer deserved the name. This was understandable. In 1914 there had been no major war for a century. That is to say, there had been no war in which all (or even a majority) of the Great Powers had been involved. There had been only one brief war in which more than two Great Powers had been in battle - the Crimean War (1854-56) between Russia on one side and Britain and France on the other. Moreover, wars involving Great Powers had all been comparatively quick. The length of war was measured in months or even in weeks. Between 1871 and 1914, there had been no wars in Europe, though in the Far East Japan fought and beat Russia in 1904-05. There had been no world wars at all. In the 18th century, France and Britain had fought a series of wars whose battlefields ranged from India through Europe to North America and across the world's oceans. Between 1815 and 1914, however, no Great Power fought another outside its immediate region. All this changed in 1914. The First World War involved all the Great Powers. What is more, troops from the world overseas were, often for the first time, sent to fight outside their own regions. Canadians fought in France, for example, and significantly the USA sent men to fight in Europe. Though military action outside Europe was not very significant, the naval war was once again global.

Adapted from 'Age of Extremes' by E. Hobsbawm, 1994

QUESTIONS

1. What does Source 1 tell us about the costs of the First World War?

2. When the First World War was over, it was described as 'the war to end all wars'. Why do you think it was described in this way? Use Sources 1 and 2 in your answer.

3. Judging from Source 2 how did the First World War differ from previous wars?

There is no single reason why war broke out in August 1914. The First World War, like all other wars, was the result of a combination of short-term and long-term factors. Different historians have offered different explanations. Most, however, would agree that the points listed in Box 1.1 were important factors in the outbreak of war.

1 The system of alliances

Allies and associates ☐ Central Powers ☐ Neutral
Neutral, later joining Allies ☐ Neutral, later joining Central Powers

Box 1.1

The origins of World War I

1. The system of alliances.

2. German militarism and fear of encirclement.

3. The Moroccan crises of 1905 and 1911 and the struggle for overseas colonies.

4. The arms race.

5. Austria's seizure of Bosnia in 1908 and the Balkan Wars of 1912-13.

6. The assassination of Archduke Ferdinand on 28 June 1914.

7. The German invasion of Belgium on 3 August 1914.

Following Germany's victory over France in 1871 (the Franco-Prussian war), the balance of power in Europe changed. In 1879, Germany and Austria-Hungary signed a secret treaty promising to protect each other if either were invaded. In 1882, Italy joined this alliance. To counter this **Triple Alliance**, France and Russia signed a treaty of alliance in 1894. In 1894, Britain's policy was to refuse to make alliances with anyone (**Splendid Isolation**). Ten years later, however, the growth of the German navy persuaded Britain that Germany was a real military threat. As a result, Britain made an agreement with France - the **Entente Cordiale**. Despite German efforts to break this Entente, it survived to 1914. Indeed, it was strengthened in 1907 when Britain and Russia signed an agreement. By 1914, therefore, the Great Powers in Europe were divided into two camps (known as the 'Allies' or 'Allied Powers' and the 'Central Powers'). Although the aim of these alliances was to keep the peace, in fact they ensured that the Great Powers became involved in the First World War.

2 German militarism and fears of encirclement

This cartoon shows Kaiser William II in the bath. It was produced in Britain in 1914.

German militarism

William II became Kaiser (German Emperor) in 1888. He was obsessed with military matters. According to the historian Gordon Craig, William spent the first 26 years of his reign 'playing at soldiers'. Military dress became an obsession with him. He wore it whenever possible. Wherever he went, he was surrounded by crowds of men in uniform and he preferred military companions, manners, and advice to any other. This gave the impression that Germany was set on military expansion.

Fears of encirclement

The gradual drawing together of France, Russia and Britain meant that German leaders became concerned about being faced with hostile powers on three sides. Between 1897 and 1905, General Schlieffen, the German Chief of Staff, worked on a plan to knock France out of a war very quickly. This plan relied on the bulk of the German army attacking France through Belgium (see p.8). Since the plan relied on an element of surprise, its success partly depended on the Germans striking before France and Russia were fully prepared for war.

③ The Moroccan crises

The first Moroccan crisis, 1905

One of the main deals made in the Entente Cordiale was that, in return for a free hand in Egypt, the British would support a French move into Morocco (Morocco was ruled by a Sultan who relied on French support). The first test of this agreement came in March 1905. The German foreign ministry persuaded the Kaiser (who was on a Mediterranean cruise) to visit Tangier in Morocco. In Tangier, the Kaiser said that he regarded the Sultan as an independent ruler and that he intended to protect Germany's trading interests in Morocco. This was a direct challenge to French interests. It seems that Germany had two main aims. First, Germany hoped that the British would refuse to support France in the crisis which was sure to follow. Second, Germany wanted to demonstrate that it intended to enlarge its overseas empire (which was smaller than that of Britain and France). In the crisis which followed, war between France and Germany was threatened. It was avoided, however, when all parties agreed to an international conference. At this conference (held in Algeciras in January 1906), Germany was isolated. With British support, France was given control of Morocco.

The second Moroccan crisis, 1911

In 1911, the Sultan asked for French help in putting down a rebellion. French troops were sent from Algeria to Fez, Morocco's capital. The German government demanded that these troops be withdrawn. Two months later, a German gunboat was sent to Agadir, a Moroccan port. Officially, the boat was sent to protect Germans from internal disorders there. In reality, the German government hoped to blackmail the French into giving up some of their colonies elsewhere in return for German recognition of French control of Morocco. As in 1905, there was the danger of war. The British government thought the Germans aimed to set up a naval base at Agadir. As in 1906, Germany had to back down and relations between Britain and France were strengthened.

④ The arms race

In the 19th century, Britain had built up a large navy to protect its interests around the world. In 1900, no other country could seriously challenge Britain's naval superiority. In that year, however, William II declared: 'Just as my grandfather reorganised his army, I shall unswervingly complete the task of reorganising my navy so that it shall be in a position internationally to win for Germany that place which we have yet to achieve.' In the early years of the 20th century, the Germans poured money into their navy. When Britain produced a new, improved warship in 1906, *HMS Dreadnought*, it seemed that Britain's naval superiority would be secure, but the Germans designed a similar ship and an arms race began. Each side tried to outproduce the other.

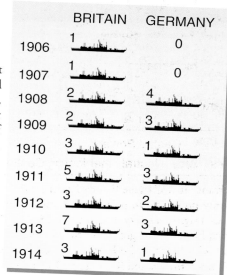

	BRITAIN	GERMANY
1906	1	0
1907	1	0
1908	2	4
1909	2	3
1910	3	1
1911	5	3
1912	3	2
1913	7	3
1914	3	1

Number of dreadnoughts built each year in Britain and Germany.

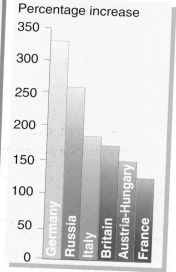

Spending on arms, 1872-1912.

⑤ The Balkans

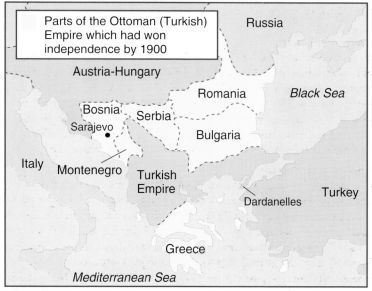

Parts of the Ottoman (Turkish) Empire which had won independence by 1900

The Balkans in 1900.

Although the Turkish Empire had once covered most of the Balkans, Greece, Serbia, Montenegro, Romania and Bulgaria had won their independence by 1900 (see map, left). This resulted in growing political tension since Serbia hoped to unite all Slav people in a single, larger Serbia whilst Austria-Hungary was determined to prevent this (not least because many Slavs lived in Austria-Hungary). In 1908, the Austrian army occupied Bosnia. Serbia appealed to its ally Russia. When Germany promised to support Austria, however, Russia was forced to back down. In 1912, Serbia, Greece, Montenegro and Bulgaria joined together in the 'Balkan League' and drove Turkey out of Europe (the First Balkan War). The system of alliances meant that a general European war would break out if Austria-Hungary declared war on the League. This was avoided by a peace conference. At the conference, Austria prevented Serbia gaining a coastline by creating a new country (Albania), but Serbia increased in size and strength. In June 1913, the Second Balkan War broke out when Bulgaria fell out with the other members of the League. Bulgaria was defeated. Serbia and Greece divided up the land Bulgaria had gained in the First Balkan War.

6 Sarajevo, 28 June 1914

This photograph shows the heir to the Austrian throne, Archduke Franz Ferdinand, and his wife during their visit to the Bosnian capital Sarajevo on 28 June 1914. Later that day, they were assassinated by a Bosnian Serb student, Gavrilo Princip. Princip was a member of the 'Black Hand', an organisation committed to forcing Austria out of Bosnia. Although there was no evidence to link Princip with the Serbian government, the Austrian government used Ferdinand's assassination as an excuse to present Serbia with an ultimatum. When Serbia did not fully meet Austria's terms in this ultimatum, Austria declared war. This started the chain of events which led to an all-out world war (see Box 1.2).

Box 1.2

The July crisis of 1914

For all the talk of war before July 1914, previous crises had not in fact led to violent conflict. The Moroccan crises had involved France and Germany, but Russia had no interest in France's African ambitions and no objection to Germany developing an African empire. The Bosnian crisis of 1908 had been resolved because the Russians knew that they were not yet militarily strong enough to stand up to Germany. In the Balkan Wars, the interests of small states had sometimes come into conflict with those of the Great Powers, but none of the Great Powers was prepared to go to war over the interests of any one Balkan state. So, what was different in July 1914? First, the desire for peace was missing - British attempts to set up a peace conference (like the one which had successfully ended the First Balkan War) were rejected. Second, the crisis of July 1914 rapidly involved all the potential sources of conflict among the Great Powers - Austro-Russian rivalry in the Balkans, Franco-German resentment and distrust, the Anglo-German naval rivalry. And third, the crisis came at a moment which seemed (especially to the Germans) to be one at which the chances of success were greatest.

From 'Europe Since 1870' by J. Joll, 1976

7 Countdown to war

28 June	5 July	14 July	19 July	23 July	28 July
Archduke Franz Ferdinand assassinated in Sarajevo.	Austrian government requests German backing if Austria-Hungary decides to use force against Serbia. German backing was agreed.	Austro-Hungarian government agrees to send ultimatum to Serbia.	Text of ultimatum agreed. If Serbia agrees to the terms, then it will have to give up independence to Austria. If it refuses, then Austria has an excuse to start war.	Ultimatum delivered to Serbia. Serbia agrees to nine out of the ten points.	Austria declares war on Serbia. Serbia appeals to Russia (its ally) for help.

30 July	31 July	1 Aug	2 Aug	3 Aug	4 Aug
Russia mobilises troops (orders them to prepare for war).	Germany sends an ultimatum to Russia, demanding that Russia suspend all warlike measures within 12 hours. Germany also sends an ultimatum to France, demanding that it stay neutral.	After Russia ignores Germany's ultimatum, Germany declares war on Russia. France (Russia's ally) mobilises troops. France also ignores Germany's ultimatum.	Germany demands from Belgium the right to send troops through its territory as part of its campaign against France.	Belgium refuses to allow German troops to cross its borders, but Germany invades Belgium anyway.	Under the 1839 Treaty of London, Britain had promised to guarantee Belgium's neutrality. Britain therefore sends an ultimatum to Germany at 11am giving it 12 hours to withdraw from Belgium. At 11pm Britain declares war on Germany.

Activity

Why did war break out?

Source A *A historian's view (1)*

It is often said that the relations between the Great Powers were especially tense and strained in the early months of 1914. This is totally inaccurate. The truth is the exact reverse. Relations between the Great Powers had never been better. It is difficult, in fact, to discover any cause of hostility between the European Great Powers in the early summer of 1914. But there was one cause of conflict. This was the system of alliances which distanced the Great Powers unnecessarily. These alliances dragged Powers into wars which did not concern them. They were supposed to make for peace, they made for war. They were supposed to make Powers secure, they dragged them into danger.

From 'The entente that ended in slaughter', an article in the 'Guardian' by A.J.P Taylor, 4 August 1984

Source B *Berlin, 9 August 1914*

Exactly what was the cause of war, nobody seems to know, although it is discussed day and night. One thing grows clearer to me every day. Neither the people here nor those in Britain wished for war. But here they are now being carried off their legs with patriotism, at seeing so many enemies on every side. It is said in England that Germany provoked the war. Here, they deny it. To me, it seems that Europe was thirsting for war and that the armies and navies were no longer to be held back.

Extract from 'An English Wife in Berlin', the diary of Evelyn, Princess Blucher, published in 1921. Evelyn and her German husband had travelled to Berlin on 6 August 1914.

Source C *A historian's view (2)*

The Great Powers did not fight because they had different religious or political beliefs. But they feared each other and felt threatened. France feared Germany and remembered the war they had fought 43 years ago (the Franco-Prussian war which ended with a German victory in 1871). Germany was afraid of Russia's military might (Russia was rearming rapidly in 1914). Austria was afraid of losing its empire in the Balkans. Britain felt that its naval power was being threatened by Germany. Each was afraid that their enemies might strike the first blow.

From 'The Twentieth Century' by J. Hamer, 1980

Source D *The 'scrap of paper'*

The Treaty of London, signed by Britain in 1839, included the promise to protect Belgium if it was ever invaded. In August 1914, German leaders gambled that Britain would overlook this treaty (which the German Chancellor described as a 'scrap of paper'). But when German troops marched into Belgium on 3 August, Britain demanded their withdrawal. When Germany ignored the ultimatum, Britain declared war.

Source E *The Entente Cordiale*

This postcard was produced in 1904 to celebrate the new friendship between Britain and France (the Entente Cordiale).

QUESTIONS

1. Judging from the information in this section, why did war break out in 1914?

2. Using Sources A-E make a list of long-term and short-term causes of the war and place them in order of importance.

3. 'The system of alliances was an important cause of World War 1.' Explain this statement using Sources A, C, D and E. Explain how historians might have reached this conclusion.

4. What does Source B tell us about people's views at the time the First World War broke out?

Why was the war not over by Christmas 1914?

When war broke out in August 1914, most people on both sides expected it to be over quickly. Few could imagine it lasting beyond Christmas 1914. Yet, by Christmas 1914, neither side had made a decisive breakthrough and it was clear that no immediate end to the war was in sight. So, what had gone wrong? Historians argue that there were three main reasons why the war was not over by Christmas 1914. First, the Schlieffen plan failed. Second, military leaders on both sides made mistakes. And third, defence proved to be easier than attack.

① The Schlieffen plan

The aim of the Schlieffen plan was to knock France out of the war within a few weeks, leaving the Germans free to fight the Russians in the east. Schlieffen planned to surprise the French with a daring pincer movement. The main part of the German army (the right wing) would make a surprise attack from the north via Belgium, whilst a much smaller force (the left wing) would fight the main French army further south. After sweeping

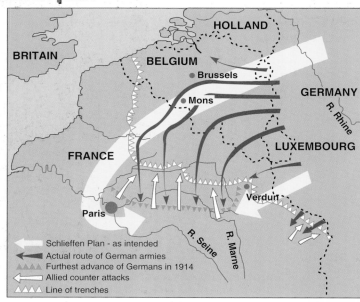

through northern France and capturing Paris, the right wing would then come up behind the main French army and crush it. Schlieffen argued that the right wing should have eight times as many troops as the left wing. He also worked out a detailed timetable. The whole operation was supposed to take 42 days. When war broke out in 1914, however, Schlieffen's successor, Moltke, had made small but significant changes to the plan (see Box 1.3).

Box 1.3

Why did the Schlieffen plan fail?

1. Moltke, the German Commander, altered the balance of forces so that the right wing had only three times as many troops as the left. Since the right wing was smaller, it advanced more slowly than had been planned.

2. There was more resistance from the Belgian army and then from British and French forces than had been expected. This slowed down the right wing and allowed the British and French forces to retreat and then to counter-attack.

3. The Russians surprised the Germans by attacking in the east. Moltke further weakened the right wing by sending troops to fight the Russians.

4. Troops marched more than 30 km every day and, by early September, were exhausted. German supply lines became stretched and central command (based in Luxembourg) became increasingly out of touch.

② The military leaders

The German commander Helmuth von Moltke (top left) was over-cautious. By altering the balance of his forces, he made it less likely that the Schlieffen plan would succeed. The French commander, Joseph Joffre (top right), made the mistake of sending the main French army to attack Alsace-Lorraine. The Germans were expecting this and the French army suffered heavy losses. This also left France's northern flank exposed to German attack. Further, although Joffre restored his reputation by winning the Battle of the Marne (see Box 1.4), the historian A.J.P. Taylor argues that Joffre missed several opportunities to win a more decisive victory over the Germans. The British commander, Sir John French (bottom), was a veteran cavalry officer. He found it difficult to work with Joffre. The historian J.M. Winter claims: 'Like other cavalry men, he was puzzled by the nature of the war in 1914-15.' All three commanders were men in their 60s. They made decisions at headquarters far from where the fighting was taking place, often on old or inaccurate information.

③ The nature of the war

The First World War was not like previous wars. It soon became clear that defence was easier than attack. One reason for this was the development of new small arms. The first machine gun, the Gatling gun, had been invented in the 1860s, but it was large and heavy. Smaller, lighter machine guns had been invented by 1914. Even if they did not have machine guns, soldiers in 1914 had guns which could fire repeated shots quickly. This changed the nature of warfare. Attacking armies tended to race at the enemy on foot. This made it easy for defenders to shoot down the massed ranks of attackers. Second, armies in 1914 made use of railways. Even if attackers were able to break through, the defending army could transport reinforcements to a new position by rail. Since the attacking army was moving on foot, the reinforcements could find a good defensive position for themselves before the attackers arrived. And third, armies in 1914 had better artillery (big guns and cannons) than in previous wars. That meant they could fire on an enemy which was some distance away.

Box 1.4 — The battle of the Marne and its consequences

The Schlieffen plan nearly succeeded. Between 4 August and 5 September, the German army advanced through Belgium and northern France, defeating any resistance it encountered. By 5 September, German troops were just 40 km from Paris. Blocking their way, however, were British and French troops who had managed to reassemble near the River Marne (see map below, Source A). The Battle of the Marne (5-10 September) was a major turning point in the war. British and French troops were able to exploit a gap between two sections of the German army and force it to retreat. Once the German army had retreated, there was no chance of it quickly knocking France out of the war. The Schlieffen plan had failed. After the Battle of the Marne, therefore, tactics changed. Both sides began to move north again, each hoping to get round the back of the other. Since neither managed to do this and the two armies ended up marching right up to the Belgian coast, this part of the war became known as the 'race to the sea'. By the end of October, the two sides had established positions opposite each other from the Belgian coast in the north right down to Switzerland. For the next four years, these positions hardly changed. The war of movement ended and trench warfare began.

Activity
The war in 1914

Source B An eyewitness account

The battle showed that well-directed fire would mow the enemy down at very little risk to the firers. The Germans did not aim, but shot anyhow and without troubling to put their rifles to their shoulders. The battle also showed that the enemy had no plan of action and did not try to make use of cover. If they had had a proper plan, they should have pushed us back in a quarter of the time they did. But they simply relied on their weight of numbers, which must have been nine to one. They must have lost ten to one in casualties, however. The value of machine guns was a lesson to us and, though ours had done good work, the enemy's had too, and they had lots of them.

Extract from the diary of a British soldier, Lieutenant T.S. Wollocombe, following his first encounter with German troops on 23 August 1914

Source A Map of the war in 1914

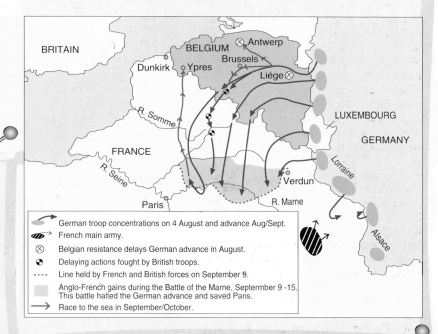

German troop concentrations on 4 August and advance Aug/Sept.

French main army.

⊗ Belgian resistance delays German advance in August.

☢ Delaying actions fought by British troops.

- - - - Line held by French and British forces on September 9.

Anglo-French gains during the Battle of the Marne, September 9 -15. This battle halted the German advance and saved Paris.

→ Race to the sea in September/October.

Source D British cartoon, 12 August 1914

The boy represents Belgium. The man represents Germany.

BRAVO, BELGIUM!

Source C A historian's account

Horses were everywhere. No army had any mechanical transport except for a few motor cars in which generals and staff officers travelled. Once they reached the end of the railway line, the men slogged along on foot. So, armies were fast in delivering men to the battlefield, but slow when they got there. The armies could move no faster than in Napoleon's time when it came to fighting. Indeed, they could not move as fast. Reinforcements could always arrive by rail to a threatened position before the attacking side could break through on foot. This is the reason why defence was stronger than attack throughout the First World War. Defence was mechanised. Attack was not.

From 'The First World War' by A.J.P. Taylor, 1963

QUESTIONS

1. Judging from the information in this section, why was the war not over by Christmas 1914?
2. Using Source A write an account of the war in 1914 from the point of view of a German. How would your account differ if it was written from the point of view of the French?
3. Judging from Sources B and C why did the Schlieffen plan fail?
4. What is happening in Source D? Why do you think the artist chose these images?

What were the effects of the military deadlock on the Western Front?

The war of movement ended when neither side managed to outflank the other in the 'race to the sea' (see Box 1.4 on p.9). From November 1914 and for nearly four years afterwards, there was military deadlock on the Western Front. This deadlock arose from the development of a new sort of warfare - trench warfare. To break the deadlock, military leaders resorted to desperate tactics. Despite great loss of life, however, the battles fought between 1915 and 1918 were inconclusive.

 ## The development of trench warfare

Once the 'race to the sea' was over, both sides took measures to defend their positions. Experience had shown that the best way to provide protection was to dig trenches. As a result, both sides dug a complex system of trenches along their front line (see right). In some places, the trenches between the two sides were less than 50 metres apart. Once they had been dug, however, they provided such good protection that neither army was able to make significant advances until 1918. The trench system allowed each side to bring troops up to the front line without exposing them to enemy fire. Trenches were deliberately dug in a zig zag shape to provide some protection from artillery shells and to prevent enemy troops simply firing down a straight line if they reached the trench. German trenches tended to be much deeper than Allied trenches. In some places, underground rooms were carved out so that the soldiers could retreat there when there was an artillery bombardment. The area between the front line trenches was known as 'No Man's Land'. Shallow trenches were often dug into this area (often to a shell crater) so that troops could crawl there and listen for signs of enemy activity.

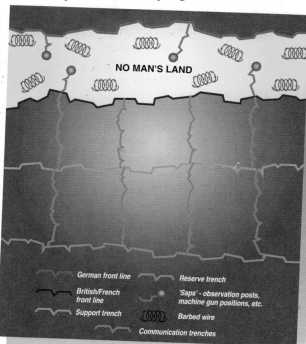

NO MAN'S LAND

German front line	Reserve trench
British/French front line	'Saps' - observation posts, machine gun positions, etc.
Support trench	Barbed wire
	Communication trenches

The trench system

 ## Weapons and tactics

The tactics used by military commanders on both sides were ineffective and resulted in great loss of life. When an offensive began, the artillery (heavy guns) would bombard the enemy trenches (see above), hoping to knock out most of the enemy, and then the infantry (foot soldiers) would be ordered to charge across No Man's Land in the hope that they would be able to occupy the enemy's trenches. The problem with this was that the artillery bombardment did not knock out all enemy troops. So, when the infantry charged, they were mown down by machine gun fire (see Box 1.5)

Box 1.5 Trench warfare

a) For three hours they sent over shells at the rate of at least 120 per minute. The noise was deafening. The trenches either side of us were blown in and, sorry to say, shells dropped in the trenches and killed and wounded many of our men. After three hours, there was a lull of five minutes and the Germans attacked. It was a relief for us to have something we could reply to and we practically stood on the parapet [low wall on top of the trench] in our excitement and mowed them down. Our fellows were so furious that any wounded man seen to move was riddled with bullets and the ground was strewn with German dead lying in all positions. Then they started shelling again. They kept it up this time from 6.30 am to 6 pm. How any of us escaped, God only knows.

From a letter written by a British soldier, Corporal Shepherd, to his sister. Shepherd was fighting in the Battle of Ypres in 1915.

b) Like most generals, Haig's weaknesses were old army weaknesses [Haig was in charge of the British army from 1915]. British army regulations of 1909 suggested action should begin with a short, sharp artillery bombardment followed by infantry advance in lines. Then a bayonet charge to cut the enemy lines. When a gap had been made, the cavalry would pour through. Haig and the other generals never gave these tactics up.

From 'Haig's Command' by D. Winter, 1991

3 Battles

Time after time, military commanders on both sides attempted to break the deadlock (see table below). But each time the result was the same. Thousands died and no more than a few kilometres were gained.

DATE	BATTLE	WHAT HAPPENED	NUMBERS KILLED*	
SEPT 1914	Marne	German attempt to advance to Paris. French force them back.	German French	300,000 250,000
		Both sides settle into trenches.		
APRIL-MAY 1915	Ypres	German attempt to capture Ypres. First use of poison gas by Germans.	German Allied	35,000 60,000
FEB-AUG 1916	Verdun	German attempt to capture Verdun. So many people died, the struggle had to be abandoned.	German French	282,000 315,000
JULY-NOV 1916	Somme	French/British attempt to break through German lines. Only a few kilometres were gained by the Allies.	German British French	500,000 420,000 200,000
		USA enters war on side of Allies.		
JULY-NOV	Passchen-daele	British advance. Gained 11 kilometres.	German British	206,000 265,000
		Russia drops out of war.		
MARCH 1918	Spring offensive	With extra troops from eastern front, Germany launches a massive attack against Allies.	German British	120,000 150,000
AUG-NOV 1918	Allied counter-attack	Allies retake lost ground and push German army back into Belgium.	No figures available	
		Ceasefire 11 November 1918.	*estimated figures	

4 Life in the trenches

Box 1.7 — A quiet sector

We have our turns on duty and off duty. If I am off in the middle of the night, my day begins with 'Stand To' at dawn. I wake up and listen to the sentries talking and the mice scuttling. Everything is grey and damp in the autumn mist. A few stray shots but little more. The order 'Stand Down' comes. The day sentry sits down and looks up into his periscope and the others stretch themselves and move off to get rations, to light fires, to clean rifles. One party pushes a trolley down to a ruined farm to get water. Soon there is the smell of frying bacon and I go round to examine rifles. After breakfast some men are sent to clean the wooden boards in the footway. Others are working at a dugout. Others sleep (they get most of their sleep in the day). I work on a trench which needs to be deepened. Then lunch and then sleep. Tea and 'Stand To'. The trenches begin to look gloomy now, with a dripping of rain and darkness coming on. Work begins again at 'Stand Down'. Then I go on night duty, visiting sentries and the listening posts and firing an occasional flare out into the darkness.

Part of a letter from a British soldier, Lieutenant Philip Brown, to his mother, written in October 1915

According to the historian Denis Winter, in a typical month a soldier would serve four days on the front line, four days in support, eight days in reserve and the remainder at rest behind the lines. Life on the front line varied according to where a soldier was stationed. In some places, there was little fighting and little for the soldiers to do (see Box 1.7). As a result, many had time to keep a diary, write letters, make sketches or compose poems (see Box 1.6). In sectors where battles took place, however, soldiers were under constant bombardment and had to endure

appalling conditions. The tinted photo above shows a British soldier on observation duty in a trench on the Western Front.

Activity
The Battle of the Somme

Source B The Battle of the Somme - a map

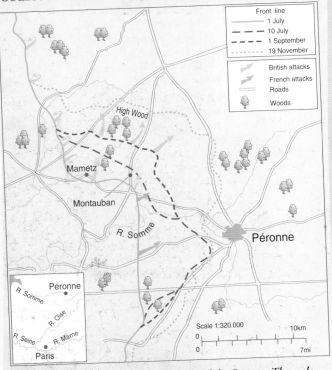

Front line
1 July
10 July
1 September
19 November

British attacks
French attacks
Roads
Woods

High Wood

Mametz

Montauban

R. Somme

Péronne

Péronne
R. Somme
R. Oise
R. Seine
R. Marne
Paris

Scale 1:320.000
0 ————————— 10km
0 ————————— 7mi

This map shows the course of the Battle of the Somme. The scale shows the distances involved.

Source A An eyewitness account

You were between the devil and the deep blue sea. If you go forward, you'll likely be shot. If you go back, you'll be court martialled and shot. So what the hell do you do? What can you do? You just go forward. We were sent in to High Wood in broad daylight in the face of heavy machine gun fire and shell fire. Everywhere there was dead bodies all over the place where previous battalions had taken part in previous attacks. It was criminal to send men in broad daylight into machine gun fire without any cover of any sort whatsoever. There was no need for it. They could have hung on and made an attack on the flanks, but we had to carry out our orders. There was one place just before we got to High Wood which was a crossroads. It was really hell there. They shelled it like anything. You couldn't get past it. There were heaps of men everywhere, all dead. Then afterwards when our battle was over, there was other battalions went up and got the same. They went on and on. They just seemed to be pushing men in to be killed for no reason. They couldn't possibly take the position, not on a frontal attack. Not at High Wood.

Account written by Private W. Hay and published in '1914-1918: Voices and Images of the Great War' by L. Macdonald, 1988

Source C The Battle of the Somme - a photograph

British troops go over the top during the Battle of the Somme.

Source D A historian's account

The battle began on the morning of 1 July when nearly a quarter of a million shells were fired at the German positions in just over an hour, an average of 3,500 a minute. So intense was the barrage that it was heard on Hampstead Heath, in North London. At 7.28 am ten mines were exploded under the German trenches. Two minutes later, British and French troops attacked along a 25 mile front. As they went over the top, British soldiers carried with them about 30 kilos' weight of equipment: a rifle, ammunition, grenades, rations, a waterproof cape, three empty sandbags, a steel helmet, two gas helmets, a pair of goggles, a field dressing, a pick or shovel, a full water bottle and a mess tin. General Edmonds has written in his official history: 'The weight of this equipment made it difficult to get out of a trench, impossible to move much quicker than a slow walk, or to rise and lie down quickly.' As many as a hundred German machine guns opened fire as the infantry moved forward from their trenches. Many of the attackers were killed as they bunched together to push through the unexpectedly small gaps in their own barbed wire. Two German held villages, Mametz and Montauban, were captured on 1 July. The human cost of the day's attack was higher than on any single day of battle in the First World War. Just over 1,000 British officers and more than 20,000 men were killed and 25,000 seriously wounded.

From 'First World War' by M. Gilbert, 1994

QUESTIONS

1. Judging from the information in this section, what were the effects of the military deadlock on the Western Front?

2. a) Using Sources A-D describe what happened in the Battle of the Somme from the point of view of (i) a British soldier and (ii) a German soldier.

   b) What do these sources tell us about the nature of war on the Western Front?

3. a) Judging from Sources A and D what were the aims of the British military leaders?

   b) Would you describe the Battle of the Somme as a British success? Give reasons for your answer.

'Gassed' by John Singer Sargent

Desperate to break the military deadlock, both sides were prepared to experiment with new weapons. Poison gas was first used on 22 April 1915. German troops near Ypres opened around 4,000 cylinders of chlorine along an eight kilometre front and used the wind to blow it towards the enemy. When the gas reached the French and Algerian troops opposite, they either fled or suffocated. German troops, advancing with gas masks on, were able take 2,000 prisoners and capture 51 big guns. Subsequent attacks in April and May were not so successful. On a number of occasions, the wind changed direction and the attackers themselves suffered casualties. Nevertheless, from April 1915, gas was used regularly by both sides. By 1918, roughly one shell in four was a gas shell and soldiers had become accustomed to fighting in gas masks. By then, other gases were used. Most devastating was mustard gas which caused the skin to blister and affected the eyes. The painting below was entitled 'Gassed'. It shows a group of British soldiers suffering after a gas attack. The artist was John Singer Sargant.

The artist - John Singer Sargant

John Singer Sargant was born in the USA in 1856. By the outbreak of the First World War, he was already a well known artist. In April 1917, the USA joined the war on the side of the Allies. A year later, Sargant was approached by the British War Memorials Committee and asked to paint a large-scale picture on the theme of Allied cooperation. Sargant came over to Britain and received a personal welcome from the Prime Minister, David Lloyd George, who wrote to him saying how much he looked forward to the production of 'great paintings'. Sargant then went over to France to visit the front for the first time. When he returned, he did not paint a scene showing Anglo-American cooperation. Rather, he produced a huge painting (3 metres by 7 metres) showing the victims of a mustard gas attack (see above). This painting was produced from sketches and notes made by Sargant during his stay in France. In March 1919, the National War Museum (which later became the Imperial War Museum) paid £600 for this painting.

A gas attack in April 1918

A photo taken by one of the British army's official photographers, Tom Aitken. It shows a group of men at a field hospital after a gas attack in April 1918

QUESTIONS

1. a) What does Sargant's painting tell us about the First World War?
   b) What message (if any) do you think the artist is trying to get across? Give reasons for your answer.

2. What does the information about the artist add to our understanding of the painting?

3. Compare the two pictures on this page. Would you describe Sargant's painting as a 'reliable record'? Give reasons for your answer.

How important was the war in the air and the war at sea?

Given that the first successful plane flight took place in the USA in December 1903 (Orville and Wilbur Wright made four short flights of which the longest was 252 metres), it is perhaps surprising that planes played a part in World War I at all. However, in its first ten years, aeroplane technology developed quickly. By 1909, for example, the French aviator Louis Blériot was able to fly a plane across the Channel for the first time and, by 1914, planes had a range of several hundred miles. So, although aviation was in its infancy when war broke out in 1914, a military role was soon found for aircraft. War at sea, of course, had a much longer history than war in the air. But, although the naval arms race was important in the build-up to the war, there were few set-piece naval battles in World War I. Both sides were aware that a single decisive naval defeat would allow the enemy to gain complete control of the seas. Control of the seas would mean control of supplies. If one side had control of supplies, it would be able to starve the other side into submission. As a result, the navies on both sides were very cautious. Despite this, there was naval action (both above water and beneath it) and the course of the war at sea made an impact on the war as a whole.

The war in the air

The war in the air was not just fought by planes. Airships also played a part (airships were known as 'Zeppelins', after their inventor). Zeppelins worked on the same principle as hot air balloons. Huge bags of gas were enclosed in a cigar-shaped rigid frame. These gas bags lifted the crew (suspended in a cockpit underneath) off the ground. In World War I, the main function performed by both Zeppelins and planes was observation. They could fly high over enemy territory, taking photographs or making records of enemy positions and movements. In addition, aircraft began to carry out bombing raids. In 1915 and 1916, for example, Zeppelins

made bombing raids on London. Although Zeppelins could carry more bombs than planes, it was easy to shoot them down (the picture above shows a Zeppelin being shot down by a British plane). By the end of the war, special planes were being used for bombing raids. To counter this threat, special fighter planes had been developed to provide protection against enemy air raids (see Box 1.8). Whilst the British Royal Flying Corps (later, the Royal Air Force) had 150 planes in 1914, by the end of the war, the number had risen to over 22,000.

Box 1.8

A dogfight above the trenches

25 July 1915: Today we have been treated to one of the most thrilling yet awful sights imaginable - a fight in mid-air. One of our airmen was scouting over our trenches when a 'Taube' [German plane] flew straight towards him. The British aviator turned tail with the German in hot pursuit. Ascending to about 3,000 feet, the Briton became hidden by a cloud. Here he outwitted the German by remaining almost stationary until the Taube passed underneath him. He then flew down as though he would crash on top of his opponent, but when quite close above him dropped a bomb. The effect was awful. The Taube burst into flames and dived downwards. We expected to see it crash to the ground, but with wonderful skill, the German got control and tried to get back to his lines. He was within 1,000 feet of the ground when he was seen to fall or jump out of the machine. He dropped like a stone. Though he was German, we admired the gallant attempt he made to get back.

From the diary of Private Raymond Grimshaw, a British soldier stationed near Ypres in France

Naval tactics and battles

When war broke out, the British navy was stronger than the German navy. Both sides, however, realised that if a full-scale naval battle was to take place, in the words of British Admiral Jellicoe: 'The war could be lost in an afternoon'. As a result, the British aimed to pin the German fleet back at port, whilst the Germans hoped to isolate and pick off small parts of the British fleet. At first, there were clashes. In August 1914, three German cruisers were destroyed in the North Sea. In November 1914, two British ships were sunk off the coast of Chile, with the British taking their revenge two weeks later. Then, after another German warship was sunk at the Battle of Dogger Bank (off the east coast of Britain) in January 1915, the Germans decided on a policy of extreme caution. From this time onwards, the main German fleet remained at port. The only exception to this came with the Battle of Jutland in May 1916 (see Activity on p.15). A measure of British naval success is the fact that, every day during the war, ships crossed the Channel and not one was lost to enemy action.

This photo shows the British navy in Kiel harbour in 1914. A Zeppelin flies over. During the war, British ships set up a blockade around Germany, making it difficult for Germany to obtain supplies from abroad.

3 Submarines, U-boats and convoys

The first submarine used in combat was that invented by the American David Bushnell in 1776. It was only in 1898, however, that a submarine was designed which could travel through the open sea. By 1914, both sides had submarines capable of crossing the Atlantic Ocean. Since the main part of the German navy was hemmed in by the British navy, in 1914-15, the Germans used their 28 U-boats (the German for submarine is 'Unterseeboot') to attack ships bringing supplies to Britain. In May 1915, a U-boat sank the *Lusitania*, a passenger liner travelling from the USA. Over 1,000 passengers were drowned (including 128 Americans). When the American government protested, the Germans agreed not to attack ships without warning and U-boat activity quietened down. By February 1917, however, Germany had produced 110 U-boats and a second U-boat campaign began. In eight weeks, over 500 ships were sunk. This was the last straw for the USA. It declared war on Germany on 6 April. At the end of April, British began to use a 'convoy' system (groups of ships carrying supplies were protected by warships). This was so successful that only five of the 800 ships travelling in convoys in July and August 1917 were sunk. The painting above shows a convoy passing the Lizard in Cornwall.

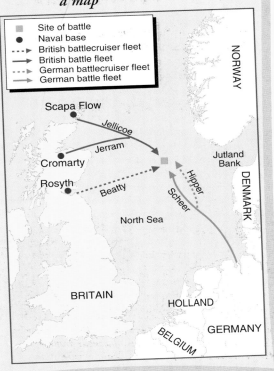

Activity
The Battle of Jutland

Source B *The Battle of Jutland - a map*

- ■ Site of battle
- ● Naval base
- - - -▶ British battlecruiser fleet
- ──▶ British battle fleet
- - - -▶ German battlecruiser fleet
- ──▶ German battle fleet

NORWAY

Scapa Flow

Jellicoe

Jerram

Cromarty

Rosyth

Beatty

Hipper

Scheer

Jutland Bank

DENMARK

North Sea

BRITAIN

HOLLAND

BELGIUM

GERMANY

Source A *A historian's account*

The great day came on 31 May. Scheer (the German commander) set his trap. Admiral Hipper was to go ahead and lure the British ships on to the main fleet. The British knew what the Germans were planning as they had broken the German code. From Scapa Flow, Jellicoe (the British commander) steamed south with the Grand Fleet to catch the Germans in their own trap. At first, everything went according to plan. Beatty, commanding the British battle cruisers, engaged Hipper in the early afternoon. Though two British ships were sunk, Beatty pushed on towards the main German fleet. Scheer thought his great chance had come. Beatty turned away, apparently in flight. For two hours, Scheer pursued him. At 6.15 pm the main British fleet appeared on the horizon. Scheer saw the trap and turned away. Jellicoe did not attempt to pursue. The battle seemed over. Then, half an hour later, Scheer suddenly reappeared, slap in the centre of the British line. The battle was renewed for some 15 minutes. Then Scheer turned away once more and Jellicoe also. Scheer slipped past the British rear and got safely home. Jellicoe found himself on an empty sea. The British lost more ships - 14 ships compared to 11 lost by the Germans. But, at the decisive moment, the German fleet fled and, in Jellicoe's eyes, that was all that mattered. He did not think he could win the war by destroying the German fleet. He thought he might lose it if he did not preserve his own. Many people in Britain did not accept this and in 1917 Jellicoe was replaced by the more aggressive Beatty. Once in command, Beatty, too, became cautious.

From 'The First World War' by A.J.P. Taylor, 1963

QUESTIONS

1. Judging from the information in this section, how important was (a) the war in the air and (b) the war at sea?
2. 'The Battle of Jutland was a disappointment to both sides.' Explain this statement using Sources A and B.
3. Suppose you were (a) a British or (b) German journalist in 1916. Design the front page of a newspaper reporting on the Battle of Jutland.

What was the significance of the war on other fronts?

The war which broke out in August 1914 soon became a world war. As the Germans launched the Schlieffen plan in the west, Russian troops attacked in the east. At the same time, Austro-Hungarian troops attacked Serbia in the south. But the war was not just fought in Europe by Europeans. The Allies and the Central Powers had overseas colonies in Africa, Asia and the Americas. Fighting took place in some of these colonies and many colonial troops fought in the European countries' armies. Whilst many historians (especially British historians) have focused on the Western Front, events elsewhere had an important bearing on the outcome of the war.

 ## The Eastern Front

When war broke out, the Russian army, with around 1.3 million men, was the largest army in Europe. Nicknamed 'the steamroller' by its allies, the Russian army advanced into Germany, only to suffer major defeats at the Battle of Tannenberg (26-30 August 1914) and the Battle of the Masurian Lakes two weeks later. This set the pattern for the war on the Eastern Front (see Box 1.10). Time after time, the Russian army (over 10 million men had been mobilised by 1917) mounted offensives which, at first, were successful but then ground to a halt. Counter-offensives were then launched by the Central Powers. Although there were periods when both sides sat defensively in their trenches, there was much more movement on the Eastern Front than in the west. For example, in the summer of 1915, the Russian army was forced to retreat through Poland. This pushed back the Russian front line by over 500 km in places. A major problem for both sides was the provision of supplies. In June 1916 and July 1917, Russian offensives brought initial gains but petered out when supplies failed to arrive. The same happened to the German army in August 1917. By the time peace was agreed, neither side had made a decisive breakthrough, though the Russians had lost much territory.

The Russian 'Steamroller'

Box 1.10

Russia & World War I

From the summer of 1914 to its collapse in 1917, the Russian army fought stubbornly and desperately under the most difficult circumstances. The offensive in August 1914, which helped France at the most critical moment, ended in a shattering defeat. Quickly the Russian army ran out of its supply of weapons and ammunition. For part of 1915, up to 25% of Russian soldiers were sent to the front unarmed, with instructions to pick up what they could from the dead. Although, later, Russian supplies improved, the Russian forces remained vastly inferior to the German and Austrian in artillery and other weapons. Yet, the Russian troops went on fighting. Despite defeats and retreats, they continued to force Germany to wage a war on two fronts at the same time.

From 'A History of Russia' by N.V. Riasanovsky, 1993

② The war in the Balkans

Although the Allies put up some strong resistance, it was the Central Powers who gained the upper hand in the Balkans. In August 1914, Austria-Hungary launched a major offensive against Serbia. This failed and trench warfare began. On 7 October 1915, however, the Austro-Hungarians (supported by German reinforcements) began a second major offensive. This was successful. The Serb army was totally defeated by 20 November and Montenegro was taken in January 1916. During the winter, the Serbian army retreated through Albania to the sea (a difficult journey on which many died). Survivors were then shipped over to Corfu. On 6 October 1915, the day before the Austro-Hungarian offensive began, Bulgaria joined the war on the side of the Central Powers. Bulgarian troops immediately moved to contain an Allied force of French and British troops which had landed at Salonika in neutral Greece on 5 October. When Romania entered the war on the side of the Allies on 27 August 1916, the Allied force in Salonika tried to break through, but failed. This left Romania exposed to a combined attack from German, Austro-Hungarian and Bulgarian troops. Romania was overrun. There was little movement in 1917, but in June 1917 Greece joined the war on the Allies' side. In September 1918, an Allied offensive broke the Bulgarian line for the first time, forcing the Bulgarians to agree to an armistice on 29 September. Then, on 3 November, Austria-Hungary which had suffered defeat at the hands of the Italians in the north (Italy had joined the war on the side of the Allies in May 1915), also agreed to an armistice.

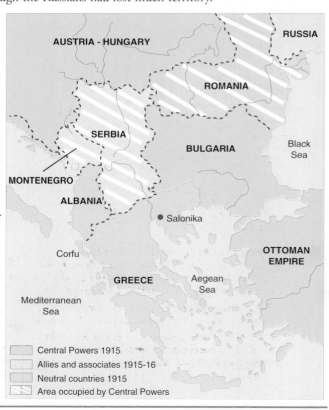

Central Powers 1915
Allies and associates 1915-16
Neutral countries 1915
Area occupied by Central Powers

3 The Gallipoli campaign

Since Britain and France were cut off from their ally Russia and since Turkey had joined the war on the side of the Central Powers, the British government planned an ambitious campaign to take control of the Dardanelles - the stretch of water leading from the Aegean Sea to the Sea of Marmara. Control of the Dardanelles would provide a base to knock Turkey out of the war and to link up with Russia. The plan was to take control of the Gallipoli peninsular, a rocky outcrop on the northern side of the Dardanelles. In practice, this proved more difficult than the military leaders imagined and, after the loss of around 200,000 troops (mainly troops from Australia and New Zealand), the plan had to be abandoned. The campaign had three distinct phases. First, in **February 1915** Allied ships bombarded Turkish forts at the entrance of the Dardanelles and minesweepers attempted to clear the straits of mines. Second, on **18 March**, an attempt to push ships through the straits ended in failure when three battleships were destroyed by mines and another three were badly damaged. And third, on **25 April**, a land expedition began. Troops were transported to Cape Helles and Anzac Cove, but they failed to make headway inland. Between April and December large numbers of Allied troops remained trapped between the sea and the hills and were unable to break through the Turkish lines. In December 1915, the surviving troops were successfully evacuated.

Activity
Gallipoli

Source B *Map of the Gallipoli campaign*

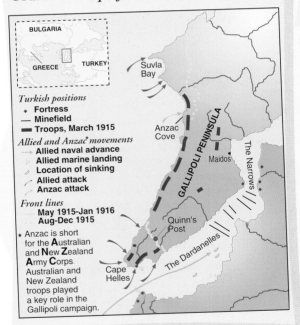

BULGARIA

GREECE   TURKEY

Turkish positions
- ◆ **Fortress**
- — **Minefield**
- ▬ **Troops, March 1915**

Allied and Anzac* movements
- ⟶ **Allied naval advance**
- **Allied marine landing**
- **Location of sinking**
- **Allied attack**
- **Anzac attack**

Front lines
  May 1915-Jan 1916
  Aug-Dec 1915

★ Anzac is short for the **A**ustralian and **N**ew **Z**ealand **A**rmy **C**orps. Australian and New Zealand troops played a key role in the Gallipoli campaign.

Suvla Bay

Anzac Cove

Maidos

GALLIPOLI PENINSULA

The Narrows

Quinn's Post

The Dardanelles

Cape Helles

Source A *An eyewitness account*

We had trouble with our boat and didn't land until well into the afternoon of 25 April. The wounded and the killed were lying about in all directions. I should say a thousand or more. The noise was terrific. I don't remember being frightened. I was anxious to get to the firing line. I never got that far, not for at least a fortnight. When I got into the trenches at Quinn's Post I found we were less than 20 yards off the Turk trenches. Between our trenches and theirs were about 15 or 20 bodies. They were there the whole time I was in Quinn's Post, about six weeks. The stink was worse at night. You were lucky to get two hours of sleep. You couldn't sleep because of the flies. We fought the flies harder than we fought the Turks. When I looked out my periscope all I could see was a heap of flies, not bodies, between us and the Turks.

Part of an interview conducted in 1983 with Hartley Palmer, a New Zealander who took part in the Gallipoli campaign.

Source C *Painting of the Gallipoli landings*

This painting shows Allied troops (Australians) landing at Gallipoli in April 1915.

QUESTIONS

1. Judging from the information in this section, how significant was (a) the war on the Eastern Front (b) the war in the Balkans and (c) the Gallipoli campaign?
2. Why did the Gallipoli campaign fail? Use Sources A-D in your answer.
3. What difficulties arise when using Sources A and C to reconstruct what happened during the Gallipoli campaign?

Source D *A historian's verdict on the Gallipoli campaign*

The new attack was fixed for 6 August. Hamilton (the British commander) took the Turks by surprise. At Anzac Cove, one column got within a quarter mile of the ridge with only 20 Turks ahead of them. It then settled down to breakfast and, by the time it had finished, the ridge was bristling with rifles. At Suvla Bay 20,000 men were put ashore almost without loss; only a thousand Turks, without machine guns, barred their way. Here, General Stopford was in command. He did not go ashore. Instead, he congratulated the men on their successful landing and settled down to his afternoon nap. On shore, the men were told to relax; they went off to bathe with no Turks between them and victory. Hamilton was too polite to interfere. On the following day, the British troops dug defences. On 8 August, they attempted to advance. By then, the Turks were too strong for them.

From 'The First World War' by A.J.P. Taylor, 1963.

The military deadlock on the Western Front lasted from the beginning of 1915 to March 1918. In March 1918, the German army made what was to be its final offensive. When this failed, the Allies were able to launch their own counter-offensive. This forced the German leaders to sign an armistice (a truce) on 11 November 1918. Historians give three main reasons why the military deadlock on the Western Front was broken in 1918. First, the development of a new weapon - the tank - made an impact on the battlefield. Second, the USA joined the war on the side of the Allies. And third, the Bolshevik revolution in Russia removed the Eastern Front and triggered the events which led to Germany's collapse.

The development of the tank

To break the military deadlock, a British military journalist, Lieutenant-Colonel Ernest Swinton, had the idea of an armoured vehicle capable of crossing difficult ground. The advantage of such a vehicle would be its ability to withstand machine gun fire, to cross trenches and to destroy machine gun positions. The new vehicle was called a 'tank'. Tanks were first used during the Battle of the Somme, on 15 September 1916, but most broke down or got bogged down. Nevertheless, they frightened the German troops and their production was encouraged. By contrast, in Germany there was little enthusiasm for tanks. A German tank had been designed by 1918, but only 20 had been built by the end of the war. In the Battle of Cambrai of November 1917, over 400 British tanks crossed No Man's Land, with the infantry following and aircraft in support. After three days, a gain of 8 km had been made for a fraction of the usual losses. The same tactics were used on a larger scale at the Battle of Amiens on 8 August 1918. Success on that day marked the beginning of the offensive which led to the German collapse.

A British tank in action. By breaking through the barbed wire and destroying machine gun posts, tanks cleared the way for the infantry. They were also designed to cross trenches. Their top speed, however, was just 6 km per hour.

The USA's entry into the war

The USA's decision to enter the war on the side of the Allies in April 1917 was a crucial factor in ending the military deadlock for two reasons. First, it was a morale boost for the Allied soldiers in the trenches. And second, when the American troops finally arrived, they arrived in great numbers (see Box 1.11). This tilted the balance of forces in favour of the Allies. Before April 1917, the USA had provided a great deal of aid and this continued to pour in. By the end of the war, for example, 89,000 tonnes of meat and 600,000 horses had been sent to Europe. Britain owed the USA $4,277 million. France owed $2,997 million.

The picture, right, is an American postcard printed in 1917. It was designed to encourage people to support the USA's entry into the war.

FOR FREEDOM!

Box 1.11

The USA joins the war

a) America's entry brought limitless resources to the Allied side, but only in the comparatively distant future. The USA had a great navy. It had virtually no army. Millions of men had to be conscripted and trained. There were few weapons factories. Tanks, guns and even rifles had to be supplied by the British and French, not the other way round. No American tanks and hardly any American planes ever reached the Western Front.

From 'The First World War' by A.J.P. Taylor, 1963

b) It took some time for the American presence to make much of a difference in the war on the Western Front. A small number of troops arrived in the early summer of 1917, and received a weary reception when they were paraded through Paris on 4 July. But, to provide additional manpower, the USA brought in conscription on 18 May 1917. By 5 June, over 10 million men were registered for service. From March 1918, 250,000 men were sent overseas per month. By the end of the war, nearly 2 million men were in Europe. This was more than the total number of British forces then in action.

From 'The Experience of World War I' by J.M. Winter, 1988

③ Germany's collapse

As soon as the Bolsheviks had seized power in Russia, they began to negotiate a peace settlement with Germany (see p.38). In March 1918, the Treaty of Brest-Litovsk ended the war on the Eastern Front and German troops were transferred to the west. On 21 March, a new German offensive began in the west. After some successes, the offensive lost its momentum and, by August, the German army was exhausted. On 8 August, the Allies began their counter-attack near Amiens. German resistance was weak and the Allies were able to push the Germans slowly back until the armistice was signed. When news of the Allied counter-attack reached Germany, morale dropped very quickly. The naval blockade of German ports meant that food was scarce. Whilst there was a chance of victory, the German people put up with this. But once the chance of victory had gone, they wanted peace as quickly as possible. Besides, Germany became isolated as its allies surrendered in quick succession (Bulgaria on 30 September, Turkey on 31 October and Austria-Hungary on 3 November).

The causes of Germany's collapse

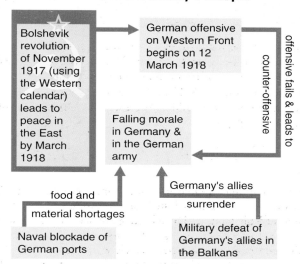

Bolshevik revolution of November 1917 (using the Western calendar) leads to peace in the East by March 1918 → German offensive on Western Front begins on 12 March 1918 → offensive fails & leads to counter-offensive → Falling morale in Germany & in the German army

food and material shortages ← Naval blockade of German ports

Germany's allies surrender ← Military defeat of Germany's allies in the Balkans

Activity
The final stages of the war

Source B   Photo taken on 8 August 1918

This photo, taken on 8 August 1918, shows a column of German prisoners captured during the Battle of Amiens. That day, the Kaiser said to Ludendorff: 'We have reached the limits of our capacity. The war must be ended.'

Source A   The final stages - a map

HOLLAND
Ostend · Antwerp
FOURTH ARMY
Ypres · River Lys · Brussels
BELGIUM
SIXTH ARMY · Mons
Arras · SEVENTEENTH ARMY
SECOND ARMY
River Somme
EIGHTEENTH ARMY
FRANCE
SEVENTH ARMY
LUXEMBOURG
FIRST ARMY · THIRD ARMY · FIFTH ARMY
GERMANY
Reims
River Marne
Verdun · DETACHMENT C

Front line 20 March
German deployments
German attacks
Land gained by Germans:
5 April
11 April
27 April
9 June
17 July
British deployments
French deployments
Belgian deployments
American deployments
Front line 10 Nov
National borders

QUESTIONS

1. Judging from the information in this section, how was the military deadlock on the Western Front broken? Make a list of factors and place them in order of importance. Explain why you have chosen this order.

2. Why was Germany forced to agree to an armistice in November 1918? Use Sources A-C in your answer.

3. Why do you think General Ludendorff described 8 August 1918 as: 'The black day of the German army in this war.' Use Sources B and C in your answer.

Source C   German commander's account

Early on 8 August, in a dense fog, the English and French attacked with strong squadrons of tanks, but otherwise in no great superiority. Between the Somme and the Lys they penetrated deep into our positions. By mid-morning I had gained a complete impression of the situation. It was a very gloomy one. I was told of deeds of glorious valour, but also of behaviour which, I openly confess, I should not have thought possible in the German army. Groups of men had surrendered to single troopers. Retreating troops, meeting a fresh division going bravely into action, had shouted things like: 'You're prolonging the war'. The officers in many places had lost their influence and allowed themselves to be swept along with the rest. Everything I had feared had here, in one place, become a reality. Our war machine was no longer efficient.

From 'My War Memories' by General Ludendorff (joint German commander-in-chief 1916-18), 1919

How did World War I change life in Britain?

The First World War affected the lives of people in Britain in many ways. First, more men were drafted into the army than in previous wars and more were killed or wounded than ever before. As a result, by the end of the war most people had a close friend or relative who had been killed or wounded. Second, the war affected the lives of some people very directly since they were the victims of enemy attacks (coastal towns were bombarded by the German navy, for example, and attacks were made from the air). Although they were infrequent, attacks like this had not been experienced before. Third, to ensure that the army was supplied with arms and equipment and that services and industries were organised efficiently at home, the British government took a more active role than it had taken in peacetime. This affected people's lives at work and at home. Fourth, the difficulty of bringing in supplies from abroad led to shortages of essential items. These shortages led to the introduction of rationing. Rationing was a new experience for everybody. And fifth, since large numbers of men were needed at the front, women were able to play an important part in the war effort by doing the jobs left vacant by men and by providing support services such as nursing. In short, the war shook up the whole of British society and life was never the same again once the war was over.

Recruitment and support for the war

When war was declared on 4 August 1914, the British government asked for volunteers aged 19 to 30 to come forward and serve in the armed forces (the age limit was raised to 35 on 11 September). At first, there was a great rush to join up - a million men had come forward by December 1914 and 2.46 million had volunteered by January 1916. Most joined up because they felt it was their duty to fight for 'King and Country' (a message repeated time and again on the recruitment posters produced by the army - see right). By January 1916, however, the number of volunteers had dropped and the army was having to spend more and more time, effort and money trying to persuade men to join up. As a result, the government introduced conscription (compulsory military service). By April 1918, conscription had been extended to include all men aged 18 to 51. By the end of the war, a further 2.5 million men had been conscripted to the armed forces. As the rush to join up 1914 in indicates, there was, at first, overwhelming support for the war. Even when the war dragged on and the casualties mounted, most people continued to support it. But there was some opposition. When conscription was introduced, 16,100 'conscientious objectors' refused to join the armed forces, claiming that it was wrong to fight. Of these, around 9,500 helped the war effort by working behind the lines in a non-fighting role or by doing essential work not connected with the armed forces. The remainder were sent to prison.

YOUR KING & COUNTRY NEED YOU

A WEE 'SCRAP O' PAPER' IS BRITAIN'S BOND.

TO MAINTAIN THE HONOUR AND GLORY OF THE BRITISH EMPIRE

2 Bombardments and bombing raids

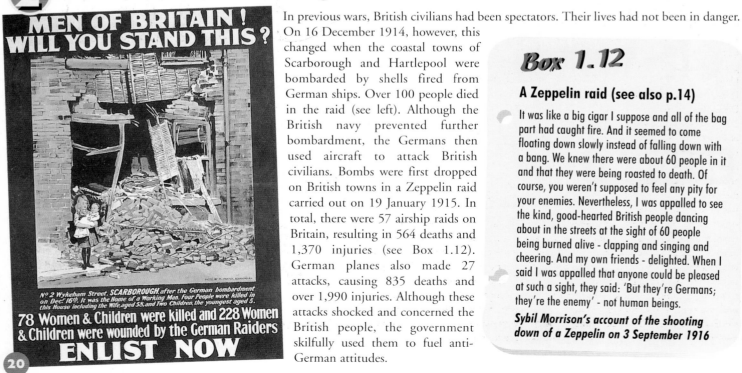

MEN OF BRITAIN! WILL YOU STAND THIS?

Nº 2 Wykeham Street, SCARBOROUGH, after the German bombardment on Dec!! 16!!º. It was the Home of a Working Man. Four People were killed in this House including the Wife, aged 58, and Two Children, the youngest aged 5.

78 Women & Children were killed and 228 Women & Children were wounded by the German Raiders

ENLIST NOW

In previous wars, British civilians had been spectators. Their lives had not been in danger. On 16 December 1914, however, this changed when the coastal towns of Scarborough and Hartlepool were bombarded by shells fired from German ships. Over 100 people died in the raid (see left). Although the British navy prevented further bombardment, the Germans then used aircraft to attack British civilians. Bombs were first dropped on British towns in a Zeppelin raid carried out on 19 January 1915. In total, there were 57 airship raids on Britain, resulting in 564 deaths and 1,370 injuries (see Box 1.12). German planes also made 27 attacks, causing 835 deaths and over 1,990 injuries. Although these attacks shocked and concerned the British people, the government skilfully used them to fuel anti-German attitudes.

Box 1.12

A Zeppelin raid (see also p.14)

It was like a big cigar I suppose and all of the bag part had caught fire. And it seemed to come floating down slowly instead of falling down with a bang. We knew there were about 60 people in it and that they were being roasted to death. Of course, you weren't supposed to feel any pity for your enemies. Nevertheless, I was appalled to see the kind, good-hearted British people dancing about in the streets at the sight of 60 people being burned alive - clapping and singing and cheering. And my own friends - delighted. When I said I was appalled that anyone could be pleased at such a sight, they said: 'But they're Germans; they're the enemy' - not human beings.

Sybil Morrison's account of the shooting down of a Zeppelin on 3 September 1916

3 The changing role of government

To win the war, it was necessary to recruit and equip a large army and to keep it supplied with food, arms and ammunition. The civilian population also needed to be fed. This required a great deal of central planning. It required, in other words, government control. Before the war, the British government had been reluctant to interfere in the way in which industries were run. Munitions (weapons) factories, coal mines and railways, for example, were all privately owned. During the war, however, it was vital that enough shells and bullets were made to supply the army. As a result, the government took control of munitions factories. To ensure that these factories were powered and that sufficient weapons were supplied, the government controlled coal mines and the railways. By giving itself the power to 'requisition' (seize) materials necessary for the war effort, the government ensured that, for example, enough steel was provided for these weapons and enough wool and leather was provided for army uniforms and equipment. And the government also took control in other ways. On 8 August 1914, the Defence of the Realm Act (DORA) was passed by Parliament. This gave the government special powers to imprison people whose actions put into danger public safety. Under this law, newspaper reports were censored and strikes were made illegal. Whenever possible, however, the government preferred not to use its new powers. After all, it was better that the unions volunteered not to go on strike (which they did on 24 August 1914) than that the government was forced to imprison strikers who broke the law.

Defence of the Realm Act
NOTICE
THE CONTINUANCE OF TRAFFIC ON THE RAILWAYS IS NECESSARY FOR THE SAFETY OF THE NATION AND FOR THE PROSECUTION OF THE WAR. ANY PERSON WHO PREVENTS OR ATTEMPTS TO PREVENT ANOTHER PERSON FROM WORKING ON A RAILWAY AT THE PRESENT TIME IS LIABLE TO SIX MONTHS IMPRISONMENT.

When unions threatened to break their no-strike agreement, notices like the one above (produced in August 1917 when a national rail strike was threatened) made union members think twice about going on strike.

4 Shortages and rationing

In 1914, Britain was by no means self-sufficient. It relied on imports to provide it with basic goods such as sugar, tea and flour. Since most imports were brought to Britain by ship and since ships ran the risk of being attacked by German U-boats, it is not surprising that, as the war dragged on, there were food shortages. At first, the government did little to organise food supply. But later in the war, discontent led to government action. When Lloyd George became Prime Minister in December 1916 (see Box 1.13), he set up a Ministry of Food. This ministry was responsible for the poster campaign which encouraged people to grow their own vegetables and not to waste food (see right). In the autumn of 1917, however, people began to panic about food shortages (even though supplies were not so bad as earlier in the year). Huge queues formed outside food shops and, in some places, fights broke out. To calm fears, the Ministry of Food introduced rationing (people were given a book of coupons allowing them to buy only a certain amount of a product each week). In February 1918, the rationing of meat, butter and margarine was introduced in London. By July 1918, a uniform system of rationing had been introduced throughout the country. This had the desired effect. There was enough food for everyone to buy their ration each week. People stopped panicking and the queues outside food shops disappeared. The rationing of some goods continued until 1921.

We risk our lives to bring you food. It's up to you not to waste it.

'A Message from our Seamen'

Box 1.13

David Lloyd George

1863	Born
1890	Elected Liberal MP
1906	President of the Board of Trade
1908-14	Chancellor of the Exchequer
May 1915	Minister of Munitions
Dec 1916	Prime Minister

Lloyd George's year at the Ministry of Munitions transformed the British economy. When he entered the requisitioned hotel which was to house the new ministry, he found no tables, no staff and too many mirrors. By the end of the war, the ministry was employing a staff of 65,000 and had over 3 million workers under its direction. Lord Kitchener (Secretary of State for War) thought that four machine guns per battalion might be useful and anything more a luxury. Lloyd George said: 'Take Kitchener's figure. Square it. Multiply by two. Then double again for good luck.' The army began the war with 1,330 machine guns. During the war, 240,506 were manufactured - thanks to Lloyd George. The War Office turned down the Stokes light mortar, one of the best weapons of the war. Lloyd George got an Indian prince to finance its manufacture out of his own pocket.

From 'English History 1914-45' by A.J.P. Taylor, 1965

5 The changing role of women

As soon as war was declared, the campaign to win the vote for women (see Box 1.14) was halted. Suffragette leaders called on women to play their part in the war effort. Women responded with enthusiasm (see Box 1.15) and they played a vital part in the war, both at home and at the front. At home, women took over jobs which had become vacant because men had joined the armed forces. During the war, the number of working women grew by around 1 million. Many of these women did jobs which had previously been thought of as jobs that only men could do. Others helped to support the men fighting at the front. Over 120,000 women trained to be nurses and, from 1917, women were allowed to join the army and serve in non-combat roles.

As Minister of Munitions, Lloyd George negotiated an agreement with the unions to allow women to work in the munitions industry. New training centres for women were set up by the government and, by the end of the war, over 750,000 women had been employed in munitions (the photo above shows a woman working in a munitions factory). A report to the British Association in 1915 stated that, except with the very heaviest tools, women could operate as efficiently as men.

This photo shows a female ambulance team which served in France during the First World War. Before the war, few believed that women could be ambulance drivers or mechanics (these women repaired their own vehicles). Many of the women who served abroad belonged to the Voluntary Aid Detachments (VADs) - groups of untrained volunteers who cleaned and cooked as well as performing basic nursing.

Box 1.14

Suffragettes

During the decade before the First World War, many women campaigned to win the vote. Those who supported the Women's Social and Political Union (WSPU), led by Emmeline Pankhurst and her daughters, were known as 'suffragettes'. Between 1906 and 1914 the WSPU used ever more violent tactics to draw attention to their cause. The picture above, for example, was produced after suffragettes smashed shop windows in London on 1 and 4 March 1912. Later, suffragettes bombed and set fire to post boxes and empty buildings (they aimed to damage property, not people). Many suffragettes were sent to prison and, after going on hunger strike, forcibly fed. The suffragettes accused the government of torture. The government accused the suffragettes of terrorism.

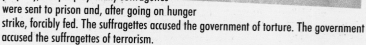

THE SUFFRAGETTES GET WILDER DAILY & SMASH SHOP WINDOWS. OH! SO GAILY

As more men joined the army, more jobs opened up for women. Women became fire fighters, chimney sweeps, painters, blacksmiths and bakers. London County Council trained women to be plumbers, carpenters and electricians. Even though, just a few months before the war began suffragettes had been fighting policemen, some women served as police officers during the war (see right). Although there was grumbling at first, most people were impressed by the contribution made by all these women.

A FAIR COP.

Box 1.15

Encouraging women to play their part

On 28 June 1915 the Minister of Munitions, Lloyd George, was informed that: 'The King feels strongly that we should do more to enlist women workers. Would it be possible for you to make use of Mrs Pankhurst?' As a result the WSPU was given a £2,000 grant from the Ministry of Munitions to pay for a parade insisting on women's 'right to serve'. On 17 July 1915, Lloyd George inspected a two mile procession of 30,000 women. Some carried banners with slogans like: 'Shells made by a wife may save her husband's life'.

From 'Rise Up Women!' by A. Rosen, 1974

Activity
The impact of the war

Source B *Representation of the People Act, 1918*

The year 1918 marks a vital turning point in British history. From this time onwards we can properly talk of 'democracy' in Britain. The Representation of the People Act of February 1918 gave the vote to women over the age of 30 and to those men over 21 who did not already have it. In the elections of 1910, about 7.5 million men had been able to vote - roughly 60% of adult (over 21) males or less than 30% of all adults in Britain. In 1918, in sharp contrast, there were over 21 million voters, including 8 million women - about 78% of the adult population. The new Reform Act also allowed women to stand as parliamentary candidates and specified that elections were to be held on a single day, instead of being spread out over a week or two as previously.

From 'Britain: Domestic Politics 1918-39' by R. Pearce, 1992

Source C *The decline of the Liberal Party*

	Labour vote	Labour % of vote	Labour MPs	Liberal vote	Liberal % of vote	Liberal MPs	PM
1900	63,304	1.8	2	1,568,141	44.6	184	CON
1906	528,797	9.4	30	2,583,132	45.9	377	LIB
1910(Jun)	505,657	7.6	40	2,880,581	43.2	275	LIB
1910(Dec)	371,772	7.1	42	2,295,888	43.9	272	LIB
1918	2,398,773	22.2	60	2,754,448	25.6	161	LIB
1922	4,237,769	29.4	142	4,183,982	29.1	116	CON
1923	4,438,508	30.5	191	4,311,147	29.6	159	LAB
1924	5,489,077	33.3	151	2,928,747	17.6	40	CON
1929	8,389,512	37.1	288	5,308,510	23.4	59	LAB
1931	6,649,630	30.7	52	2,318,510	10.7	72	LAB
1935	8,325,491	37.8	154	1,422,116	6.5	21	CON
1945	11,967,985	48.2	394	2,227,400	8.9	12	CON

This table shows the performance of the Labour Party and Liberal Party at elections between 1900 and 1945. It also shows which party the Prime Minister who took office after each general election belonged to.

Source E *The general election, 1918*

This photo shows a woman voting in the general election held on Saturday 14 December 1918. The election was won by the coalition headed by David Lloyd George. This coalition was dominated by the Conservatives who won 332 seats. It also included 136 'Lloyd George' Liberals and 14 others. The Labour Party won 60 seats and 'Asquith' Liberals (those who opposed Lloyd George) won 27 seats. Lloyd George remained Prime Minister.

Source A *Impact of the war*

The whole texture of British daily life could be said to commemorate the war still. It is remembered in the odd pub closing hours which survived into the 1990s (a result of the Defence of the Realm Act). Afternoon pub closing was designed to discourage the munitions workers of 1915 from idling away their afternoons over beer. Summer time is a legacy of the Great War. So are cigarette smoking, the use of wristwatches (originally a trench fad) and the cultivation of garden allotments ('Food Will Win the War'). So is the use of paper banknotes, entirely replacing gold coins. The playing of 'God save the King' in theatres began in 1914 and continued until the 1970s. Every day, the *Times* and the *Telegraph* still print the little 'In Memoriam' notices - 'sadly missed' and so on - with the military ones separated from the civilian. Even what we eat commemorates the war. Egg and chips became popular during the war because both bacon and steak were scarce and costly. The current economic bankruptcy of Britain is another way the war is remembered. Between 1914 and 1918 Britain's gold reserves were reduced drastically. The USA benefited from this and emerged as an undisputed Great Power.

From 'The Great War and Modern Memory' by P. Fussell, 1975

Source D *Remembrance Day*

This photo shows veterans of the First World War about to lay a wreath in remembrance of their colleagues who died in the war. This ritual takes place every year on 11 November, the day when the Germans agreed to an armistice.

QUESTIONS

1. Judging from the information in this section, how did life in Britain change *during* the First World War?

2. How did life in Britain change (a) in the short term and (b) in the long term *after* the First World War? Use Sources A-E in your answer.

3. Judging from Sources A and D, why do you think the First World War has been described as 'a turning point in British history'?

4. 'Politics in Britain were never the same after the First World War.' Explain this statement using Sources B, C and E.

How was propaganda used by the British government?

The First World War was not just fought with bullets and shells, it was also fought with propaganda. Governments on both sides controlled and restricted the information made available to the public and they bombarded their own people (and sometimes their friends and enemies abroad) with publicity which promoted their point of view. The propaganda produced in Britain during the war had four main aims. First, some propaganda was designed to raise morale and keep it high - to make the British people feel that the war was worth fighting and that they would win. Second, some propaganda was designed to inflame the population against the enemy. It encouraged people to think of the enemy as less than human. Third, some propaganda encouraged people to act in certain ways - ways which would be helpful from the government's point of view. And fourth, some propaganda was aimed at friends and enemies abroad. It encouraged overseas friends to support Britain's war effort and it hoped to persuade enemies to end the war. It should be remembered that the First World War was fought in the age before mass communications - television had not been invented and radio was in its infancy. As a result, governments relied on newspapers, posters, leaflets and word of mouth.

1 Raising morale and encouraging action

When people believe that they are fighting for a good cause and are convinced that they will win, they are more likely to work hard and to suffer hardships without complaint. Realising this, the British government produced posters which portrayed Britain as a nation working happily together to defeat the enemy. Often such posters were produced because the government wanted people to act in a certain way. For example, when there were food shortages later in the war, posters encouraged people not to waste food. The poster (right) was designed by Robert Baden Powell, the founder of the Scout movement in 1908. Baden Powell was a senior army officer. He produced this poster for the Parliamentary Recruiting Committee in 1915.

Are YOU in this?

2 Influencing the views of friends and enemies

Some British propaganda was designed to influence friendly nations. For example, the British government set up a propaganda centre whose aim was to encourage the USA to join the Allies. This centre, headed by Sir Gilbert Parker, produced pamphlets, books and leaflets which it sent, for example, to editors of local newspapers in the USA. Much was made of the fact that 128 Americans were drowned after a U-boat torpedoed the *Lusitania* in 1915. The propaganda from the centre helped to prepare American public opinion for war. British propagandists also tried to influence German public opinion. In 1917 and 1918, over 2 million leaflets were dropped on German towns. The aim was to persuade the German people to give up. There is some evidence that morale dropped, especially in the final months of the war.

3 Inflaming people against the enemy

One way of convincing people that they are fighting for a just cause is to stir up hatred of the enemy. During the war, the government produced many posters which showed atrocities (acts of brutality) supposedly carried out by the enemy. In addition, government propagandists were responsible for spreading hostile rumours about the enemy. For example, in August 1914, newspapers reported that the Kaiser had described the British army as 'a contemptible little army'. In fact this phrase was invented by British propagandists who hoped to keep up spirits during the difficult retreat to Paris. Similarly, British propagandists invented the rumour that the Germans sent corpses to a factory which then used human fat to make candles and boot polish. The poster (right) is typical of this kind of propaganda.

HOW THE HUN HATES!

THE HUNS CAPTURED SOME OF OUR FISHERMEN IN THE NORTH SEA AND TOOK THEM TO SENNELAGER. THEY CHARGED THEM WITHOUT A SHRED OF EVIDENCE WITH BEING "MINE LAYERS". THEY ORDERED THEM TO BE PUNISHED WITHOUT A TRIAL. THAT PUNISHMENT CONSISTED IN SHAVING ALL THE HAIR OFF ONE SIDE OF THE HEAD AND FACE. THE HUNS THEN MARCHED THEIR VICTIMS THROUGH THE STREETS AND EXPOSED THEM TO THE JEERS OF THE GERMAN POPULACE.

BRITISH SAILORS! LOOK! READ! AND REMEMBER!

4 The cinema as propaganda

In 1914, the newest means of informing and influencing the masses was the cinema. By 1917, there were 4,500 cinemas in Britain. The first film to be made as propaganda was Britain Prepared, released in December 1915. Perhaps the most striking film of the war, however, was the Battle of the Somme. This was filmed with the army's permission in late June and early July 1916 and it was released in August 1916, weeks before the real battle had ended. It was the first film to show trench warfare and it even included wounded and dead British soldiers. Some parts were filmed at the front and others were reconstructions. The film was a sensation in Britain. It was even shown to soldiers fighting the real battle in France.

Activity
The film of the Battle of the Somme

Source A A *historian's view*

Although it proved to be an extremely successful government propaganda film, it would be wrong to claim that the *Battle of the Somme* was an attempt by government propagandists to hide the scale of the losses at the start of the Battle of the Somme. Rather, the aim was to use the example of the men at the front to rally civilian support behind the war effort. It would also be wrong to say that there was a plan to make a record of the battle for historians to look back on. In 1916, the War Office had only recently, and without much enthusiasm, relaxed its earlier ban on film and photography at the front. A small number of cameramen (never more than three) was allowed to cover activities on the Western Front. The first material to be produced was a series of short films. It was only after the Somme material was viewed in London that a much longer and grander film was planned.

From 'The Battles of the Somme and Ancre', edited by Roger Smither, 1993

Source B *Invitation to the first screening of the 'Battle of the Somme'*

SCALA THEATRE,
CHARLOTTE STREET, FITZROY SQUARE, W.
Proprietor: Dr. E. Distin Maddick.

THE BRITISH TOPICAL COMMITTEE FOR WAR FILMS
request the pleasure of the company of Bearer and Friend on
THURSDAY NEXT, AUGUST 10th, at 11.30 a.m. prompt,
when they will present
OFFICIAL PICTURES
of the

"BATTLE of the SOMME,"

Taken by Special Arrangement with the
WAR OFFICE
and under their direction.

No "Exclusive Rights" of this film will be granted.
Schedule of prices can be obtained from the sole booking director, W. F. JURY.

The 'Battle of the Somme' was first shown to an invited audience on 10 August 1916. From 21 August, the film was shown in 34 cinemas in London. By October, it had 2,000 bookings all over the country.

Source C *Memoirs of a film maker*

The Somme film has caused a great sensation. I really thought that some of the dead scenes would offend the British public. And yet why should they? They realised that it was their duty to see for themselves. They had been told by the press, by Parliament and by lecturers what was happening, but to no purpose. They must be shown. They must see with their own eyes. I put these questions to all who have seen the film. Did you realise until you saw it what this vast battle front was like? Did you realise what the army was doing - how our wonderful soldiers were driving the Huns back, how they were going to their death with a laugh upon their faces, fighting and dying like true Britons? Yes. The truth has at last dawned upon you.

Extract from 'How I filmed the war' by Geoffrey Malins, one of the two men to film the 'Battle of the Somme', 1920

Source D *Reaction to the film*

Today I went to see the Somme War film. It is not a cheerful sight, but it does give a wonderful idea of the fighting and the front, especially of shelling and its effects. Also, it shows the marvellous courage and cheerfulness of our soldiers in every emergency. As usual, all the pictures move too fast, even the wounded seem to fly along. The most impressive of them to my mind is that of a regiment scrambling out of a trench to charge and of one man who slides back shot dead. There is something appalling about the instantaneous change from fierce activity to death. Indeed, the whole horrible business is appalling. War has always been dreadful, but never, I suppose, more dreadful than today.

From the diary of Henry Rider Haggard, 27 September 1916

Source E *Still from the 'Battle of the Somme'*

This still from the film shows part of an attack sequence which was probably filmed several days before the real attack took place. It is now believed that some scenes were filmed away from the front, possibly at a training school. This, however, has never been confirmed by the War Office.

QUESTIONS

1. a) **Judging from the information in this section, how did the British government use propaganda?**

   b) **Look back through the chapter and find examples of propaganda. Explain how you know they are propaganda.**

2. **What does Source A tell us about the British government's use of film in the First World War?**

3. **What is the evidence in Sources B, C and E to suggest that the 'Battle of the Somme' was a propaganda film?**

4. a) **Why do you think the 'Battle of the Somme' caused a great sensation? Use Sources C and D in your answer.**

   b) **What lessons can be learned from the 'Battle of the Somme' about the use of film as propaganda?**

THE RUSSIAN REVOLUTION

Themes

The year 1917 was a momentous year in Russia. It was a year of revolution. First, Tsar Nicholas II was overthrown. Tsars had ruled Russia, almost exactly as they pleased, for over 500 years. Then, just eight months later, there was a second revolution in which the Bolsheviks (Communists) seized power. Communists remained in power until 1991. This chapter starts by looking at Russia in the early years of the 20th century. By examining the problems faced by Tsar Nicholas before 1917, it is possible to explain why the people rose up against him in that year. Once the Tsar had abdicated (resigned), however, a new set of problems arose. The chapter therefore goes on to explore these new problems and to consider why a second revolution followed the first.

The chapter focuses on the following questions.
* What were the problems facing Russia between 1900 and 1914?
* Why was there a revolution in Russia in February 1917?
* Why was there a second revolution in October 1917?
* How did the Bolsheviks hold on to power after October 1917?

Note

Before 1918, the Russians used a calendar which was slightly different from that used in the rest of Europe (it was 13 days behind the European calendar). Since the Russians themselves refer to the two revolutions in 1917 as the 'February revolution' and the 'October revolution', the old calendar is followed in this chapter. As far as the rest of Europe was concerned, however, the first revolution took place in March and the second in November.

Key Events

1894

Nicholas Romanov (left) becomes Tsar Nicholas II in 1894. He is an autocrat (he has almost unlimited powers). He claims to be God's chosen ruler.

1903

In 1903, a Marxist party, the Social Democrats, splits into two groups - the Mensheviks (majority) and Bolsheviks (minority). The Bolsheviks develop into a small, professional revolutionary group led by Lenin (left).

1904

Russo-Japanese war ends in humiliating defeat for Russia in 1904.

1905 Stolypin's reforms

The 1905 revolution
Peaceful demonstrators shot on 'Bloody Sunday' (22 Jan). This sparks a year of unrest. The Tsar promises reforms but later goes back on his word.

1911

Stolypin (left), the Tsar's chief minister, tries to win support for the Tsar by allowing some peasants to buy land. He was assassinated in 1911.

1914

In August 1914, Russia enters the First World War. After initial gains, it suffers heavy defeats.

1915

In 1915, the Tsar makes himself commander-in-chief of the army.

1916

The government is in the hands of Tsar's wife Alexandra. She relies heavily on the advice of Rasputin (left). Rasputin was assassinated in December 1916.

1917

In February 1917, the first revolution begins. The Tsar abdicates.

1917

In October 1917, the second revolution begins. The Bolsheviks seize power.

1918

Between 1918-21, a civil war is fought. Trotsky (left) organises the Red Army.

1921

In 1921, a New Economic Policy (NEP) is introduced to help recovery after the civil war.

1924

Lenin dies on 21 January 1924.

Why was it difficult to rule Russia in the early 20th century?

Source 1

A historian's description of Russia in the early 20th century

In January 1917, the Russian Empire stretched from Vladivostok in the east to Poland in the west, from the frozen Arctic circle down to the arid lands of central Asia. A population of roughly 125 million inhabited the huge continent, a population whose dominant group of Slavs had spread to all parts of the Empire. More than 100 different nationalities - Armenians, Uzbeks, Mongols and Kazakhs, to name but a few - lived within its boundaries. In terms of religion, Orthodox Russians were joined by Muslims in the south, Lutherans and Catholics in the west. Around 80% of the population were peasants, and illiterate. By the turn of the century, however, industry had made its appearance. The railways had spread their network across the country. Large industrial centres and huge shipyards employed both skilled and raw unskilled labour. Modern technology operated alongside wheelbarrows. The country was ruled by Tsar Nicholas II whose brutal autocratic regime was supported by an aristocracy happier speaking French than Russian, by the army with its smart officer corps and by the Russian Orthodox Church. Rule was carried out through the state bureaucracy centred in St Petersburg, the capital of the Empire. In the provinces, governors ruled with the help of the army and new local government institutions. In February 1917, Tsarism collapsed, brought down when the soldiers joined the women protesting in the bread queues. Nine months of turmoil followed. Revolution gathered speed as social and economic conflict deepened. In October 1917, the Bolsheviks took power in the capital and the revolution spread across the country.

From 'Soviet Politics 1917-1991' by Mary McAuley, 1992

Source 2

A map of Russia in 1900

Great Britain
Arctic Ocean
N
Pacific Ocean
Norway
Sweden
1
B
Germany
Baltic Sea
Kronstadt
C
St Petersburg ★
Eastern Siberia
Western Siberia
1
1
M
3
Austria-Hungary
D
Odessa
Moscow
A
Ural Mountains
RUSSIAN EMPIRE
L
E
3
K
Black Sea
Sebastopol
3
3
F
Turkey
Caspian Sea
G
J
Caucasus Mountains
2
China
Vladivostok
H
I
Korea   Japan
Persia
Afghanistan   India

★ In 1914, St Petersburg was renamed Petrograd
In 1924, Petrograd was renamed Leningrad

CLIMATE AND VEGETATION	PEOPLES		COMMUNICATIONS
1 TUNDRA (Arctic wasteland Frozen all year round. No Crops)	A Russians F Georgians K Mongols		┼┼┼ Trans-Siberian railway
2 DESERT/SEMI-DESERT (Some livestock)	B Finns G Armenians L Tartars		Centres of industry
3 STEPPES (Flat and fertile farmland)	C Poles H Uzbeks M Yakuts		Black Earth region - very fertile soil
	D Ukrainians I Kirghiz		
	E Cossacks J Kazakhs		

QUESTIONS

1. Suppose you had travelled through Russia in 1900. Using Sources 1 and 2 write an account of what you saw.

2. Using Source 1 make a list of the main characteristics of Russia in the early 20th century. Which of these characteristics is illustrated in Source 2?

3. What do Sources 1 and 2 tell us about the difficulties of ruling Russia in the early 20th century?

What were the problems facing Russia in 1900?

In 1900, Russia was a divided and increasingly unstable country. Its problems arose from a dangerous combination of economic change and political inequality. Since Russia was an autocracy (it was ruled by a monarch with absolute power called the Tsar), opposition was focused on the Tsar. In 1905, Tsarist rule came under serious challenge for the first time, but the Tsar survived by promising reforms.

1 Russian society

In 1900, Russian society was divided and top heavy. Those in the top layers of society (the Tsar and the nobles) were few in number and far removed from the mass of the people. They relied on the next levels (the priests and the army) to keep control for them. Sandwiched between the upper levels and the mass of the people came the new middle class (see Box 2.1). Most middle class people had enough money to enjoy life. At the bottom were the workers - people who worked in factories and peasants (poor farm workers). About 80% of Russia's 130 million people were peasants. Although peasants had been freed from serfdom (slavery) in 1861, little had really changed in terms of their everyday life since the middle ages. The cartoon above shows the workers and peasants struggling to hold up the rest of Russian society.

The Tsar
The nobles
The priests
The army
The middle class
The workers and peasants

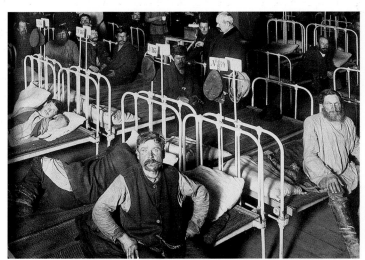

By 1900, large numbers of peasants were leaving the countryside to find factory work in the new industrial towns. They were used as cheap labour in the cotton factories and ironworks of cities such as St Petersburg and Moscow. Living and working conditions were appalling. The photograph above shows workers in a St Petersburg dosshouse in 1900. Many men had to live away from their families in cramped conditions like this.

Box 2.1   The new middle class

Recent economic change had led to the growth of a middle class which made up about 3% of the population. Groups like civil servants, factory owners and teachers belonged to the middle class. Although, in other countries, middle class people tended to support the government, in Russia many did not. They wanted to share political power through an elected Parliament and a free press, neither of which existed in Russia in 1900. In Russia, ministers carried out the Tsar's orders without reporting to any Parliament and the newspapers were carefully censored so that only news favourable to the Tsar was reported. It was even illegal to try to set up or belong to a political party in Russia in 1900.

2 Economic change

In 1900, the Russian economy was old fashioned. It relied mainly on agricultural rather than industrial production. Large landowners rented their land out to peasants who were so poor they could not afford modern tools. Farming techniques were out of date and farming was therefore inefficient. When, from the 1880s, the Tsar attempted to modernise the Russian economy by promoting new industries, he introduced high taxes. Peasants were forced to sell their grain to pay these taxes. This grain was then exported to pay for machinery. The result was food shortages in both the towns where industry was based and in the countryside. In the picture (left), peasants are so poor they have to feed their animals with thatch off the roof.

Political inequality

In 1900, Russia was ruled by Tsar Nicholas II (see picture right and Box 2.2). Some historians have argued that the root of some of the problems faced by Russia in the early 20th century was the personality of Nicholas II. Since the Tsar had such great power, the way in which he behaved was of great importance. But there is evidence that Nicholas never really wanted to be Tsar. He was, some historians claim, a shy, family man who found the day-to-day business of government boring. Despite this, they argue, Nicholas believed that he had been appointed to rule by God and that people should obey his commands without question. This caused problems because he was either ignorant of or chose to ignore the hardships suffered by many ordinary Russians and used his brutal secret police, the Okhrana, to crush any opposition. This gave him the reputation for being uncaring and cruel and dented his popularity with the mass of people. Nicholas also gained the reputation for being a weak man, dominated by his wife Alexandra and her friend and adviser Rasputin (see p.32). In the long term, this undermined his reputation with some members of the nobility and made it more difficult for him to keep control.

The cartoon above shows Nicholas II and Alexandra in the clutches of Rasputin

Box 2.2 — The key features of Tsarist autocracy

* The Tsar had absolute power. He could make laws as there was no elected Parliament.

* The Tsar hand-picked his own ministers - usually his own close friends.

* The Tsar relied on the following groups to carry out his orders: (a) the priests and the army (b) the huge, inefficient civil service which collected taxes and provided local government (c) the secret police who spied on opponents and stamped out opposition and (d) the nobility who were responsible for the peasants who lived on their land.

Box 2.3 — Opposition groups

* **Liberals** - mainly supported by middle class professionals (for example, teachers, doctors, lawyers) and some landowners. They wanted a parliamentary democracy like that which existed in Britain and France.

* **Socialist Revolutionaries** - supported by many students and some industrial workers, but mainly by peasants. They aimed at a violent uprising by the peasants against the Tsar and used terrorist tactics (such as the assassination of members of the nobility).

* **Social Democratic Party** - mainly supported by industrial workers, though some students and middle class professionals joined. This party supported the ideas of Karl Marx and hoped for a revolution in which the industrial working class would overthrow the Tsar and seize power.

Opposition groups

By 1900, three main strands of opposition to Tsarist rule had emerged (see Box 2.3). Whilst the Liberals hoped for gradual reform, the other two groups aimed at violent revolution. The Socialist Revolutionaries hoped to persuade the majority of peasants to rise up against the Tsar, but found that many remained loyal to their 'father' Tsar and blamed their misfortunes on the nobles. The Social Democratic Party hoped that the ideas of Karl Marx (see right) could be adapted to Russian conditions. In 1903, the Party split into two. The Mensheviks (majority) wanted to build a mass party, whilst the Bolsheviks (minority), led by Lenin, aimed to build a small group of professional revolutionaries who would dedicate their lives to the struggle against Tsarist rule.

The ideas of Karl Marx

1. Industrial society is divided into two main groups. At the top is the 'ruling class' - people who own businesses and land. At the bottom is the 'working class' - people who work in factories and on the land. In time, the workers become fed up because they remain poor no matter how hard they work. The ruling class has money and power but refuses to share them with the workers.

Karl Marx (1818-83)

2. Eventually, Marx claimed, the workers would become so fed up that they would start a revolution. Their aim would be to make things more equal. Marx argued that there would be two phases in this revolution.

3. First, the workers would take control of government and work out how best to share out money and power between everybody.

4. Second, as things became more equal, there would be no need for government. People would share out things without being told to do so. There would no longer be different classes. This is Communism.

5 The 1905 revolution

Between 1900 and 1904, there were signs that even some members of the nobility were growing dissatisfied with Nicholas' rule. To divert attention, the Tsar's chief minister, Plehve, argued that a 'small, victorious war' was necessary. In 1904, therefore, Russia provoked a war with Japan, Russia's rival for power and territory in China. At first, this war was welcomed as a means of rallying the country behind the Tsar. But, as news of serious setbacks spread, so unrest grew. When the war ended with humiliating defeat in January 1905, the economic, social and political tension exploded in what later came to be known as the 1905 revolution. In St Petersburg, the police had secretly set up a trade union to draw factory workers away from the more extreme revolutionary groups. Membership of the union grew rapidly and, it seems, the union's leader, a Tsarist police agent named Father Gapon, became genuinely converted to the workers' cause. Early in 1905, he organised a major strike at the Putilov ironworks and on 22 January he led a procession of 200,000 workers to the Tsar's Winter Palace. The aim was to present a petition calling for better working conditions. Nicholas had, in fact, left the city. As the marchers approached the Palace, they were attacked by the Tsar's armed guards. The massacre of 'Bloody Sunday' sparked a year of unrest (see Box 2.4). It was the first serious challenge to Nicholas' rule.

'Bloody Sunday' - troops attack protestors

6 The aftermath of the 1905 revolution

Box 2.4   The 1905 revolution

JAN	FEB	MAR	JUN	OCT
'Bloody Sunday' At least 96 killed and over 300 injured	Assassination of Tsar's uncle Grand Duke Sergei	Increased peasant unrest	Battleship Potemkin mutinies in the port of Odessa. Over 2,000 die in street fighting which follows. Two other mutinies in Kronstadt and Sebastopol	2.5 million workers join a general strike. Soviets (workers' councils) set up in St Petersburg and Moscow

Box 2.5   The October Manifesto

* Duma (elected Parliament) to be created with the power to make new laws and to supervise the work of the Tsar's ministers.

* Duma to be elected by peasants (43%), landowners (33%) and townspeople who owned property (23%). Most industrial workers did not qualify. No women were allowed to vote.

* New civil rights promised - eg the freedom to meet, the freedom of speech, the freedom to form political parties and the freedom of worship.

Peter Stolypin (above) has been described as a 'potential saviour of Tsarism'.

By October 1905, Nicholas realised that, if Tsarist rule was to survive, reforms would have to be promised. The result was the October Manifesto (see Box 2.5). This suggested Nicholas would become a figurehead, leaving the important decisions to elected politicians - rather like the monarch in Britain. The Manifesto made an immediate impact. By the beginning of 1906, the unrest had died down. But Nicholas soon went back on his promises. After just three months, the first Duma was dissolved (shut down) because it demanded more reforms (changes in taxation, the abolition of the death penalty and the right to strike). The second Duma was also dissolved in June 1907. Then, ignoring the new constitution (which said that the Duma must approve constitutional changes), the Tsar's chief minister, Peter Stolypin, changed the voting laws. A landlord's vote became worth 600 times that of a peasant. As a result, the Duma became the tool of the Tsar. The third and fourth Dumas lasted for their full five year terms, but they opposed reform and supported whatever measures the Tsar and his ministers proposed. Stolypin had become chief minister in 1906. He had two main policies. First, he took a hard line against opponents - in 1906 alone over 1,000 people were executed for terrorist offences. And second, he introduced land reforms to encourage the growth of richer, landowning peasants (kulaks). For the first time, peasants were allowed to leave their local commune (mir) and farm their own land. Government loans helped them to buy land. Stolypin's goal was that these kulaks would not only help to modernise the Russian economy, but that they would also support the system of Tsarist rule which favoured them. However, before his goal could be achieved he was assassinated in 1911.

Activity
Tsarist Russia

Source A *Tsar Nicholas II - Contemporary views*

He has infantile judgements.
Tsar Alexander III, 1892

I shall maintain the principles of autocracy just as firmly and unflinchingly as did my late, unforgettable father.
Nicholas II, 1895

I am not prepared to become Tsar. I never wanted to become one. I know nothing of the business of ruling. I have no idea of even how to talk to ministers.
Nicholas II on hearing that his father had died, 1894

Nicholas II is not fit to run a post office.
A government minister

His family did not endow him with one quality which would have made him capable of governing an empire.
Leon Trotsky, an opponent of Tsarism

His real affection was for his family. Well-meaning, his character did not allow him to respond to the gigantic events of his reign.
Count Beckendorff, a member of the nobility

The Tsar did not appear mentally or physically strong. He was slim, not very tall, and delicate looking. He entered the room shy, uncertain, indecisive and awkward.
A British MP, 1896

My poor Nicky's cross is heavy. He remains brave and full of faith in God's mercy. He tries so hard.
Tsarina Alexandra (Nicholas II's wife)

His mentality and his circumstances kept him wholly out of touch with his people. He found the daily routine of monarchy very boring. When it came to defending his divine right to be Tsar, his usual indifference left him. He became cunning, obstinate, cruel and merciless at times.
Alexander Kerensky, an opponent of Tsarism

The Tsar can change his mind from one minute to the next. He's a sad man. He lacks guts.
Rasputin, a friend and adviser to the Tsar's family

Source B *Tsar Nicholas II - a historian's view*

It is hard to imagine anyone less well equipped to steer Russia into the 20th century than Nicholas II. A family man first and foremost, as an autocrat he was hopeless. Nicholas' personality did not help him overcome the limitations of his education. A short, neat figure of a man, 5 feet 7 inches tall, he was timid, introverted and weak in the sense that he was incapable of making up his mind and sticking to his decisions. However, it must be said that he always commanded great love and loyalty in his immediate circle, together with a considerable amount of respect. He had great charm. Yet, despite his majesty of manner, he lacked that taste for power which is vital for an autocrat.

From 'The Life and Times of Rasputin' by A. de Jonge, 1983

Source C *Russian economic growth, 1861-1913*

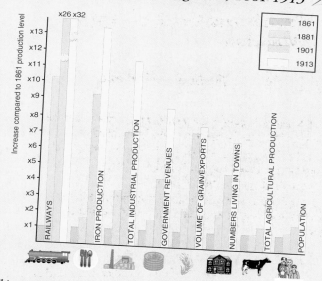

This graph shows how economic production increased in Russia between 1861 and 1913.

1. Judging from the information in this section: **(a) What were the main problems faced by Russia between 1900 and 1914? (b) How successfully were they solved?**
2. a) **Using Source A describe the strengths and weaknesses of the Tsar's character.**
   b) **'Nicholas II's character was the main obstacle to the survival of Tsarist rule after 1900.' Do you agree with this view? Explain your answer.**
3. **How reliable is the historian's account in Source B? Give reasons for your answer.**
4. a) **What conclusions about Russia's economic development can you reach from Source C?**
   b) **What problems might arise from this economic development?**

'Revolution' is a label used by historians to describe a sudden moment of great change in a country's history. Often, a revolution involves the overthrow of one kind of government and the setting up of a new system. In Russia in 1917, there were two revolutions. The February revolution led to the overthrow of Tsarist rule and the setting up of a provisional government. Then, the October revolution resulted in the overthrow of the provisional government and the setting up of a Bolshevik (Communist) government. Historians usually try to explain why revolutions happen by examining both long-term and short-term causes (see Box 2.6). Although, by 1914, it seemed that the Tsar had been able to solve some of the problems which faced Russia in 1900 (see previous section), these continued to act as the long-term basis for discontent. Then, between 1914 and 1917, the extra strains imposed by the First World War finally stretched Tsarist Russia to breaking point. The impact of the war is therefore central to an explanation of why Tsarist rule collapsed in February 1917. The events in February 1917 which triggered the revolution, however, must also be considered.

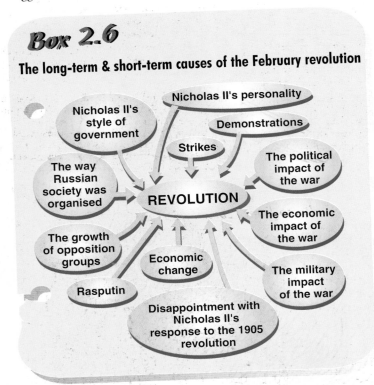

Box 2.6

The long-term & short-term causes of the February revolution

Nicholas II's style of government — Nicholas II's personality — Demonstrations — Strikes — The political impact of the war — The way Russian society was organised — REVOLUTION — The economic impact of the war — The growth of opposition groups — Economic change — The military impact of the war — Rasputin — Disappointment with Nicholas II's response to the 1905 revolution

1 Military impact of the First World War

In 1914, the Russian army was the largest in the world with 6.5 million troops. Although the first few weeks of the war were a success, old fashioned tactics and mistakes by the aristocratic generals led to crushing defeats in the Battle of Tannenburg (27-30 August 1914) and the Masurian Lakes (two weeks later). By June 1916, over 1 million Russian soldiers had been killed and another million taken prisoner. Many more were sick. Equipment, weapons and food were in short supply. Morale was very low. In June 1916, the Russian commander, General Brusilov, attacked Austria. Again the Russian army made quick gains. By October, however, lack of equipment and arms had ensured that this offensive, too, had failed. In the winter of 1916, many soldiers began to desert the army.

2 Political impact of the First World War

In August 1915, the Tsar took personal control of the army for the first time. This was a mistake for two reasons. First, it ensured that people would blame the Tsar himself (rather than the commander he had appointed) if the army suffered any defeats. And second, it meant that Nicholas had to leave St Petersburg for the army headquarters. In his absence, Nicholas left the government in the hands of his wife, Alexandra. This caused resentment amongst the nobility. Alexandra was accused of being too easily led by her favourite, Rasputin (see Box 2.7). Although Rasputin held no formal office and there is little evidence that he actually influenced policy decisions, he did have some influence over appointments. Between August 1915 and December 1916, more than 20 new ministers were sacked and appointed by Alexandra. Not only did this rapid turnover of ministers increase resentment amongst the nobility, it also resulted in greater inefficiency. The supply of food, fuel and equipment to the troops and to towns dried up. As a result, unrest grew. More and more soldiers deserted. Workers went on strike and demonstrated against Tsarist rule.

Box 2.7 Rasputin

'Rasputin' is a nickname meaning degenerate or immoral.

c.1862 Born Grigory Yefimovich in Siberia. His parents were peasants.

1904 Birth of Alexis, Tsar's son. Alexis has haemophilia (a disease which prevents blood from clotting).

Nov 1905 Grigory (Rasputin), a 'man of God' meets the Tsar and stops Alexis' bleeding. Regular visits to the Tsar's family follow.

1911 Rumours spread about Rasputin's behaviour. He is hated by many nobles because of his background, his supposed influence (especially over Alexandra) and his supposed affairs with women from the nobility.

Jun 1914 He survives an assassination attempt and encourages the Tsar to avoid war.

1915 When the Tsar leaves St Petersburg in August, rumours suggest that Alexandra does whatever Rasputin tells her to do. Certainly, he is a trusted adviser.

Dec 1916 A group of nobles invites Rasputin to a dinner party and then kills him. He is poisoned with potassium cyanide and then shot. Still alive, he is thrown into the freezing River Neva. Some historians argue that Rasputin's murder was the first step to revolution because, by killing Rasputin, even members of the nobility showed they had little respect for the Tsar.

③ Economic impact of the war

The First World War put an enormous strain on Russia's economy. Industry suffered because of supply problems (shortages of fuel and labour) and because it relied on imports (which did not arrive). Agriculture suffered because many peasants left to join the army and because Russia's transport system broke down. Food was produced, but it did not reach the towns. In some places there were food shortages (the photo above, for example, shows a bread queue in Petrograd in February 1917). In other places, piles of excess food lay rotting. Lack of food in the big cities, combined with high prices, led to strikes and demonstrations. The war, therefore, made existing economic problems worse and showed the government's inability to cope in a crisis.

④ The events of February 1917

22 Feb	23 Feb	26 Feb	27 Feb	28 Feb	1 Mar	2 Mar

Workers locked out of a steel factory in Petrograd after pay talks break down.

The Duma sends a message to the Tsar warning him that there is a crisis. The Tsar orders the Duma to stop meeting. The Duma refuses.

The Soviet issues 'Order Number 1' calling on troops to obey nobody except the Soviet.

The Tsar leaves army HQ for Petrograd. His train is stopped by revolutionaries. His generals tell him he no longer has the support of the army.

International Women's Day. Marches and strikes in Petrograd as a protest against fuel and food shortages and in support of locked out workers. Over the next three days, marches and strikes spread.

The Tsar agrees to abdicate (resign).

Crowds demand the removal of the Tsar. Soldiers mutiny. They join the demonstrators. The Duma sets up a committee of 12 to take over the government - the **provisional government**. At the same time, workers and soldiers set up a council (a **Soviet**) to take over the government.

Activity
The February revolution

Source A *A historian's view*

It was war which paved the way for the revolution. First there was the humiliation of the war against Japan and then the First World War. Russian soldiers were hurled at German machine guns by aristocratic officers using old fashioned tactics. Sometimes they were ordered to charge armed only with bayonets and hand grenades. At first, the soldiers responded with courage which exposed them to fearful casualties. Well over a million men were killed. More than 4 million were wounded (of whom at least 350,000 died of their wounds) and a further 2 million were captured. Their hardships were increased by inadequate supplies and disease. Life was also very difficult for civilians. So many men had gone to the war that both farming and industry were crippled. By January 1917, the transport system had broken down and the bread and fuel needed in cities failed to reach them. Tens of thousands of workers were out of work or on strike. Revolutionary propaganda made them increasingly restless. Alexander Briansky was alive in 1917. Interviewed recently, he said: 'We lived very badly. It got so bad there wasn't even a piece of bread.' He decided to join the revolutionaries: 'There were many reasons - hatred for the Tsarists, the shooting of ordinary strikers, this endless war that didn't show any mercy to people.'

Adapted from 'The People's Century' by G. Hodgson, 1995

Source B *Photo from February 1917*

This photo shows a group of Cossacks demonstrating against the Tsar in February 1917. Traditionally, the Cossacks had been the most loyal of the Tsar's troops. In February 1917, however, they joined the demonstrators.

QUESTIONS

1. List all the causes of the February revolution saying whether each is a long-term or a short-term cause. Then write a paragraph explaining why there was a revolution.

2. 'Without the war, there would have been no revolution'. Give arguments for and against this view. Use Source A in your answer.

3. What does Source B tell us about the mood in February 1917? Why was the behaviour of the Cossacks important?

Why was there a second revolution in October 1917?

By the time that the Tsar had abdicated, two different centres of power had emerged - the provisional government (a moderate, mainly middle class committee made up of members of the Duma) and the Petrograd Soviet (an increasingly revolutionary council of workers and soldiers). At first, power was shared by the two groups in what became known as 'dual government'. Dual government, however, soon resulted in confusion as the two groups struggled for power. Between May and August 1917, the provisional government made a number of mistakes. These mistakes were then brilliantly exploited by the Bolsheviks (Communists) who were able to seize power in October. Without the confusion caused by the February revolution, it is unlikely that the Bolsheviks would have been able to seize power. It can be argued, therefore, that the February revolution was itself a major reason why there was a second revolution in October (see Box 2.8).

Dual government

The provisional government had difficulties from the start (see Box 2.9). Its members had belonged to the Duma (which was loyal to the Tsar until the last moment). They were not elected. And they lacked the power to enforce their decisions. The main reason they were tolerated was because the government was provisional (temporary) - it was to be in charge only until full-scale elections were held. The Petrograd Soviet, on the other hand, had great popular support. It was an elected body and its decisions were accepted by the mass of workers and soldiers in Petrograd. Similar soviets sprang up throughout Russia and followed the lead given by the Petrograd Soviet. Since the Petrograd Soviet had popular support and widespread influence, the provisional government had to consult it and take its wishes into account ('dual government'). Dual government was only possible, however, as long as there was agreement between the two bodies. At first, the Petrograd Soviet was led by moderates who supported the provisional government. As this support faded, the best hope for the provisional government seemed to come from the leadership of Alexander Kerensky (see Box 2.10).

Box 2.8 **The causes of the October revolution**

- Lenin's arrival in Petrograd
- Dual government created tension
- The February revolution
- Provisional government continues war
- Role of Lenin
- No land reforms
- **OCTOBER REVOLUTION**
- No elections held for new Parliament
- Trotsky organises Red Guard
- The Kornilov revolt
- Bolsheviks oppose provisional government
- Bolsheviks win control of Petrograd
- Kerensky's military offensive fails

Box 2.9 **The provisional government**

'The February revolution had been made in the streets of Petrograd without leaders and without a programme. The Tsar had gone. Otherwise nothing was changed. The provisional government simply carried on the old system, just as a hen continues to run round the yard when its head has been cut off.'

A.J.P. Taylor (a British historian), introduction to 'Ten Days that Shook the World' by John Reed, 1977

2 The role of Lenin and the Bolshevik Party

At the time of the February revolution, Lenin was in exile in Switzerland. The German government, however, allowed Lenin and other revolutionaries to travel back to Russia in a special train in the hope that they would encourage Russians to end the war. Before Lenin's return, Bolsheviks in Russia had supported the provisional government. But when Lenin arrived in Petrograd on 3 April he made a speech to his supporters calling for 'peace, bread and land' and 'all power to the soviets'. Lenin had no time for the provisional government. He wanted a further revolution which would give power to the Bolsheviks. To achieve this, he encouraged the Bolsheviks to oppose everything that the provisional government did. At first, the Bolsheviks were the only group to oppose the provisional government. As a result, when the provisional government lost popularity, support for the Bolsheviks grew rapidly.

An artist's impression of Lenin's arrival in Petrograd (at the Finland Station) on 3 April 1917. The speech he made on his arrival was written up as a pamphlet known as the 'April Theses'.

③ The mistakes made by the provisional government

Between May and October 1917, the provisional government made a series of mistakes which played into the hands of the Bolsheviks. First and most important, no steps were taken to end the war. Although large numbers of troops had deserted after hearing about the February revolution and although supplies of equipment and arms had not improved, Kerensky (see Box 2.10) organised a new offensive against the Germans and Austrians in June. By July, this offensive had failed. Military failure led to discontent. Second, the provisional government announced in April that there would not be full-scale elections until November. This gave the impression that the provisional government did not want to let go of power. Third, the provisional government failed to pass promised land reforms (it was argued that these, like other measures, should wait until the new Parliament was elected in November). But after the February revolution, many peasants simply began to grab land for themselves. The result was chaos in the countryside. The provisional government could not keep order. Food supplies were no better than they had been under the Tsar. By the summer of 1917, therefore, Lenin's demand for 'peace, bread and land' had begun to have great appeal, especially since the Bolsheviks had carefully distanced themselves from the provisional government.

④ The Kornilov revolt

General Kornilov. His revolt had failed by 29 August 1917

Following the military defeat in July, discontented crowds gathered in the big cities (the 'July Days'). The Bolsheviks hoped the demonstrations would lead to a second revolution. Kerensky, however, was able to restore order since the troops remained loyal to the provisional government. Some leading Bolsheviks were imprisoned and others (including Lenin) went into hiding. It seemed that the Bolshevik threat had been overcome. In August, however, the new commander-in-chief of the army, General Kornilov, appears to have plotted some kind of military takeover (see Box 2.11). To defend Petrograd from attack, Kerensky released Bolshevik leaders from prison and armed their supporters. Although Kornilov never reached Petrograd (railway workers refused to allow his train to move), the damage was done. The Bolsheviks came to be seen as the defenders of Petrograd, and now they were armed.

⑤ The events of October 1917

Events after Kornilov's revolt moved very quickly: **6 Sept** Bolsheviks win control of the Petrograd Soviet and on **23 Sept** a leading Bolshevik, Leon Trotsky, is elected to chair it. **10 Oct** Lenin argues that the Bolsheviks must seize power before the November elections. Bolshevik leadership (the Central Committee) agrees. **12 Oct** Trotsky sets up the Military Revolutionary Committee (MRC). This issues orders to soldiers and plans the uprising. Soldiers obey MRC rather than the provisional government. **24 Oct** Trotsky wins support of Petrograd garrison. Kerensky moves against Bolsheviks, closing down their press. **25 Oct** Bolshevik uprising. Winter Palace stormed. Kerensky flees, hoping to raise support from troops at the front (he fails and goes into exile). **26 Oct** Bolsheviks begin to take control in other cities. Bitter fighting in Moscow for a week before Bolsheviks win control there.

An artist's impression of the storming of the Winter Palace, the provisional government's headquarters. In reality, when the Red Guards (Bolsheviks) attacked, there was virtually no resistance.

Activity
Lenin in 1917

Source B Lenin returns to Russia in April 1917

An artist's impression of Lenin arriving at the Finland station in April 1917.

Source E Lenin in disguise

This photograph shows Lenin in disguise in the summer of 1917. After the July Days, Lenin was forced to flee to Finland to escape arrest. He remained in hiding until secretly arriving in Petrograd on 10 October to attend a meeting of the Bolshevik Central Committee. At this meeting, Lenin urged the other Bolsheviks to agree to an immediate armed uprising. Although a date for an uprising was agreed, it was the date suggested by Trotsky, not Lenin. Also, several leading Bolsheviks argued against an armed uprising.

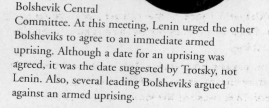

Source A Lenin on the Kornilov revolt

The Kornilov revolt is an unbelievably sharp turn in events. Like every sharp turn, it calls for a revision and a change of tactics. Even now we must not support Kerensky's government. We will be asked: aren't we going to fight against Kornilov? Of course we must! We shall fight, we are fighting against Kornilov, just as Kerensky's troops do. But we do not support Kerensky. On the contrary, by fighting Kornilov, we expose how weak Kerensky is. We must use the fight against Kornilov to bring revolution nearer - by drawing the masses in, by arousing them and by inflaming them.

This extract from Lenin's 'Selected Works', vol.2, was written at the time of the Kornilov revolt in August 1917

Source C Lenin calls for an uprising in October

Now that the Bolsheviks have a majority on the Petrograd Soviet and the Moscow Soviet, they can and must take state power into their own hands. They can do so because the revolutionary element in both cities is strong enough to carry the people with it, to overcome opposition and to gain and keep power. By immediately proposing peace, by immediately giving land to the peasants and by re-establishing the democratic institutions shattered by Kerensky, the Bolsheviks will form a government which nobody will be able to overthrow. The Bolsheviks must take power now because the imminent surrender of Petrograd will reduce our chances a hundred times. And, it would be a mistake to wait for a majority in the new Parliament. No revolution ever waits for that. History will not forgive us if we do not take power now.

Part of a letter written by Lenin to the Central Committee of the Bolshevik Party in October 1917

Source D A historian's view

Lenin, from the time of his return to Russia in April 1917, was the overall strategist of the revolution. He also dealt with internal divisions within the Party and provided a degree of discipline and unity which the other parties lacked. Above all, he was entirely responsible for the timing of the October revolution. He had realised that the rising of July 1917 was premature and therefore urged restraint on that occasion. But by October he calculated that circumstances had changed sufficiently to warrant immediate action and he urged: 'We must not wait! We may lose everything!'

From S.J. Lee 'The European dictatorships', 1987

QUESTIONS

1. **Judging from the information in this section, why was there a second revolution in Russia in October 1917?**

2. **'Lenin spent most of 1917 in exile. His role was not that important.' Using Sources A-E give arguments for and against this view.**

3. **What evidence is there in Sources A and C to support the arguments made in Source D?**

4. **Compare Source B with the picture on p.34. How useful are these pictures to someone studying the Russian revolution?**

Ten Days which Shook the World by John Reed

John Reed was born in 1887 in Portland, Oregon in the USA. He studied at Harvard University and became a journalist. Despite his wealthy background, he became a socialist and in 1913 was briefly jailed for helping to organise a strike. The following year, he made his name with the publication of *Insurgent Mexico*, an account of his experiences during the Mexican revolution. In 1917, Reed travelled to Russia. He reached Petrograd in late August 1917 and stayed in Russia until 1919. In 1919 he returned to the USA and helped to found the Communist Party of the USA. His account of the October revolution, *Ten Days which Shook the World*, was first published in March 1919. Reed returned to Russia and died of typhus in 1920.

Ten Days which Shook the World - a historian's view

Dazzled by Reed's achievement, we may fail to appreciate exactly what it was. The book provides first-hand evidence when Reed describes what he saw and experienced. But much of it was not first hand. Often, Reed sat in the quiet of his hotel room tapping away on his typewriter. He would piece together fragments of conversations, add imaginative detail of what was likely to have happened and crown all with a brilliant phrase. For instance, Reed often says that Smolny (headquarters of the Petrograd Soviet) was 'humming with activity'. There is little detail about what people were actually doing there because Reed did not know. He was a foreign journalist, though a sympathetic one, and the Bolsheviks revealed to him few of their secrets. A further warning is necessary. In 1927, Eisenstein, the famous film director, made a film for the 10th anniversary of the Bolshevik revolution. He used Reed's book as his script. It is tempting to see the film as somehow confirming what is written in the book. This is not the case. Much of the film is fiction, as indeed is much of Reed's book.

Adapted from A.J.P. Taylor's introduction to 'Ten Days which Shook the World' by John Reed, 1967.

Extract from *Ten Days which Shook the World*

When we came out into the chill night, the front of Smolny was one huge park of arriving and departing automobiles, above the sound of which could be heard the far-off, slow beat of the cannon. A great motor truck stood there, shaking to the roar of its engine. Men were tossing bundles into it, and others receiving them, with guns beside them. 'Where are you going?' I shouted. 'Downtown - all over - everywhere!' answered a little workman, grinning. We showed our passes. 'Come along!' they invited. 'But there'll probably be shooting.' We climbed in. The truck jerked forward past the huge fire by the gate and then the fire by the outer gate, glowing red on the faces of the workmen with rifles who squatted around it, and then bumping at top speed down the Suvorovsky Prospect...One man tore the wrapping from a bundle and began to hurl handfuls of paper into the air. We imitated him. Passers-by stopped to pick them up; the patrols around bonfires on the corners ran out with uplifted arms to catch them. I picked up a copy of the paper and under a fleeting streetlight read: *TO THE CITIZENS OF RUSSIA! The provisional government is deposed. The state power has passed into the hands of the organ of the Petrograd Soviet of Workers' and Soldiers' Deputies, the Military Revolutionary Committee, which stands at the head of the Petrograd workers and garrison...LONG LIVE THE REVOLUTION OF WORKERS, SOLDIERS AND PEASANTS.*

An actor playing Lenin arrives at the Finland Station in Eisenstein's film 'October' which was made in 1927 and based on 'Ten Days which Shook the World'.

QUESTIONS

1. Lenin said that John Reed gave 'a truthful and most vivid' account of the October revolution. Do you agree? Describe the problems historians face when using John Reed's account as source material.

2. What evidence is there in the extract above to suggest that John Reed was not impartial about the events he was describing?

3. Would you expect Eisenstein's film 'October' to provide an accurate account of the October revolution? Give reasons for your answer.

When the Bolsheviks overthrew the provisional government in Petrograd in October 1917, Russia did not suddenly become a Bolshevik country. Rather, this was just a first step in that direction. Outside large cities like Petrograd and Moscow support for the Bolshevik Party was small. Other parties expected and demanded a share in government. But the Bolshevik leaders were determined to govern alone. The result was that, within six months, civil war had broken out between those who supported the Bolsheviks (the 'Reds') and those who supported their opponents (the 'Whites'). By winning the civil war, the Bolshevik Party (renamed the Communist Party in 1918) hung on to power. At the same time, the experience of civil war shaped the type of government which emerged.

All power to the soviets

The Bolsheviks came to power on the slogan 'all power to the soviets'. They did not believe in dual government. They wanted the soviets (the workers', soldiers' and peasants' councils) to rule on their own. As a result, the Bolsheviks timed their uprising in Petrograd so that it took place when representatives from soviets from all over Russia were meeting there at the second All-Russian Congress of Soviets. As soon as the Congress found out that the Bolsheviks had seized power, it voted to set up a new Soviet government. A Council of People's Commissars or 'Sovnarkom' was appointed. These Commissars (ministers) had the power to issue decrees (orders). Significantly, all members of the Sovnarkom were Bolsheviks. The Bolsheviks also timed their uprising in Petrograd so that it took place before elections to a new Constituent Assembly (Parliament) were held, knowing that they were unlikely to win a majority in these elections. Elections went ahead for the new Assembly as planned (see Box 2.12) and it met for the first and only time on 5 January 1918. At this meeting, Bolshevik members proposed that the Assembly accept a declaration giving power to the soviets. When a majority voted against the declaration, the Sovnarkom ordered Red Guards to close the Assembly down.

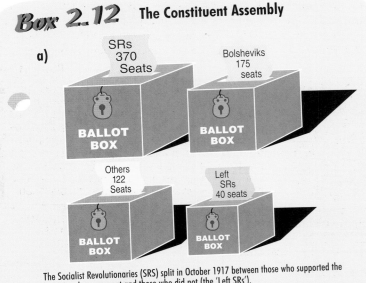

Box 2.12 **The Constituent Assembly**

a)

SRs 370 Seats — BALLOT BOX

Bolsheviks 175 seats — BALLOT BOX

Others 122 Seats — BALLOT BOX

Left SRs 40 seats — BALLOT BOX

The Socialist Revolutionaries (SRS) split in October 1917 between those who supported the provisional government and those who did not (the 'Left SRs').

b) Take any parliamentary country from America to Switzerland, from France to Britain, Norway and so forth - in these countries the real business of state is performed behind the scenes. Parliament is given up to talk for the special purpose of fooling the common people.

Extract from 'State and Revolution', written by Lenin when in hiding in the summer of 1917

Peace, bread and land

— Boundary of Russia 1914
— Territory lost at Brest-Litovsk but regained after the war
— Territory lost at Brest-Litovsk but not regained after the war

FINLAND, Petrograd, Estonia, Baltic Sea, Latvia, Moscow, Lithuania, RUSSIA, POLAND, Brest-Litovsk, UKRAINE, Caspian Sea, GEORGIA, Black Sea

This map shows the territory Russia lost by signing the Treaty of Brest-Litovsk. Some territory was regained after Germany's defeat in 1918.

The Bolsheviks also came to power on the slogan 'peace, bread and land'. To show that the Bolsheviks meant business, on 26 October (the day after the uprising in Petrograd) Lenin (President of the Sovnarkom) announced two decrees. The first ordered that peace negotiations should begin. The second abolished the private ownership of land - all land owned by the Tsar, the Church and other landlords was to be given to the peasants to divide between themselves. The land decree legalised what was happening anyway (all over Russia peasants were seizing land for themselves). The peace decree led to immediate negotiations with Germany. These negotiations were carried out by the new People's Commissar for Foreign Affairs, Leon Trotsky, and took place in the town of Brest-Litovsk. The Germans knew that the Bolsheviks were desperate to end the war and would therefore accept peace on almost any terms. At first, Trotsky thought the German demands so severe that he withdrew from negotiations. But Lenin insisted that an agreement to end the war was essential. In March 1918, the Treaty of Brest-Litovsk was signed. Peace was secured, but at a heavy price (see map, left, and Box 2.13).

Box 2.13 **The Treaty of Brest-Litovsk**

a) Terms of the Treaty
Russia loses:
* Poland and the Baltic states
* 27% of its agricultural land
* 80% of its coal mines
* 26% of its population
* 75% of its iron and steel works
* 26% of its railway network

b) Lenin on the Treaty
'It is a question of signing the terms now or signing the death sentence of the Soviet government three weeks later'.

③ Civil war, 1918-21

By the time that the Treaty of Brest-Litovsk was signed, the Bolsheviks (or Communists as they were known from March 1918) had already made many enemies. Not only did they face opposition from those who had supported the Tsar or the provisional government, they upset landowners who lost their land, industrialists who lost their factories (all factories were placed under the control of elected committees of workers in December 1917) and those supporters of parties whose elected representatives had been locked out of the Constituent Assembly. In addition, by negotiating a separate peace with Germany, the Bolsheviks greatly annoyed their former wartime allies. In May 1917, Czech prisoners of war overpowered their Communist guards and seized control of part of the Trans-Siberian railway (the main communication between the west and east). Other enemies of the new government (including soldiers from abroad) joined them and a civil war began. This war lasted for three years, ending in victory for the Red Army. During the war, both sides acted with great brutality and there was great suffering. When the Red Army finally won victory, opposition parties were banned and Russia was run as a one-party state. Some historians argue that the Communists were moving towards a one-party state even before the civil war broke out. They point out that, even before the end of 1917, the new government had closed down the Constituent Assembly and had banned non-Bolshevik newspapers and an opposition party (the pro-Tsarist 'Cadets'). Other historians argue that it was the experience of the civil war which pushed the government in this direction.

The civil war

The Red Army

The Red Army was brilliantly organised by Leon Trotsky. At first, it was untrained and undisciplined. But Trotsky used ex-Tsarist officers to train and lead the soldiers. By including in each unit a political commissar from the Communist Party, he secured the loyalty of the officers. By travelling around the war zone in an armoured train, Trotsky kept up morale. Any indiscipline was severely punished.

Leon Trotsky on board his train during the civil war

The Cheka & the Red Terror

In December 1917, the new government set up a secret police force, the Cheka, led by Felix Dzerzhinsky. When, in August 1918, Lenin was shot (he survived), this led to the 'Red Terror'. During the war, several thousand people suspected of helping or fighting for the Whites were arrested and executed by the Cheka. Often they were tortured. The most famous victims of the Red Terror were the Tsar and his family. They were shot in 1918.

Felix Dzerzhinsky, Chief of the Cheka

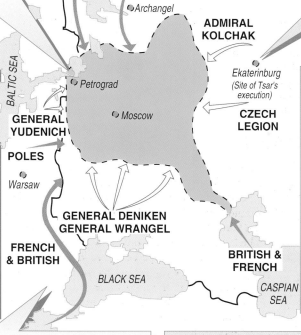

- ☐ Area under Communist control 1918
- → White Russian forces
- ⇒ Non-Russian anti-Bolshevik forces
- — Border of Soviet territory

AMERICAN BRITISH, FRENCH

Archangel

ADMIRAL KOLCHAK

Ekaterinburg (Site of Tsar's execution)

CZECH LEGION

BALTIC SEA

Petrograd

Moscow

GENERAL YUDENICH

POLES

Warsaw

GENERAL DENIKEN GENERAL WRANGEL

FRENCH & BRITISH

BLACK SEA

BRITISH & FRENCH

CASPIAN SEA

Reasons for the Reds' victory

* Trotsky's tactical ability
* The Whites had no single leader and no clear plan.
* The Whites were made up of many different groups with different aims. All that united them was opposition to the Reds.
* The Reds controlled the central region of Russia, including Moscow and Petrograd.
* The Reds had good internal lines of communication and could use the railways to move their troops from front to front as needed.
* The White armies did not receive as much aid from their foreign allies as they hoped.

War Communism

During the war, it was crucial that the Red Army had enough food and weapons. To ensure that this happened, the government took charge of the economy. All factories were nationalised (came under government control) and private trading was banned. The government fixed the price of grain and peasants had to hand their produce over to the government, They could not sell it for profit. Food was carefully rationed, especially in the cities. Peasants who refused to hand over their produce were imprisoned or executed.

Foreign intervention

The civil war in Russia was complicated by foreign intervention. This began in 1918 and involved 14 countries. The Japanese sent over 60,000 troops. Britain sent around 40,000. The USA sent about 10,000. Other countries sent smaller forces. Allied forces helped White armies by providing military supplies (for example, General Denikin was given British tanks). But they often avoided actual fighting. Once World War I was over it was less easy to justify the intervention. All foreign troops (except the Japanese) had left by the end of 1920.

War Communism: key features

* state control of factories, mines & railways.

* abolition of private trading - money became worthless.

* grain was requisitioned (forcibly taken) from peasants.

* lack of success - peasants refused to cooperate, growing only what they needed for themselves.

④ The failure of War Communism

War Communism had two aims. First, by keeping the Red Army fed and equipped, the government hoped to win the military struggle. And second, by sharing out resources more equally, the government hoped to create a Communist state (see p.29). The problem with the policy, however, was that peasants did not see the point of working hard to produce a surplus when they knew they would receive nothing in return. Besides, the forced seizure of grain contributed to the climate of violence created by the Cheka's Red Terror. Peasants started to produce just enough to feed themselves. This, combined with the collapse in foreign trade, resulted in a terrible famine in 1921 - it has been estimated that as many as 5 million people died of hunger and disease. Although, by then, the Red Army had won the military struggle, the government seemed to be losing the battle of ideas. In March 1921, Red sailors at the naval base of Kronstadt mutinied in protest at government policy. This was a major blow to the government since the

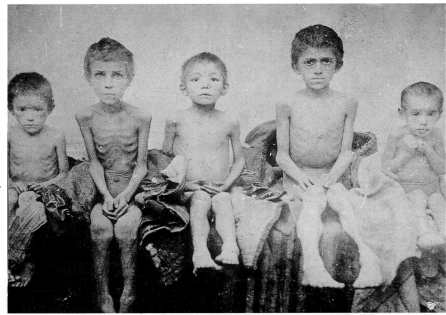

These children were victims of the famine which broke out in 1921. Weakened with hunger, many died of diseases such as cholera and typhus.

sailors had been strong Bolshevik supporters during the struggle for power. The Kronstadt mutiny quickly led to a revision of policy.

⑤ The New Economic Policy (NEP) 1921-24

Results of NEP

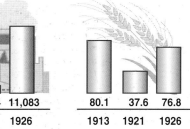

Factory production (millions of roubles)

10,251	2,004	11,083
Date 1913	1921	1926

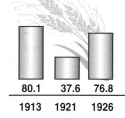

Grain (million tons)

80.1	37.6	76.8
1913	1921	1926

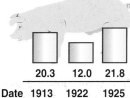

Pigs (millions)

20.3	12.0	21.8
Date 1913	1922	1925

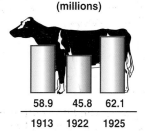

Cattle (millions)

58.9	45.8	62.1
1913	1922	1925

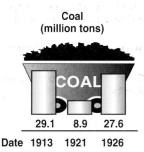

Coal (million tons)

29.1	8.9	27.6
Date 1913	1921	1926

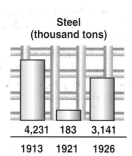

Steel (thousand tons)

4,231	183	3,141
1913	1921	1926

Box 2.14 — Key features of the New Economic Policy (NEP)

* Small-scale industry returned to private ownership.
* Private trade legalised.
* Reintroduction of currency so that workers were paid in money.
* New foreign investment encouraged.
* Major industries (such as coal, steel and railways) remained under state control.
* Grain no longer requisitioned (forcibly taken) from peasants. Peasants to pay tax according to how much grain they produced.

Although the Kronstadt mutiny was quickly crushed, the government realised how unpopular its policies had become. Lenin later described the mutiny as 'the spark which lit up reality'. It was clear that War Communism would have to be abandoned if the Communist government was to survive. At the Communist Party Congress in 1921, Lenin announced a New Economic Policy (see Box 2.14). This reversed many of the rules made under War Communism. Some small factories, for example, were given back to their owners and money was reintroduced. Also, peasants were once again allowed to sell their surplus produce for profit. And, to encourage them to produce more, a taxation system was introduced. The more peasants produced, the less tax they had to pay. These measures quickly made an impact. By 1925, production levels were almost back to the levels they had been when World War I began. A new class of trader emerged, sometimes called 'nepmen'. They began to set up small factories which were allowed to employ up to 20 workers. Many Communists, however, felt that the NEP was wrong and they criticised Lenin for taking one step backwards towards capitalism. Lenin himself described the NEP as a 'breathing space' designed to help Communism recover from the strains of war.

Activity
The civil war

Source B *Trotsky in the civil war*

This photo shows Leon Trotsky on board the armoured train which toured the fronts during the civil war. Trotsky wrote: 'For 2$\frac{1}{2}$ years I lived on a railway coach. The work of the train was to build up the army, to educate, administer and supply it.' On board the train was a printing press, a telegraph station, a radio station, an electric generator and a library.

Source E *White propaganda*

Anti-Bolshevik cartoon produced in the civil war. The caption reads 'Russia sacrificed on the altar of Communism.' Lenin is the man wearing a red robe. Trotsky is on his right.

Source A *Red propaganda*

This poster was produced by the Soviet government in 1919. The caption reads: 'Either death to capitalism or death under the heel of capitalism.'

Source C *White terror*

Having surrounded the village, the White army cut off the ford with machine guns and fired a couple of rounds in the direction of the village. Then the mounted platoon entered the village, met the Bolshevik committee and put its members to death. The platoon then demanded the surrender of those responsible for murdering and torturing four Whites. They were delivered to us and executed on the spot. After the execution, the houses of the culprits were burned and the whole male population under the age of 45 whipped soundly. Then the population was ordered to deliver without pay the best cattle, pigs, fowl and bread for the whole platoon, as well as the best horses. All this they kept bringing over until nightfall. 'An eye for an eye'.

From the diary of the White Colonel Drozdovsky, March 1918

Source D *A historian's view of the civil war*

There were many reasons for the victory of the Red Army in the civil war, but most of them add up to one simple fact - the people as a whole, despite the unpopularity of the Communists, preferred the Soviet government to the available alternatives. The peasants disliked both sides and wished above all to be left alone. But they preferred the Communists who gave them land to the Whites who took, or threatened to take, it away. Trotsky regarded this as the main cause of victory. One must also consider the state of the armies themselves. Banditry, corruption and desertion were rampant on both sides, but the better morale was on the side of the Red Army, especially in units with a large number of Communists. These Communists were at any rate united about what they were fighting for. There was no common aim on the White side. Towering above other reasons were the energy, skill and ruthless determination of Trotsky, the main architect of the new Red Army.

From '1917' by L. Shapiro, 1984

QUESTIONS

1. Judging from the information in this section, how did the Bolsheviks manage to hold on to power after October 1917?

2. What point is being made by each of the posters in Sources A and E? Why do you think each side chose to produce these images?

3. Why do you think the Whites failed to win the civil war? Use Sources A-E in your answer.

4. 'Trotsky was a key figure in the Soviet government's early years.' Explain this statement using Source B.

All major wars result in important changes in the relationships between states. Certainly, this is true of the First World War. Long before the end of the fighting, it was clear that the world would never be the same again. Yet, when the war ended, it took the victors by surprise. The Allies had been concentrating on winning the war rather than on what might happen after it. As a result, when the victors gathered in Paris to decide what should happen to those defeated in the war, there was little common ground between them. Over 1,000 politicians from 30 different countries attended the Paris Peace Conference which met throughout 1919 and 1920 in an attempt to resolve the problems caused by over four years of war. In reality, however, the Conference was dominated by the decisions of the so-called 'Big Three' - Woodrow Wilson, President of the USA, David Lloyd George,

Prime Minister of Britain, and Georges Clemenceau, Prime Minister of France. There is no doubt that all three wanted to create a world in which the horrors of the First World War could never be repeated. However, many historians have criticised their decisions on the grounds that there was no unity or direction in their thinking about how this was to be achieved. Indeed, as it turned out, the treaties drawn up in Paris were themselves responsible for the growth in international tension which led to the Second World War just 20 years later. This chapter explores the impact of the peace settlement on international politics in the 1920s. In particular, it considers the following questions.

* What were the aims and motives of the Big Three in Paris?
* How did Germany respond to defeat in the First World War?
* What problems did the Weimar Republic face, 1920-23?
* How successful was the League of Nations in the 1920s?

Key Events

Note It is important to realise that, although much discussion at Paris focused on the treatment of Germany (the Treaty of Versailles), the peace makers also drew up individual treaties with each of the countries defeated in the war. The terms of these treaties are outlined below. Collectively, the settlement is known as the 'Peace of Paris' with each separate treaty taking its name from a palace in the Parisian region.

AUSTRIA: TREATY OF ST. GERMAIN
* The Habsburg Empire to be broken up - Austria and Hungary to become separate countries.
* Land to be lost to Italy.

* Armed forces to be reduced in size.
* New and independent nations (Czechoslovakia and Yugoslavia) to be created from land that used to be part of Habsburg Empire.
* Reparations to be paid.

HUNGARY: TREATY OF TRIANON
* Hungary to accept break-up of Habsburg Empire.
* Territory of Hungary to be reduced to about 1/4 of its area and 1/3 of its population.
* Land to be lost to Czechoslovakia and Yugoslavia.
* Armed forces to be limited.

GERMANY: TREATY OF VERSAILLES
* Germany to accept responsibility for causing the war - the 'War Guilt' clause.
* Germany to pay reparations to the value of £6600 million in gold and goods (finalised in 1921).
* Land to be lost to France, Belgium, Denmark and Poland (about 10% of Germany's territory).
* All overseas colonies to be taken away and governed as mandates (areas under control of League of Nations until self-government organised).
* German army to be reduced to 100,000 soldiers. Navy to be cut back and no submarines allowed. No airforce. Rhineland to become a demilitarised zone.
* Union with German - speaking Austria to be forbidden.

BULGARIA: TREATY OF NEUILLY
* Land to be lost to Yugoslavia and Greece.
* Armed forces to be reduced.
* Reparations to be paid.

TURKEY: TREATY OF SÈVRES
* Ottoman Empire to be broken up.
* European territory to be lost to Greece.
* Middle Eastern territory to be lost to Britain and France as mandates (areas under control of League of Nations until self-government organised).

A = Albania
B = Belgium
C = Czechoslovakia
D = Denmark
H = Holland
P = Portugal

Was the Peace of Paris a 'good' peace?

Source 1 — Map of Europe after 1919

ESTONIA
LATVIA
LITHUANIA
BRITAIN
GERMANY
POLAND
CZECHOSLOVAKIA
SOVIET UNION (RUSSIA)
AUSTRIA
HUNGARY
FRANCE
ITALY
YUGOSLAVIA
ROMANIA
BULGARIA
SPAIN
GREECE
TURKEY

A = Albania
B = Belgium
D = Denmark
H = Holland
P = Potugal
S = Switzerland

'New' countries

Germany split by the 'Polish Corridor'

Source 2 — A historian's view of the peace settlement

The end of the First World War came suddenly and left the victors with enormous problems. Germany was defeated. Austria-Hungary was breaking up. The Ottoman (Turkish) Empire was in ruins and the future of Russia was uncertain. Had the Allies been united, the peacemakers would still have faced a difficult task. In fact, they were badly organised and distrusted each other. France's major concern was to gain security against its more powerful German neighbour. Before the war, its security had rested on its alliance with Russia. But the Bolshevik revolution of 1917 had replaced a friendly government with a hostile one. The British wanted a peace which would establish their empire as the leading world power. At the same time, they wanted to preserve Germany as a sound trading partner and as a useful counterweight to France. President Wilson of the USA pressed for a new system of international relations. The Peace Conference met in Paris for the first time on 18 January 1919, with the most important decisions taken by the 'Big Four' (Britain, France, the USA and Italy). The Italians soon realised that they were to be denied the territories promised to them under the 1915 Treaty of London and their Prime Minister, Vittorio Orlando, withdrew in protest on 24 April 1919. This left matters firmly in the hands of Clemenceau (French Prime Minister), Lloyd George (British Prime Minister) and President Wilson. Although people hoped that they would produce a settlement which would make another world war impossible, they failed. Within 20 years, the world was once again at war.

From 'From Weimar to Wall Street' edited by P. Furtado, 1993

Source 3 — A British cartoon

This cartoon, drawn by William Dyson, appeared in the 'Daily Herald' on 17 May 1919. It shows the 'Big Four' emerging from the Peace Conference (from the left Lloyd George, Orlando, Clemenceau and Wilson). Behind the pillar is a weeping child (who has just looked at the discarded peace treaty) and the words '1940 class'. The child, therefore, represents people who would be of military age in 1940. Clemenceau was nicknamed 'The Tiger' because of the skill with which he demolished a number of French governments. It is he who says: 'Curious! I seem to hear a child weeping!'

The Tiger: "Curious! I seem to hear a child weeping!"

QUESTIONS

1. Compare the map in Source 1 with that on the previous page. How did Europe change after the First World War?

2. Judging from Source 2 what were the aims of the victors? What problems did they face?

3. What point is being made in Source 3? Why do you think this cartoon later became famous?

43

What were the aims and motives of the Big Three in Paris?

The Paris Peace Conference was dominated by the Big Three - the American President, Woodrow Wilson, the French Prime Minister, Georges Clemenceau, and the British Prime Minister, David Lloyd George. Each man had his own ideas about how peace could best be secured. This made it difficult for decisions to be made. The Peace Conference had to answer a number of questions. First, there was the issue of the damage and destruction caused by the war. How should those who suffered be compensated for their losses? Second, the collapse of the German, Habsburg (Austro-Hungarian), Russian and Ottoman (Turkish) empires had created dangerous levels of political instability in central Europe. How should the map of Europe be redrawn? And third, since October 1917 the Allies had been terrified that Bolshevism (Communism) would spread from its breeding ground in Russia. How could they prevent this from happening? This section examines the aims and motives of the Big Three and how these aims and motives affected the peace settlement that emerged.

 ## The aims of the Big Three

Some historians have argued that the peace settlement was fatally flawed by a basic tension between President Wilson's idea of a fair and just peace (as laid out in his Fourteen Points - see p.47) and the more narrow aims of Clemenceau and Lloyd George who wanted to satisfy public opinion in France and Britain. The painting below is by William Orpen. It was painted in 1920 and shows Wilson, Clemenceau and Lloyd George signing the peace treaty drawn up for Germany in the Hall of Mirrors at the Palace of Versailles.

WOODROW WILSON (USA)

Wilson had become President in 1912 after a successful career as a History lecturer in one of the USA's leading universities. His aims included:

* A fair and just peace based on his general framework known as the 'Fourteen Points'. This was a list of ideas written down before the end of the war in January 1918 (see p.47).

* The creation of new, independent nations whose borders were based on the principle of self-determination (see Box 3.1)

* The setting up of an international peacekeeping organisation (the League of Nations) whose job would be to prevent future war.

* The prevention of the spread of Communism.

GEORGES CLEMENCEAU (FRANCE)

Clemenceau was 78 years old in 1919 and was therefore old enough to remember France being invaded by Germany twice - in the First World War and in the Franco-Prussian war of 1871. He had three basic aims:

* To make Germany so economically and militarily weak that it would never be able to attack France again.

* To make Germany pay for the damage caused to France during the war.

* The prevention of the spread of Communism

In particular, Clemenceau wanted an independent Rhineland (see map on p.46) to act as a defensive buffer against future German attacks. This, however, went against Wilson's idea of self-determination.

DAVID LLOYD GEORGE (BRITAIN)

Lloyd George had become Prime Minister in 1916. When he arrived in Paris, he had recently been re-elected on the basis of promises to treat Germany harshly. From a personal point of view, however, he favoured a moderate approach. His aims included:

* The need to fulfil his election promises to a British public calling for revenge.

* The need to protect the British Empire. Although Lloyd George was sympathetic to self-determination in Europe, he refused to allow the idea of self-determination to be applied to British colonies.

* The need to revive British trade (much of which had previously gone on with Germany).

* The prevention of the spread of Communism.

Lloyd George found himself in a dilemma, caught between his personal beliefs and his role as Britain's representative. He was more willing to compromise than the other two and often tried to bring the other two together.

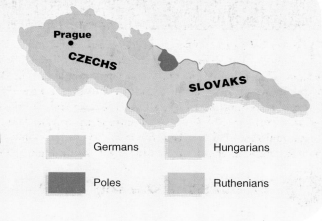
② The negotiations

The relationship between the Big Three became increasingly strained as the peace talks developed. Although all three agreed about the basic aim of making a lasting peace, there were fundamental differences about how this could best be achieved. In particular, there was confusion about the extent to which the victors should take revenge on the defeated nations. Certainly, Paris was not the best venue for peace talks to take place (see Box 3.2). The delegates found themselves constantly under pressure from a French public which wanted harsh terms to be imposed on Germany (see Box 3.3). David Lloyd George records the pressures that the negotiators were under. He wrote of: 'Stones clattering on the roof and crashing through windows and sometimes wild men screaming through the keyholes.' Some historians have argued that the personal relationship between the Big Three was important. It was not just that all three had different aims. There were personality clashes. In particular, it was difficult to persuade Clemenceau to tone down his demands for revenge on Germany. Therefore, the treaties were the result of a series of compromises rather than the product of a unified vision (Box 3.4 illustrates the sort of tensions that surfaced during the negotiations). It should be remembered that neither the defeated nations nor Communist Russia were invited to attend the Peace Conference. The peace settlement, therefore, was not a negotiated settlement. It was imposed on the defeated nations.

Activity

How satisfactory were the terms of the peace settlement to the victors?

Source B *Lloyd George's view*

It is comparatively easy to patch up a peace which will last for 30 years. What is difficult is to draw up a peace which will not provoke a struggle when those who took part in the war have passed away. You may strip Germany of her colonies, reduce her armaments to a mere police force and her navy to that of a fifth rate power. All the same, if she feels that she has been unjustly treated, she will find ways of getting revenge. Injustice or arrogance in the hour of triumph will never be forgiven or forgotten. For these reasons, I am strongly opposed to transferring more Germans to the rule of some other nation than can possibly be helped.

Part of a memorandum written by D. Lloyd George shortly before the signing of the Treaty of Versailles

Source D *A British cartoon*

THE RECKONING.

This cartoon appeared in the magazine 'Punch' on 23 April 1919. The sum to be paid as compensation by Germany (the 'indemnity' mentioned in the cartoon) was not fixed by the Treaty of Versailles. Long before the Treaty was signed, however, it was clear that Germany would have to pay something. According to a caption below the cartoon, the German man is saying: 'Monstrous, I call it. Why, it's fully a quarter of what we should have made them pay, if we'd won.'

Source A *The terms of the Treaty of Versailles (1)*

—— Germany's border in 1914

land taken from Germany and given to other countries | land put under League of Nations control | demilitarised zone

Source C *The terms of the Treaty of Versailles (2)*

Germany agrees:
1. To accept the new frontiers and to keep the peace.
2. To accept decisions made by the League of Nations.
3. To limit the size of its army to 100,000 soldiers and navy to six battleships (no submarines and no air force were allowed).
4. To give up its empire to the League of Nations.
5. To accept blame for starting the war (the 'War Guilt' clause) and to pay compensation* to countries which suffered damage in the war.

Adapted from the Treaty of Versailles, 28 June 1919

* This compensation was later set at £6,600 million, to be paid in cash and materials.

Source E *A historian's view*

None of the Big Three lasted long in office after the Peace Conference. French voters thought that Clemenceau had not done enough and that Germany had been left alarmingly strong. Lloyd George lost the support of voters and never held office after 1922. Wilson returned to the USA to campaign for active American involvement in world affairs. By the end of 1919, however, he had fallen ill and in 1920 American voters rejected his party. Nevertheless, the peace settlement aimed, ambitiously, to do far more than merely share out the recent spoils of war. Most problems were addressed. Undoubtedly, it could have been more consistent. Parts of the settlement were vindictive [revengeful]. But if organisations such as the League of Nations did not work as successfully as the peacemakers hoped, the fault lay less with them than with the next generation of politicians.

From '20th Century World Affairs' by J. Watson, 1984

QUESTIONS

1. Judging from the information in this section, what were the aims of the Big Three?
2. Look at Sources A-C. Would you expect Lloyd George to be satisfied with the final version of the Treaty of Versailles?
3. What point is being made by Source D? What does it tell us about attitudes in Britain?
4. How satisfactory were the terms of the peace settlement to the victors? Use Source E in your answer.

SOURCE WORK

President Wilson's 'Fourteen Points'

In January 1918 (11 months before the armistice and a year before the peacemakers met in Paris), President Wilson drew up his 'Fourteen Points for Peace'. The aim was to provide a framework for discussion once the war was over. Certainly, they appeared reasonable to Germany and in October 1918 the German Chancellor, Prince Max von Baden, tried unsuccessfully to bypass Britain and France by negotiating an armistice with the USA on the basis of the Fourteen Points. Wilson's peace plan was based on the idea that new and democratic states would work together in a League of Nations to prevent any future war. The new states would be created using the principle of self-determination (see Box 3.1 on p.45). During the Peace Conference, the original shape of the Fourteen Points became lost, although aspects of it were reflected in the final treaties. Wilson himself argued that, although the settlement was harsher than he hoped, there were opportunities for progress through the new League of Nations. Unfortunately, American public opinion did not share Wilson's enthusiasm for the more active role that the USA would have to play in the League. In 1920, the Republican-controlled Senate refused to allow the USA to join the League. Wilson's energetic campaigning ruined his health and, following a stroke, he remained an invalid until his death in 1924.

In 1917, the Bolsheviks published the secret treaties made between the Tsar and Western governments. This proved that secret deals had been made and that the First World War had resulted from such deals. To prevent similar wars breaking out, Wilson argues that no secret deals should be made in the future.

General principles to be enforced by the League of Nations.

The armies of the defeated powers were limited, but there was nothing to prevent the victors building up their armies.

Unlike Britain and France, the USA did not have colonies. It was especially difficult for Britain to agree to this point since self-determination in the colonies might mean the break-up of the British Empire.

Russia was not invited to the Peace Conference and land taken from Russia by the Germans was made into independent states (Estonia, Latvia and Lithuania).

Agreed. See map on p.46.

Program for the Peace of the World
By PRESIDENT WILSON January 8, 1918

I. Open covenants of peace, openly arrived at, after which there shall be no private international understandings of any kind, but diplomacy shall proceed always frankly and in the public view.

II. Absolute freedom of navigation upon the seas, outside territorial waters, alike in peace and in war, except as the seas may be closed in whole or in part by international action for the enforcement of international covenants.

III. The removal, so far as possible, of all economic barriers and the establishment of an equality of trade conditions among all the nations consenting to the peace.

IV. Adequate guarantees given and taken that national armaments will reduce to the lowest point consistent with domestic safety.

V. Free, open-minded, and absolutely impartial adjustments of all colonial claims, based upon a strict observance of the principle that in determining all such questions of sovereignty the interests of the population concerned must have equal weight with the equitable claims of the government whose title is to be determined.

VI. The evacuation of all Russian territory and such a settlement of all questions affecting Russia as will secure the best and freest cooperation of the other nations of the world in obtaining for her an unhampered and unembarrassed opportunity for the independent determination of her own political development and national policy, and assure her of a sincere welcome into the society of free nations under institutions of her own choosing. The treatment accorded Russia by her sister nations in the months to come will be the acid test of their goodwill and of their intelligent and unselfish sympathy.

VII. Belgium, the whole world will agree, must be evacuated and restored, without any attempt to limit the sovereignty which she now enjoys in common with all other free nations. No other single act will serve as this to restore confidence among the nations in the law which

they have themselves set and determined for their government of their relations with one another.

VIII. All French territory should be freed and the invaded portions restored, and the wrong done to France by Prussia in 1871 in the matter of Alsace Lorraine, which has unsettled the peace of the world for nearly fifty years, should be righted, in order that peace may once more be made secure in the interest of all.

IX. A readjustment of the frontiers of Italy should be effected along clearly recognisable lines of nationality.

X. The people of Austria-Hungary, whose place among the nations we wish to see safeguarded and assured, should be accorded the freest opportunity of autonomous development.

XI. Romania, Serbia and Montenegro should be evacuated; occupied territories restored; Serbia accorded free and secure access to the sea; and the relations of the several Balkan states to one another determined by friendly counsel along historically established lines of allegiance and nationality.

XII. The Turkish portions of the present Ottoman Empire should be assured a secure sovereignty, but the other nationalities which are now under Turkish rule should be assured an absolutely unmolested opportunity of autonomous development, and the Dardanelles should be permanently opened as a free passage to the ships and commerce of all nations under international guarantees.

XIII. An independent Polish state should be erected which should include territories inhabited by indisputably Polish populations, which should be assured a free and secure access to the sea, and whose political and economic independence and territorial integrity should be guaranteed by international covenant.

XIV. A general association of nations must be formed under specific covenants for the purpose of affording mutual guarantees of political independence and territorial integrity to great and small states alike.

Agreed. See map on p.46

Italy gained territory from Austria (including a German-speaking minority) and part of the Dalmatian coast. But, it was not satisfied with its gains.

Agreed. Austria and Hungary became independent nations.

Romania gained its independence. Serbia and Montenegro were joined to make Yugoslavia. See map on p.43.

Agreed. See map on p.43.

An independent Poland was created, but it contained a large minority of German speakers - see maps on pages 43 and 46.

A League of Nations was set up - see pages 54-57. It was the first truly international organisation. But the USA refused to join.

QUESTIONS

1. The language in the source above is difficult. Make a list of the key words and phrases in each of the Fourteen Points and then rewrite the Fourteen Points in modern language.

2. What are the strengths and weaknesses of the Fourteen Points as a basis for peace?

3. 'During the Peace Conference, the original shape of the

Fourteen Points became lost, although aspects of it were reflected in the final treaties'. Explain this statement using the information on pages 44-46 and on this page.

4. Why do you think the source above is a useful source for historians studying the peace settlement?

How did Germany respond to defeat in the First World War?

The last months of the First World War created political chaos in Germany. For a while it looked as though the country was on the verge of a revolution like that in Russia the previous year. As defeat came nearer, the old political order began to crumble. Once the Kaiser (German Emperor) had been forced to abdicate (resign) on 9 November, Germany became, for the first time, a democratic republic (known after January 1919 as the Weimar Republic). But the period between the end of the war in November 1918 and early 1920 was a very testing time for the new republic (see Box 3.5 below). First, it had to deal with a series of left wing uprisings which threatened to bring about a Communist revolution. The brutal methods used to defeat the Communists did much to undermine the popularity of the new government. And then, in June 1919, representatives of the new government had no choice but to sign the Treaty of Versailles. Although the new government had not been responsible for Germany's actions during the war, it was then blamed for what was seen in Germany as a humiliating peace settlement. So, having survived the threat from the left, the new government then found itself challenged from the right.

 The old order collapses

Many Germans were not prepared for defeat in the war. Military setbacks in August 1918, however, made defeat inevitable (see p.19). On 3 October, in an attempt to deflect criticism away from the military leaders, Max von Baden, a civilian, was appointed Chancellor (Prime Minister). On 28 October, however, sailors at two ports mutinied and refused to put to sea in a final attack on the British navy. At this point, the old order collapsed. The naval mutinies sparked workers' protests and Russian style 'soviets' (councils) sprung up across the country. To prevent the disorder becoming a revolution, Chancellor von Baden asked for an armistice. But President Wilson insisted this was only possible if the Kaiser abdicated.

 The Kaiser abdicates

Pressure for the Kaiser's resignation came from inside Germany as well as from abroad (see Box 3.6). On 9 November, a general strike took place in Berlin. Crowds marched in protest towards government buildings and soldiers did nothing to stop them. The Kaiser was reluctant to go, but even his generals refused to support him. As a result, he left Germany, never to return. He took refuge in Holland. This British cartoon entitled 'Wanted' shows the Kaiser as a criminal hiding from British and French police officers behind a Dutch woman. A caption below the cartoon said: 'William the Gallant (to Holland): 'Courage! I will never desert you.'

WANTED.

Box 3.5 — Germany in chaos 1918-20

1918

3 Oct Prince Max von Baden appointed Chancellor

28 Oct Naval mutinies at Wilhelmshaven and Kiel. Nationwide strikes and establishment of soviets across Germany.

1 Nov Von Baden attempts to secure an armistice

9 Nov Kaiser William II abdicates. Von Baden resigns. Ebert becomes leader of a provisional government.

11 Nov Armistice agreed.

1919

Jan Communist uprising in Berlin led by the extreme Spartacist group. Uprising crushed with the help of right wing Freikorps. Spartacist leaders murdered by Freikorps.

Nov 1918-Jan 1919 Struggle develops between Ebert's largely moderate socialist government and the Communists.

April Separate soviet republic established in Bavaria. Overthrown by government.

28 June Provisional government accepts the Versailles Treaty.

July The new Weimar constitution is accepted.

1920

March 1920 Freikorps attempt monarchist coup in Berlin (the Kapp Putsch).

Box 3.6 — The Kaiser must go

Your abdication has become necessary to save Germany from civil war and to fulfil your mission as the peacemaking Emperor until the end. The blood would be laid upon your head. The great majority of the people believe you to be responsible for the present situation. This belief is false, but it is held. If civil war and worse can be prevented through your abdication, your name will be blessed by future generations. Disorders have already occurred. It might at first be possible to put them down by force, but once the blood has flowed, the cry for vengeance will everywhere be heard. The troops are not to be depended on. We are steering straight for civil war.

Part of Prince Max von Baden's appeal to Kaiser William on 8 November 1918, recorded in his memoirs published in 1928

3 Ebert and the new republic

The Chancellor, von Baden, resigned on the same day as the Kaiser. He was replaced by Friedrich Ebert, leader of the Social Democratic Party. The aim of the Social Democrats was to set up a new democratic political system. Ebert, therefore, called for elections to a National Assembly. This National Assembly would then draw up a new constitution for Germany. The constitution would, in turn, lay down how future governments were to be elected and what powers they were to have. But not all socialists supported the Social Democratic Party. Some argued that the situation in Germany was like that in Russia after the February revolution and they called for a Communist uprising (see paragraph 4 below). On 19 January 1919, however, the elections to the new National Assembly took place, with Ebert becoming President. The Assembly then met in the small town of Weimar where it spent six months drawing up a constitution. Although this constitution protected people's rights (see p.66), many Germans never forgave Ebert and the new republic for the brutal methods used to defeat the Spartacists in January 1919.

Friedrich Ebert

4 The Spartacist uprising, January 1919

At the end of the war, German socialists split into three groups - the Social Democrats, the Independent Socialists and the Spartacists (Communists). All three groups wanted greater power for ordinary working people, but their tactics were very different. Social Democrats aimed to work through Parliament. Independent Socialists organised strikes in the hope that this would bring

A poster produced by the Spartacists (renamed the German Communist Party in January 1919). The caption reads: 'Who protects us against collapse? The armed workers.'

change. The Spartacists (named after the gladiator Spartacus who led a slave revolt in ancient Rome) believed that there should be a Communist uprising like that in Russia in October 1917. When Ebert called for national elections, the Spartacists opposed him because these elections would allow non-socialists to decide the future of Germany. On 6 January 1919, the Spartacists attempted an uprising in Berlin. Following the call for a general strike, armed Communists took over important buildings. This uprising was opposed by Ebert's government. They armed the Freikorps, a right wing volunteer force (see paragraph 5), and sent them to Berlin. The Freikorps arrived on 11 January and there were four days of brutal street fighting. Several hundred workers and Communists were killed, including the Spartacist leaders Rosa Luxemburg and Karl Liebknecht. The uprising had failed.

5 The Freikorps and the Kapp Putsch of 1920

Although some soldiers were socialists (many were active in the soviets that were set up in late 1918), many were not. Once the war ended, these soldiers returned to Germany to find themselves unemployed and their country in chaos. Many refused to recognise that the army had been defeated. Instead, they believed that politicians had 'stabbed them in the back' by agreeing

A Freikorps recruitment poster from 1919. The caption reads: 'Temporary volunteers, let's go!'

to stop the fighting. In particular, they hated the Communists whom they blamed for creating the crisis which had forced the government to agree to make peace. When the Spartacist uprising began, Ebert's government did not have enough regular troops to oppose it. As a result, it turned to the Freikorps - a volunteer army. Having crushed the Spartacist uprising in Berlin, the Freikorps then fought the Communists who had gained power in Bavaria (see Box 3.5). Although the Freikorps helped to crush the Communists, they had no love for Ebert's socialist government. Indeed, once the government had signed the Treaty of Versailles, the Freikorps joined other opponents who aimed to overthrow Ebert. In March 1920, the Freikorps launched an uprising, hoping to make Wolfgang Kapp Chancellor. The so-called 'Kapp Putsch' (a 'putsch' is an attempt to seize power) was defeated by a general strike of German workers. Many members of the Freikorps later joined the Nazis.

Activity
German reactions to the Treaty of Versailles

The immediate effect of signing the Treaty of Versailles was a blaze of indignation in the press and depression among the people. In Berlin, an atmosphere of profound gloom settled on the city. Several papers appeared with black borders around their Versailles articles and had such headings as 'Germany's Fate Sealed' and 'Peace with Annihilation'. The right wing Deutsche Zeitung was banned for printing the headline 'Vengeance! German Nation!' Some churches set aside 6 July as a day of mourning. In Berlin, on 24 June, a number of German officers and soldiers seized 15 flags which had been captured from the French in 1870 and publicly burned them. More or less serious mob violence was in evidence, especially in Berlin and Hamburg throughout the week in which the Treaty was signed.

Part of an article printed in the 'New York Times' in July 1919

Source B *A German newspaper*

Vengeance!
German Nation!

Today in the Hall of Mirrors at Versailles, a disgraceful treaty is being signed. Never forget it! On that spot where, in the glorious year of 1871, the German Empire in all its glory began, today German honour is dragged to the grave. Never forget it! The German people with unceasing labour will push forward to reconquer that place among nations to which they are entitled. Then there will be vengeance for the shame of 1919.

Part of the front page of the Deutsche Zeitung (a right wing newspaper) from 28 June 1919, the day the Treaty of Versailles was signed. The article was surrounded by a thick black band to symbolise mourning.

Source C *Photograph taken in June 1919*

This photo shows a large crowd of people which had gathered in Munich to protest at the terms of the Treaty of Versailles.

Source D *A German cartoon*

This German cartoon from 1919 shows the devil examining the terms of the Treaty of Versailles. He is surrounded by figures who represent revenge, greed and lust for power.

Source E *Historians' views*

a) In the eyes of many German patriots, the Weimar Republic was only there at all because Germany had been defeated. Indeed, to patriots, the people who set up the Republic had helped in that defeat. The Weimar Republic had also agreed to the peace terms and would always be blamed for them.

From 'The Age of Upheaval' by J.M. Roberts, 1981

b) Severe as the Treaty of Versailles seemed to many Germans, it should be remembered that Germany might easily have fared much worse if Clemenceau had had his way, instead of being restrained by Britain and the USA. However, the Germans as a nation were not inclined to count their blessings. Most of all they resented the War Guilt clause which put blame on them which they did not feel. Further, the fact that the Treaty was not negotiated but dictated to Germany and signed in humiliating circumstances made it certain that the German people would accept no responsibility for its fulfilment.

From 'A History of Germany 1815-1945' by W. Carr, 1985

QUESTIONS

1. Judging from the information in this section, how did Germany respond to defeat in the First World War?
2. a) Judging from Sources A-D what was the initial reaction in Germany to the Treaty of Versailles?
   b) Using Source E describe the political impact of the Treaty of Versailles.
3. What point is being made by the cartoon in Source D?
4. Using the information in this section, explain how the Treaty of Versailles contributed to Germany's political problems between November 1919 and March 1920.

What problems did the Weimar Republic face, 1920-23

The Kapp Putsch was by no means the last political crisis that the Weimar Republic faced in its early years. Indeed, the general strike which had successfully defeated the Kapp Putsch spread, requiring the government to send in the Freikorps to restore order once again. But then, in an attempt to fulfil the terms of the Treaty of Versailles, the government took steps to disband the Freikorps (Germany was only allowed an army of 100,000 soldiers). As a result, although the Weimar government had the support of most people, it was hated by groups on both extremes. Those on the left (Communists and others) hated it because it had used the Freikorps against the workers. Those on the right (people who served in or supported the Freikorps) hated it because it had ended the war, signed the Treaty of Versailles and then disbanded the Freikorps. The threat from the political extremes, however, was not the only problem faced by the Weimar government between 1920 and 1923. In 1921, the amount Germany had to pay in compensation for damage caused during the war (reparations) was set. It was much more than Germany could afford. When Germany failed to pay, the French army invaded the Ruhr, one of Germany's key industrial areas. This invasion added to Germany's economic problems and in 1923 inflation spiralled out of control. The result was economic chaos and great hardship for many people.

Political extremism

In the years 1919-23 it has been calculated that nearly 400 political murders were carried out by groups on the extreme right and the extreme left (see table, right). Most notably, in August 1921 the former Finance Minister, Matthias Erzberger, was assassinated while taking a walk in the Black Forest and in June 1922 the Foreign Minister, Walter Rathenau, was ambushed and killed. Both murders were the work of a well organised terrorist organisation, most of whose members had been in the Freikorps. One of those responsible for Rathenau's murder, Ernst von Salomon, recalled in 1954: 'Actually, there was only one political belief that held together the national movement. It amounted to this. We must make an end to the policy of accepting the Versailles Treaty and cooperating with the West. We had no wish to become a political party with mass support. But we did desire basic change. The only course open was to "eliminate" every politician who accepted the Versailles Treaty. To eliminate means, of course, to kill.'

Political murders in Germany 1919-22

	Extreme Left	Extreme Right
Number of murders	22	354
Number of murders resulting in punishment	17	28
Average length of prison sentence	15 years	4 years
Number of murderers executed	10	0

Figures from 'Nazi Germany' by K.P. Fischer, 1995

2 Reparations and the occupation of the Ruhr

The 'War Guilt' clause in the Treaty of Versailles led to the demand that Germany should pay for the entire cost of the war. German objections that this would ruin their economy were ignored and a Reparations Committee set up. When, in 1921, this committee announced that Germany would have to pay France and Belgium £100 million per year for 66 years (mostly in the form of goods such as iron, coal and timber), the German government resigned in protest. But the Germans simply had to pay or face an Allied invasion. The new German government paid the first instalment on time. But, at the end of 1922, it failed to deliver 140,000 telegraph poles to France. This was the excuse that the French Prime Minister, Poincaré, had been waiting for. On 11 January 1923, a French-Belgian force invaded the Ruhr valley (see map on p.46) and seized its industries and mines. The German government responded by supporting a policy of 'passive resistance' - Germans in the Ruhr were told not to cooperate with the invaders in any way. Industrial production ground to a halt, preventing the invaders seizing German goods. But the invading force acted with brutality against those who resisted and the policy added to Germany's economic problems. The occupation of the Ruhr ended in 1924 when the new German Chancellor, Gustav Stresemann (see p.67) called off passive resistance and negotiated a withdrawal on the basis of renewed reparations payments.

The poster (right) was produced by the German government to encourage the policy of passive resistance in the Ruhr. It shows a German miner being threatened by French soldiers. The caption reads: 'No! I will not be forced'.

3 Economic problems - hyperinflation

Four years of war and the British naval blockade had already weakened the German economy. The Treaty of Versailles further weakened it by taking away much of the country's most valuable industrial land and its overseas colonies and by

Number of marks to the dollar

July 1914	4
July 1920	40
July 1921	80
July 1922	500
January 1923	18,000
July 1923	350,000
September 1923	100,000,000
November 1923	4,000,000,000,000

This photo was taken in 1923. The cash register is too small to hold the day's takings in this shop because banknotes have become worth so little. Instead, the shopkeeper is storing the money in a tea chest.

forcing Germany to pay reparations. In addition, other countries had little confidence that the German economy would recover and this reduced the value of the mark. Imports became more expensive which forced up prices within Germany. In 1919, Germany was already suffering from high inflation. In 1923, inflation went completely out of control and the economy collapsed. The immediate cause of this collapse was the invasion of the Ruhr. First, industrial production in the Ruhr ground to a halt, reducing the amount of goods in circulation. And second, to support the policy of passive resistance, the German government printed money to compensate those who resisted. But this only made prices rise since there was too much money in circulation chasing too few goods. The result was hyperinflation. The more money the government printed, the higher prices rose. Money became almost worthless. At one point it cost 5 million marks to buy a stamp or 80 million marks to buy an egg. One man recalled: 'In 1923, I was advertising chief of a rubber factory. I had a monthly salary of 200 billion marks. We were paid twice a day and then everyone had a half hour break so they could rush to the shops and buy something before the next quotation on the dollar came out, at which time the money would lose half its value' (quoted in *Germany 1866-1945* by G.A. Craig, 1978). Hyperinflation brought political as well as economic damage. Many people became unemployed. Some starved. Even the better-off suffered - many found that their life's savings simply became worthless.

This cartoon appeared in the German magazine 'Simplicissimus' in November 1922. It criticises the government's decision to print banknotes. Gutenburg, who invented the movable type printing press in the 15th century, stands dismayed as 1,000 mark notes are produced. The caption reads: 'I had not intended this!'.

4 The Munich Putsch, November 1923

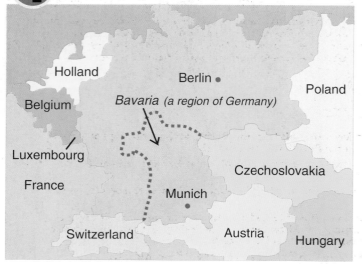

Map of Germany in 1923

The invasion of the Ruhr and the economic crisis caused such discontent that another putsch was attempted. This time, the attempt took place in Munich in Bavaria (see left). It was organised by the National Socialist German Worker's Party (NSDAP) whose leader was Adolf Hitler (at the time, the Nazi Party was just one of many small groups opposed to the Weimar Republic). On the night of 8 November 1923, Hitler and his supporters stormed into a meeting in a large beer cellar where the Governor of Bavaria, von Kahr, was making a speech. The Nazis, supported by General Ludendorff (a commander in the First World War), declared that they were seizing power and would march to Berlin to take over the government. They persuaded leading members of the Bavarian government to support them. But, the next day, as the Nazis and their supporters marched through Munich, they were confronted by armed police officers. Firing broke out and 16 Nazis were killed, including the man marching next to Hitler. The leaders of the Putsch were then arrested. The Putsch had failed, but Hitler used his trial to publicise his views.

Activity
The Munich Putsch

Source B An eyewitness account (1)

The Governor of Bavaria, von Kahr, was on his feet droning away at some boring speech. I said to myself: 'This waiting is dull enough, but there's no need to go thirsty.' So I went over to the serving hatch and bought three litre jugs of beer. I remember they cost a billion marks each. Then the door burst open and in burst Goering (one of the leading Nazis) and around 25 brownshirts with pistols and machine guns. What an uproar. Everything happened at once. Hitler began to plough his way towards the platform and the rest of us surged behind. Tables were overturned and people threw themselves on the floor. Hitler climbed onto a chair and fired a shot at the ceiling. 'The national revolution has broken out', he said, 'The army is with us. Our flag is flying on their barracks.'

The memories of Ernst Hanfstaengl recorded in 'Unheard Witness', 1957

Source D An eyewitness account (2)

Von Kahr had spoken for half an hour. Then there was movement at the entrance as if people were wanting to push their way in. I saw Hitler emerge between two armed soldiers. He climbed on a chair to my left and then he made a sign to the man on his right who fired a shot at the ceiling. Hitler called out (I cannot remember his exact words): 'The revolution has begun. The hall is surrounded.' He may have mentioned the exact number, I am not sure.

Memories of Professor von Mueller who gave evidence at Hitler's trial in 1924, recorded in 'Documents on Nazism' by J. Noakes & G. Pridham, 1974

Source E A historian's account

The failure of the Putsch meant that the Weimar Republic was secure from internal threats for several years to come. Indeed, Hitler drew the lesson that state power could only be achieved from within. Putsches were unlikely to succeed. But popular faith in the Weimar Republic (never very strong) had been badly, and in some cases permanently, shaken by the events of 1923. The collapse of the currency left behind a legacy of resentment, especially amongst the middle classes. The mark was revalued and became stable. But this revaluation was damaging for farmers and small businesspeople. Legal cases about debt repayment during the inflation dragged on for years and caused much bitterness. All these economic difficulties were not without political effects. When the time came, Hitler was to be the beneficiary.

From 'Weimar and the Rise of Hitler' by A.J. Nicholls, 1979

Source A The Beerhall Putsch

The Munich Putsch is also known as the 'Beerhall Putsch' since Hitler burst into the Burgerbraukeller, a large restaurant complex near the centre of Munich. This painting was produced in 1933, the year Hitler became Chancellor.

Source C Nazi leaflet

Although the Putsch failed, Hitler was able to use his trial to promote his cause. From the witness box, he condemned the 'November criminals' (the politicians who made peace in November 1918) and the peace settlement. Also, the Munich Putsch provided the Nazis with martyrs. The leaflet above honours the men who died during the Putsch.

QUESTIONS

1. a) Judging from the information in this section, what problems did the Weimar Republic face 1919-23?
   b) To what extent were these problems the result of the peace settlement?
2. How accurate is the painting in Source A? Give reasons for your answer.
3. Look at Sources B and D and list the similarities and differences. What difficulties do historians face in trying to reconstruct what happened during the Munich Putsch?
4. Why did the Munich Putsch take place? What were its consequences? Use Sources C and E in your answer.

How successful was the League of Nations in the 1920s?

The call for a permanent and international peacekeeping organisation was the last of President Wilson's Fourteen Points (see p.47) and, to him and his supporters, was the most important. Until the League of Nations was set up in 1920 there had never been a truly international organisation where disputes and problems between countries could be discussed and settled. At the Paris Peace Conference, President Wilson insisted that the creation of a League of Nations must be a priority. As a result, the covenant (constitution) of the League of Nations was incorporated into all the treaties signed by the defeated powers. The main aim of the League was to provide peace through collective security. In other words, if one member was attacked, then all the other members would take action against the aggressor in order to restore peace. But the League also had other functions. Permanent committees and agencies were set up to deal with international problems such as bad health, drug smuggling and poor working conditions. However, even before it was up and running, the League suffered a massive blow. The American Senate refused to accept the League's covenant and so the USA failed to become a member. Many historians believe this helps to explain the League's ineffectiveness in the 1930s. However, it is important to realise that during the 1920s the League did play a significant role in addressing a wide range of postwar problems.

 How the League of Nations was organised

Actions were decided by these two bodies, although the Council took really key decisions

Elects 4 Members

The Council (key decisions)
- Five permanent members: Britain, France, Italy, Japan and (from 1926) Germany.

- Four non-permanent members.
- Met four times a year.
- All decisions had to be unanimous.

The Assembly (policy and finances)

- All members of the League had one vote each.
- Met once a year.
- All decisions had to be unanimous.

The Secretariat
A staff of civil servants to carry out the League's decisions.

PERMANENT COMMITTEES
- Health Organisation
- International Labour Organisation
- Intellectual Cooperation
- Economic and Financial Organisation

SPECIAL COMMITTEES
- Drugs traffic
- Women's rights
- Child welfare
- Refugees

SPECIAL COMMITTEES
- Mandates
- Disarmament
- Military affairs
- Minorities

 **PERMANENT COURT OF JUSTICE**
- 11 Judges
- Sat at the Hague

Dealt with legal not political disputes between countries.

No peace-keeping army

 **The covenant of the League**

The 26 articles of the covenant (constitution) of the League of Nations were drawn up at the Paris Peace Conference. They set out the aims of the organisation and explained how it would work (see Box 3.7).

> ## Box 3.7   The 26 articles
>
> **Article 1. Membership.** Originally the Allies who signed the peace treaties and 13 states neutral in World War I. New members required support of two thirds of the Assembly.
>
> **Articles 2-6. Basic machinery. (i) The Assembly** was an annual gathering of all members. Resolutions had to be passed unanimously. If they were passed, they were only recommendations which could be ignored. **(ii) The Council** was a smaller body which met more often and could act quickly. If its members were unanimous, the Council could call for economic or military sanctions against an aggressor. Economic sanctions meant cutting off trade. Military sanctions meant declaring war. **(iii) The Secretariat** was a civil service led by a Secretary-General and financed by the members.
>
> **Article 7.** League's headquarters to be based at Geneva.
>
> **Articles 8-9.** Members agreed to reduce arms and a **Disarmament Commission** was set up to advise the Council.
>
> **Articles 10-12.** Members agreed to protect all members against aggression, to refer disputes to the Council and not to go to war for three months after a Council decision.
>
> **Articles 13-15.** Members agreed to allow disputes to be settled by the judgement of a third party such as the **Permanent Court of Justice**.
>
> **Article 16.** Members agreed to take action against a member who went to war and broke the covenant. The Council could ask members to provide soldiers for military action. Offending members could be expelled.
>
> **Article 17.** Non-members could be asked to agree to the League's rules.
>
> **Articles 18-21.** All treaties should be made public and should not break any of the rules of the League.
>
> **Article 22.** The colonies of the defeated powers were to become mandates, governed by the League.
>
> **Articles 23-25.** Members agreed to cooperate for the common good - for example, over the control of disease, drugs and working conditions.
>
> **Article 26.** Listed the rules by which the covenant could be changed.

3 The membership of the League

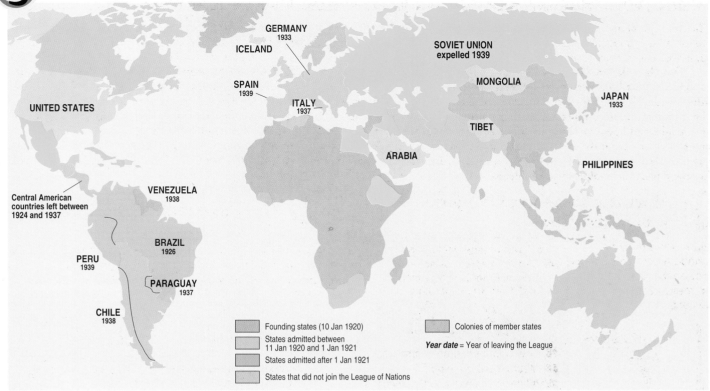

GERMANY 1933
ICELAND
SOVIET UNION expelled 1939
MONGOLIA
SPAIN 1939
ITALY 1937
JAPAN 1933
UNITED STATES
TIBET
ARABIA
PHILIPPINES
VENEZUELA 1938
Central American countries left between 1924 and 1937
BRAZIL 1926
PERU 1939
PARAGUAY 1937
CHILE 1938

Founding states (10 Jan 1920)
States admitted between 11 Jan 1920 and 1 Jan 1921
States admitted after 1 Jan 1921
States that did not join the League of Nations
Colonies of member states
Year date = Year of leaving the League

At first, none of the countries defeated in the First World War was allowed to join the League (nor was the Soviet Union). There were 48 founder members. By 1923, the number of members had risen to 54 and included Austria, Bulgaria and Hungary. Germany was allowed to join in 1926. The Soviet Union joined in 1934.

4 The weaknesses of the League

The League of Nations suffered from two main weaknesses. First, the USA refused to join. Since Germany and the Soviet Union were at first excluded, that meant that three of the most powerful nations in the world were not part of the League. This reduced the League's effectiveness since it could not claim to speak for the world as a whole. Nor could it claim to have the backing of these states when it tried to settle disputes. As the Comte de St Aulaire, the French Ambassador in London between 1920 and 1924, put it: 'A cloud of tiny states do not equal in value one Great Power absent from the League.' The cartoon above suggests that the USA's refusal to join the League was of crucial importance. The USA is shown as the keystone (Uncle Sam, representing the American people, is using it as a pillow). Without its keystone, the bridge is in danger of collapsing.

THE GAP IN THE BRIDGE.

The second major weakness of the League was its lack of real fire power. Although, in theory, the League could ask its members to provide troops for a special force, in practice this never happened. Rather, the League relied on persuasion.

The trouble was, as the historian Hugh Brogan observed: 'The League depended on the good will of the nations to work, though it was the absence of good will which made it necessary.' The cartoon above suggests that the League is helpless. The rabbit (representing the League) faces a snake (representing international conflicts) and all it can hope to do is outstare the snake.

5. The work of the League's agencies in the 1920s

The League was set up not just to settle international disputes. Its aim was also to promote international cooperation and to help solve international problems. In the 1920s, the League's agencies proved themselves successful in many different areas. The most important successes were as follows:

1. The **Commission for Refugees**, led by the Norwegian explorer Fridtjof Nansen, found homes for around half a million former prisoners of war between April 1920 and April 1922.

2. The **Mandates Commission** successfully governed the German and Turkish colonies put under its control at the Paris Peace Conference.

3. The League organised **plebiscites** (referendums) in various areas so that local people could decide whether or not they wanted to be part of Germany - for example, in the Saarland in 1935, 90.8% voted to join Germany.

4. The League's **Health Organisation** did effective work to help prevent the spread of diseases - especially when a typhus epidemic in Russia threatened to spread across Europe.

5. The **International Labour Organisation (ILO)**, under the leadership of the French socialist Albert Thomas, helped to encourage the formation of trade unions and improved working conditions across the world. Significantly, the ILO was the only body set up by the League which continued to operate in its original form after the Second World War.

6. The League and international disputes during the 1920s

1920: Åland Islands
In 1920, both Sweden and Finland laid claim to these islands. Their inhabitants were of Swedish descent, but the islands had been part of the Russian Empire. Sweden accepted the League's decision to give the islands to Finland.

1923: The Corfu incident
Three Italian army officers were shot while working on a boundary dispute between Greece and Albania (Albania was under Italian protection). The Italian government blamed the Greeks and demanded compensation. When the Greeks did not pay, Italian soldiers occupied Corfu. Greece appealed to the League, but the Italian government ignored the Council's ruling, only leaving Corfu when compensation had been paid.

1923: Memel
Memel on the coast of Lithuania was one of the ports placed under control of the League. In 1923, however, the Lithuanian army seized the port. The League then agreed to give the area to Lithuania provided the port became an 'international zone'. Lithuania agreed.

1920-23: Vilna
Both Poland and Lithuania wanted control of the town of Vilna. It had once been the capital of Lithuania, but most of its people were Polish. In 1920, the Polish army siezed Vilna and both sides rejected a frontier line proposed by the League. The dispute was settled by the Conference of Ambassadors (a committee set up by the Treaty of Versailles to settle border disputes). Poland kept control of Vilna.

1921: Upper Silesia
Both Germany and newly formed Poland wanted control of the important industrial area of Upper Silesia. The League decided to split the area between the two.

1925: Greece/Bulgaria
Following a Greek invasion of Bulgaria, the League ordered both armies to stop fighting. An investigation by the League blamed Greece for starting the dispute. Greece accepted the blame and was ordered to pay compensation.

1922-26: Mosul
Both Turkey and Iraq claimed the oil-rich area of Mosul. Although its population was mainly Kurdish (one of Turkey's peoples), the League ruled in favour of Iraq.

7. The failure to achieve disarmament

PEACE (SADLY): "THIS LOOKS VERY LIKE THE POINT WE STARTED FROM."

If the ILO was the League's biggest success in the 1920s, then the **Disarmament Commission** was probably its greatest failure. In 1919, member states agreed to work together to reduce and limit their stocks of weapons and the level of recruitment into their armed forces. This commitment, which formed part of the covenant, proved very difficult to fulfil and it was not until 1932 that a disarmament conference was held in Geneva. The cartoon (left) makes the point about very slow progress by showing peace (the woman) sitting on a donkey (donkeys move slowly). The milestone shows that little progress towards disarmament has been made. The only evidence of change is a top hat and empty bottle - signs that politicians have held parties to discuss disarmament, but done nothing to achieve it.

Activity
Why did the USA fail to join the League?

Source A *A historian's account (1)*

When President Wilson returned to the USA, he found three groups preparing to fight against him. One, led by Senator Lodge, was determined to defeat anything Wilson recommended. A second group was made up of progressives like Herbert Hoover. This group did not personally dislike Wilson (Hoover had been one of Wilson's advisors in Paris), but it was afraid that the League of Nations' covenant would reduce the control Congress had over domestic affairs. A third group, led by Republican William Borah of Idaho, refused to agree to American participation in any international organisation. One common thread united the three groups. All wanted to maintain maximum American freedom of action in the world, particularly so that Americans could freely take advantage of their new economic power without having to worry about political restraints.

From 'The American Century' by W. Lafeber, R. Polenberg & N. Woloch, 1992

Source B *A senator opposes the League*

I object in the strongest possible way to having the USA agree, directly or indirectly, to be controlled by an organisation which may at any time be drawn in to deal with internal conflicts in other countries, no matter what these conflicts might be. It must be made perfectly clear that American soldiers can never be engaged in war or ordered anywhere except by the constitutional authorities of the USA.

Part of a speech made by Senator Henry Cabot Lodge to the Senate in August 1919

Source C *A historian's account (2)*

On 6 November 1919, the Bill proposing American participation in the League of Nations completed its committee stage. Senator Lodge, however, made 14 amendments [changes] to the Bill. President Wilson wanted the USA to join the League on his own terms. He therefore refused to support the Bill and instructed Democrats in the Senate to vote against the amended Bill. The Bill failed in the Senate. This brought calls for compromise, but neither Lodge nor Wilson budged. The amended Bill came up for vote again on 19 March 1920. Again, President Wilson instructed the Democrats in the Senate to vote against it. The amended Bill failed for a second time. For Wilson, one chance remained - the presidential election of 1920. If the Democrats won, the USA would join the League on Wilson's terms.

From 'America: Past and Present' by R. Divine, T. Breen, G. Fredrickson & R. Williams, 1995

Source D *American cartoon from 1919*

This cartoon shows President Wilson (left) and Senator Borah (right) tripping up the American Senate (which is too busy to see where it is going). A caption below it said: 'The two willful gentlemen who are holding up the world'. On Wilson's end of the rope, a piece of paper says 'No Reservations'. Although President Wilson wanted the USA to join the League of Nations, he refused to support the Bill that came before the Senate because his opponents had amended (altered) it (see Source C). Senator Borah, on the other hand, refused to support the Bill because he opposed American participation in the League. The piece of paper on his end of the rope makes this clear.

Source E *The 1920 presidential election*

ELECTION RESULT 1920		% VOTES CAST
Republicans (Harding)	16,152,200 votes	
Democrats (Cox)	9,147,353 votes	
Minor parties	1,240,170 votes	

5.5
34.5
60

The diagram above shows the result of the 1920 presidential election. Wilson was too ill to stand (he suffered a stroke on 2 October 1919). The Democrats chose as its candidate James Cox of Ohio. During the campaign, Wilson declared that the election would be 'a great and solemn referendum' on the Treaty. In fact, the Democrats were well beaten.

QUESTIONS

1. Judging from the information in this section, how successful was the League of Nations in the 1920s?

2. a) Why did the USA refuse to join the League of Nations? Use Sources A-E in your answer.
   b) Why was the USA's failure to join the League important?

3. Using Sources A, B and C explain the point being made in the cartoon in Source D.

4. 'The American presidential election of 1920 was a turning point in the history of the League of Nations.' Explain this statement using Sources C, D and E.

Themes

across much of Europe, the interwar years were years of dictatorship and undemocratic government. In the Soviet Union, Joseph Stalin set up a Communist dictatorship in the late 1920s (see chapter 6). In western Europe, first Benito Mussolini in the 1920s and then, most successfully, Adolf Hitler in the 1930s set up Fascist dictatorships. By 1939, most of western Europe was under Fascist rule. 'Fascism' is the broad term used to describe a new political movement which developed after the First World War and spread rapidly around western Europe and beyond. This new movement had five main characteristics. First, it was violently opposed to Communism. Second, it was opposed to democracy. Third, it was opposed to the peace settlement made after the First World War. Fourth, it was strongly militaristic - the dictators saw themselves as great military leaders and tried to organise Fascist states along military lines. And fifth, Fascist movements rapidly gained support in times of economic depression. It is important to note, however, that there were different variations of Fascism across Europe and that it was certainly stronger in some areas than others. Oswald Mosley's British Union of Fascists, for example, never managed to gain the sort of mass following that Hitler's Nazi Party enjoyed in the 1930s. This chapter explores the rise of the Fascist dictatorships through the following key questions.

* What is Fascism?
* To what extent was Mussolini responsible for the Fascists' rise to power in Italy?
* To what extent did Fascism change Italian society?
* Was the Weimar Republic doomed from the start?
* What were the Nazis' aims and tactics after 1923?
* How did the Nazis manage to win power in Germany?
* To what extent did the Nazis change life in Germany during the 1930s?
* What impact did World War II make on life in Nazi Germany?
* Was Nazi Germany a totalitarian state?

Key Events

Oct. 1922	Mussolini seizes power in Italy.
Oct. 1923	Kemal Ataturk elected in Turkey.
Jan. 1925	Ahmed Zogu seizes power in Albania.
May 1926	Pilsudski seizes power in Poland.
Dec. 1926	Smetona seizes power in Lithuania.
Jan. 1929	King Alexander seizes power in Yugoslavia.
Jul. 1932	Salazar sets up dictatorship in Portugal.

Europe in 1919

Europe in 1939

Jan. 1933	Hitler seizes power in Germany.
Mar. 1933	Dollfuss seizes power in Austria
Mar. 1934	Pats sets up dictatorship in Estonia.
May 1934	Ulmanis sets up dictatorship in Latvia.
Jun. 1934	Boris III sets up dictatorship in Bulgaria.
Aug. 1936	Metaxas sets up dictatorship in Greece.
Sep. 1936	Franco sets up dictatorship in Spain.
Jan. 1938	King Carol II sets up dictatorship in Romania.

What is Fascism?

Source 1

A historian's definition of Fascism

The word 'Fascism' is difficult to define. It is used today as a term of abuse, directed against people who believe that strong government is more important than individual freedom. But the word originally referred to a political movement which developed in Italy at the end of the First World War. The first Fascist Party was founded by Benito Mussolini in 1919. Later, other political movements which resembled Mussolini's were also described as Fascist. The most powerful of these was Adolf Hitler's German Nazi Party. Fascism's most striking characteristic was its **nationalism** - the love of the nation. Fascist nationalism was aggressive - Fascist states would become strong by conquering other, weaker nations. A second characteristic of Fascism was its aim of **totalitarianism**. The state was to take control over the lives of individual citizens. There was only one political party in the state and that party controlled all sources of information. Organisations were set up to brainwash the young. There was constant propaganda putting forward the party view. Opposing viewpoints were suppressed [crushed] by censorship and behind everything was the fear of arrest by the secret police. Related to Fascism's totalitarianism was its **militarism**. The Fascist parties, with their uniforms and parades, were closely modelled on the army and they wanted to impose military values on the whole nation. War was glorified as a source of nobility. The main Fascist virtues were discipline and unquestioning obedience. In the Fascist state the ultimate source of authority was the leader. The devotion Fascist leaders inspired could be religious in its intensity.

From 'The Rise of Fascism' by P. Crisp, 1991

Source 2

The impact of Fascism

Mussolini was Europe's first postwar dictator. The success of Italian Fascism in the 1920s had an effect on other countries. Other would-be dictators copied Mussolini's style and tactics. This postcard shows Mussolini as the Roman wolf which nursed Romulus and Remus (the mythical founders of Rome). The wolf is suckling Hitler (Chancellor of Germany from 1933), Ataturk (President of Turkey from 1923), Metaxas (Greek Prime Minister from 1936), General Franco (dictator in Spain from 1936) and Oswald Mosley (leader of the British Union of Fascists). All five aimed to create a one-party state like that in Italy . The word 'Fascist' comes from the Latin 'fasces'. The fasces were bundles of rods and axes carried in front of the ancient Roman Consuls. These bundles were a symbol of the Consul's power of life and death over Roman citizens. A fasces can be seen on the left of the cartoon, the axe stuck into the base of the statue.

LUPA CAPITOLINA

QUESTIONS

1. Using the information on these pages, describe Fascism in no more than 150 words. Why do you think the meaning of the word has changed today?

2. Judging from Source 1 what were the main features of a Fascist state? How does the Fascist system of government differ from the British system today?

3. Use Source 1 to explain the main points being made by Source 2. Why do you think Mussolini was portrayed as the wolf?

4. Why do you think Mussolini and his colleagues chose to name their party the 'Fascist Party'?

To what extent was Mussolini responsible for the Fascists' rise to power in Italy?

Fascism was born in Italy in 1919. Three years later, the leader of the Fascist Party, Benito Mussolini, was invited to form a government. He and his colleagues used this opportunity to overthrow the parliamentary system and to set up a dictatorship. Historians have identified three main factors behind Mussolini's rise to power. First, political and economic instability had been a feature of life in Italy ever since it first became a single, unified state in 1870. This instability helped to provide the environment in which Mussolini and his colleagues were able to make a bid for power. Second, Italy had a parliamentary system. When the terms of the peace settlement of 1919 were announced, many Italians were bitterly disappointed and blamed the government for failing to win a better deal. This helped those who opposed the parliamentary system (such as Mussolini's Fascists) to win support. And third, there was Mussolini himself. According to some historians, his energy and charismatic leadership helps to explain how the Fascists were able to gain sufficient support to win power. Other historians, however, are not so complimentary about Mussolini's leadership qualities. For example, the British historian A.J.P. Taylor described Mussolini as: 'A vain, blundering boaster without either ideas or aims'. This section considers the extent to which Mussolini was responsible for the Fascists' rise to power.

1 Italy 1870-1915

When the First World War broke out in 1914, Italy was a young country. Until the mid-19th century, it had been split up into separate regions which were under foreign rule. Unification was only achieved in 1870. From the start, its parliamentary system had problems. Between 1870 and 1914, for example, there were 31 changes of government - more than one every two years. Many people had little faith in the political system and rumours of corruption were widespread. Also, despite unification, the country was still deeply divided - especially between the more prosperous, industrialised north and the poor, rural south. On top of this, problems arose from the uneasy relationship between the new state and the Catholic Church. When war broke out in 1914, Italy at first remained neutral. In 1915, however, the Allies persuaded it join on their side by offering the Treaty of London (see Box 4.1).

Box 4.1 — Italy and the Paris Peace Conference

Territory gained by Italy in 1919

Territory claimed by Italy but not gained in 1919

In 1915 in the Treaty of London, Britain and France promised Italy South Tyrol, Dalmatia, Albania and overseas territory. But at the Paris Peace Conference the American President, Wilson, argued that self-determination should be used to draw new frontiers. The result was that, although Italy was given South Tyrol and other small areas, the other promises in the Treaty were ignored.

Box 4.2 — D'Annunzio and the occupation of Fiume

Under the terms of the peace settlement, the port of Fiume (promised to Italy in the Treaty of London) was placed under international control. Arguing that Italy had been 'cheated' of territory, the patriotic poet Gabrielle D'Annunzio led a band of 100 ex-soldiers into the city and claimed to have won it back for Italy. His followers all wore black uniforms and saluted D'Annunzio with outstretched arms in the 'Roman style'.

After 15 months of resistance, D'Annunzio was forced out of Fiume and the port became independent again.

D'Annunzio's actions and style of leadership undoubtedly influenced Mussolini. Also, Mussolini was able to use the episode as propaganda against the parliamentary government (which refused to send in the Italian army to support D'Annunzio as that would have meant war).

2 Italy after World War I

Involvement in the war only increased Italy's long-term problems. Despite ending up on the winning side, the Italian army suffered a crushing defeat by the Austrians in 1917. In addition, involvement in the war threatened to bring about economic collapse. The war cost 148,000 million lire, over twice the total spent by all Italian governments between 1870 and 1915. Then, with the demobilisation of the army and the closing of the munitions factories at the end of the war, unemployment soared to over 2 million. By 1919, Italy seemed on the brink of a Communist revolution. Inflation and unemployment led to a wave of strikes and peasant uprisings. This atmosphere of mounting tension was further heightened by a wave of disappointment at the terms of the peace settlement (see Box 4.1). When the poet Gabrielle D'Annunzio led a private army into Fiume to reclaim it for Italy, he instantly became a national hero (see Box 4.2).

3 The early development of Fascism

The historian Ernst Nolte has written: 'The origin of the Right can always be found in the challenge of the Left'. Certainly, the early development of the Fascist Party owes a great deal to what opponents of the Left saw as the Communist threat. The Fascist movement was launched at a meeting in Milan in March 1919. The meeting was chaired by Mussolini and he remained the figurehead throughout the movement's history. The new Fascist groups provided a focus for those who opposed both the Communists and the government. Many of the first to join were unemployed ex-soldiers. These Fascist groups failed to win a single seat in the 1919 elections, but from October 1920 rapidly gained support (see above). In October 1920, Italy seemed on the verge of a Communist revolution. When a series of strikes broke out, the government did nothing. Fascist groups, on the other hand, took action to break the strikes. Towns were surrounded by Fascist squads, Socialist Party buildings were burned down and their leaders beaten up. In 1920, there were over 1 million strikers. The next year, due mainly to the Fascists, there were just 80,000. These tactics paid off politically. In the 1921 elections, the Fascists won 35 seats.

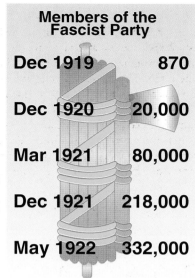

Members of the Fascist Party

Dec 1919	870
Dec 1920	20,000
Mar 1921	80,000
Dec 1921	218,000
May 1922	332,000

4 Benito Mussolini

Mussolini was born in a village in the Romagna region of north Italy. His father was a blacksmith and his mother a school teacher. In the passage below, the historian Stephen Lee points out how, during his early political career, Mussolini went through several major changes in direction:

'Mussolini's original beliefs were of the Left, not the Right. He became a member of the Italian Socialist Party (PSI) and in 1912 was appointed editor of the Party's paper *Avanti*. In 1914, he devoted his energies to putting the case against Italian involvement in the First World War. Then the first major change in direction occurred. By 1915, he was pressing openly for Italy to join the war. He was promptly sacked and expelled from the PSI. He set up his own paper *Il Popolo d'Italia*. His personal contribution to the Italian war effort was a spell of loyal but undistinguished service, ended in 1917 by wounds after a grenade exploded in his trench. In March 1919, Mussolini chaired the meeting in Milan which gave birth to the Fascist movement. The 'Fasci' soon spread to other cities and towns. In 1921, Mussolini underwent a second change. He abandoned his revolutionary inclination and prepared Fascism for a parliamentary struggle. He set up a political party - the National Fascist Party (PNF) - and appealed to as wide a cross section of society as possible.'
From 'The European Dictatorships' by S. Lee, 1987

This poster shows the Italian Fascist leaders in the 1920s. Mussolini (the 'Duce') is at the top.

5 The March on Rome, October 1922

One reason why the Fascists won seats in the 1921 election was that they had the support of the Prime Minister, Giolitti. He hoped to 'tame' the Fascists into supporting official government policy. But the Fascists refused to support either him or his two successors Bonomi (Prime Minister 1921-22) and Facta (Prime Minister 1922). During the summer of 1922, the breakdown of law and order in Italy was so great that many of Mussolini's colleagues urged him to seize power. By then, Mussolini had won the support of many industrialists and he had been careful to make it clear that Fascism was no threat to the monarchy or to the Catholic Church. At first, Mussolini resisted the call to force the government to surrender. But, in October, he agreed to a plan to march on Rome and take power by force if necessary. As Fascists gathered on the outskirts of Rome, the government declared martial law. At first, the King, Victor Emmanuel, agreed to this. But then he changed his mind and invited Mussolini to become Prime Minister. The plan had worked. Mussolini had bluffed his way into power without a shot being fired.

Fascists from all over Italy gathered on the outskirts of Rome (Italy's capital) on 28 October 1922. The next day, Mussolini was made Prime Minister. Only then did the Fascists (or 'blackshirts' as they became known) enter the city. The photo (left) shows Fascist leaders during the March on Rome - from the left - Balbo, De Bono, Mussolini, De Vecchi and Bianchi.

Activity
The Fascist rise to power

Source A *Mussolini the orator*

Mussolini was an excellent public speaker (orator). In 1921, an Italian journalist described his speech at the Fascist Congress in Rome as follows: 'He is a most expert orator. Before his public, he always puts on the manner which best suits his subject and the moment.' In an age before mass media were available, public speaking was particularly important.

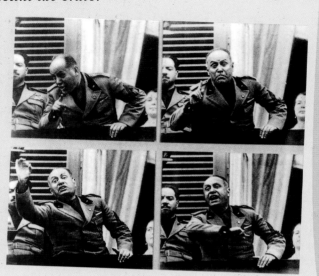

Source B *The March on Rome*

On 29 October 1922, King Victor Emmanuel invited Mussolini to form a new government. The heavily armed garrison of Rome could easily have defeated the poorly armed blackshirts. So, why was there no effective resistance? To fire on Fascists might have resulted in a civil war, leading to a Communist revolution. In any case, the King could not be sure of the loyalty of the army (Marshall Diaz is reported to have said: 'Your Majesty, the army will do its duty, however, it would be well not to put it to the test'). Six generals actually took part in the March on Rome and the military had even misled the King, telling him there were 100,000 armed Fascists outside the city (in reality there were around 30,000, most of whom were unarmed). The King's position was also weakened by the claim to the throne of his cousin, the pro-Fascist Duke of Aosta. In September, Mussolini had offered his support to the monarchy, if it did nothing to oppose the 'Fascist revolution'.

From 'The Rise of Fascism' by P. Crisp, 1991

Source C *Fascist propaganda (1)*

1919—*Bolscevismo*—   1923—*Fascismo*—

After seizing power, the Fascists created their own myths about what had happened and used propaganda like this postcard (which reads '1919 Communism; 1923 Fascism') to encourage support for the Fascist government.

Source D *Fascist propaganda (2)*

The Fascist leader was not satisfied with something as unspectacular as a royal appointment. He needed to develop the myth of a March on Rome by 300,000 armed Fascists who forced the King to accept Mussolini's ultimatum. Eventually a story was invented of Mussolini on horseback leading his legions across the Rubicon. Mussolini admitted in private that the Fascist squads did not arrive in Rome until 24 hours after he had been asked to form a government. But the photographers were waiting to picture their arrival and the myth was launched of Fascism winning power by arms after a civil war and the loss of 3,000 men. These 'Fascist martyrs' soon took their place in government-sponsored History textbooks.

From 'Mussolini' by D. Mack Smith, 1981

QUESTIONS

1. **Judging from the information in this section, to what extent was Mussolini responsible for the Fascists rise to power in Italy?**

2. **'Mussolini bluffed his way into power'. What is the evidence in Sources A-E to support this view?**

3. **Judging from Sources A and E what were Mussolini's qualities and failings?**

4. **Using Sources B-D, explain how the Fascists used propaganda to gain support.**

Source E *Mussolini's leadership skills*

a) Mussolini provided Fascism with a national structure and a national identity. His first contribution to Fascism was its organisation. Second, he showed the importance of action. By taking action, he made full use of the chaotic conditions in postwar Italy. He also learned from D'Annunzio during the Fiume escapade how to create a sense of power among his followers.

From 'The European Dictatorships' by S. Lee, 1987

b) Mussolini never stopped being a journalist. He had a great eye for a catchy headline, but his 'stories' contained little truth or substance. In other words, his rise to power was a huge confidence trick. He conned the Italian people into thinking that he and the Fascists were the only answer to the threat from the Communists.

From 'Mussolini' by D. Mack Smith, 1981

To what extent did Fascism change Italian society?

Mussolini (or 'il Duce' as he was called - 'Duce' is Italian for 'leader') remained in power for 21 years. At first, his main concern was to make sure that he himself and the Fascist Party secured themselves in power. Once his own position was secure, he began to talk about his long-term aims. His goal was to build a new society, summed up in the slogan 'everything within the state, nothing outside the state, nothing against the state'. Clearly, it was Mussolini's aim to bring permanent change to Italian society. Yet, many historians argue that Mussolini's brand of dictatorship was never as complete or as secure as that of Stalin in the Soviet Union (see chapter 6) or as that of Hitler in Germany (see pp.76-85). They point out, for example, that Mussolini never achieved complete control over many aspects of Italian life and that the monarchy and Catholic Church continued to command the loyalty of many sections of the Italian population. This section looks at the key features of the Italian Fascist state and considers the extent to which Fascist rule brought deep and long-lasting change.

1 The Fascists' consolidation of power

When Mussolini became Prime Minister, the Fascist Party only had 35 seats in Parliament. His first Cabinet was therefore a coalition and his position was weak. Over the next six years, however, Mussolini took a number of steps to strengthen both his own position and that of the Fascist Party.

1. **The Acerbo Electoral Law (1923).** The party gaining most votes would automatically gain two thirds of seats in Parliament. Mussolini argued that the old system produced weak and unstable governments. In April 1924, the Fascists won 64% of the vote and two thirds of seats.
2. **The Press Laws (Dec. 1925).** Newspapers were only allowed to print news approved by the government. Anti-Fascist papers were closed down.
3. **The Decree Law (Dec. 1925).** The Head of State (Mussolini) could only be removed by the King (not Parliament). And, no future law could be discussed by Parliament unless it was first agreed by the Head of State. This marks the beginning of Mussolini's dictatorship.
4. **Banning of opposition parties (Nov.1926).** Following an assassination attempt, Mussolini banned all opposition parties and trade unions.
5. **Grand Fascist Council (Dec. 1928).** A leading group of Fascists was chosen to replace Parliament.

In May 1924, the Socialist leader, Giacomo Matteotti, made a speech in Parliament accusing the Fascists of using violence and fraud in the elections in April. Eleven days later, he was kidnapped and murdered by Fascists. When his body was discovered in August, it led to a serious crisis. Although Mussolini was not personally involved in the murder, the involvement of Fascists led to calls for his resignation (the Italian cartoon above suggests Mussolini was responsible for Matteotti's death). But then the opposition played into Mussolini's hands by walking out of Parliament in protest. The King, who still feared a Communist revolution, continued to back Mussolini. Mussolini then took advantage of the absence of opponents by passing laws which damaged them and strengthened his position.

2 A military regime

A Fascist parade in Rome

It is an important characteristic of Fascist states that they are organised along military lines. Discipline and obedience are promoted as virtues. Fascist leaders spend much of their time in uniform. Marching and parades are designed to impress audiences at home and abroad. All this was certainly true of Fascist Italy. The sight of Fascists marching through the streets with military precision (left) became common. Slogans such as 'Believe, obey, fight' decorated public buildings. In 1934 Mussolini said: 'We are becoming a military nation and shall become so increasingly because that is our desire. We are becoming warlike in the sense that what matters is the virtues of obedience, sacrifice and dedication to country. This means that the whole life of the nation must be directed towards our military requirements.' In the 1930s, Mussolini's foreign policy became more aggressive as he aimed to create a 'second Roman Empire'. The most notable conquest was that of Abyssinia (Ethiopia) in 1935 (see p.137).

3 The removal of opponents

Unlike democratic states, Fascist states refuse to allow organised opposition to the government. In Italy, the banning of opposition political parties and trade unions in 1926 was followed by the removal of many top civil servants (replaced by Fascists). In addition, in December 1926, the Law for the Defence of the State set up a new court for political trials - the 'Special Tribunal' - and a secret police force (the OVRA). Unlike in the Soviet Union and Nazi Germany, however, the death penalty was rare (26 political prisoners were executed). The usual punishment was internal exile. It was not just political opponents who were seen as enemies of the state. In the late 1930s, following the example of Nazi Germany, the Fascists passed a number of anti-Jewish laws. By 1939, Jews were prevented from teaching in schools, owning land or owning businesses which employed over 100 people. They were banned from the Fascist Party and were not allowed to marry non-Jews. Although, as a result, many people's lives and careers were disrupted, there was no policy of extermination like that in Nazi Germany.

4 Education and young people

Education in Fascist Italy was strictly regulated. The historian Stephen Lee notes that: 'In 1936, textbooks became a state monopoly. The number of approved History texts, for instance, was reduced from 317 to one.' The one remaining History textbook, of course, gave the Fascist view of history. It was not only at school, however, that young people were exposed to Fascist views. They were also encouraged to join the Fascist Youth Movement, the **Balilla**. Children from the age of six could join (in 1937 it became compulsory to join). Members wore uniforms and swore the following oath of allegiance: 'I believe in the genius of Mussolini, in our holy father Fascism and in the rebirth of the Roman Empire'. Much of their time was spent on parades or doing PE. The picture above is from a Balilla magazine published in 1931.

5 Censorship and the cult of the personality

'Editors were forbidden to print news about crime, financial or sexual scandals, traffic accidents or indeed anything which suggested the government had problems. By the late 1920s, newspaper staff were expected to become members of the Fascist Union of Journalists. Mussolini's press office told editors what to print, sending them the comments they were expected to make after a speech by the Duce or after an event. No foreign news was to be published without permission. Foreign newspapers were banned. From the early 1930s, there was much greater emphasis on the cult of the Duce. It was forbidden to mention any illnesses suffered by Mussolini, his birthday was to be ignored as was the fact that the Duce had become a grandfather - the Duce must possess eternal youth. He must also be photographed and portrayed not only as a statesman and warrior, but as a man of the people, gathering in the harvest or visiting schools. He was often featured driving cars, riding horses, sitting in aeroplanes and even taming lions.'

From 'Fascist Italy' by J. Whittam, 1995

Above, a photo showing Mussolini as a motorboat sportsman.

6 Economic policy and the corporate state

The main aim of Mussolini's economic policy was self sufficiency. To achieve this, the government fought 'battles' like the **Battle for Births** or the **Battle for Grain**. These had limited success. For example, although grain production rose by 100% between 1922 and 1939, production of other crops and dairy farming fell. A second emphasis was on great public works. For example, the ancient Romans had tried and failed to drain the Pontine Marshes, but the Fascists used modern technology to drain them so a new city could be built. This was a propaganda victory and created some jobs. But schemes like this failed to make a major impact on jobless figures in the 1930s. A third feature of economic policy was the development of the **corporate state**. The economy was to be run by corporations which set prices and wage levels and settled disputes. Although this was to be the 'third way' (a better way of organising the economy than capitalism or Communism), it failed to prevent Italy suffering from the Depression of the 1930s and was dropped. Instead, the government took direct control of large parts of the economy.

A poster from 1929 promoting the 'Battle for Grain'. 1929 is described as 'Year Seven' (ANNO VII) as it was seven years after the March on Rome.

Activity

How successful was Italian Fascism?

MUSSOLINI
THE EMPEROR OF
THE MEDITERRANEAN

MUSSOLINI
THE GHASTLY FLOP

On 10 June 1940, Mussolini announced that Italy would enter the Second World War on the side of the Nazis. Italy was ill-prepared for war, but Mussolini gambled that the war would soon be over. On 29 May 1945, two days before committing suicide, Hitler wrote: 'I have to admit my undying friendship for the Duce could be added to my list of mistakes. The Italian alliance was of more service to the Allies than to ourselves.' The cartoon above was entitled 'The dream and the nightmare'. It shows Mussolini weighing up the arguments for and against joining the war on the side of the Nazis. Note the peace offer from Roosevelt and the orders from Hitler on the table.

Source B *A cartoon published in 1929*

Mussolini never gained the same degree of power or control as Hitler or Stalin because he made agreements with existing institutions like the monarchy and the Catholic Church (King Victor Emmanuel, Mussolini and the Pope all have Italy under their control in this cartoon). The army remained loyal to the King throughout the Fascist era. And, in 1929, Mussolini signed a treaty with the Catholic Church (the 'Lateran Accord'). This granted independence to the Vatican (the Catholic headquarters in Rome) and made Catholicism Italy's official state religion. In return, the Church recognised the Italian state.

Source C *An extract from a novel*

The local gentry were all members of the Fascist Party. The Party stood for power and they felt entitled to a share in it. For the opposite reason, none of the peasants were members. Indeed, it was unlikely that they should belong to any party (if, by chance, others existed). They belonged to another world. What had peasants to do with power, government and the state? The state meant 'those fellows in Rome'. 'Everyone knows', they said, 'that those fellows in Rome don't want us to live like human beings'. On the day when Italy's invasion of Abyssinia was announced, about 25 peasants, roped in by the police and Fascist Youths, stood woodenly in the square to listen to the radio. The outbreak of war was greeted with stony indifference. Mayor Don Luigi spoke from the balcony of the Town Hall. He talked about the eternal grandeur of Rome, the wolf that suckled Romulus and Remus, and the Roman Empire which was about to be revived. Huddled against the wall below, the peasants listened in silence.

From 'Christ Stopped at Eboli' by Carlo Levi, 1944. This novel is based on the author's experience of internal exile in a small village in the south of Italy in 1933-35. He was sent there as punishment for anti-Fascist activity.

QUESTIONS

1. Judging from the information in this section, to what extent did Fascism change Italian society?

2. Explain the point that is being made by each of the cartoons in Sources A and B. In what ways might historians find them useful?

3. What do Sources A-D tell us about the nature of Fascism?

4. Is there any evidence in Sources A-D to suggest that Fascism was not very successful in the long term? Give reasons for your answer.

Source D *The view of a British diplomat*

Mussolini knew very little about the machinery of government or economics or foreign countries. His ignorance was sometimes staggering. Figures meant little to him. One million was a large figure. So was 10 million or 100 million and he found it difficult to distinguish between them. Since he had no stomach for the grind of administrative work, it was Mussolini's practice in the early days to leave to his ministers the management of their departments. He kept for himself only major decisions of policy and the right to intervene on a whim. For example, he personally decided on which date the Rome police changed into their white summer uniforms.

From 'Mussolini: Study of a demoagogue' by I. Kirkpatrick, 1964. Kirkpatrick served as a diplomat in the British Embassy in Rome in the 1930s and interviewed many former Fascist leaders after 1945.

Was the Weimar Republic doomed from the start?

Fascism first gained a grip in Italy and so Italian Fascism provided an important model for Fascists in other countries. As early as 1923, Hitler's Nazis tried to copy Mussolini's March on Rome with their own March on Berlin - the Munich Putsch (see pp.52-53). Although the Munich Putsch failed, the Nazis continued their struggle for a German version of Fascism. Ten years later, Hitler was appointed Chancellor (Prime Minister) and, like Mussolini before him, he used this position to destroy the democratic constitution and to replace it with a personal dictatorship. Many historians have argued that the collapse of German democracy was somehow inevitable. They point to the problems facing the Weimar Republic in its early years (see pp.49-53) and argue that these problems meant that large sections of the population (especially the middle classes) never felt any loyalty towards the Weimar constitution. Although there is no doubt that the Weimar Republic did face severe problems between 1919 and 1923, it is equally clear that there was a period of stability between 1923 and 1929 - the period when Gustav Stresemann was Chancellor and then Foreign Minister. Given this period of stability, some historians argue that the collapse of German democracy was not inevitable. It can only be explained by examining the particular circumstances that led to the appointment of Hitler as Chancellor. This section examines both the period of stability in Germany between 1923 and 1929 and the historical debate.

The Weimar constitution

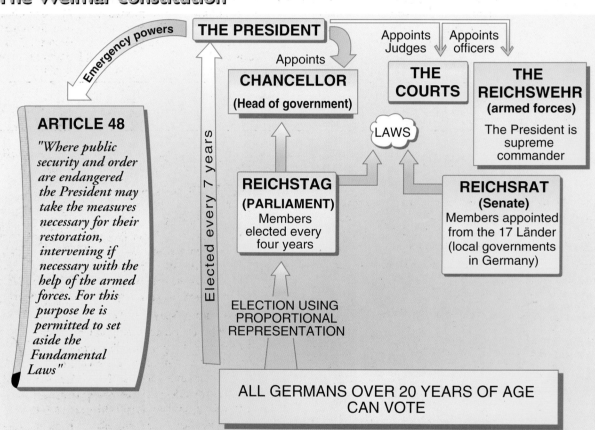

THE PRESIDENT

Emergency powers

Appoints

Appoints Judges

Appoints officers

CHANCELLOR
(Head of government)

THE COURTS

THE REICHSWEHR
(armed forces)
The President is supreme commander

LAWS

Elected every 7 years

ARTICLE 48

"Where public security and order are endangered the President may take the measures necessary for their restoration, intervening if necessary with the help of the armed forces. For this purpose he is permitted to set aside the Fundamental Laws"

REICHSTAG (PARLIAMENT)
Members elected every four years

REICHSRAT (Senate)
Members appointed from the 17 Länder (local governments in Germany)

ELECTION USING PROPORTIONAL REPRESENTATION

ALL GERMANS OVER 20 YEARS OF AGE CAN VOTE

THE FUNDAMENTAL LAWS *(the rights of all German citizens)*

(1) Personal freedom
No one can be arrested unless they have broken the law.

(2) Freedom of Expression
All Germans can express their opinion in speech, writing or picture.

TRADE UNION

(3) The freedom to hold peaceful meetings and form unions and societies.

Some historians argue that there were two major flaws in what was otherwise regarded as a 'model' constitution. First, the electoral system allowed small parties (like the Nazi Party) to gain a foothold in the Reichstag (Parliament). It also prevented a single party gaining an overall majority. The result was a series of coalition governments. Since each coalition did not last for long, there was a lack of stability. And second, the President had extensive emergency powers (see Article 48 above). These could be abused. Certainly, they made it easier for Hitler to set up his dictatorship once he was appointed Chancellor.

Political parties

PARTY	Communists (KPD)	Social Democrats (SPD)	German Democratic Party (DDP)	Centre (Zentrum)	German People's Party (DVP)	German National People's Party (DNVP)	National Socialist German Workers Party (NSDAP or Nazi Party)
SUPPORT	Working Class.	Largely working class.	Largely middle class.	Roman Catholics from all classes.	Middle class. Largely businessmen.	Middle and upper classes. Mainly officials and ex-soldiers.	The unemployed (mainly ex-soldiers). Some members of middle and upper classes.
POLICIES	Anti-Republic. Wanted workers' revolution.	Pro-Republic. Wanted reforms to help the working class.	Pro-Republic. Believed in individual freedom.	Pro-Republic. Supported the interests of the Catholic Church.	Pro-Republic. Preferred monarchy, but accepted the Republic. Promoted trade and industry.	Anti-Republic. Wanted strong government. Pro-monarchy. Extreme nationalists.	Anti-Republic. Wanted strong government. Anti-democrat and anti-Communist. Wanted Germany to be a great nation again.
THE POLITICAL SPECTRUM	LEFT WING						RIGHT WING

 From stability to crisis

Many historians have looked on the years when Gustav Stresemann was Chancellor and then Foreign Minister (see Box 4.3) as a period of hope and recovery - a time when it looked as though the Weimar Republic might succeed after all. Stresemann's main achievements were as follows:

1. **Stabilising the currency** - a new currency, the 'rentenmark' was introduced, ending hyperinflation.
2. **The Dawes Plan, 1924** The USA agreed to lend Germany money to help it to pay for reparations.
3. **The Locarno Pact, 1925** Germany, France and Belgium agreed to recognise their existing borders.
4. **Joining the League of Nations** Germany was allowed to join in 1926.

As the German economy recovered, some people became prosperous again. During the Stresemann era, Berlin became a centre of culture. The painting above illustrates both the sort of art produced in Berlin in the 1920s and the gap between the rich and the poor.

Box 4.3

Gustav Stresemann
1878 Born.
1919 Leader of DVP.
1923 Chancellor in August. Head of a coalition of centre parties. Became Foreign Minister from November to his death in October 1929.

a) Stresemann's 'hundred days' as Chancellor marked a real turning point in the Republic's history. He took office when the Republic was at its lowest ebb. By the time his coalition collapsed in November 1923, the Republic was well on its way to recovery. Stresemann was one of the few really outstanding political figures in the Weimar period. A statesmanlike figure of immense ability and industry, he was a gifted orator and strong personality.

From 'A History of Germany 1815-1945' by W. Carr, 1969

b) During the 'Stresemann era' the currency was stabilised and an agreement on reparations made with the Allies in 1924 (the Dawes Plan). Massive investment followed, mainly from the USA. This enabled German industry to recover almost to 1913 levels, despite the losses of land in 1919. At the same time, Stresemann stabilised Germany's relations with the rest of Europe. He negotiated treaties with Russia in 1922 and 1926. He helped form a collective defence pact with four other countries at Locarno in 1925 and took Germany into the League of Nations in 1926. During this period there was relative political stability as coalition governments functioned more or less effectively. But it did not last. Stresemann died in 1929.

From 'The European Dictatorships' by S. Lee, 1987

Activity
The collapse of the Weimar Republic

Source A Portrait of Hindenberg

The first President of the Weimar Republic, the Social Democrat Friedrich Ebert, had the power to govern through emergency decree. But Ebert used this power to protect the young state against putsches from the right and attempts at revolution from the left (see pp.49-53). This shows that the personal and political views of the President were of some importance. The second President, Paul von Hindenberg (elected in 1925 - see right), was a First World War commander who was a devoted monarchist, a conservative and a nationalist. At first, his election strengthened the Republic since it encouraged Conservatives to support the Republic. But, in the crisis which developed from 1930, he too governed through emergency decree. His conservative views and his determination to create a strong government were then crucial factors in Hitler's rise to power and the collapse of the Republic.

Source B A historian's view

A new President was elected every seven years. The President represented Germany in foreign affairs, appointed all ministers (including the Chancellor), was supreme commander of the armed forces and was responsible for calling meetings of the Reichstag (Parliament). A President could only be removed from office by a vote of two thirds of the Reichstag. In an emergency, the President could suspend the fundamental laws and take whatever measures were considered necessary to restore law and order. Unfortunately, the use of these special powers was never properly defined so that, during the emergency which existed in Germany after 1930, governments gained their power from the President rather than from the Reichstag. This problem was not foreseen by those who drew up the constitution. In fact, in 1919 it was felt that the President was a rather weak figure in danger of being overshadowed by the Reichstag. To counter this, the President was to be elected by the whole people. Only later did it become clear that a popularly elected President could make the presidency the real centre of power.

From 'A History of Germany 1815-1945' by W. Carr, 1969

Source C Election results 1919-33

All figures show number of seats won	6 June 1920	5 May 1924	7 Dec. 1924	20 May 1928
Communist (KPD)	4	62	99	54
Social Democrat (SPD)	103	103	131	153
Centre	64	65	69	61
Bavarian People's Party (BVP)	21	16	19	17
German Democratic Party (DDP)	39	28	32	25
German People's Party (DVP)	65	45	51	45
German National Party (DNVP)	71	95	103	73
National Socialist (Nazi, NSDAP)	–	32	14	12

All figures show number of seats won	14 Sept. 1930	31 July 1932	11 Nov. 1932	3 March 1933
Communist (KPD)	77	89	100	81
Social Democrat (SPD)	143	133	121	120
Centre	68	75	70	74
Bavarian People's Party (BVP)	19	22	20	18
German Democratic Party (DDP)	20	4	2	5
German People's Party (DVP)	30	7	11	2
German National Party (DNVP)	41	37	52	52
National Socialist (Nazi, NSDAP)	107	230	196	288

　　Anti-Republic (left wing)　　　　　　Pro-Republic
　　　　　Anti-Republic (right wing)

From 'Modern Germany' by V.R. Berghahn, 1982

Source D A historian's view

Hitler neither understood nor was interested in economics, but he was alive to the consequences of events which, like the hyperinflation of 1923, affected the life of every family in Germany. Unemployment in Germany rose from 1.3 million in September 1930 to a peak of over 6 million in 1932. Translate these figures into terms of men standing hopelessly on street corners, of houses without food and warmth and one may begin to guess something of the human anxiety burned into the minds of millions of ordinary Germans. The Depression was not limited to the working class. It affected the middle class just as sharply since they were threatened with the loss not only of their livelihood, but of their respectability. Nor was the slump limited to towns. In many parts of Germany, the peasants and farmers were in an angry and desperate mood. Like men and women in a town stricken by an earthquake, millions of Germans saw the apparently solid framework of their existence cracking and crumbling. In such circumstances, people no longer listen to reason. They have fantastic fears, extravagant hatreds and extravagant hopes. In such circumstances, the speeches of Hitler began to attract a mass following as they had never done before.

From 'Hitler: a Study in Tyranny' by A. Bullock, 1962

QUESTIONS

1. Judging from the information in this section, was the Weimar Republic doomed from the start?

2. What do Sources A and B tell us about the Weimar constitution? Does this mean its collapse was inevitable?

3. 'Hitler would never have won power if it had not been for the catastrophic events of 1929'. Explain this statement using Sources C and D.

During the Stresemann era, the Nazi Party was a small group with little influence and few supporters. The supporters it had, however, were extremely loyal and the Party's main aims remained consistent - to gain power and then to overthrow the Weimar Republic, replacing it with a new, strong government led by Hitler (see Box 4.4 for his background). Following the failure of the Munich Putsch in November 1923 (see pp.52-53), Hitler spent nine months in prison, along with other Nazi leaders. On his release, he immediately reorganised the Nazi Party and changed the Party's tactics. The overall aims of the Nazi Party remained the same, but Nazis were no longer to work towards winning power by force. Instead, they were to concentrate on building the Nazi Party into a nationwide network in the hope that this would result in greater support in elections. The Nazis still stood out as bitter opponents of the Weimar Republic and they were still involved in violence (usually on a local basis in fights against Communists), but the hope was that this would appeal to voters opposed to Communism. When elections for the Reichstag were held in 1928, it seemed that the Nazis had made little progress - they won just 12 out of 440 seats. But, as soon as the impact of the Wall Street Crash and economic slump which followed it began to bite, support for the Nazis rose dramatically. This section examines the new tactics adopted in the Stresemann era and the impact that the death of Stresemann and the onset of the Great Depression had on the Nazi Party. The Activity considers what sort of people became supporters of the Nazi Party.

J Hitler in prison

Following the failure of the Munich Putsch (see pp.52-53), Hitler and other senior Nazis were imprisoned in Landsberg Fortress near Munich. Hitler was sentenced to five years, but served just nine months. Not only was the prison term short, it was comfortable. The Nazis were allowed to meet daily. They were well fed and the prison guards left them to their own devices. This spell in prison was very important in the development of the Nazi Party. In prison,

English translation of 'Mein Kampf'.

Hitler dictated his autobiography *Mein Kampf* (which means 'My Struggle'). This laid out his views and aims (see Box 4.6). Also, it is clear that Hitler learned the lesson of the failed Putsch. In prison, he came to the conclusion that Nazi tactics should change (see Box 4.5).

Box 4.5

Hitler in prison - an eyewitness account

'From now on', Hitler said, 'we must follow a new line of action. It is best to attempt no large reorganisation until I am freed which may now be a matter of months rather than years. When I resume active work, it will be necessary to pursue a new policy. Instead of working to achieve power by an armed coup, we shall have to hold our noses and enter the Reichstag against Catholic and Communist MPs. If outvoting them takes longer than outshooting them, at least the results will be guaranteed by their own constitution. Sooner or later we will have a majority - and, after that, Germany.

From 'I knew Hitler' by Kurt Ludecke (who visited Hitler in prison), 1937

Box 4.4 Adolf Hitler

1) Adolf Hitler was born in 1889 in the small border town of Braunau-am-Inn in Austria (he was an Austrian citizen). His father was a customs official (he died in 1903), his mother a housewife (she died in 1907). Hitler left school in 1905 with no qualifications. In 1907, he went to Vienna, hoping to become an art student. But the art school rejected him. For six years, he made a poor living painting postcards. Then, in 1913, he moved to Munich to avoid conscription into the Austrian army.

2) When the First World War began, Hitler immediately volunteered to join the German army. In the war, he served with distinction, winning medals and promotion to lance corporal. He was wounded and gassed. For him, the war was a turning point. He enjoyed the camaraderie and believed in the cause of fighting for a greater Germany. When the armistice was announced, Hitler was devastated. He felt that the army had been betrayed by politicians.

Hitler (right) during the First World War

3) The failure of the Munich Putsch was the next major turning point in Hitler's life. Hitler used his trial to promote his cause (his comments were widely reported in the press). He admitted responsibility for the Putsch, but claimed: 'It is not you, gentlemen, who pass judgement on us. That judgement is spoken in the eternal court of history. That court will judge us as Germans who wanted only the good of their people and fatherland - who wanted to fight and die.' The photo below shows Hitler (on the left) in prison with other leading Nazis.

2. The Nazi Party 1924-29

Reichswettkampf der SA

When Hitler was released from prison, his first and most important task was to re-establish his authority in the Nazi Party. On 27 February 1925, he held a special meeting in Munich to relaunch the Party (4,000 Party loyalists met in the Beer cellar where the failed Putsch had taken place). In his speech, Hitler made it quite clear that he intended to lead the Party and would accept no opposition. After that meeting, Hitler was banned from speaking in public and so he concentrated on reorganising the Party behind the scenes (see Box 4.7). Germany was divided into 34 districts (Gaus), each controlled by a Nazi official (Gauleiter) - Mussolini's Fascist Party had a similar set-up. Gauleiters were appointed by Hitler and were responsible for recruiting members, raising funds and promoting Nazism. Like Mussolini, the image that Hitler wanted to promote was that of a disciplined and uniformed force, loyal to its leader. Central to this image and to Nazi tactics was the SA, the military wing of the Party. The SA was prominent at all Nazi events. For example, in 1927 the first of the Nazi rallies was held at Nuremberg - 30,000 members of the SA marched past Hitler and then stood in line, listening to a rousing speech. This became an annual event which grew in size and splendour. The poster above advertises for SA recruits.

3. The Nazi breakthrough

The economic slump coincided with a breakdown of coalition government in Germany. In March 1930, the government headed by Hermann Muller broke down and President Hindenberg appointed Heinrich Bruning as Chancellor. Bruning did not have a parliamentary majority, but ruled by emergency decree, using the President's special powers. From March 1930, therefore, the Weimar Republic ceased to function as a parliamentary democracy. As all the fears and disappointments of the early years of the Weimar Republic began to return with the Depression, people began to look for alternatives. A revival in support for the Communists played into the Nazis' hands. As in Italy in 1920 (see p.61), the government seemed incapable of action whereas Nazi troops (the SA) were quick to fight against the Communists on the streets. The result was a rapid growth in both votes (see right) and in membership of the Nazi Party. Between 1925 and December 1929 membership rose from 27,000 to 178,000. A year later it had reached 389,000 and by December 1931, it had reached 800,000.

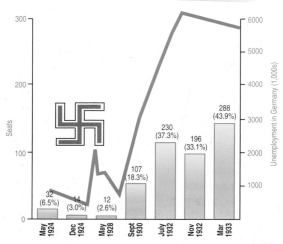

The figures above each bar show the number of Nazi MPs and their percentage of the total vote. The graph in the background shows the number of people unemployed.

70

Activity

Who supported the Nazis?

Source B Nazi militarism

Nazi militarism appealed to ex-soldiers and conservatives who feared a Communist takeover. The Nazis quickly became very skilled at organising set piece events like that pictured above.

Source E A Nazi election poster, 1932

This poster was produced for the presidential elections of 1932. The caption reads: 'Our last hope - Hitler'.

Source A A historian's view (1)

The nucleus of the Nazi Party's support was formed by the small farmers, shopkeepers and skilled workers of the old middle class. They made up the most stable and consistent group in the Nazi Party between 1924 and 1932. It was among these groups that the fear of economic insecurity and hatred of Communism was most common. By 1932, the Party had also won considerable support among university students, civil servants and even amongst the wealthy in big cities like Berlin and Hamburg. The reason for this support varied, but often included fear of the Communists and resentment because rich people no longer felt respected in the way they once had. It is important to note that these groups cannot be described as uneducated or as victims of the Depression. At the same time as the Nazis won support from the lower and upper middle classes, they also won significant support from the working class. By 1932, therefore, the Nazis could claim to be a people's party. Yet even at the height of its popularity, this was only partly true. If the party's support was a mile wide, it was, in places, an inch deep. The basis of this extraordinary electoral alliance was dissatisfaction, resentment and fear.

From 'The Nazi voter' by T. Childers, 1985

Source C A historian's view (2)

Nazism became the voice of the small townsman, the anxious officials and small businessmen, the peasant who felt he had had a raw deal from the Republic, the teachers and state employees who felt they had lost out in terms of status and income to other groups. The Nazi Party was made up and led by people like this. Nazi leaders voiced their fears and desires and promised to end the crisis. Nazism expressed the nationalism (extreme patriotism) of the conservative masses by blaming the Allies and reparations for Germany's ills. Above all, Nazism was violently anti-Communist. It was the only party visibly combating the threat of Communism on the streets. Although the violence put many respectable Germans off, they hated Communism more.

From 'Hitler and the Third Reich' by R. Overy in 'Modern History Review', November 1989

Source D An eyewitness account

Here, it seemed to me, was new hope. Here were new ideals, a new understanding, new tasks. The perils of Communism, which seemed to be on their way, could be halted. Hitler persuaded us that, instead of hopeless unemployment, Germany could move towards economic recovery. He had mentioned the Jewish problem only in passing. But such remarks did not worry me, even though I was not antisemitic [hostile towards Jews]. Indeed, I had Jewish friends from my school days and university days, like virtually everyone else. It must have been during these months that my mother saw an SA parade in the streets of Heidelberg. The sight of discipline in a time of chaos, the impression of energy in an atmosphere of hopelessness seems to have won her over also.

In this extract (from 'Inside the Third Reich', 1970), Albert Speer remembers hearing Hitler speak in 1931. Speer was a lecturer in architecture at the Berlin Institute of Technology. He later became the official Nazi architect and a minister.

QUESTIONS

1. Judging from the information in this section, what were the Nazis' aims and tactics after 1923?

2. Who supported the Nazis? Use Sources A-C in your answer.

3. What does Source D tell us about the impression made by the Nazis in the late 1920s and early 1930s?

4. Who was the election poster (Source E) designed to appeal to? What does this tell us about the tactics used by the Nazis?

How did the Nazis manage to win power in Germany?

The Nazis' breakthrough came in the election of September 1930 when they won 107 seats and 18.3% of the vote. Before the election, the Nazi Party had been an insignificant force in the Reichstag, but overnight it became the second biggest party. Given that the Nazis had made it very clear that they were opposed to democracy and to the Weimar Republic, this was a major headache for those politicians who supported the Republic. For two years, these politicians managed to keep the Nazis out of government. But, for two years, electoral support for the Nazis continued to grow. After the election in July 1932, the Nazi Party became the single biggest party in the Reichstag (though it still did not have an overall majority). Despite losing some support in the election of November 1932, the Nazi Party remained the largest party and, after months of political manoeuvring, President Hindenberg finally invited Hitler to become Chancellor on 30 January 1933. Although there were only two other Nazis in the Cabinet when Hitler became Chancellor, he was determined not to lose power once he had it. Over the next 18 months, he pushed through a series of measures which effectively destroyed the Weimar Republic and set up a dictatorship in its place. As in Italy, the Nazis did not force their way into power. They used the existing system to pass laws which destroyed that system. Historians have described this process as a 'legal revolution'. By 1935, Hitler's position was all-powerful. The Weimar Republic was dead. It had been replaced by the **Third Reich**.

1 Political manoeuvring in 1932-33

The parliamentary system broke down when Bruning was appointed Chancellor in March 1930. Bruning governed by emergency decrees, signed by President Hindenberg. As a result, power shifted from the Reichstag to the President. In the presidential election of 1932, Hitler stood as a candidate against Hindenberg and did much better than expected. The election went to two ballots and, although Hindenberg won with 19.4 million votes, Hitler polled 13.4 million votes. This was enough for Hindenberg to sack Bruning in May 1932 and to appoint Franz von Papen as Chancellor. Von Papen then called an election for July. Although Hindenberg refused to invite Hitler to form a government after the election (when the Nazis won more seats than any other party), Hitler was in a very powerful position. He refused to serve under von Papen, thus forcing another election in November 1932. Although the Nazi Party's vote dropped slightly, it remained the largest party in the Reichstag. Hitler then refused to serve under the next new Chancellor von Schleicher, making instead a secret deal with von Papen. Von Papen agreed that Hitler could be Chancellor on condition that his party, the Nationalist Party, had a majority of places in the Cabinet. When von Schleicher resigned on 28 January 1933, Hindenberg had no choice but to invite Hitler to become Chancellor.

President Hindenberg receives his new Chancellor Adolf Hitler. Hindenberg looked down on Hitler because he was an ex-lance corporal. Hindenberg had been a commanding officer during the First World War.

2 The Reichstag fire

The Reichstag building burning on 27 February 1933.

Once he became Chancellor, Hitler decided that there must be one last election. He hoped to win an overall majority so that he could be rid of his coalition partners. The election date was set for 5 March. During the campaign, the Nazis tried to scare the electorate by claiming that the Communists were preparing an uprising. Then, on 27 February, the Reichstag building was burned down and a young Dutch Communist, Marinus van der Lubbe, caught red-handed at the scene. The Nazis claimed that this was proof that the Communists were planning a revolution and they persuaded Hindenberg to sign an emergency decree allowing the police to search houses, ban meetings and shut down newspapers in the interest of national security. Over 300 leading Communists and socialists were immediately arrested. Opponents of the Nazis, however, claimed that the fire was actually started by Nazis and that Lubbe was a scapegoat (Lubbe admitted responsibility but said he was working alone). Whatever the truth, the timing was certainly convenient for the Nazis.

3 The legal revolution

This British cartoon (right) appeared in the magazine *Punch* on 8 March 1933. It shows Hindenberg (left) and Hitler as Roman senators (In Roman times, senior senators were appointed to the special post of dictator to deal with emergencies). In the background, a building (very like the Reichstag) burns. In the caption, Hindenberg says to Hitler: 'This is a heaven sent opportunity, my lad. If you can't be dictator now, you never will be.' The point is clear.

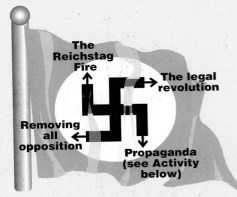

THE RED PERIL.

THE OLD CONSUL (to HITLER). "THIS IS A HEAVEN-SENT OPPORTUNITY, MY LAD. IF YOU CAN'T BE A DICTATOR NOW, YOU NEVER WILL BE."

Hitler would use the burning of the Reichstag to set up a dictatorship. And, in the next two years, that is exactly what he did. The elections of March 1933 were a disappointment to the Nazis. They won 43.8% and 288 seats, but not an overall majority. They then launched an attack on the Weimar Republic from above and below. At a local level, the Nazis simply took over - SA squads marched into town halls, police stations and newspaper offices and placed Nazis in charge. At a national level, Hitler skilfully used constitutional means to destroy the constitution. Two days after the new Reichstag met, an Enabling Act was passed (see Box 4.8). After this, it no longer mattered that the Nazis did not have an overall majority. Hitler was then able to remove his opponents and set up a one-party state.

4 Removing the opposition

Once in power, it was Hitler's aim to create a new Germany in which every aspect of life was controlled by the Nazis (see Box 4.9). To achieve this goal, the Nazis moved quickly to remove opponents at all levels in society. In April 1933, the elected state governors were dismissed and replaced with Nazis. On 2 May, trade union offices were raided, officials beaten and arrested and the unions closed down. A new Nazi organisation (the **German Labour Front**) took their place. Then, in July, a law was passed banning all political parties except the Nazi Party. At the same time, civil servants began to be replaced by Nazis and steps were taken to secure the support of lawyers. In October, for example, 10,000 lawyers were forced to swear an oath of loyalty to Hitler. Anybody who resisted any of these measures risked imprisonment - or worse. On 21 March 1933, a Nazi newspaper announced that the first concentration camp was to be opened that week. The photo above shows political prisoners arriving at Oranienburg concentration camp in August 1933.

Box 4.8

The legal revolution

When he was appointed Chancellor, Hitler's power was by no means absolute. It seemed, therefore, that von Papen was right to believe Hitler could be tamed. Within two months, von Papen argued, 'we will have pushed Hitler so far into a corner that he'll squeak'. Yet within six months Hitler was able to kick away the ladder by which he had climbed to power and set up a dictatorship based in effect on a permanent state of emergency. Part of the process was accomplished within the framework of the constitution. The results, however, were so devastating that they amounted to a legal revolution. After the March election, the new Reichstag met on 21 March and Hitler hoped to secure his Enabling Act which would reduce the Reichstag's powers. Such a change needed a two thirds majority. Hitler's solution was ingenious. He used the emergency decree of 28 February to expel all Communist MPs from the Reichstag. He then negotiated an agreement with the Centre Party. They would vote for the Enabling Act in return for special guarantees for the Church. On 23 March, the Enabling Act was passed with only the socialists voting against it. It allowed the Chancellor to issue laws without consulting the Reichstag. The legal revolution now gathered momentum as the new power was used to eliminate other political parties. Another election was held in November 1933 in which a single party list was put to the electorate. The result was that the Nazi Party took all the seats in the Reichstag. Germany was officially a one-party state.

From 'The European Dictatorships' by S. Lee, 1987

Box 4.9   Hitler's consolidation of power

The Nazi revolution proceeded along two related paths. First, efforts were made to ensure that all government institutions were controlled by the Nazis. And second, there was an attempt to persuade all German citizens to support the Nazi cause. The first approach involved the removal of all political opponents. The second involved the creation of mass organisations for mass control.

From 'Nazi Germany' by K. Fischer, 1995

5 The 'Night of the Long Knives'

Like Mussolini before him, Hitler made great use of organised violence during his rise to power. Most of this violence was carried out by the Storm Troopers, the SA (the military wing of the Nazi Party). By 1934, however, the SA was becoming both a liability and a danger. Ernst Rohm, the leader of the SA, wanted the SA to be the basis of a new German army - an idea which worried regular army commanders. Rohm also began to make speeches calling for a 'second revolution' that would speed up the changes made since Hitler became Chancellor. This annoyed Hitler who, by contrast, wanted a period of stability in order to win the confidence of the army and big business. In June 1934, Hitler decided to act. He made a deal with regular army commanders, guaranteeing their support. Then, on the night of 29-30 June, SS officers (the SS was Hitler's personal bodyguard) arrested Rohm and other SA leaders at a hotel near Munich. They claimed that Rohm was planning to overthrow Hitler (historians argue that it is unlikely that this was true). Although it is difficult to be certain about the figures because the SS destroyed all records, it is thought that around 85 people were executed and many thousands arrested on that night and in the days which followed. As well as Rohm and SA officers, the victims included political opponents such as the former Chancellor von Schleicher. The French cartoon (right) describes Hitler as 'The Butcher of Berlin'. Box 4.10 contains a historian's assessment and Hitler's attempt to justify his actions.

6 The death of Hindenberg

One reason for the timing of the Night of the Long Knives was the ill health of the elderly President, Hindenberg. When Hindenberg died on 2 August, Hitler declared himself **Der Fuhrer** (leader). He took over the post of President and became commander-in-chief of the armed forces. The Night of the Long Knives had cleared the path for this. Not only did army commanders support Hitler, they (along with all the troops) swore an oath which bound them to him personally: 'I swear by God this sacred oath, that I will give unconditional obedience to the Fuhrer of the German Reich, Adolf Hitler, the Supreme Commander of the Wehrmacht [armed forces], and, as a brave soldier, will be ready at any time to lay down my life for this oath.' Hitler was now in a position of supreme power. As the American cartoon from 1936 (above) suggests, he used this power to suppress (crush) individual freedom throughout German society. The following caption was included beneath the cartoon: 'In these three years, I have restored honour and freedom to the German people!'

Box 4.10

The Night of the Long Knives

a) Hitler consolidated his alliance with the army leaders by agreeing that the army alone should have the right to bear arms in Germany. This meant checking the power of the SA and its leader Ernst Rohm who regarded the SA as the Party's army and as destined to replace the old military class. In a series of swift, brutal murders on the night of 29-30 June 1934, Rohm and his leading associates were killed on Hitler's orders. For good measure, Hitler took advantage of the general blood bath to remove others who might be potential rivals or who had crossed his path in the past. It was a sign of Hitler's stability, compared with that of Mussolini at the time of Matteotti's murder (see p.63) that these acts of cold treachery raised little opposition and even abroad hostile comment was soon over and forgotten.

From 'Europe Since 1870' by J. Joll, 1976

b) If anyone criticises me and asks why I did not turn to the regular courts for conviction of the offenders, then all I can say to him is this. In this hour I was responsible for the fate of the German people and I thereby became the supreme judge of the German people. I gave the order to shoot the ringleaders in this treason. Let the nation know that its existence (which depends on its internal order and security) cannot be threatened with impunity [without punishment] by anyone. And let it be known for all time to come that if anyone raises his hand to strike the state, then certain death is his lot.

Part of a speech made by Hitler in which he attempted to justify the Night of the Long Knives. It was delivered in the Reichstag on 13 July 1934

Activity
Nazi propaganda

Source B   A Nazi rally - an eyewitness account

More than 100,000 people had paid to squeeze inside, while another 100,000 packed a nearby race track where loud speakers had been set up to carry Hitler's words. And, at home, millions were waiting by the radio. Around the stadium, banners were silhouetted against the darkening sky. Row under row, the seats stepped down to the centre field. Opposite them reared the dramatic speaking stand, its bold, cubical masses hung with giant swastikas. Draperies, also with swastikas, made a simple and thrilling background. Picked men were drawn up in close ranks below the stand. Twelve huge SA bands played military marches with beautiful precision and terrifying power. Behind the bands, on the field itself, solid squares of uniformed men stood in strict military order. Suddenly, a word was tossed from man to man. Hitler is coming! Hitler is here! A blare of trumpets split the air and 100,000 people leaped to their feet. All eyes were turned towards the stand, awaiting the approach of the Fuhrer. There was a low rumble of excitement and then, releasing its pent-up emotion, the crowd burst into a tremendous ovation, the 'Heils' swelling until they were like the roar of a mighty waterfall.

From 'I Knew Hitler' by K. Ludecke, 1937

Source D   A propaganda poster

Posters like this were produced by the Ministry of Enlightenment and Propaganda. The caption says: 'Children, what do you know about your Fuhrer?'

Source A   A Nazi rally - a photo

This photo shows Hitler speaking at a mass rally in Nuremberg in 1935. Events like this were organised by the Ministry of Enlightenment and Propaganda.

Source C   The Ministry of Enlightenment and Propaganda

We have set up a Ministry for Enlightenment and Propaganda. Propaganda is something active. We cannot be satisfied with just telling the people what we want and enlightening them as to how we are doing it. We must rather replace this enlightenment with an active government propaganda, a propaganda which aims at winning people over. It is not enough for people to move to a position where they are neutral towards us. We want rather to work on people until they are addicted to us. I am of the opinion that the press must help the government. The press may criticise the government, but it must not misrepresent the government to the people. The press must not only inform, it must also instruct. The press should be like a piano in the hands of government and on which the government can play. The press is an enormously important and significant instrument of mass influence that the government can make use of in the work for which it is responsible. It is possible for the government and press to work together. I see it as one of my principal tasks to achieve that aim.

Part of a speech made Joseph Goebbels, the new Minister for Enlightenment and Propaganda, 15 March 1933

QUESTIONS

1. Judging from the information in this section, how did the Nazis manage to win power and then to hold on to it?

2. 'Propaganda, propaganda. All that matters is propaganda' (Hitler, 1923). Judging from Sources A-D what do you think Hitler meant by this?

3. a) Judging from Sources A and B why do you think the Nazis organised mass rallies?
   b) Suppose you had been a British journalist who attended a rally. Write a report explaining what happened and why.

4. Using Sources A, C and D describe the role played by the Ministry of Enlightenment and Propaganda. How did it help the Nazis to remain in power?

To what extent did the Nazis change life in Germany during the 1930s?

The Nazis' aim was to create a new Germany with a new set of values and a new way of life. As Goebbels pointed out (see Source C on the previous page), it was not enough for German citizens to be neutral about Nazism. He (like the other Nazi leaders) was determined that every German citizen should become an active supporter of Nazism. The Nazis' mission, therefore, was to create a new sense of purpose. In part, this could be manufactured by propaganda. In part, it required the close supervision and control of all aspects of everyday life. At home, at work, at school and at play the Nazis aimed to make an impact on people's lives. The approach adopted by the Nazis tended to be a 'carrot and stick' approach. Those whose behaviour fitted in with Nazi thinking were rewarded. Those who opposed the Nazis or did not fit in were punished. By 1939, the apparatus of a police state had been set up, with many people living in fear of arrest. It is especially important to note that the Nazis were racists. In particular, they were extremely antisemitic - prejudiced against Jewish people. During the 1930s, this antisemitism made an impact on German society.

The economy in the 1930s

The Nazis had three main economic aims in the 1930s. First, they aimed to reduce unemployment - to fulfil the promises they had made before gaining power. Second, they aimed to revive the defence industry - so that Germany became a strong military power again. And third, they aimed for economic self-sufficiency - so that Germany would be able to survive if other countries refused to trade with it. The first task was to tackle unemployment. In 1933, the Economics Minister, Schact, set in motion the **Battle of Labour**. The government spent money financing schemes such as a house building programme and a road building programme (the new motorways, 'autobahn's, provided routes for military vehicles and therefore furthered the Nazis' military plans). After the Nazis came to power, unemployment dropped rapidly and the economy grew (see below). It is unclear, however, whether this was due to an upturn in the world economy, the 'Battle of Labour', the rearmament programme or a combination of these factors. The rearmament programme was launched by Hitler in 1936. He ordered a **Four Year Plan** to be set up and demanded: 'The German economy must be fit for war within four years'. The Four Year Plan's targets were not reached, however. For example, in 1939, the army only had enough ammunition for six weeks fighting. The target was for six months' supply. Nor was Germany self-sufficient by 1939, though the conquest of other nations brought control of new supplies and raw materials.

This poster was produced by the 'Strength Through Joy' organisation which was part of the German Labour Front, the Nazi controlled organisation which had been set up to replace trade unions (see p.73). The Strength Through Joy organisation's job was to organise leisure activities for working people and to encourage hard work by providing incentives. The biggest programme provided workers with cheap holidays. This poster shows happy workers on a cheap package holiday cruise. The slogan says: 'You too can now travel.' In practice, the Strength Through Joy organisation was just another way of extending Nazi control over people's lives. It was only the most loyal and hard working Party members who received places on these holidays. The German Labour Front provided other incentives to work hard. For example, it set up a scheme which encouraged workers to buy their own Volkswagen (German for 'people's car') on hire purchase. People began to pay a sum each week even before the factory building Volkswagens had gone into production. But the scheme was a con. Nobody had received their car by 1939 when the factory was converted to arms production.

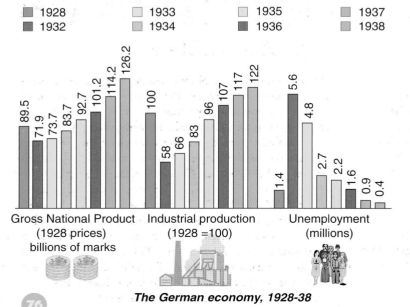

Key:
- 1928
- 1932
- 1933
- 1934
- 1935
- 1936
- 1937
- 1938

	Gross National Product (1928 prices) billions of marks	Industrial production (1928 =100)	Unemployment (millions)
1928	89.5		1.4
1932	71.9	58	5.6
1933	73.7	66	4.8
1934	83.7	83	2.7
1935	92.7	96	2.2
1936	101.2	107	1.6
1937	114.2	117	0.9
1938	126.2	122	0.4
(1928 index)		100	

The German economy, 1928-38

2 Antisemitism

One important way in which Nazism differed from Italian Fascism was that the Nazis were extreme racists. Today, people usually think of racism in terms of skin colour. Racists believe white people are superior to black people. The Nazis believed this, but they went further. They believed that the 'Aryan' race was the master race (the ideal Aryan has white skin, blond hair and blue eyes). Race was more than just appearance, however. It depended on belief and behaviour, too. The Nazis believed that Jews were 'racially impure', as were gypsies, Communists and homosexuals. In *Mein Kampf*, Hitler spent page after page attacking Jewish people and blaming them for all the problems that Germany faced after the war. Although antisemitism (hatred of Jews) was fairly common in other European countries, it was only in Nazi Germany that it formed the basis of government policy. As early as April 1933, the Nazis passed a law preventing Jews from working in the civil service and they organised a boycott of Jewish shops and businesses. Over the next few months, Jewish judges and lawyers were dismissed, books by Jewish authors were burned in public and the number of Jewish students entering schools and universities was fixed at a maximum of 5%. And this was just the start of a campaign that grew in intensity as time went on. By 1939, the German people had been bombarded with antisemitic propaganda for six years. This paved the way to the Holocaust (see pp.81-83). The poster (right) is typical of antisemitic propaganda. It was produced to advertise an exhibition of 'degenerate' art (art opposed by the Nazis) entitled 'The eternal Jew'.

The Jew on this poster is a money lender who has sold Germany to Bolshevik Russia. Jews were often linked with the Communists by the Nazis.

3 Nazi education

The education system under the Nazis was designed to ensure that young people understood and accepted Nazi values. As the historian Gerhard Wilke explains: 'In Nazi Germany, the household lost its dominant role in the rearing and training of children. The school became an instrument for the spreading of racial propaganda. It helped to win young minds for the system and it made children receptive to militaristic ideas and practices.' To achieve their aims, the Nazis laid down strict guidelines about what could be taught and how it was to be taught. There was, for example, a great emphasis on PE since the Nazis wanted young people to develop into fit and strong soldiers. Biology under the Nazis was used to promote the Nazis' theories on racism. And History followed the Nazi line (see Box 4.11). The picture (right) appeared in a school textbook in 1938. It encourages Aryans to dislike Jews.

Box 4.11

Nazi education

a) From all the innumerable great names of German history, the greatest must be picked out and introduced to children so often that they become the source of an unshakable pride. The curriculum must be built up along these lines so that when a young man leaves school he is not a half pacifist or democrat, but a whole German. The crown of the state's entire work of education and training must be to burn the racial sense and racial feeling into the heart and brain of every youth. No boy and no girl must leave school without understanding the necessity and essence of blood purity.

From 'Mein Kampf' by A. Hitler, 1924

b) Racial instruction is to begin with the youngest pupils (six years of age) in accordance with the wish of the Fuhrer that: 'No boy or girl must leave school without having been led to a realisation of the necessity and essence of blood purity.'

Order issued by the Education Minister, 1935

4 A police state

On the one hand, the Nazis encouraged enthusiasm and a sense of national unity. On the other, they clamped down hard on any sign of opposition. After 1933, the security services were greatly expanded and reorganised. By 1936, all police officers were under the control of the SS whose commander was Heinrich Himmler. The most feared branch of the SS was the Gestapo (secret police) whose job was to identify and punish opponents. It was led by Reinhard Heydrich. The Gestapo had the power to arrest people on suspicion and to punish them without trial. It has been estimated that 150,000 people were detained in concentration camps between 1933 and 1939 and that 32,500 Germans were executed for political crimes between 1933 and 1945. Fear of spies and arrest made many people reluctant to express their views openly.

5 The Hitler Youth movement

'Nazi youth policy aimed to secure the younger generation's total loyalty to the government (see Box 4.12) and their willingness to fight in the war which lay ahead. The main arm of the Nazis' youth policy was the Hitler Youth. By the end of 1933, all youth organisations, apart from the Catholic ones (which were protected by an agreement made between Hitler and the Vatican), had either been banned or 'coordinated' (merged with the Hitler Youth). By the end of 1933, therefore, the Hitler Youth already contained 47% of boys aged 10-14 and 38% of boys aged 14-18. However, only 15% of girls aged 10-14 and 8% aged 15 and 21 were organised. The Hitler Youth Law of December 1936 called for all German youth to join and this was backed up with pressure on those remaining outside to enrol voluntarily. In 1939, membership became compulsory.'

From 'Youth in the Third Reich' by D. Peukart, 1985

Box 4.12   Hitler Youth - an eyewitness account

I had already been a member of the Hitler Youth for 10 months. In our village on the French border the Hitler Youth leader was our teacher. He had already talked to us about the Jews: 'You have to fight them wherever you can'. We boys had the job of convincing our parents not to do business with Jews. And here was a Jew called Levi sitting in our kitchen. He wanted to escape to France (his family had escaped there in 1938). I was in despair. Although my father opposed my teacher and refused to buy me a brown shirt, I respected my teacher. He was big and strong. 'The Fuhrer', he said, 'expects you boys to be as fast as greyhounds, tough as leather and hard as Krupp steel.' And here was my father, a friend of Jews. I just couldn't figure it out. After dark, my father took Levi across the border. 'Are you sure nobody saw you?', my mother asked father on his return. 'You can rest assured', he said. At that moment I saw a smile light up my mother's face. And for the first time in my life, I wished I wasn't my parents' son.

Memories of Albert Bastian, interviewed in 1989

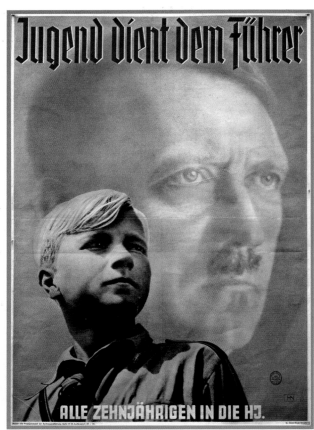

A poster designed to recruit boys to the Hitler Youth. The caption says: 'Youth serves the Fuhrer. All 10 year olds join the Hitler Youth'. The Hitler Youth organised hikes, sports, camps and competitions - as well as military-style drills and discussions on political texts.

6 How popular were the Nazis in the 1930s?

No opinion polls were conducted in Germany in the 1930s and no elections were held in which the Nazis competed with other parties. As a result, it is difficult to be sure how popular the Nazis were. Historians have to rely on the evidence from referendums and elections organised by the Nazis (Box 4.13) and from eyewitness accounts (Box 4.14). Significantly, the historian Ulrich Herbert records that: 'As late as 1951, almost half of those citizens of West Germany questioned in an opinion poll survey described the period between 1933 and 1939 as one in which things had gone best for Germany.'

Box 4.14   An eyewitness account

Whilst most people I met did not accept everything about the Nazis, they all said there was quite a lot to be said for how they ran the country. What had Hitler provided to persuade the Germans to give up their freedom so happily? Well, there was something for everyone in his political stew pot. Work for the unemployed, an army for the generals, a phoney religion for those easily fooled, a strong foreign policy for those who still smarted under the indignity of the lost war. Hitler knew he needed the support of the middle class and so he threw up a smokescreen of respectability. But there were also concentration camps and carefully broadcast hints about what was in store for anyone who questioned Hitler's methods, let alone openly disapproved of them.

Extract from the diary of Christabel Bielenberg, written in 1934

Box 4.13   Referendums and elections

a) Results, 1933-38

(i) Referendum, Nov. 1933
YES 95.1%
NO 4.9%

(ii) 'Election', March 1936
For Nazis 98.8%
Against 1.2%

(iii) Referendum April 1938
YES 99.08%
NO 0.92%

Turnout 99%

The referendum in 1933 asked the German people if they wanted to leave the League of Nations. The referendum in 1938 asked the German people if they supported the Auschluss (union with Austria - see p.142). In both cases, the Nazis wanted people to vote 'yes'.

b) In March 1936, the Nazi Party exerted more direct pressure on voters than ever before. In factories, offices and even schools the same slogans were heard over and over again for three weeks: 'No one must miss this election!' 'Every vote for the Fuhrer!' 'Anyone who does not vote for Hitler is a traitor!'. When Goebbels announced that 99% had voted for Hitler and the Nazi Party, nobody was surprised. Everyone had felt the pressure. An entire nation had bowed to a system of terror.

From 'In Hitler's Germany' by B. Englemann, 1988

Activity
Women in Nazi Germany

A photo of an ideal Nazi family. To protect the 'purity' of German blood, members of the SS were only allowed to marry women who had passed tests designed to prove that they were biologically and politically suitable. They were then given training for motherhood in special schools.

Source B *Hitler's view*

If one says that the man's world is the state, one might be tempted to say that the world of the woman is a smaller world. Her world is her husband, her family, her children and her home. But what would become of the greater world if there was nobody to tend and care for the smaller one? We do not consider it correct for women to interfere in the world of the man. We consider it natural if these two worlds remain separate. To the one belongs the strength of feeling, the strength of the soul. To the other belongs the strength of vision, of toughness, of decision and of the willingness to act. The programme of our Nazi Women's Movement has in reality but one single point and that point is the child. Every child that a woman brings into the world is a battle, a battle waged for the existence of her people.

Extract from a speech made by Hitler at the Nuremberg Party rally on 8 September 1934

Source C *A historian's view*

What the Nazis wanted from German parents was more children. The birth rate, which had been at an all-time high around the turn of the century, had levelled off by the 1930s, causing much alarm among Nazi leaders. To plant the German seed throughout Europe, the Nazis encouraged large families by blocking women's access to equal opportunities. They also offered money. The government paid child subsidies and a generous family allowance. The government constantly complained about selfish couples who did not want children. Exhibitions were staged to show that great Germans, such as the composer J.S. Bach, had fathered dozens of children. In addition, a cult of the mother was launched. Each year on 12 August, the birthday of Hitler's mother, awards were handed out to the most fertile mothers. The 'Honours Cross' of the German mother came in three classes - gold for more than eight children, silver for more than six and bronze for five. Large families presupposed that women stay at home rather than go to work. For this reason, the image of women cultivated by the Nazis was a traditional one of mother and home maker. Magda Goebbels, a blonde, tall and attractive woman became the officially promoted ideal of womanhood in the Third Reich. Her husband, the Propaganda Minister said: 'The mission of women is to be beautiful and to bring children into the world.'

From 'Nazi Germany' by K. Fischer, 1995

Source D *Nazi poster*

This poster says 'The Nazi Party looks after the people's community'. It shows an ideal German family protected by the wings of an eagle (a symbol of the Nazi Party). The image of a young mother with blonde hair and small baby appeared over and over on Nazi posters.

QUESTIONS

1. Judging from the information in this section, to what extent did the Nazis change life in Germany during the 1930s?

2. Using Sources A-D describe the role women were expected to play in Nazi Germany. What do these sources tell us about the nature of Nazism?

3. Look at Sources A and D and explain why they are good examples of Nazi propaganda.

4. How would you expect ordinary German women to respond to the appeals to women made by the Nazi government? Use Sources B and C in your answer.

Total war placed a considerable strain on the political, economic and social structure developed by the Nazis between 1933 and 1939. In the first two years of the war, military success helped to ensure that morale remained high. But even when the tide turned against the Nazis, there was little opposition to Nazi rule. Unlike in Mussolini's Italy (where morale and fighting spirit collapsed), most Germans were prepared to make sacrifices to the end. Whether they would have done so if they knew the true nature of Nazi rule during the war is a matter of debate. During the war, Nazi rule became much more extreme. Indeed, the Nazis used the cover of war to pursue policies that would not have been acceptable in peacetime. In particular, it was during the war that the Nazis set up programmes whose sole purpose was to rid Europe of Jews and other 'undesirables' by killing them. By 1942, a series of death camps had been set up. In these death camps, inmates were used as slave labour and then shot or gassed to death. By the time the Germans surrendered in 1945, at least six million people had died in the Holocaust (holocaust is a word meaning complete destruction). How much ordinary people knew about the Holocaust and whether they could or should have done something to stop it are some of the questions that have been asked since evidence of the Holocaust came to light in 1945.

1 The wartime economy

Although the Nazis' economic policies in the 1930s had been successful to some extent, the German economy in 1939 was by no means self-sufficient and the rearmament programme had produced insufficient arms and ammunition to fight a long war against strong opposition. Conquest brought important new resources such as gold reserves and raw materials. It also provided a pool of cheap labour. Indeed, by the beginning of 1941, there is no doubt that Germany was in a strong position. But, in June 1941, the decision was made to invade the Soviet Union and then, in December, the USA entered the war. By the end of 1941, Germany's position was much less secure and the economy was reorganised in preparation for total war. A Central Planning Board was set up in April 1942. This decided where raw materials should be sent. If more planes were needed, for example, the Central Planning Board directed raw materials to aircraft factories. If tanks were needed, raw materials went to tank factories. In addition, steps were taken to solve the problem of a labour shortage (which arose as men left to join the armed forces). Prisoners of war and civilians from countries under Nazi occupation were brought to Germany and made to work for low wages in very poor conditions. In many cases, they were treated as slave labour. Unsurprisingly, this slave labour was less efficient than normal labour and production could not keep up with demand. In addition, in 1944-45, Allied bombing raids on Germany were very damaging. By the beginning of 1945, the German economy was collapsing. The poster (right) was produced by the Nazis in an effort to recruit French workers for German industry in 1943. Its caption says: 'The bad days are over! Father is earning money in Germany'.

Finís les mauvais jours !

Papa gagne de l'argent en Allemagne !

2 Morale in Germany during the war

As soon as they gained power, the Nazis put Germany on a war footing. This was not just a matter of rearmament. Everything in Nazi Germany had a military flavour. Education was all about training boys to be good soldiers. Unemployment was a 'Battle of Labour'. Women were expected to play their part in the 'Battle for Births'. From the start, Nazi foreign policy was aggressive and Nazi leaders made it clear that Germany's enemies might declare war on it at any time. By 1939, therefore, the German people should have been well prepared for war and, provided they had swallowed the Nazi propaganda, they should have been more than willing to sacrifice their lives for the Third Reich. The historian's account in Box 4.15, however, suggests that, although morale did not collapse during the war, there was little enthusiasm.

Box 4.15   German morale - a historian's view

Hitler was determined to maintain support at home for the war effort. The means of doing this were provided by the fruits of his conquests. Occupied Europe was forced to supply foodstuffs, raw material and labour which cushioned the German home front for much of the war. The strategy worked. Throughout the war, there was virtually no open defeatism and, far less, any popular rebellion against the Nazis. But that does not mean that there was enthusiasm for the war. The memory of World War I remained horrifically vivid. Germany's early victories were popular, but there was clear evidence of war weariness virtually from the start. Even the victorious campaigns in Poland and western Europe in 1939-40 brought casualties and grief. The Russian campaign, in particular, caused great anxiety. Especially after the Germans were defeated at Stalingrad early in 1943, there was increasing despair. But there was also apathy [an unwillingness to do anything] as reality became too terrible to face. Together with increasing Nazi terror, this ensured that Hitler's government would not be overthrown from within.

From 'World War II', edited by J. Campbell, 1992

3 German women in the war

Unlike Britain and the USA, Germany only introduced conscription for women as a last resort. The Nazis believed that a woman's place was in the home and did not want women to be forced to do war work. Besides, the availability of cheap labour from the occupied countries meant that there was less need for women to fill the jobs left by men who joined the armed forces. Nevertheless, as the poster (right) shows, the requirements of total war meant that some women (mainly young, single women) were needed for important war work. Faced with defeat in 1943, conscription for women was introduced, but it was not strictly enforced. Between 1939 and 1944, around 3 million German men left jobs in industry. However, the number of employed women in September 1944 (14.9 million) was only slightly higher than that in May 1939 (14.6 million).

Box 4.16   German women in the war - an eyewitness account

It was the autumn of 1944. My father was at war and the rest of my family had moved to Bavaria. I was 19 and decided to stay in Berlin. I was drafted into the labour service and had to work in an ammunition factory. Thank God I didn't end up in the main hall, but instead was sent to work in a small room. It was said we were doing solder work on a secret weapon, but all I remember soldering were pots and pans. I got up at 5 am each morning and rode my bike to the factory to begin at 6 am. I worked 64 hours per week for 'our Fuhrer'. About that time, we really began to feel the food shortage at home. We had used up everything in reserve and relied totally on official rations. Our noon meal consisted of cabbage and potatoes, while in the evening we ate potatoes and carrots. I remember having to divide up a tiny piece of butter into daily portions which were never even enough to spread on one piece of bread.

Memories of Juliane Hartmann, interviewed in 1989

This poster was produced in 1941. It shows a factory worker, a nurse and a farm worker and says: 'You, too, must help!'.

4 The euthanasia programme

During the war, the Nazis' ideas about the purity of German blood were taken to an extreme. People who were mentally ill or disabled were regarded as 'racial inferiors' whose lives were not worth living. As soon as war broke out in September 1939, Hitler issued a secret order beginning a programme of **euthanasia** (mercy killing). A committee of doctors examined lists of patients with disabilities and decided which should be given lethal injections (see Box 4.17). Significantly, in 1935 Hitler told Dr Wagner (the Nazis' chief doctor) that large-scale euthanasia would have to wait until wartime because then it would be easier to administer.

Box 4.17   Euthanasia - a historian's account

The actual killings were carried out in six selected asylums. Specially trained SS teams of doctors and nurses moved in and prepared the way. Patients were killed in gas chambers disguised as shower rooms or in mobile vans (techniques later used in the death camps). The corpses were then incinerated [burned]. Since these actions took place in Germany, word soon leaked out. Ugly scenes occurred when regular staff tried to protect their patients. Relatives of the victims informed clergymen and lawyers. In August 1941, Hitler ended the programme, possibly because of criticism, but more likely because it had reached its target. When the killings stopped, 70,273 people had been exterminated.

From 'Nazi Germany' by K. Fischer, 1995

5 Steps towards the Holocaust

Before the war, the Nazis aimed to make Germany a racially pure country by persuading non-Aryans to go and live elsewhere. This 'persuasion' took two forms - a steady stream of antisemitic propaganda and a gradually escalating series of measures. The photo above from 1933 shows a married couple - an Aryan woman and a Jewish man - being bullied by Nazis (the first stage). In 1935 the Nuremberg Laws were passed. They made it illegal for Aryans to marry Jews and took away German citizenship from Jews (the second stage). Then, on the night of 9-10 November 1938, throughout Germany Nazis attacked Jews (the third stage). About 90 were killed and over 300,000 sent to concentration camps. Jewish businesses and synagogues (places of worship) were wrecked. This was known as 'crystal night' because of all the broken glass. It was a small taste of what was to follow.

Activity

The Holocaust

Source A *The number of people killed*

The Nazis kept records of those killed, but some of these records have been lost. One leading Nazi, Adolf Eichmann, was captured and put on trial in 1961. He said that he knew that at least six million Jews had been killed. The figures in the two tables (right) are based on the Jewish population before and after the war. In addition, several thousand gypsies, homosexuals, Communists and other political opponents were killed.

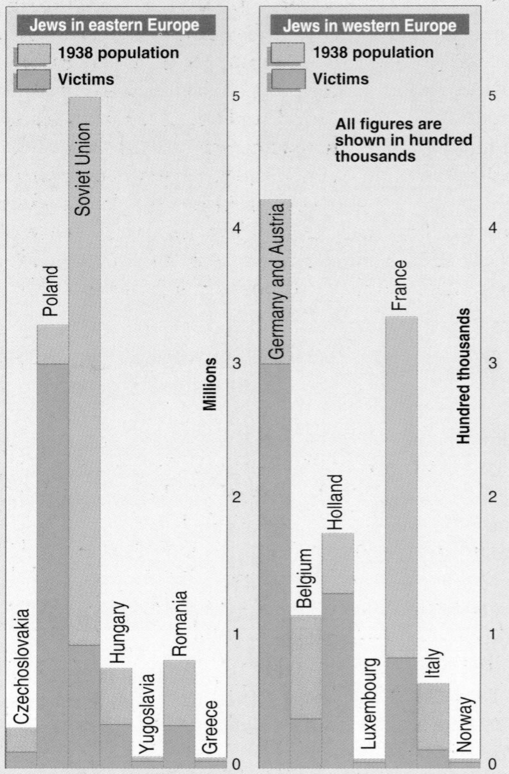
Jews in eastern Europe
1938 population
Victims
Millions
0
1
2
3
4
5
Czechoslovakia
Poland
Soviet Union
Hungary
Yugoslavia
Romania
Greece
Jews in western Europe
1938 population
Victims
All figures are shown in hundred thousands
Hundred thousands
Germany and Austria
Belgium
Holland
Luxembourg
France
Italy
Norway

Source B *The Wannsee Conference*

In pursuance of the final solution, the Jews will be conscripted for labour in the east under appropriate supervision. Large labour gangs will be formed from those fit for work, with the sexes separated. These gangs will be used for road construction and undoubtedly a large number of them will drop out through natural wastage. The remainder who survive - and they will certainly be those who have the greatest powers of endurance - will have to be dealt with accordingly. For, if released, they would, as a natural selection of the fittest, form a germ cell from which the Jewish race could regenerate itself. That is the lesson of history. In the process of carrying out the final solution, Europe will be combed from west to east.

From the minutes taken at the Wannsee Conference held in January 1942. This conference was organised by Reinhard Heydrich, deputy leader of the SS. It was attended by 15 members of government. According to Adolf Eichmann, who was present, the discussion was much more open and frank than the minutes suggest.

Source C *Eyewitness account*

When we got to Auschwitz the first thing we noticed was the big sign saying 'freedom through work'. Then the first selection came, where people were picked out to go straight to the gas chamber. We all had to undress and march naked past a group of SS officers. My older sister was absolutely terrified of dying. I said to her: 'Don't be afraid. You go in first. I'll be right behind you. If you are gassed, I'll be with you. I won't leave you alone.' Then all the hair on our bodies was shaved off by prisoners. Next we were sent to a very large room with nozzles on the walls. We still didn't know if we were going to be gassed. When water came out, we knew we were going to stay alive. We were beaten a lot and hardly given anything to eat. You could watch human beings turn into animals. Many people lost all sense of human dignity. We were forced to carry heavy rocks from one place to another. We had to carry a rock about half a mile, set it down, pick up another rock and carry that back to where we had originally come from. And of course there was the fire, the bright fire rising from the chimney. You couldn't help but notice it. It burned night and day. People came from Hungary and we said: 'Today the Hungarians are burning'. When was it going to be our turn?

Memories of Dora Volkel, interviewed in 1989

Source D *Arrival at Auschwitz*

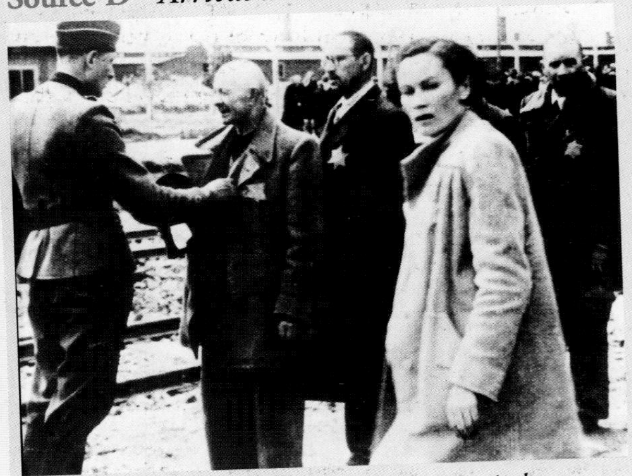

This photo shows Nazi guards sorting out new arrivals at Auschwitz. The stars on the prisoners' coats show they are Jews. When prisoners arrived, the Nazis decided who should be killed immediately and who should be used as slave labour. The old, the weak and children were usually killed. They were taken to a changing room and told to take off their clothes as if they were to have a shower. When they were inside the shower chamber, pellets of deadly gas were released, killing them. In 1944, 12,000 people were killed in the gas chambers at Auschwitz every day. Once the prisoners were dead, gold fillings and rings were removed and they were cremated in huge ovens.

QUESTIONS

1. **Judging from the information in this section, what impact did World War II make on life in Nazi Germany?**
2. **Using Sources A-D explain how the Nazis attempted to bring about the 'final solution to the Jewish problem'.**
3. **What do Sources B and C tell us about the attitudes of Nazis involved in the Holocaust?**
4. **Who was to blame for the Holocaust? Use Sources A-D in your answer.**

SOURCE WORK

Oral history - the Holocaust

When it became clear that Germany would be defeated in the war, the Nazis tried to hide what they had been doing. Gas chambers were blown up. Mass graves were reopened and the corpses cremated. Despite these efforts, a great deal of evidence about the Holocaust survives. Much of this evidence is 'oral' evidence - the memories of those who lived through the Holocaust. Oral evidence is very useful for historians, but it must be handled with care. People do not always tell the truth. Besides, they always look back with hindsight (the knowledge of what happened afterwards). Also, people, deliberately or unconsciously, invent details or exaggerate. The chances are, for example, that if ten people witnessed an event and were interviewed a year later, there would be ten very different accounts. Once the Nazis had been defeated and the full horror of the Holocaust became known, a number of questions arose. For example, just how many people were involved in and knew about the Holocaust? And, was it just the top Nazis and their henchmen who were responsible or should the wider German public take some of the blame? The accounts on this page were given by ordinary German people who lived through the war. These people were interviewed more than 40 years after the events they discuss actually happened.

Eyewitness account (1)

We knew about the 'protective custody' camps, as we called them. I was a young girl. As far as we knew, nobody ever called them concentration camps. We were told that the Jews were kept in these camps for their own safety, so that they wouldn't be killed by people who hated Jews. At the end of the war, they were supposed to leave the country. Once I talked to an SS soldier home on leave. I asked him about the camps. He said: 'No problem. I visited the camp in Bergen Belsen, not far from here. All I can say is that they are receiving the best treatment and are eating well.' When you're young, you believe it, you want to believe it. Not even those who had been interrogated by the Gestapo ever said a word to their families about what had happened to them. They were probably told: 'You open your mouth about any of this, we'll kill you and your family'. So how were we to find out anything if those who knew didn't even talk?

Memories of Ines Lyss who lived in Hamburg during the war

Eyewitness account (2)

It wasn't until January 1947, after I voluntarily saw a documentary film on Auschwitz, that I was forced to believe that the horrible crimes that I had heard were committed by the Nazis were really true. Ever since then, down to the present day, my life has been one of terrible shame. Still, I don't believe in collective guilt because, as troops at the front, we had no way of suspecting that Jews or other groups were being liquidated far behind the front. And I swear that I personally never once witnessed German soldiers liquidating Jews, prisoners or civilians. The troops at the front knew that the penalty for rape, pillage or plunder was death.

Memories of Hans Ulrich Greffrath, an officer in the German army during the war

Eyewitness account (3)

It is absolutely out of the question that the military leaders of the day didn't know about the existence of concentration camps and the atrocities which were going on at the time. Even we common soldiers who witnessed the 'transports' [prisoners being sent to the camps by train] and heard that people were being beaten knew that something wasn't right. It is impossible that staff who otherwise had their nose in just about everything didn't know that the Jews were being annihilated.

Memories of Willi Weisskirch, an infantryman during the war

When Allied troops reached the concentration camps and found scenes of devastation, they forced German citizens who lived locally to come and see the scenes for themselves. This photo shows German civilians inspecting a mass grave at Flossenburg under American army supervision.

QUESTIONS

1. **What problems might historians face when dealing with oral evidence? How is it possible to overcome these problems?**

2. **What do the eyewitness accounts tell us about the way in which ordinary Germans came to terms with the Holocaust? Do you think ordinary Germans can be blamed for what happened?**

3. **Separate the facts in each extract from the opinions. What does this tell you about the nature of oral evidence?**

4. **Think of an event which happened about a year ago. Interview three of your friends about the event. How do their accounts differ? Using their accounts, write an account which explains what really happened.**

Was Nazi Germany a totalitarian state?

A totalitarian state is a state which aims to take complete control of the lives of its citizens. To achieve this, it relies on three main factors - the widespread use of propaganda, the setting up of a large-scale police force whose job is to terrorise the population into obedience and an emphasis on strong, almost godlike leadership. Although it has often been assumed that Nazi Germany is an excellent example of a totalitarian state, in recent years historians have begun to question whether this is so. In particular, they have raised two important questions. First, to what extent did the Nazis manage to win over the hearts and minds of the majority of the German people? Some historians argue that the Nazis were simply not in power long enough to do this. It is true that they were able to persuade the vast majority of people to vote for them in referendums (see p.78) and there was a growing acceptance of Nazi attitudes, but many people gave their support reluctantly, often because they were scared of what might happen if they did not. In the words of the historian David Schoenbaum, the Nazis never did achieve a 'social revolution'. And second (and more controversially), was Hitler really in total control in Germany? Although there are many historians who believe that Hitler deliberately kept the Nazi system of government confused to ensure that his position of supreme power was not challenged, others now argue that the confusion was actually due to Hitler's personal weakness as a leader. In reality, they argue, Hitler was not at all like his public image. He was, in fact, a weak dictator. The Activity below explores the arguments for and against this view.

Activity
Hitler the leader

Source A
Portraits of the Fuhrer

Ein Volk, ein Reich, ein Führer!

The caption on the poster (right) reads: 'One people, one state, one leader'. The photo above shows Hitler meeting girls dressed in traditional German costume.

Source B   *The Nazi system of government - a historian's view*

Despite the so-called 'Nazi revolution', central government experienced a surprising degree of continuity. All the ministries of the Weimar Republic remained and their power was increased by the Enabling Act. There was no attempt to destroy existing institutions and to replace them with new Nazi agencies. In fact, Hitler was never very enthusiastic about the idea of undiluted Nazi Party rule. He preferred to set up parallel agencies which competed with each other. For example, he appointed Special Deputies who were outside the government ministries but whose job was the same. So, the work of Fritz Todt, General Inspector for Roads, overlapped and came into conflict with the Minister for Transport. Untidiness and overlapping were also apparent in local government. The traditional authorities under the Minister-President of each state remained. But a second type of official emerged (one based more directly on the Party) - ten senior Nazis were appointed as Reich Governors whose job was to enforce the Fuhrer's orders. The result was open competition between the Ministers-President and Governors. There are two possible explanations for this type of set-up. First, Hitler used a process of divide and rule to strengthen his personal power. His strength, in other words, depended on him being the only one to sort out the jumble which came from the competing agencies. A second explanation, however, is that the overlapping and inefficiency was the result of a haphazard exercise of power. Hitler was, in fact, incompetent. The question boils down to whether Hitler was strong and decisive or weak and uncertain.

From 'The European Dictatorships' by S. Lee, 1987

Source C *Hitler at work - an eyewitness*

When, I would often ask myself, did he really work? Little was left of the day. He rose late in the morning and conducted one or two official conferences. But from the subsequent dinner on, he more or less wasted his time until the early hours of the evening. His rare appointments in the late afternoon were ruined by his passion for looking at building plans. The assistants in his office often asked me: 'Please don't show any plans today'. Then the drawings I had brought with me would be left by the telephone switchboard at the entrance and I would dodge Hitler's questions. Sometimes he would see through this game and would go himself to look for my roll of plans. In the eyes of the people, Hitler was the leader who watched over the nation day and night. This was hardly so. Hitler's lifestyle was characteristic of the artistic temperament. According to my observations, he often allowed a problem to mature during the weeks when he seemed entirely taken up with trivial matters. Then after the 'sudden insight' came, he would spend a few days of intensive work giving final shape to his solution. Once he had come to a decision, he fell back again into idleness.

From 'Inside the Third Reich' by Albert Speer, 1970. Speer was the official Nazi architect and a minister.

Source D *Hitler as leader - a historian's view*

Hitler was Nazi Germany and Nazi Germany was Hitler. The personality and leadership style of Hitler shaped the nature of government and life during the Third Reich. Hitler believed in the rule of men and not the rule of law. In practice, decision making was inspired by personal desire not formal laws. The spirit of the new regime was summed up by Hitler's claim that there could only be one will in Germany - his own - and all had to obey it. However, it was not always clear what the Fuhrer's will was on any given question (except those issues like race and territorial expansion where his views were unshakable). His habit of making decisions by fits and starts caused confusion. The result was often a kind of chaos which has misled some historians into believing Hitler was a weak dictator who was often absent in his government and encouraged competition and conflict which caused strife and confusion. It is true that Hitler was little seen in government in the sense of being involved in the daily routine of government work. But this would only be a sign of weakness if his role had been questioned or if his major decisions had been defied. Neither happened. Rather there was the belief among decision makers that Hitler was sensitive to the deepest needs of the German people. His will was never seriously challenged. His orders (usually spoken not written) had the force of law. In short, Hitler was all-powerful.

From 'Nazi Germany' by K. Fischer, 1995

Source E *Nazi poster*

The main caption on this poster says: 'This hand guides the Reich'.

Source F *Hitler's place in history*

The unending fascination with Hitler undoubtedly has something to do with the continued readiness to see the past in terms of 'the history of great men', even where 'greatness' means 'evil genius'. Only an extraordinary individual with quite outstanding talent could have done what Hitler did, it is presumed. But rather than as a demonic [devil-like] figure, Hitler should be seen as a mediocre person whose immense historical impact can only be explained through external conditions and through the weakness, ambitions and stupidity of others. His personal actions were indeed of critical importance at key moments. He did take the 'big' decisions that determined war or peace. But the circumstances and conditions were seldom of his own choosing and his actions were usually those of a bully or a 'go-for-broke' gambler. That they came off so often and for so long was not because Hitler was a brilliant politician, but because his opponents were weak, external powers were ready to appease him and powerful groups in Germany were ready to collaborate.

From 'Herr Hitler: Man of the Volk' by I. Kershaw, 'The Guardian', 22 April 1995

QUESTIONS

1. **Look back through the chapter and find evidence to support the view that Nazi Germany was a totalitarian state. Is there any evidence to suggest that the Nazi grip on power was not as total as some historians have claimed?**

2. **What image is being promoted by the pictures in Sources A and E? To what extent does that image fit with reality?**

3. **Was Hitler a weak dictator? Give arguments for and against, using Sources B, C, D and F in your answer.**

4. **'An extraordinary individual' or 'a mediocre person' (Source F). Which phrase best describes Hitler? Give reasons for your answer.**

5 ▶ THE USA, 1918 - 41

Themes

For many (but by no means all) Americans the 1920s were years of prosperity and a freer way of life. By contrast, the 1930s were years of economic depression and insecurity.

The prosperity of the 1920s had a number of causes. Perhaps most important, the American economy had been stimulated by the demand to provide the Allies with supplies during the First World War. At the same time, new techniques of mass production were being developed by industrialists like Henry Ford. The result was that more goods were bought by Americans who had more money to spend. These Americans could also enjoy a freer style of life because moral attitudes began to change and people became able to travel more easily as cars became cheap and widely available. The prosperity of the 1920s, however, was not shared by everyone. Americans who were poor, black or foreign-born immigrants had a very different experience of the 1920s. The 1930s was the decade of the Great Depression. This started with the Wall Street Crash of 1929. Production fell and unemployment rose to record levels. Some people even feared the collapse of the American system. The election of a new Democratic administration in 1932 under the energetic leadership of Franklin D. Roosevelt, however, offered some hope. Roosevelt promised Americans a 'New Deal'. This did not solve the problems brought about by the Great Depression, but it did restore confidence in the American system. This chapter looks at the contrasting fortunes of the USA in the 1920s and 1930s. It examines the following questions.

* What was the impact of the First World War on the USA?
* To what extent were the 1920s a time of economic boom in the USA?
* Was the USA a free society in the 1920s?
* What were the causes of the Great Depression? What impact did it make?
* Why did Roosevelt win the 1932 presidential election?
* What was the New Deal?
* Who opposed the New Deal in the 1930s?
* How successful was the New Deal?

Key Events

1919
1. The Senate refuses to join the League of Nations.
2. A Prohibition amendment is passed making alcohol illegal.
3. The 'Red Scare' reveals fears of Communism.

1920
Warren Harding (right) wins the presidential election - the start of 12 years of Republican government. Women voted for the first time.

1922
The annual production of cars reached over 3 million. The car industry is central to the economic boom.

1927
1. First talking movie - 'The Jazz Singer' (right).
2. Sacco and Vanzetti, poor Italian immigrants, are executed.

1929
The Wall Street Crash. The New York stock market collapses, beginning the Great Depression.

1932
Franklin D. Roosevelt (right), a Democrat, is elected President. Over 13 million people are unemployed at the time of his election.

1933
Roosevelt's '100 days' in which the New Deal is launched. The federal government takes responsibility for looking after people in need for the first time.

1935-36
Second phase of the New Deal. Roosevelt is then re-elected in 1936 (he wins all but two states).

WORK PROMOTES CONFIDENCE
WORKS PROGRESS ADMINISTRATION

1940
OURS...to fight for

For the first time, an American President wins a third term of office. Roosevelt then prepares the USA for war. The USA enters World War II in December 1941.

The American system

Source 1

A historian's view

Historically, the most difficult problem for the federal government has been building sufficient political support for effective policy making. The separation of the powers (see Source 3) means that each branch of government - the executive, the legislature and the judiciary - has a great amount of independent power. In addition, federalism gives the states and local governments a great deal of power. Therefore, if the federal government is to act effectively, it must have the support of Congress, the Supreme Court and the state governors, at least for part of the time. This, of course, assumes that the government needs to act. In fact, for most of the 19th century and for the first 30 years of the 20th century, the federal government was required to do very little. American capitalism flourished without much state involvement. All this changed after 1929 when the country was plunged into economic depression. From 1932, there was much greater federal spending and more federal government involvement in the American economy and society generally.

From 'Politics and Power in the USA' by D. McKay, 1987

Source 2

Presidential elections 1920 & 1936

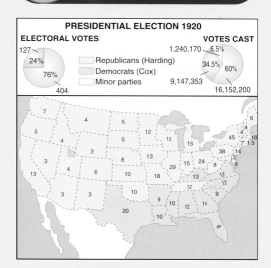

PRESIDENTIAL ELECTION 1920

ELECTORAL VOTES

127
24%
76%
404

VOTES CAST

1,240,170 5.5%
34.5% 60%
9,147,353
16,152,200

☐ Republicans (Harding)
☐ Democrats (Cox)
☐ Minor parties

PRESIDENTIAL ELECTION 1936

ELECTORAL VOTES

8 votes
1.5%
98.5%
523 votes

VOTES CAST

16,674,665 1,200,982
36.53% 2.66%
60.81%
27,752,869

☐ Republicans (Landon)
☐ Democrats (Roosevelt)
☐ Minor parties

The numbers on the maps above show the number of 'electoral votes' returned by each state. The candidate who wins the most votes in a state wins all that state's electoral votes. The candidate with most electoral votes overall is elected President. The number of electoral votes for a state depends on its population at the time of each election.

Source 3

WRITTEN CONSTITUTION
The USA is governed by a written constitution, drawn up in 1789. Since then, 26 amendments (changes) have been made. Of these, eight amendments have been made since 1918.

FEDERAL GOVERNMENT
The federal government is divided into three - the **legislature** (which makes laws), **executive** (which proposes and oversees laws) and the **judiciary** (which decides whether laws have been broken). These powers are exercised by different people. This is known as the **separation of the powers**. The aim is to avoid the concentration of power into the hands of a single person or group.

LEGISLATURE (CONGRESS)	EXECUTIVE (PRESIDENT)	JUDICIARY (SUPREME COURT)

Congress has two houses - the **Senate** (made up of two members elected from each state) and the **House of Representatives** (made up of 435 members).

The President is the head of the executive. A new President is elected every four years. Since 1951, Presidents have only been allowed to serve for a maximum of two terms.

This is the final court of appeal. It decides whether laws are valid under the constitution. Its nine justices are appointed by the President for life.

STATE GOVERNMENTS

In a federal system, different levels of government exist side by side. Matters which concern the country as a whole are dealt with by the federal government. Matters only concerning a particular state are dealt with by the state government. Like the federal government, state governments have an executive, legislature and judiciary. Since state and federal powers overlap, there are often disputes between the two layers of government.

QUESTIONS

1. a) **Judging from Sources 1-3, how does the American system of government differ from the British system?**

   b) **Why is it difficult for American Presidents to make big changes? Describe the problems they might face.**

2. **'An ideal democracy'. Do you agree with this view of the American system? Give reasons for your answer.**

3. **Using Sources 1 and 2 and information on the opposite page, explain why 1929 was a turning point in American history.**

What was the impact of the First World War on the USA?

When war broke out in Europe in August 1914, the USA at first remained neutral. Indeed, for the first two and half years of the war many Americans were able to prosper from the growth in business which the war in Europe brought. Private American banks provided loans to the Allies which the Allies then used to buy arms, food and equipment - mainly from the USA. The result was an economic boom. The position of neutrality, however, was increasingly difficult to maintain. The main problem was that American ships or Americans travelling in other countries' ships fell victim to attacks made by German U-boats. In 1916, Germany promised not to attack unarmed ships without carrying out search procedures first. In early 1917, however, U-boats were instructed to ignore this promise and a number of American ships were sunk. Then, in March 1917, a German plot to use Mexico as the base for a possible attack on the USA was discovered. This was enough to persuade the American government to declare war on Germany and it did so in April 1917. The USA then played an important part both in the final stages of the First World War and in the peacemaking of 1919. Participation in the war affected the position of the USA as a world power. The impact of the war was also strongly felt in the economic and social development of the nation in the 1920s (see Box 5.1).

① A limited world role - the rejection of the League of Nations

After the war, President Wilson wanted the USA to play a part in shaping the peace. His Fourteen Points (see p.47) were adopted as the basis of the peace settlement and other countries agreed to his idea of a League of Nations (see pp.54-56). Wilson hoped that, through the League of Nations, the USA would play a leading world role. He attended the Paris Peace Conference in person and played an important part in the decisions reached there. But Wilson's political position had been weakened even before he left for Paris. Many Americans were worried by the squabbles of the Europeans at the Peace Conference and feared that membership of the League would involve the USA permanently in the affairs of Europe. The American Senate rejected the peace treaties and the USA never joined the League (see p.57).

> ## Box 5.1   Impact of the war
>
> 1. A limited world role: rejection of the League of Nations.
> 2. A major world role: the world's leading economy.
> 3. Republican victory in 1920, followed by 12 years of Republican government.
> 4. Two major constitutional changes:
>   Prohibition (18th amendment, 1919)
>   Votes for women (19th amendment, 1920).
> 5. Wartime intolerance continues:
>   (a) against immigrants
>   (b) against black Americans.

② A major world role - a leading economy

Increases in production

	Iron ore Million Tons	Coal Million Tons	Petrol Million Tons	Wheat Million Tons
1914	41.4	422.7	265.7	763.4 (1913)
1917	75.3	551	335.3	1,025.8 (1915)

Exports

	Chemicals exported	Iron & Steel exported	Meat exported	Wheat exported
1914	21.9	251.5	143.3	87.9
1917	281	1,133.7	353.8	298.2

All figures in $ millions

Food, industrial goods and loans poured across the Atlantic to the Allies throughout the war. Older industries were modernised and new ones flourished. By 1919, the American economy led the world and many countries owed it large amounts of money.

③ Republican government

One result of the war was a change from Democratic to Republican government. The Democrat Woodrow Wilson was first elected President in 1912. He was re-elected in 1916, but only by a small margin. When mid-term elections were held in November 1918, the Republicans won a majority in both the Senate and the House of Representatives. In the autumn of 1919, Wilson collapsed and was forced to retire (he died in 1924). He was replaced by James Cox as leader of the Democrats. But, in the presidential election of 1920, the Republican Warren Harding won a sweeping victory. The Republicans remained in power for 12 years.

A portrait of President Harding (right). His Vice President, Calvin Coolidge, became President when Harding died in 1923. Coolidge then won the 1924 presidential election. In 1928 Coolidge stood down and Herbert Hoover (also a Republican) was elected.

4 Constitutional changes

After the war, two amendments were made to the American constitution as a result of campaigns which had gained momentum during the war. First, the need for sober wartime workers and the fact that most brewers were German-Americans were useful weapons for the anti-alcohol crusaders. In 1919, the constitution was amended to make the brewing or drinking of alcohol illegal. This was known as the **prohibition** amendment since alcohol was prohibited. And second (as in Britain), women's contribution towards the war effort helped them to gain the vote in 1920. This also required an amendment to the constitution.

5 Wartime intolerance continues

Between 1890 and 1917, nearly 18 million immigrants arrived in the USA, many of them from countries involved in World War I. When the USA joined the war on the side of the Allies, many Americans feared that immigrants from the Central Powers (such as German-Americans) would cause trouble. News of the Bolshevik revolution in Russia added to these fears. Some immigrants were suspected of promoting dangerous Communist ideas. Such fears brought intolerance. During the war, for example, German was banned in schools in several states and the government limited the number of immigrants entering the USA and imprisoned leading critics. After the war, this intolerance continued. In 1919, for example, a **Red Scare** led to arrests and dismissals (see Activity below). Intolerance also continued towards another group - black Americans. They had hoped that their contribution to the war effort would lead to a better deal. Instead, black soldiers were grouped together in separate black units with white officers. Also, black workers who moved to northern cities to work in war industries were forced to live in ghettoes (poor inner city areas) and were often violently attacked by whites.

Activity

The Red Scare, 1919

Source A *The Red Scare, 1919 (1)*

In 1919, 4 million workers took part in 3,600 strikes. The leaders were accused of aiming for a Communist revolution. Moreover, a series of bombings in the Spring frightened the American people. Fear of violent revolution led to drastic measures. No fewer than 28 states passed Acts making it illegal to criticise the government in public. As a result, 1,400 people were arrested and 300 convicted. In November 1919, the House of Representatives refused to allow a socialist, Victor Berger, to take his seat. When he won re-election, the House refused again. In January 1920, the New York State government expelled five socialists, even though most had held office during the war. States required school teachers to sign loyalty oaths. Immigration laws were tightened. In the first week of January 1920, federal agents arrested 3,000 alleged Communists in 33 cities. Many were imprisoned, though no charges were brought against them and 550 were deported.

From 'The American Century' by W. LaFeber, R. Polenberg & N. Woloch, 1992.

Source B *The Red Scare, 1919 (2)*

This cartoon was published in the 'Philadelphia Inquirer' in 1919.

Source C *The population of the USA in 1920*

GERMANY 1,683,298
ITALY 1,607,458
RUSSIA 1,398,999
POLAND 1,139,578
GREAT BRITAIN 1,133,967
CANADA 1,117,136
IRELAND 1,035,680
SWEDEN 624,759
AUSTRIA 574,959
MEXICO 476,676
HUNGARY 397,081
NORWAY 363,599
DENMARK 189,051
GREECE 175,701
FRANCE 152,792
FINLAND 149,671
HOLLAND 131,262
SWITZERLAND 118,647
ASIA 110,586
ROMANIA 103,007

This diagram shows the number of foreign-born people living in the USA in 1920. In 1920, the total population numbered 106.5 million. The total number of foreign-born Americans was 12,683,907.

QUESTIONS

1. Judging from the information in this section, what was the impact of the First World War on the USA?

2. a) Why was there a Red Scare in 1919? Use Sources A and B in your answer.

   b) What do these sources tell us about the atmosphere in the USA after the war?

3. a) What does Source C tell us about the population of the USA in 1920?

   b) How does Source C help to explain the intolerance which developed in the USA during and after the war?

To what extent were the 1920s a time of economic boom in the USA?

In the 1920s, many Americans enjoyed a prosperity never before experienced. They earned more money, worked shorter hours and owned more goods than had ever been the case before. By contrast, however, some Americans remained poor, particularly those who worked in agriculture or the older industries (Box 5.2 illustrates these contrasting fortunes). This section considers why the 1920s was a time of economic boom for some, but not for others. It begins by examining the development of new industries and a mass market and then turns to those groups which did not benefit from what has been described as 'America's second industrial revolution'.

A second industrial revolution

In the second half of the 19th century, the USA had become an industrial giant. This first industrial revolution, based on coal, brought steam engines, steel, railways and mechanisation. The second industrial revolution, based on electricity and oil, was sparked by the First World War. Wartime demands encouraged the development of new materials and new techniques. These new materials and new techniques were then used as the basis of new industries (see Box 5.3).

Box 5.3 — New materials and new techniques

a) The war, with its demands for speed in production, greatly hastened technical changes that were already on the way. In peacetime, these changes might have come more slowly. Increasingly, machines did the work once done by men.

From 'Republican Ascendancy' by J.D. Hicks, 1963

b) The years between 1917 and 1929 witnessed major industrial breakthroughs, such as the manufacture of continuous strip-sheets in steel and tin and of machines to make glass tubing. New machines revolutionised the construction [building] industry - including power shovels, belt and bucket conveyors, pneumatic tools, concrete mixers and dumper trucks. The communications industry developed automatic switchboards, dial phones and teletype machines. Innovations in chemicals included rayon, bakelite and cellophane.

From 'America in the Twentieth Century' by J.T. Patterson, 1976

The value of some new industries

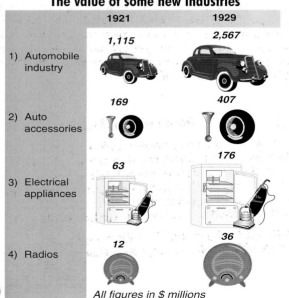

	1921	1929
1) Automobile industry	1,115	2,567
2) Auto accessories	169	407
3) Electrical appliances	63	176
4) Radios	12	36

All figures in $ millions

Box 5.2 — Prosperity and poverty in the USA in the 1920s

a) Prosperity

Share dividends — 1920 = 100
Business profits — 1920 = 100
Wages — 1920 = 100
Unemployment — 1920 = 100

(graph, 1920 to 29, vertical scale 25 to 200)

b) Poverty - income in 1929

* Those who earned less than $1,500 lived below the poverty line

71% earn less than $2,500

42% earn less than $1,500 *

21% earn less than $1,000

The diagram above shows the distribution of income in the USA in 1929.

The 'new' industries

Some of the successful industries in the 1920s, like steel and construction, were in fact old industries which had been modernised. Other industries, like the automobile (car) and aircraft industry had been in a pioneering stage in 1900 and only flourished for the first time after the war. Perhaps the most important development was the introduction of electric power which became widely available for the first time (whilst just 16% of homes had electric power in 1916, 63% of homes had it by 1927). This transformed existing industries and encouraged the development of new industries. Many new products, for example, were developed for the American home. There was a great boom in newly invented labour-saving devices - such as vacuum cleaners, washing machines and toasters. Increasingly, kitchens were equipped with electric ovens and refrigerators, while families were entertained at home by the radio. What all these products had in common was that they were powered by electricity.

3 Mass production: the car industry

An assembly line at a Ford factory in Detroit, 1920.

Henry Ford set up the Ford Motor Company in 1903. By designing a car with standardised parts (the **Model T**), Ford was able to keep the cost down. Then, in 1914, the moving assembly line was introduced. Cars were assembled as they moved along a conveyor belt (see above). Workers stayed in one place adding parts. This reduced the time it took to make a car from 14 hours to 93 minutes. More cars were produced at a lower cost. As a result, the price of the Model T fell and more people could afford to buy them. The car industry was central to the prosperity of the 1920s. It was the first industry to experiment with mass production. It employed 5 million workers directly and millions more indirectly in support industries. The steel, oil, rubber, glass, leather and machine tool industries were only some of those who benefited from the boom in car sales.

6 Mass consumption

Mass production could only work if there was a mass market for the goods produced. It was necessary, therefore, to encourage people to buy the new products which became

An advert from 1928.

available. As a result, there was a huge increase in advertising (in 1914, for example, $250 million was spent on advertising in magazines. This figure had doubled by 1919 and reached $3 billion by 1929). The radio, with its commercial breaks, and the cinema were new means of reaching the public with adverts. Also, to provide more purchasing power, there was a great expansion of hire purchase (buying by instalments). Three out of four radios were bought on hire purchase in the 1920s, for example, as well as over half of all cars and furniture.

4 The boom in construction

New York in 1924.

After the war, the landscape of the USA was transformed. Economic growth led to more offices and factories being built. This, in turn, led to the building of new houses, schools, hospitals and public buildings of all kind.

New materials enabled the construction of new types of building. The skylines of the great cities, for example, were transformed by skyscrapers (see above). The car also played a part in the building boom since thousands of miles of new roads were built and people began to move out to new estates in the suburbs since they could travel to work in their cars.

5 The role of the federal government

The USA's second industrial revolution was not planned or organised by the federal government, though the Republicans were keen to take credit for it. During the 1920s, the Republicans' main aim was to give business leaders a free hand to make maximum profits. So, the regulation of businesses by federal agencies was reduced to a minimum (see Box 5.4). Government expenditure was kept low. Taxes were cut on high incomes and profits. And, most important, American goods were protected against foreign competitors by tariffs (taxes or 'duties' on goods coming into a country). High tariffs make imports more expensive and therefore 'protect' goods produced locally. The Fordney-McCumber Tariff Act of 1922 raised duties on foreign goods to the highest level ever known in American history (on average, adding 33% to the price of an import). This was welcomed by those who sold their products within the USA. But it prevented other nations from selling their goods to the USA. As a result, these countries could not earn enough money either to repay their war debts to the USA or to buy American goods. American exports suffered, especially when the other countries responded by raising their own tariffs. This ensured that world trade remained at a lower level than it otherwise might have reached. Some historians suggest that the Fordney-McCumber Tariff Act, like the refusal to join the League of Nations, was a sign of **isolationism** (the policy of cutting the USA off from the rest of the world).

Box 5.4   Government and business

- During the war, we turned to the government to solve every difficult economic problem. When the Republican Party came to power, it restored the government to its position of umpire instead of player. For these reasons the American people have gone forward in progress. Our opponents propose that we must thrust government into business. It would stifle initiative and invention. It would undermine the development of leadership.

- *Herbert Hoover, looking back on the 1920s in a speech made during the presidential election campaign in 1928*

7 Rural poverty

If, during the 1920s, you were a white American living in an urban area and working in one of the new industries, you were likely to be better off than ever before. But many Americans were not so lucky (see Box 5.5). This was especially true of those who worked in agriculture. The First World War had been good for American farmers since they had helped to supply western Europe with food and other agricultural produce (the USA had exported 600,000 horses to the Allies during the war, for example). In the 1920s, however, European farming had recovered and there was a glut of many farm products. American agricultural exports were worth $3.8 billion in 1919-20, but they were worth just $1.9 billion a year later. Greater worldwide production led to lower prices and this meant a cut in American farmers' income. The problem was that too much was being produced. This was made worse by new, improved farming techniques and better farm machinery. The Republican governments were more interested in business than agriculture and did almost nothing to help farmers.

Box 5.5 — Poverty in the 1920s

a) The main site of mass poverty was the farm. 54% of America's 5.8 million farm families got less than $1,000 a year. That was about 17 million people who had long been the poorest of the nation's poor. Poverty hit certain other groups hard. Old people were much more likely to be poor than people under 55 or 60. Members of female headed families were almost universally poor. So were the disabled and migrant workers. And blacks, as ever, clung to the lower edges of the income pyramid.

From 'The Welfare State in America' by J.T. Patterson, 1982

b) My father was a farmer and a coal miner, ten kids and I'm the oldest. The coal industry was hit in 1926 and never did fully recover. Coal and lumber [timber], they were the two things hit hard. There was a dip in 1919, then it picked up some. But in '26 there was another one. Coal and lumber never did recover. 1929 is when it hit banking and big business. But we had been suffering and starvation long before that. In the early 1920s, the mines shut down. Nothing for the people to live on. Children fainted in school from hunger. Long before the stock market crash.

Joe Morrison, a coal miner in Indiana, quoted in 'Hard Times' by S. Terkel, 1970

8 Declining industries and weak unions

Some industries, once prosperous, were overtaken by new rivals. For example, many coal mines were closed down in face of competition from oil and electricity (see Box 5.5b). Similarly, textiles such as wool and cotton now faced competition from newly invented artificial fibres such as rayon. Many of these older industries paid their workers low wages and provided poor working conditions. In some places, child labour was still used because it was cheap. Although **labor unions** (the American equivalent of trade unions) campaigned to improve wages and working conditions, they did not have a great deal of success in the 1920s. The photo above, for example, was taken in April 1926 during a strike at the Gera cotton mill in Passaic, New York State. The police used violence to break the strike. There were many similar incidents in the 1920s. For example, in 1928, workers at the Loray cotton mill in Gastoniaa, North Carolinaa, called a strike. They were expected to work 70 hours a week. Men were paid $18 per week and women were paid $9 per week. At that time, the average weekly wage in New York was around $200. When the strike began, the employers sent in security guards to break it and one of the union leaders, Ella May Wiggins, was shot dead.

9 Black Americans

A sharecropper in the 1920s.

At the beginning of the 20th century, the majority of black Americans lived in the southern states. Most worked in agriculture and lived in poverty. Many were **sharecroppers** - small farmers who had to give a share of their crops to their landlords. Before the First World War, there was a steady flow of blacks to the north and west. Then, during the First World War, there was an explosion in migration with around 300,000 black people moving north and west, mainly to the cities. Many found jobs, usually unskilled ones. Pay was low, but better than in the South. Living conditions in the city ghettoes were often dreadful, however, and hostility from the white population was strong. Black Americans generally remained poor and were the victims of racial discrimination. In many states there was 'segregation' (separate seating for blacks and whites on buses and trains, separate waiting rooms and toilets, separate schools and so on). Between 1918 and 1927, 416 black Americans were 'lynched' (rounded up by mobs of angry white Americans and killed by hanging or burning).

Activity
Henry Ford and mass production

Source B *Henry Ford's autobiography*

A Ford car contains about 5,000 parts. At first, we simply put a car together at a spot on the floor. The workers brought to it the parts they needed. The first step in the assembly lines came when we took the work to the men instead of the men to the work. The net result was the reduction of the necessity for thought on the part of the worker and the reduction of his movements to a minimum. He does as nearly as possible only one thing with one movement. Every piece of work in the factory moves on hooks on overhead chains. Each piece is assembled in the exact order in which parts are required. It may travel on a moving platform or it may go by gravity. But the point is that there is no lifting or trucking of anything other than materials.

Extract from Henry Ford's autobiography, 'My Life and Work', published in 1922

Source C *Production and price of Ford cars*

YEAR	No. PRODUCED	PRICE
1909-10	18,664	$950
1910-11	34,528	$780
1911-12	78,440	$690
1912-13	168,220	$600
1913-14	248,307	$550
1914-15	308,213	$490
1915-16	533,921	$440
1916-17	785,432	$360
1917-18	706,584	$450
1918-19	533,706	$525
1919-20	996,660	$575 to $440
1920-21	1,250,000	$440 to $355

QUESTIONS

1. Judging from the information in this section, was the 1920s a time of economic boom in the USA?

2. 'Mass production brought progress'. Using Sources A-F give arguments for and against this view.

3. Look at Sources B and E. Suppose you had interviewed (a) a worker and (b) a manager at a Ford factory in the 1920s, how might each have described the assembly line system?

4. Judging from Source D how did the mass production of cars affect people's attitudes and behaviour?

Source A *Advert for a Ford Sedan, 1929*

Henry Ford argued: *'It is better to sell a large number of cars at a reasonably small profit margin than a few cars at a large profit margin.'* His aim was to get prices as low as possible so that as many people could afford Ford cars as possible. Following the success of the first car to be mass produced, the Model T or 'Tin Lizzie' as it was nicknamed, the range of Ford cars was extended in the 1920s. Model Ts were all painted black and had the same size engine. This reduced production costs. Later, models like the Sedan, came in a limited range of colours and engine sizes.

Source D *A banker's view*

A few years ago, a car was considered a luxury. Now the ambition of every man is to own a car. The car indicates a social position. Given the choice of a fine home without a car or a modest home with a car, the latter will win. Not just the wealthy, but clerks and salaried men on limited incomes want to own a car. Many workers - carpenters, masons, bricklayers and so on - live in the suburbs and use their cars to go to work. There was a time when a bicycle or trolleycar was good enough. Walking is a lost art. Even my laundress comes to work in a taxi.

Extract from an article by William Ashdown, a banker, in 'Atlantic Monthly', June 1925

Source E *Extract from a novel written in 1971*

Neither pay nor other benefits could change the grim, dispiriting nature of the work. Most of it was physically hard. But the greatest toll was mental - hour after hour, day after day of deadening boredom. The nature of their jobs robbed individuals of pride. A man on an assembly line lacked a sense of achievement. He never made a car. He merely made, or put together, pieces - adding a washer to a bolt, fastening a metal strip, inserting screws. And it was always the identical washer or strip or screws over and over again. Some had mental breakdowns. Almost none liked the work. So, an assembly line worker's ambition, like that of a prisoner, was centred on escape. A breakdown of the line provided a partial escape. So did a strike.

From 'Wheels' by Arthur Hailey, 1971

Source F *A historian's view*

The automobile industry employed over 7% of all factory workers and accounted for over 12% of the value of America's manufactures. It consumed 15% of US steel, over 70% of glass and rubber and large quantities of leather and paint. It laid the foundation of another huge industry - oil - and stimulated the building of roads.

From 'The Limits of Liberty' by M.A. Jones, 1983

The 1920s in the USA have been called the 'Roaring Twenties' or the 'Jazz Age'. These labels are meant to suggest that a stuffy prewar Victorian society was replaced by a freer, more permissive world. Certainly, there were new opportunities for those who benefited from the prosperity of the 1920s. Many ordinary people had more money and more leisure time than before. They were, therefore, able to take advantage of the new products and new entertainments which were on offer. It was in the 1920s, for example, that the radio first became widespread and cinemas first found a mass audience. Jazz became all the rage (See Box 5.6) and sports like baseball gained wide appeal. But it was not just the range of products and entertainments which changed. The 1920s were also a time of changing attitudes. Many people, especially the young, were influenced by what they saw at the cinema and heard on the radio. Their dress and behaviour began to change accordingly. This shocked and threatened some sections of society, however, and attempts were made to control what was filmed or broadcast.

1 Jazz music and dancehalls

King Oliver's Creole Jazz Band in 1920.

American popular music had been influenced by African rhythms since 'ragtime' became popular in the 1890s. By the 1920s, as black Americans moved north in search of work, so their jazz music made its way to Chicago and other northern cities. The liveliness and improvisation of jazz appealed to the young, both black and white. Dance halls played jazz and dances like the Charleston and the Black Bottom replaced the Victorian waltz. The great black jazz players of the 1920s, such as Louis Armstrong (see above, kneeling at the front) could be heard by a wide audience on the radio.

2 The movies

The American film industry was one of the most successful of the 'new' industries of the 1920s. Its centre was Hollywood with its large studios and star system. Cinema audiences were massive, with the weekly average growing from 40 million in 1922 to 95 million by 1929. The arrival of **talkies** in 1927 stimulated new interest as millions went to hear Al Jolson speak for the first time on film in 'The Jazz Singer' (right). To its audiences, the movies were an escape from reality. Cinemas, decorated in crimson velvet and marble, were like a palace which all could afford. What people could watch, however, was carefully censored - see Box 5.7.

Warner Bros. Supreme Triumph
AL JOLSON
THE JAZZ SINGER

Box 5.6 — The impact of jazz music

Horrified at the sensual rhythms and lyrics of the new music, some Church leaders and others warned that young people's morals were at risk, but this only made jazz more popular with the rebellious young:

(i) Jazz music causes drunkenness. Reason and reflection are lost and the actions of the persons are directed by the stronger animal passions.

Dr E. Elliot Rawlings, spokesperson for the medical profession

(ii) Jazz lyrics, written in the Negro brothels of the South, are an offense against womanly purity, the very fountainhead of our family and civil life.

Fenton Bott, head of the National Association of the Masters of Dancing

(iii) My body got light. Every note Louis hit was perfection. I ran to the piano. I had never heard the tune before but somehow I knew every note.

Hoagy Carmichael talking about Louis Armstrong

Box 5.7 — Film censorship

The movies attracted criticism similar to that directed at popular music. Films, it was claimed, encouraged the breakdown of moral values. In 1922, the film industry appointed its own censor, a former federal government officer, William Hays. He produced a code which laid down what could and could not be shown in films. The following instructions appeared in the code.

* No kiss should last longer than seven feet of film.

* Members of the clergy should not be used as comic characters or villains.

* Nudity is forbidden.

* No sympathy is to be shown to murder, safecracking or arson. Acts like this should not be shown in such detail as to tempt amateurs to try their hands.

③ The radio

Although the first radio signal was transmitted (in morse code) across the Atlantic in 1901, it was not until the 1920s that radio reached a mass audience. From the start, radio in the USA was in the hands of commercial companies whose programmes were frequently interrupted by adverts. Until the late 1930s, radio broadcast little news. The National Broadcasting Company (NBC) argued, for example, that its job was to entertain. Current affairs should be left to the newspapers. In addition to music and comedy, the radio brought sports events to a mass audience and helped to create a cult of leading sports personalities - such as heavyweight boxing champion Jack Dempsey. His title fight with Gene Tunney in 1927 had around 60 million radio listeners.

1922
100,000

1927
3,500,000

Number of radios produced per year

④ The car

There is no doubt that the mass production of cars did bring greater freedom of movement to many Americans in the 1920s. They could live further from their work in the suburbs. They could take off to previously distant areas for their holidays. Rural areas became less isolated. Critics argued, however, that the car was responsible for debts and even for the decline of morals since young couples could now more easily go off out of reach of their parents and elders.

Activity
Women in the USA in the 1920s

Source B A historian's view

The symbol of the Jazz Age was the 'flapper'. This was the name given to fashionable, usually wealthy, young women whose clothes and behaviour seemed deliberately to challenge the older generation. The flapper bobbed her hair and dyed it raven black. In 1919, her skirt was 6 inches above the ground. By 1927, it had edged above her knees. The well-dressed flapper wore a tight felt hat, two strings of beads, bangles on her wrists. They were out for a good time. 'None of the Victorian mothers', wrote Scott Fitzgerald, 'had any idea how casually their daughters were accustomed to be kissed.' The flapper was the most obvious but by no means the only example of the new American cult of youth.

From 'The Perils of Prosperity' by W.R. Leuchtenburg, 1966

Source A 'Flappers'

This photo shows two flappers in the USA in the 1920s. Old fashioned Americans were shocked to see women smoke cigarettes in public or drive motorbikes.

Source C A newspaper's view

There has been a change for the worse during the past year in feminine dress, dancing, manners and general moral standards. The causes are the lack of an adequate sense of responsibility in the parents or guardians, a decline in personal religion, a failure to realise the serious consequences of immodesty in girls' dress and the absence of courage and determination to resist fashion when this is opposed to decency.

From an article by Samuel Byrne, editor of the 'Observer' in Pittsburgh, June 1922

Source D A reader's view

The word 'flapper' to us means not a female who smokes, swears and kisses her gentlemen friends goodnight, although there is no harm in any of that. We think of the flapper as the independent young woman who feels like punching someone when called the 'weaker sex', who resents being put on a pedestal and who is responsible for the advancement of women's condition in the world.

Letter to the editor, 'Daily Illini', 1922

Source E

Fashion in the early 1900s

This picture shows the sort of clothes fashionable wealthy women wore at the turn of the century.

QUESTIONS

1. a) Judging from the information in this section, what is the evidence of new freedom in the USA in the 1920s?
   b) Are there any signs that this freedom was limited?

2. a) Judging from Sources A-E what do you understand by the term 'flapper'?
   b) Why do you think some older Americans disapproved of flappers?

3. How do Sources A, D and E help us to explain the views expressed in Source C?

Was the USA a free society in the 1920s? (2)

The previous section showed that many Americans living in the Roaring Twenties seemed to have much more freedom than their Victorian parents. But there was a less attractive side to life in the USA in the 1920s. There was a great deal of intolerance towards foreign-born immigrants, racial minorities and towards anyone seen to hold radical ideas about politics, religion or almost anything else. Many people believed that the traditional values of their country were under threat from these groups. As a result, they supported measures which appeared to protect traditional values. Intolerance led to prohibition, tighter immigration controls, the harsh treatment of some immigrants, the growth of the Ku Klux Klan and the 'Monkey' trial.

1 Prohibition

For many years, religious groups in the USA had argued that the drinking of alcohol was immoral. Drunkenness, they claimed, led to many of the problems facing American society. In 1919, their campaigning paid off. The government passed the 18th amendment to the constitution, banning the manufacture and sale of alcohol. This became known as **prohibition**. But banning alcohol only seemed to make people want it more. The result was a growth in organised crime. Gangsters took over the business of the brewers. They manufactured and sold alcohol illegally (known as 'bootlegging' - see left) and they set up illegal bars (known as 'speakeasies').

Federal government agents were appointed to control this activity, but there were too few of them to deal with the problem effectively. In 1933, the law was repealed.

Police Chief, John E. Panter, of Gloucester, Massachusetts in disguise as a woman. Using this disguise, he hoped to catch bootleggers.

2 Immigration control

Between 1820 and 1920, more than 35 million immigrants reached the USA. At first, most came from Britain and northern Europe. Most, therefore, were Protestants. From the 1880s, increasing numbers arrived from central, southern and eastern Europe, Japan and China. Most, therefore, were not Protestants. The changing character of the immigrants led to calls for restriction. For many Americans in the 1920s, the ideal citizen was a 'WASP' - **W**hite, **A**nglo **S**axon and **P**rotestant. Asian immigrants were not white and many recent European immigrants were Catholics, Greek Orthodox or Jewish. The First World War added to suspicions of foreigners and the Russian revolution brought fears of a Communist takeover (see above p.89). The result was a series of Acts which reduced the number of immigrants entering the USA from around 350,000 a year between 1918 and 1921 to 150,000 a year from 1924.

3 Sacco and Vanzetti

Two of the most famous victims of intolerance towards foreigners were Nicola Sacco and Bartolomeo Vanzetti. They were poor Italian immigrants who were accused of the murder of two men in the course of a robbery in 1920. Both were anarchists who had avoided military service in the First World War. Both spoke little English (see Box 5.8). They were put on trial, found guilty and sentenced to death. But doubts about their guilt grew and there were protests both in the USA and abroad. The evidence against the two men appeared inconclusive (witnesses swore they were elsewhere at the time of the robbery). The judge, Webster Thayer, was openly biased against them (in public he described them as 'wops' and 'those anarchist bastards'). After seven years of legal argument and protest, however, their appeals were dismissed and the two men were executed by electric chair on 24 August 1927. The photo above shows Nicola Sacco and Bartolomeo Vanzetti in 1921.

Box 5.8

Vanzetti's last statement

Bartolomeo Vanzetti made the following statement just before he was executed in 1927:

I not only am not guilty of these crimes, but I never commit a crime in my life - I have never steal and I have never kill and I have never spilt blood. I would not wish to a dog or a snake, to the most low and misfortunate creature on the earth - I would not wish to any of them what I have had to suffer for things I am not guilty of. I am suffering because I am a radical and indeed I am a radical. I have suffered because I was an Italian, and indeed I am an Italian. I am so convinced to be right that if you could execute me two times and if I could be reborn two other times, I would live again to do what I have done already.

4 The Ku Klux Klan

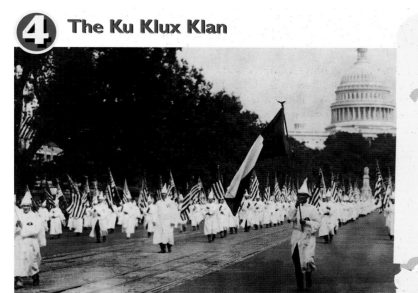

This photo shows members of the KKK from 22 states marching in Washington on 19 August 1925.

Box 5.9

The KKK

(a) Klansmen appeared as self appointed judges, juries and executioners. They resumed the reign of terror against Negroes. They tarred and feathered men and women (white and black) whom they suspected of adultery and they lynched, mutilated or lashed hundreds of others. They tortured Jewish shopkeepers and claimed that Catholics were villainous conspirators against the USA. There was a special Klan Kalendar in which 1867 became year 1 and a special language - for example, 'sanbog' meant 'strangers are near, be on guard.'

Extract from 'Time' magazine, 9 April 1965

(b) The Kloran (the KKK's 'bible')

1. Are you a native-born, white, non-Jewish American?
2. Are you absolutely opposed to any sect or ruler that is foreign to the USA?
3. Are you a Christian?
4. Do you believe in white supremacy?

These questions all appeared in the Kloran

A further sign of intolerance was the revival of the Ku Klux Klan (KKK) in the early 1920s. This secret society was originally set up to terrorise blacks after the civil war of 1861-65. Blacks were hunted by hooded 'knights' and beaten up or even killed in the hope that this would deter them from registering to vote. Although the original KKK had faded by the end of the century, it was revived in 1915 by William J. Simmons and rapidly gained support. Unlike previously, the new KKK did not just attack blacks. It also attacked Jews, Catholics and anybody else who was not a native-born WASP. The new KKK's message of hatred, its elaborate rituals, its secret language (see Box 5.9) and its menacing hooded costume appealed to many whites - especially those living in small towns and rural areas in the south and west of the USA. Many of these people (especially farmers) missed out on the prosperity of the 1920s and therefore looked for a scapegoat to blame. It has been estimated that membership of the KKK had reached 5 million by 1925. However, a scandal in 1925 involving the Grand Dragon (leader) of the KKK in Indiana led to a decline in membership and influence in the second half of the decade.

5 The 'Monkey' trial

The 1920s was an age of new ideas, new ways of living, new fashions, new forms of entertainment and new inventions. This frightened many people. Some groups longed for a return to certainty, stability and unchanging truths about the world they lived in. One such group was the Christian fundamentalists (Christians who believed that everything in the Bible

This poster advertises the 1960 film of the 'Monkey' trial.

Box 5.10

Extracts from the trial

Bryan: I believe everything in the Bible should be accepted as it is given there.

Darrow: Do you believe in Jonah and the whale?

Bryan: You are in the realm of miracles. It is easy to believe the miracle of Jonah.

Darrow: Do you believe that Joshua made the sun stand still?

Bryan: I believe what the Bible says.

Darrow: Did Eve really come from Adam's rib?

Bryan: Yes.

Darrow: Do you say you do not believe that there are any civilisations on this earth that reach back beyond 5,000 years?

Bryan: I am not satisfied by any evidence I have seen.

Extracts from the transcript of the trial.

was literally true). Fundamentalism was particularly strong in the southern and western rural areas of the USA and it was in a southern state, Tennessee, that the 'Monkey' trial took place in 1925. In 1924, pressure from fundamentalists in Tennessee led to an anti-evolution law being passed. The law made it illegal to teach about evolution in schools in such a way that it clashed with the biblical story of creation. This meant that it was therefore illegal to teach Darwin's theory that humans were descended from apes. When a High School Biology teacher called John Scopes taught Darwin's theory in his class, he was prosecuted. The case aroused national interest, not least because the defending lawyer, Clarence Darrow, was an atheist and the prosecuting lawyer, William Jennings Bryan, was a fundamentalist (see Box 5.10). Scopes lost the case and was fined $100, but he claimed he had won a moral victory since the publicity surrounding the case made fun of fundamentalist beliefs.

Activity
Restrictions on immigration in the 1920s

EUROPE

GATE

3%

Source B *Immigration Acts, 1917-24*

1917 Immigration Act - forbade entry of foreigners over the age of 16 who were unable to read a 40 word passage.

1921 Emergency Quota Act - limited the number of immigrants to 357,000 per year. The numbers allowed from each country ('quotas') limited to 35% of the foreign born of that nationality who had been living in the USA in 1910.

1924 National Origins Act - limited the number of immigrants to 150,000 per year. The quotas were readjusted so that they related to the proportion of each nationality living in the existing population of the USA. The effect was that some countries (such as Britain) did not take up all their places. Others, like Italy, had a waiting list.

Source C *Immigration and the Quota Laws*

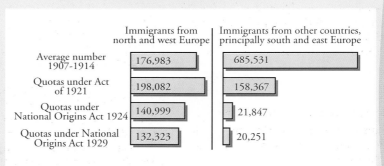

	Immigrants from north and west Europe	Immigrants from other countries, principally south and east Europe
Average number 1907-1914	176,983	685,531
Quotas under Act of 1921	198,082	158,367
Quotas under National Origins Act 1924	140,999	21,847
Quotas under National Origins Act 1929	132,323	20,251

Source D *Opposition to immigration*

(i) The steamship companies haul them over to America and, as soon as they step off the ships, our problem has begun. Bolsheviks, anarchists and kidnappers challenge the authority of our flag. They are loyal to some other country while they live in ours. They fill places which belong to the loyal wage-earning citizens of the USA. They are a menace and a danger to us every day.

Part of a speech made in 1921 by Senator Heflin

(ii) The foreign-born flood is a threat to the happiness of individual Americans. It is no wonder that Americans everywhere are insisting that their land no longer shall offer free asylum to the rest of the world. The USA is our land. If it was not the land of our fathers, at least it may be, and it should be, the land of our children. We intend to maintain it so.

Part of a speech made in 1924 by Senator Albert Johnson of Washington state

QUESTIONS

1. **Judging from the information in this section, was the USA a free society in the 1920s? Give reasons for your answer.**

2. a) **Using Sources B, C and D write a passage explaining the point made by Source A.**

   b) **Which Europeans, according to Source C suffered most from restrictions on immigration. Why do you think these Europeans were excluded?**

   c) **Why do you think many Americans wanted to restrict immigration? Use Sources C and D in your answer.**

3. **What evidence is there in Sources A-D to suggest that the USA became a less tolerant society in the 1920s?**

SOURCE WORK

'Strange Fruit' - lynching in the 1920s

Although slavery had been abolished after the American civil war (1861-65), whites in the southern states found new ways to control the black population (black people were commonly referred to as 'negroes' until the 1960s). Many states passed 'Jim Crow' laws. Jim Crow was a comic stage character played by a white man who blacked up. It was, therefore, an insulting name for blacks. Jim Crow laws ensured that blacks and whites remained segregated (see p.92). But it was not just laws which made blacks second class citizens. Customs developed which emphasised white superiority. For example, regardless of their age, whites called black men 'boy' and black women 'auntie' or 'girl'. Similarly, a black person could only enter a white person's house via the back door. Behind these laws and customs lay an atmosphere of hatred. Occasionally, this hatred erupted in violence. After the First World War, lynchings became commonplace. Black people suspected of crimes against whites were seized by mobs before they could be put on trial and they were hanged or burned. Those responsible for the lynchings were very rarely punished.

This famous photograph of a lynching is alleged to have inspired the Blues singer Billie Holiday to write the song 'Strange Fruit' (see below). The photo appears in the collection of two picture agencies in Britain. Each agency is able to provide different information about it. According to the John Hilleldon Agency, the photo was taken in the summer of 1930. The victims are Abe Smith and Tommy Shipp who had been accused of murder. The second agency, Popperfoto, was unable to provide a date for the photo or the names of the victims, though it agreed that the lynching took place in Marion, Indiana. The caption on the back of the copy owned by Popperfoto says that the two victims were accused of murdering a white man and of attacking his 19 year old fiancée. They were dragged from the local jail by a crowd of 5,000 townsfolk and hanged. Neither picture agency knows who took the photo or where it first appeared.

'Strange Fruit' by Billie Holiday

Southern tree bear a strange fruit
Blood on the leaves and blood on the root;
Black body swinging in the southern breeze,
Strange fruit hanging from poplar trees.

Pastoral scene of the gallant south,
The bulging eyes and the twisted mouth;
Scent of magnolia sweet and fresh
And the sudden smell of burning flesh.

Here is a fruit for the crows to pluck,
For the rain to gather, for the wind to suck,
For the sun to rot, for the tree to drop,
Here is a strange and bitter crop

A description of a lynching in the 1920s

The negro was taken to the grove where each one of more than 500 people in Ku Klux Klan dress had placed a pine knot around a stump, making a pyramid to the height of ten feet. The negro was chained to the stump and asked if he had anything to say. Castrated and in indescribable agony, the negro asked for a cigarette, lit it and blew smoke in the face of his tormentors. The pyre was lit and 100 men and women, old and young, grandmothers among them, joined hands and danced around while the negro burned. A big dance was held in a barn nearby that evening in celebration of the burning, many people coming by car from nearby cities.

Extract from the 'Washington Eagle', 1920

QUESTIONS

1. **What do the sources on this page tell us about American society after the First World War?**

2. **Explain how the photo might have inspired Billie Holiday to write 'Strange Fruit'.**

3. a) **Would you say that the photo is an important historical record? Give reasons for your answer.**
   b) **What are its limitations as a piece of historical source material?**

4. **What points of comparison are there between the photo and the extract from the 'Washington Eagle'?**

What were the causes of the Great Depression? What impact did it make?

The boom of the 1920s ended abruptly with the Wall Street Crash of October 1929. By October 1929, the price of shares had become unrealistically high. When people began to sell their shares, prices fell. This led to panic. More and more shares were sold and the prices of shares went down and down. On 29 October, the stock market collapsed completely. By the end of that day, thousands of individuals were ruined. Companies were forced to shut down. Unemployment grew rapidly. Within months, an economic depression had spread not just around the USA, but around the world. This depression, known as the 'Great Depression', lasted until the late 1930s. Although the Wall Street Crash marks the end of the years of prosperity, most historians agree that the Crash was not itself the cause of the Great Depression. Rather, it simply made existing economic problems worse. This section, therefore, examines not just the Crash, but also other, underlying causes of the Great Depression. The Activity which follows examines the impact that the Depression made on ordinary American people.

1 The Wall Street Crash

The graph (right) shows that between 1927 and 1929 the price of shares climbed rapidly to dizzy new heights. In fact, by 1929, share prices had become so inflated that they no longer

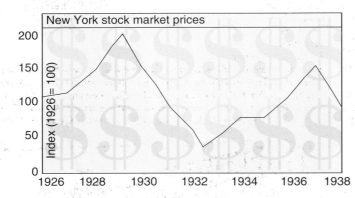

New York stock market prices

reflected the true value of companies (see Box 5.11 and Box 5.12). The bubble burst in October 1929. On 23 October, over 6 million shares were sold. This rose to 12.9 million the next day (**Black Thursday**). Efforts to stop the slide failed. On Monday 28 October a further 9 million shares were sold. Then, on 29 October (**Black Tuesday**) there was total panic. Major companies like General Electric and Woolworths collapsed. By the end of the day, 16,383,700 shares had been sold at a loss of $10,000 million. After the Crash, share prices continued to slide until 1932.

Box 5.11 — Boom and bust

(a) It seemed as if a mania for quick profits had infected everyone from bank presidents to street corner grocers. Between 1923 and 1926, share prices rose by 54%, representing the normal response of the market to higher earnings in industry. Then a tremendous upward surge of the stock market began in 1927 and the boom was totally out of control by 1929. The average price of shares increased by nearly 300%.

From 'American Epoch' by A. Link, 1963

(b) Stock prices virtually collapsed yesterday, swept downwards with gigantic losses in the most disastrous trading day in the stock market's history. Billions of dollars in market values were wiped out. The market on the rampage is no respecter of persons. It wasted fortune after fortune yesterday and financially crippled thousands of individuals in all parts of the world.

From the 'New York Times', 30 October 1929

Box 5.12 — Falling demand and over-production

(a) The boom roared on. You bought a share only to sell it at a profit. You bought 'on margin' (with credit, that is, not cash). You assumed there would always be another sucker. Yet, by late summer 1929, warehouses were choked with unsold goods and factories were therefore beginning to reduce their output. It dawned on some stockbrokers in September that it might be a good idea to sell their shares.

From 'History of the United States', by H. Brogan 1985

(b) The most serious weakness of the economy was the fact that capacity to produce had outrun capacity to consume. A large part of the population - farmers, for example, and workers in the declining industries like coal and textiles - had not shared in the prosperity of the 1920s. The mass of people, though better off than before, were unable to buy their share of consumer goods and support the level of mass production.

From 'The Limits of Liberty' by M.A. Jones, 1983

Victims of the Wall Street Crash ranged from wealthy stockbrokers like the man trying to sell his car above to ordinary pensioners who had invested their life savings in the stock market. On the day after the collapse, stories emerged of company directors jumping to their deaths from the top of skyscrapers and elderly couples committing suicide to avoid spending their final years in poverty.

2 Weaknesses in the economy

Box 5.12 shows that the American economy was suffering from falling demand and over-production. This was the result of poor income distribution. Too much of the income from the prosperous 1920s was going into too few hands. By 1929, 5% of the American population was receiving 33% of total income. By reducing top rates of tax, Republican governments helped the wealthy to become wealthier. Some of this wealth was spent or invested. But there was a limit to what the wealthy could consume. Although many wage earners were better off than they had been before the 1920s, average income remained low. Higher wages would have meant greater consumption of goods and therefore greater demand. But trade unions remained weak in the USA and so little pressure was put on employers to raise wages. In addition, the Crash in 1929 revealed many weaknesses in the way in which business was carried out. During the 1920s, companies had been given maximum freedom by the Republican government. But, after the Crash, it became clear that many large corporations were badly structured. Some were plainly fraudulent (corrupt). Banks often lacked proper cash reserves and lent money too easily. In 1929, 650 banks went bankrupt. By 1933, 4,000 banks had collapsed.

4 World trade

President Hoover blamed the Depression on international economic problems. It was true that world trade had not recovered well from the First World War. But American policies such as raising tariffs (see p.91) and demanding the repayment of war debts made the position worse (the cartoon, right, makes the point that European countries found it hard to repay their war debts). During the 1920s, American banks made loans to European countries and these loans produced a degree of recovery. But the Crash of 1929 meant an end to the loans. As a result, the Depression spread rapidly, affecting much of the world.

3 The vicious circle of depression

This diagram shows that once a depression begins, it gains a momentum of its own. That makes the depression worse and makes it all the harder to reverse. After the Wall Street Crash, businesses lost confidence and began to cut back. Many people were sacked and became unemployed.

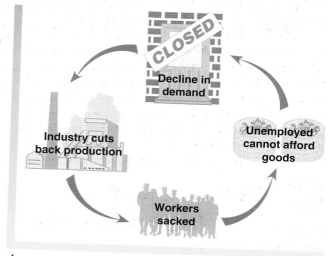

Since the unemployed could not afford consumer goods, there was a fall in demand. This led to further cutbacks which meant more unemployment. More unemployment meant a further fall in demand and therefore pressure to cut back further. In real terms, this vicious circle meant that unemployment rose from 1.55 million (3% of the workforce) in 1929 to 12.83 million (25% of the workforce) in 1933.

5 President Hoover's response

Herbert Hoover (left) was unlucky to become President only months before the Crash. He was then widely blamed for failing to lift the USA out of the economic slump. Like many Americans, Hoover believed that the Depression would eventually cure itself. He was reluctant to use the powers of government to aid recovery. Unlike European countries (like Britain and Germany) which provided at least some help (such as government funded unemployment relief), Hoover thought that government help would stop people trying to help themselves. At first, he relied on voluntary efforts. He called on industry to create jobs and on private charities to look after the elderly, sick and unemployed. When these voluntary efforts were seen to have failed, Hoover then reluctantly began to try limited government action. He set up the Reconstruction Finance Corporation (RFC) to lend money to banks, insurance companies and railways and he passed the Federal Home Loan Act (which provided loans to Building Societies) and the Relief and Construction Act (which provided loans to state and municipal governments). Hoover believed in the 'trickle down' effect. He hoped the loans would encourage investment and eventually provide jobs. Later, however, his policies were described as 'too little, too late'.

Activity
The effects of the Depression

Source A *Homelessness*

I rode the subways for the night and found hundreds doing the same. The trip takes two hours. A good corner seat gives the rider a chance to get a fair nap. When morning came, I went to Grand Central Station where I washed for two cents. Sleeping in parks I found much less satisfactory. Tired, hungry and cold, I stretched out on a bench. The soles of my feet were swollen with blisters - I had tramped the sidewalks for three days.

Account of K. Munroe, an out of work journalist, 1930

Source B *Hoovervilles*

Many people blamed the Depression on President Hoover and they named some of the results after him. 'Hoovervilles' were places where the unemployed lived in makeshift houses (see above). 'Hoover blankets' was the nickname given to newspapers because homeless people used them to keep warm when they slept outside. 'Hoover flags' was the name given to empty trouser pockets, turned inside out to show there was no money in them.

Source C *Unemployment*

You'd get word that somebody's gonna build a building. So, the next morning you get up at 5 am and you dash over there. There's 3,000 men there - carpenters, cement men, guys who knew machinery and everything else. More and more men were after fewer and fewer jobs.

Memories of Ed Paulsen who left the Midwest in 1930 to look for work in California. The photo (left) shows an unemployed man.

Source D *Hunger (1)*

A soup kitchen run by a charity.

Source F *Hunger (2)*

Every day we find children who come to school without breakfast and who state that they have nothing to eat in their homes. Many are ill through lack of nourishment. There are homes where the father has not worked for three years. And, in some of the homes, we have families of 10 to 13 and no wage earner. Milk is a luxury in most of the homes where black coffee and bread is a large part of the diet. The number of underfed children is alarming and seems to be growing.

Chicago school officials asking for food for their schools, US Senate hearings, January 1933

Source E *Cartoon from 1930*

In 1930, after much discussion, the Senate rejected a Bill to give direct aid to the unemployed. A caption below this cartoon said: 'While Washington makes up its mind...'.

Source G *The rich*

Until the late 1920s, everything was going pretty well with us. The Depression hit us like everyone else. Most of my friends who were wealthy were in some way affected. We had to readjust our way of living. We did more for ourselves. I did away with my chauffeur and so forth. I drove my own car, my wife did the cleaning and all that sort of thing.

Memories of Edward A. Ryerson, chair of the board of the Inland Steel Company in the 1930s

Source H *On the road*

Probably only in the USA could you see beggars in automobiles. You can buy a second-hand Ford for $25 and money for food and petrol is begged along the way. In pleasant weather, the tourists camp out in the fields. When it storms, they can always find some charitable soul to take them in or they can apply to one of the organised charities in the towns. There are, of course, an enormous number who lack even the $25 for a car and these make their way on foot or hitchhike (many others steal lifts on goods trains).

From the 'Guardian', 14 October 1932

Source I *Protest (1)*

England, Arkansas, 3 January 1931. The long drought that ruined hundreds of Arkansas farms last summer had a dramatic sequel late today when some 500 farmers marched on the business section of this town. Most of them were white men, many of them were armed. Shouting that they must have food for themselves and their families, the invaders announced their intention to take it from the stores unless it was provided from some other source without cost.

Indiana Harbor, Indiana, 5 August 1931. Around 1,500 jobless men stormed the plant of the Fruit Growers Express Company here, demanding that they be given jobs to keep them from starving. The company's answer was to call the city police. They used clubs to force the jobless to retreat.

Newspaper reports from 1931

Source J *Protest (2) - the 'Bonus Army'*

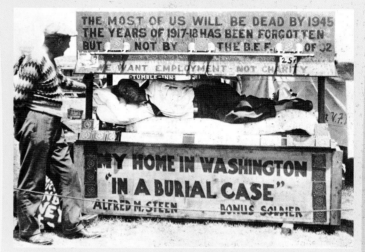

In May 1932, a group of veterans who had fought in the First World War demanded the immediate payment of the bonus which the government had promised to pay them in 1945. They were poor and they needed the money now. About 22,000 marched from all over the country to Washington where they set up camp near the Capitol (see above) and refused to move until they had been paid. They became known as the 'Bonus Army'. On 28 July, President Hoover, convinced the protest was led by Communists, sent in General MacArthur with troops and tanks to clear the camp. MacArthur said: 'The mob was a bad looking mob. It was revolutionary. It is my opinion that, had the President not acted today, he would have faced a grave situation.'

Source K *Black Americans*

The percentage of negroes among the unemployed runs sometimes four, five, six times as high as it should be given their numbers. In almost any community where jobs are scarce, preference is given to the white worker for any vacancy. Worse than this is the tendency to replace negro workers with white.

From an article entitled 'Negroes Out of Work' in 'The Nation', 1933

We have a great many farmers who rent their land here. Many, especially the negro tenants, are now, in the middle of winter, practically without food and clothes. Many of these local counties have no charitable organisations. There is no place to turn.

Part of a speech made by Congressman Huddleston of Alabama to a Senate Committee in 1932

Unemployed blacks queuing in 1937

QUESTIONS

1. a) **Judging from the information in this section, what were the causes of the Great Depression?**

   b) **What impact did the Depression make on the lives of Americans?**

2. a) **Judging from Sources A-K, what sort of people were affected by the Depression?**

   b) **Who was most affected? Who was least affected? Give reasons for your answers.**

3. **Using sources A-C and K, explain why people took the action described in Sources I and J.**

4. **Look at Sources D-H. What sort of help was available to people affected by the Depression? Do you think this help was adequate?**

5. **What is the message of the photo in Source K?**

Images of the Depression

The best known images of the Depression are the black and white photographs taken of the plight of poor farmers in the south and west of the USA. Often working for government agencies like the Farm Security Administration (FSA), photographers provided visual evidence to back up reports on the wretched conditions caused by the Depression. Among the main subjects of these photographers were poor farmers struggling with poverty and natural disasters like the great dust storms of the mid-1930s. The photographs below were taken by Walker Evans, a member of the FSA photography unit. They were published in 1941 in a book called *Let Us Now Praise Famous Men*. Evans' photos became some of the best known records of the period. He set out to record the poverty he saw and not to sensationalise it. At the same time, he hoped to influence people by what he photographed and by which photos he selected for his book.

1. This photo of George Gudger appeared in 'Let Us Now Praise Famous Men'.

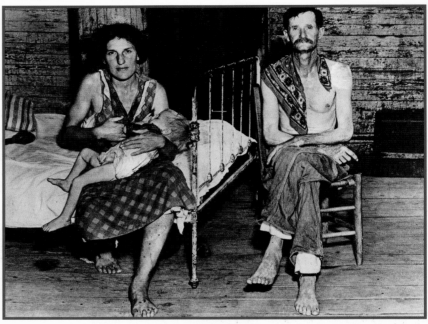

2. This photo of Bud Fields, his wife and baby appeared in 'Let Us Now Praise Famous Men'.

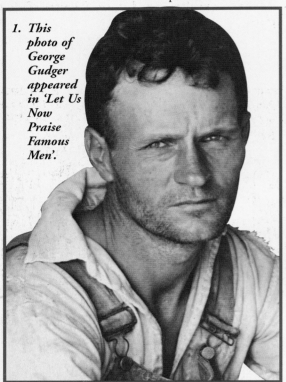

3. This photo of the Gudger family in their Sunday best was taken by Walker Evans, but it did not appear in 'Let Us Now Praise Famous Men'.

Walker Evans and the selection of photos

(a) American documentary photos of the 1930s had a romantic view. They come to us only in images meant to break our hearts. The poor are helpless yet still unconquered. Never are they responsible for their misery. The photos do not include those who are poor through laziness. The poor are shown to have 'simple dignity'. They are honest and decent. Or at least when the audience sees them they are. We see them only in selected, sentimental poses.

(b) Walker Evans was not cold hearted. He would do what he could to help the farmers. He chose the pictures for his book to benefit what he felt was a good cause. The photo which most reveals Evans' bias did not appear in the book. It is a posed family portrait of the Gudgers in their Sunday best, standing beside their cabin. Evans showed George Gudgers unshaven hangdog face after a day in the fields, but not his Sunday face.

Both extracts from 'Documentary Expression and Thirties America' by W. Stott, 1973.

 QUESTIONS

1. 'Reality in black and white'. Would you agree with this description of the value of photos to historians? Explain your answer.
2. What is the evidence in photos 1 and 2 to support the views in passage (a)?
3. Why do you think Walker Evans chose to include photos 1 and 2 in his book, but not photo 3?

Why did Roosevelt win the 1932 presidential election?

The Republican Party was given credit for the prosperity of the 1920s and remained in office for 12 years. But, in 1932, the Republican President, Herbert Hoover, faced an uphill task in seeking re-election. Many people blamed the Republicans for the Depression which had lasted for three years and showed no sign of lifting. There were even fears that the American system of government might not survive the crisis. In 1932, Hoover and the Republicans faced a formidable presidential candidate for the Democrats, Franklin Delano Roosevelt (or 'FDR' as he was often known). Roosevelt campaigned on a programme of taking action against the Depression, a programme which he called 'a New Deal for the American people'. Looking back, it is clear that Roosevelt's election as President in 1932 was a turning point in American history. There are four main reasons why Roosevelt was able to win the 1932 election. First, Roosevelt's background and experience counted in his favour. Second, the state of the USA in 1932 was such that a majority of people wanted change. Third, Roosevelt managed to win the battle of ideas about how to tackle the Depression. And fourth, Roosevelt fought a skilful election campaign.

1 The background and experience of Franklin Delano Roosevelt (FDR)

FDR was born in 1882 into a wealthy family which lived in New York State (he was a distant cousin of Theodore Roosevelt who was the Republican President of the USA between 1901 and 1909). FDR enjoyed a privileged background, attending private school and Harvard University. He trained as a lawyer and then entered politics as a Democrat in 1910 when he was elected as a Senator for New York State. Three years later, FDR was a member of President Wilson's Cabinet and in 1920 he was vice presidential candidate for the Democrats. Then, in 1921, FDR became seriously ill with polio and was never again able to walk unaided (he was able to stand for short periods in iron leg braces, but this was always very painful for him). He slowly regained his health, re-entered politics and in 1928 was elected Governor of New York (he was re-elected in 1930). As Governor of New York, FDR proved he was willing to take positive action to relieve the suffering caused by the Depression (see Box 5.13). His success as Governor not only helped him to gain the Democratic nomination for the presidential election of 1932, it also helped him to develop ideas about how best to fight the Depression.

FDR (1882-1945) in the late 1930s

2 The state of the nation in 1932

Box 5.13

FDR as Governor of New York

There is considerable evidence that Roosevelt's four years as Governor of New York led him to the conclusion that government must take responsibility for the health of the economy and the welfare of its citizens. Once he saw the need for action, Roosevelt set up a Committee on Prevention of Unemployment and persuaded New York State to spend $20 million on home and work relief. As early as 1928, Roosevelt had urged a pension scheme and unemployment insurance scheme to be set up.

From 'Franklin Roosevelt and the New Deal' by D.K. Adams, 1979

Unemployment was rising rapidly throughout the USA in 1932 (see right) and relief for the unemployed was running out. Big cities like Chicago and Philadelphia suspended relief. As a result, the poor ate at soup kitchens (see above) or waited at the back doors of restaurants for left overs. The rural areas were in crisis as farm prices collapsed. On several occasions, violence broke out as farmers dumped food or blocked the roads to stop the transport of food to the cities until prices went up. It was in the summer of 1932 that the Bonus Army (see p.103) set up camp in Washington. Some Americans thought that the country was heading for revolution. Others were deeply shocked at the violence used by troops against the veterans in the Bonus Army. It was against such a background that the presidential election of 1932 took place.

Unemployment 1929-32

1929	1.5 million
1930	5 million
1931	9 million
1932	13 million

3 The election campaign

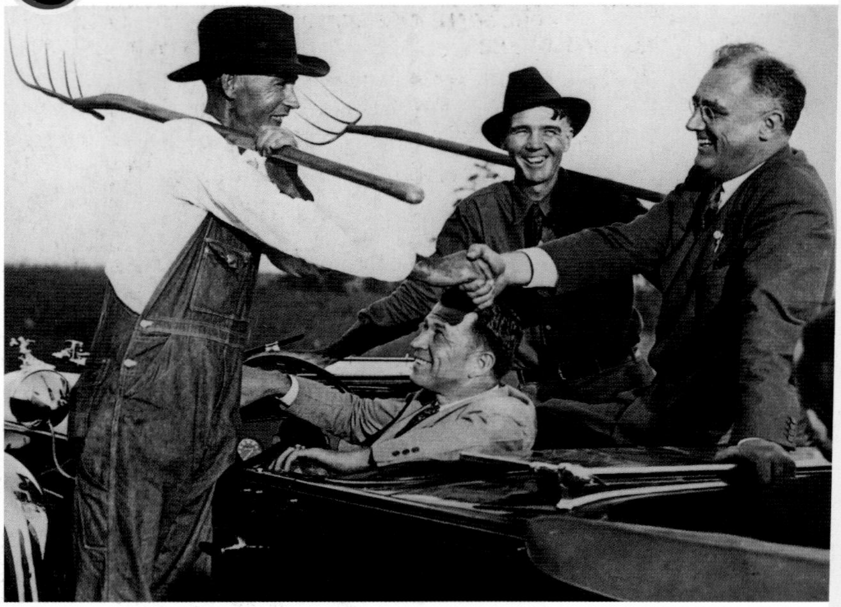

FDR campaigning for votes in West Virginia in October 1932

Box 5.14 **Campaign speeches**

a) Millions of our citizens cherish the hope that their old standards of living and thought have not gone forever. Those millions cannot and shall not wait in vain. I pledge you, I pledge myself to a New Deal for the American people. This is more than a political campaign. It is a call to arms. Give me your help, not to win votes alone, but to win in this crusade to restore America. I am waging war against destruction, delay, deceit and despair.

Part of Roosevelt's acceptance speech in Chicago, July 1932

b) This campaign is more than a contest between two men. It is more than a contest between parties. It is a contest between two philosophies of government. We are told by the opposition that we must have a change, that we must have a New Deal. It is not the change to which I object, but the proposal to alter the whole foundation of our national life. The whole American system is founded upon the idea of responsibility of the individual to the community, of the responsibility of local government to the state, of the state to federal government. New Deal measures would transfer vast responsibilities to the federal government from the states, the local governments and the individuals. They would break down our form of government.

Part of a speech made by Herbert Hoover in October 1932

Hoover was not a good election campaigner and he found himself on the defensive in 1932. He had promised the Americans 'the final triumph over poverty' in 1928, but now seemed unable to offer any solutions to the collapse of the economy. During the campaign, he was gloomy, distant and not at all at ease with people. Roosevelt, by contrast, loved politics and was a natural campaigner. He was cheerful, optimistic and a good communicator. Summing up the campaign, a historian wrote in 1969: 'Roosevelt showed himself to the voters in every part of the country. He demonstrated that his physical affliction was no barrier to his goal. The result was all he could have hoped for. The country gained a picture of him as a smiling, warmhearted man with the poise and self-assurance of an experienced politician. The thousands who saw him found his optimism infectious and exhilarating. As the earnest, plodding defender of the existing government, Hoover was no match for Roosevelt's fast-paced offensive.' (from *From the Crash to the Blitz* by C. Phillips).

4 The battle of ideas

A license plate emphasising the Democrats' anti-prohibition policy. Roosevelt promised to end prohibition, a promise which was increasingly popular and which played a surprisingly important part in the 1932 election campaign. Garner was the Democrats' candidate for Vice President.

When Roosevelt won the Democratic Party's nomination in July 1932, he broke with tradition by flying to Chicago to accept in person. In Chicago, he made a speech in which he used the term 'New Deal' for the first time (see Box 5.14a above). Although many of the details were hazy, it was clear that Roosevelt's New Deal would mean the federal government playing a much more active role than had been the case before. Roosevelt's idea was that, by setting up programmes and spending money, the government would create jobs. Once people had jobs, they would begin to spend money and this would increase demand for new goods. Increased demand would lead to companies taking on more workers. The wages spent by these workers would increase demand still further and so on. Not only was Roosevelt's idea new and daring (the federal government had never played such an important role in the economy before), it was also the opposite point of view to that held by President Hoover (Box 5.14b above). Hoover argued that it was wrong for government to interfere in the working of the economy. It was the government's job, he claimed, to encourage rather than to spend. As a result, Hoover refused to set up relief programmes to help the unemployed and he argued that it was up to individuals to turn around the economy.

Activity
Roosevelt's inauguration

Source B FDR's first inaugural address

This is the time to speak the truth, the whole truth, frankly and boldly. My firm belief is that the only thing we have to fear is fear itself. The withered leaves of industrial enterprise lie on every side. Farmers find no markets for their products. The savings of many years in many thousands of families are gone. More important, a host of unemployed citizens face the grim problem of existence and an equally great number toil with little return. Only a foolish optimist can deny the dark realities of the moment. This nation asks for action, and action now. Our greatest task is to put people to work. This task can be helped by definite efforts to raise the value of agricultural products. It can be helped by the unifying of relief activities which today are often scattered, uneconomical and unequal. It can be helped by national planning for and supervision of all forms of transport and of other utilities which have a definitely public character. There are many ways in which it can be helped, but it can never be helped merely by talking about it. We must act, and act quickly. I shall ask the Congress for the one remaining instrument to meet the crisis - broad executive power to wage a war against the emergency as great as the power that would be given me if we were invaded by a foreign foe.

Part of FDR's first inaugural address, delivered on 4 March 1933, the day on which he took over from Hoover as President

Source C Reactions to FDR's inaugural address

As a candidate, Roosevelt had pledged himself to 'a New Deal for the American people' and on Inauguration Day, 4 March 1933, tens of millions of Americans crowded around their radios to hear him tell them what they might expect from that promise. Louise Armstrong heard the speech sitting in the lobby of a Chicago hotel. 'When it was over', Louise Armstrong remembered eight years later, 'the clerk came out from behind the desk and stood beside the radio for a moment. "God, Mrs Armstrong!" was all he said. He took out his handkerchief and wiped his forehead.' Armstrong and the hotel clerk knew that they had heard an address of a kind no President had given since Abraham Lincoln had given his own second inaugural address 60 years before. Then, Lincoln had called for a great national healing in the wake of the American civil war. Roosevelt had called for a similar commitment and made it clear he would ask for powers that no President had ever been given in peacetime.

From 'The Great Depression' by T.H. Watkins, 1993

Source A Election results, 1928 and 1932

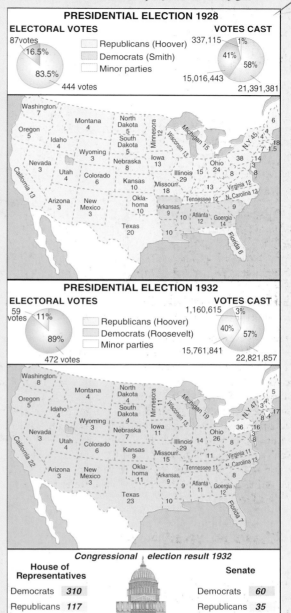

QUESTIONS

1. Judging from the information in this section, why do you think Roosevelt won the 1932 presidential election? Using Source A describe the size of his victory.

2. How would Hoover's inaugural speech have differed from that made by Roosevelt, if he had won?

3. Why do you think Roosevelt's speech (Source B) made an impact? Would you expect the reaction described in Source C to be typical? Explain your answer.

4. One American newspaper's headline for 5 March 1933 was 'Roosevelt asks for dictator's role'. Judging from Source B why do you think the newspaper chose this headline?

What was the New Deal?

The idea of a New Deal caught on with the American people. It became the label attached to a programme of government action that began as soon as Roosevelt took office in 1933. In his inaugural address (see previous page), Roosevelt said that he would 'wage a war against the emergency'. His main aim was to provide relief for victims of the Depression and to work towards economic recovery. He also believed that, if recovery was to last, then important areas of American life had to be reformed. The speed of government action surprised many people, especially the amount that was done in the first hundred days. Roosevelt believed in 'bold, persistent experimentation'. There was no overall plan and not everything worked. But the New Deal restored hope and reassured people that the government would take responsibility for the welfare of its citizens. Politically, the New Deal was extremely successful. Roosevelt was re-elected three times and the Democratic Party dominated American politics until 1948. Roosevelt used the powers of the presidency to the full, but he kept within the rules of the American constitution. As a result, the USA avoided a dictatorship like that in Germany where Hitler came to power at around the same time as Roosevelt. The main elements of the New Deal were delivered in two phases - the first hundred days of Roosevelt's presidency and in 1935. Legislation passed in these two phases resulted in the growth of the so-called 'alphabet agencies'.

I The 'Hundred Days' (March-June 1933)

Roosevelt had promised action and in the first hundred days of his administration, he kept up a hectic pace of activity. During the months between his election (in November 1932) and inauguration (in March 1933), the economic crisis deepened. In particular, bank failures rocketed (4,004 banks failed in the first two months of 1933 alone). FDR's first task, therefore, was to restore confidence in the banking system. This was skilfully handled (see Box 5.15) and set the pattern for what followed. The most important Acts of Congress passed in the Hundred Days were those which tried to bring about relief for the unemployed and recovery from the Depression in both industry and agriculture. Congress, usually slow to act (see cartoon below), rushed through a series of measures, urged on by the President. Federal government agencies (known by their initials and therefore called the **alphabet agencies -** see right) were set up to put the Acts into practice. The result was that the federal government played a much greater role in American life than had ever been the case before.

Alphabet agencies created during the Hundred Days

ACT		PROVISIONS
NIRA:	National Industrial Recovery Act	Allowed workers to join trade unions. Set up the NRA (National Recovery Administration) to regulate prices and working conditions.
CCC:	Civilian Conservation Corps	Employed young men in a massive countryside conservation programme. The men were housed, educated, fed and part of their wages went to their families.
AAA:	Agricultural Adjustment Administration	Set up a quota system to limit the amount of food produced in order to guarantee fair prices for farmers.
FERA:	Federal Emergency Relief Act	$500 million of government money was made available to cities and states in order to provide relief for the unemployed.
TVA:	Tennessee Valley Authority	Aided one of the poorest regions of the country by employing people to build dams and using them to generate electricity for the homes in the area and to irrigate farmland.
HOLC:	Home Owners Loan Corporation	Helped people who were having difficulty paying their mortgage by lending money at a low interest rate.
CWA: **PWA:**	Civil Works Administration Public Works Administration	Provided employment schemes in hundreds of areas: hospitals, schools, roads, bridges, artistic and cultural projects.

The Galloping Snail - a cartoonist's view of the Hundred Days

Box 5.15   FDR and the banking crisis

When Roosevelt took the oath of office on 4 March 1933, the nation's economy was on the brink of collapse. Unemployment stood at nearly 13 million. Banks were closed in 38 states. Within the next ten days, Roosevelt won his first great New Deal victory by saving the nation's banks. On 5 March, he issued a decree closing the nation's banks and called Congress back into session. His aides drafted new banking legislation and presented it to Congress on 9 March. A few hours later, both Houses passed it. The measure provided for government supervision and aid to the banks. Strong ones would be opened with federal support, weak ones closed and those in difficulty helped by government loans. On 12 March, FDR addressed the nation by radio in the first of his 'fireside chats'. In conversational tones, he told the public what he had done. Some banks would reopen the next day with the government standing behind them. Others would open later. By the end of 13 March, customers had deposited more cash than they withdrew. The crisis was over. Gradually, other banks opened and the failures ceased.

From 'America Past and Present' by R. Divine, T. Breen, G. Frederickson & R. Williams, 1995

2   Phase two: the legislation of 1935

The whirlwind activity of the Hundred Days was followed by a slower pace of reform until 1935 when another series of major Acts was passed by Congress. It had become clear in 1934 that recovery from the Depression was partial and slow. The new public works programmes, for example, were still not absorbing a large enough percentage of the unemployed (see right). In addition, there were still many areas of American life that the Roosevelt government wanted to reform. Most important, Roosevelt was keen to take measures to ensure that the federal and state governments provided welfare measures (such as old age pensions, disability pay or unemployment benefit) as a matter of course. The Acts passed in 1935 shifted the focus of the New Deal. Whereas the main aim of the measures passed in the Hundred Days had been to provide relief and recovery, the aim of the 1935 legislation was to provide long-lasting change. The reforms of 1935 expanded the New Deal into new areas of government activity.

Unemployment in the USA 1933-37

1933	12.8 million
1934	11.3 million
1935	10.6 million
1936	9 million
1937	7.7 million

Main measures passed in 1935	
WPA: Works Progress Administration	Provided employment schemes in hundreds of areas: hospitals, schools, roads, bridges, artistic and cultural projects.
Social Security Act:	Set up pension schemes and unemployment insurance.
RA: Resettlement Administration	Helped farmers in drought-hit areas to resettle on better land.
REA: Rural Electrification Administration	Gave financial aid to private companies to supply electricity to areas previously not supplied.
National Labour Relations Act	Stated that employers must allow unions in their industries (known as the 'Wagner Act' after the politician who introduced it).

3   The main Acts and agencies

a. Reviving industry - the National Industrial Recovery Act 1933 (NIRA)

NIRA was the government's main weapon in its battle to bring about industrial recovery. It was an attempt at government planning on a voluntary basis. The Act set up the National Recovery Agency (NRA) whose job was to draw up codes of fair competition. At first, codes were drawn up for large-scale industries like textiles, coal and car manufacture. These codes regulated levels of production and prices, aiming to prevent further job losses and wasteful price-cutting wars. The

codes also provided minimum wages, maximum hours and better working conditions. Joining the NRA was voluntary, but firms were persuaded and sometimes bullied into signing up to the codes and, by the end of 1933, over 500 codes had been drawn up. Firms taking part in the scheme were seen as patriotic and as helping the USA out of Depression. They were allowed to display the blue eagle sign on their goods (see above). The results, however, were mixed. Large firms dominated and there were accusations of price fixing. But child labour was stopped and there was much enthusiasm.

b. The Civilian Conservation Corps (CCC)

Members of the CCC setting out seedlings in the St Joe National Forest, Idaho.

The CCC was an effort to help young unemployed men (those aged 18 to 25). Living in camps, they carried out conservation work, planting new forests and helping with flood control projects. In total, the CCC provided employment for about 2.5 million men (see Box 5.16).

Box 5.16   Working again

I saw old friends of mine digging ditches and laying sewer pipes. They were wearing their regular business suits because they could not afford overalls and rubber boots. I felt sick at heart, but one said, pulling some coins from his pocket: 'Do you know, this is the first money I've had in my pocket in a year and a half. I've had nothing but tickets that you exchange for groceries.' He was happy to be working.

Comment made by F. Walker, President of the National Emergency Council, 1934

c. Public works - the PWA, CWA, WPA and FERA

WORK PROMOTES CONFIDENCE

WORKS PROGRESS ADMINISTRATION

Some people criticised the programmes of public works, accusing them of wasting money and not creating 'real' jobs. But between 1935 and 1943, the WPA (see poster, above) built 2,500 hospitals, 2,900 schools and 57,000 miles of road. When the WPA programme for artists was attacked, Harry Hopkins replied: 'Hell, they've got to eat just like other people.'

The PWA, CWA and WPA all provided for the same thing - investment in schemes that would provide employment. The Public Works Administration (PWA) was set up as part of NIRA (see p.109). Over $3 billion was spent on large-scale building projects designed to be both useful and to put people back to work. Schools, hospitals and town halls were built and around a million people employed. But, progress was slow. By the autumn of 1933, it was clear that there was going to be no quick economic upturn. To help the unemployed through the winter, additional help was necessary. Four million people were eventually on the payroll of the Civil Works Administration (CWA). The CWA paid wages for building roads, schools, playgrounds and airfields. Money was also paid to teachers and other professionals on CWA schemes. The Works Progress Administration (WPA) was a large-scale work relief programme and the most imaginative of them all. By 1941, over $11 million had been pumped into the economy. Its projects included the usual sorts of building programmes, but also a wide variety of other schemes employing actors, artists, writers and young people. The aim of the Federal Emergency Relief Administration (FERA) was slightly different. It was set up in 1933 to distribute aid to the needy as rapidly as possible and it combined cash relief with work relief. Its head, Harry Hopkins, wasted no time, spending $5 million within two hours of taking office. Money was given to individual states with $1 being donated by the federal government for every $3 the state spent on relief.

e. The Social Security Act 1935

For the first time, the federal government took responsibility for providing old age pensions and, with the help of the states, unemployment benefit and disability pay. The system was based on an insurance scheme. Both employers and employees paid. It was a modest scheme which excluded farm and domestic workers and made no provision for sickness. But it was a very important development since, for the first time, the government accepted responsibility to provide at least a minimum standard of welfare.

d. Reviving agriculture - the AAA, RA and REA

FDR's Secretary of Agriculture, Henry Wallace, believed that the only way to raise farm prices (which collapsed after 1929) was to cut down production. Under the guidance of the Agricultural Adjustment Administration (AAA), farmers who cut back production received a subsidy raised by a tax on items like flour. The scheme was voluntary. Since there was a glut of some products, the first cuts had to be drastic. Crops already planted and young animals were destroyed. In general, the scheme was successful in raising prices and therefore farmers' incomes. Other Acts also affected agriculture. A Federal Farm Mortgage Corporation was set up in 1934 to prevent the eviction of farmers who could not pay their mortgages. The Resettlement Administration (RA), set up in 1935, helped poor farmers to find new land. The Rural Electrification Agency made electricity generally available to rural USA for the first time.

YEARS OF DUST

The effects of the Depression were made worse by natural disasters. For example, in the early 1930s a drought in huge areas of the Midwest led to dust storms with the fertile topsoil simply blowing away. The area became known as the 'dust bowl' and many poor farmers were forced to move away. The Resettlement Administration attempted to find these farmers land elsewhere. The poster above, by Ben Shahn, promotes the work of the RA.

f. The National Labour Relations Act 1935

This Act (known as the **Wagner Act**) recognised the right of workers to organise into trade unions and to negotiate with their employers. It set up a National Labour Relations Board (NLRB) which could sort out any disputes that arose. Companies which refused to recognise properly formed unions or which set up tame company-controlled unions could be referred to the Board. The Act was successful in increasing the power of unions and unions were set up in industries like steel and the Ford Motor Company for the first time.

Activity
The Tennessee Valley Authority (TVA)

Source B *The Norris dam*

The Norris dam (named after the Senator who promoted the development of the Tennessee Valley - see Source E) was completed in 1936.

Source C *The Tennessee Valley Authority - a map*

Ohio R.
Cairo Paducah
KENTUCKY
Cumberland R.
VIRGINIA
Bristol
Mississippi R.
NORRIS DAM
Tennessee R.
Nashville
Knoxville
TENNESSEE
Duck R.
NORTH CAROLINA
Asheville
Chattanooga
Tennessee R.
SOUTH CAROLINA
Sheffield
Muscle Shoals
GEORGIA
MISSISSIPPI
ALABAMA

--- State line
▮ Dams
～ Rivers
⌂ Power plants
⌂ Chemical plants

Source D *Two views on the TVA*

a) It all boils down to this. Those who ran the TVA, aided and abetted by the government in Washington, looked upon the TVA as a great revolutionary movement which would break down borders between states, ignore local self-government and set up a huge, centralised, regional body which would dispense the 'blessings' of a new social order to the 'backward' inhabitants of the Valley.

Comment made by a Tennessean looking back on the 1930s, 1952

b) This is an entirely different region from what it was ten years ago. You can see the change almost everywhere you go. You can see it in the copper lines strung along back country roads and in the fresh paint on the houses these lines were built to serve. You can see it in the new electric water pumps in the farmyards, in the community refrigerators at the crossroads, in the feed grinders in the woodsheds. You can see the factories that stand where there were worn-out cotton fields and rows of tenant shacks a few years ago. You can see the new houses by the thousand on the edges of towns - new houses of the men who take away as much cash from a few trips to the payroll window as they used to earn in a year.

From 'TVA: Democracy on the March' by D. Lilienthal (who chaired the TVA from 1941), 1944

Source E *A historian's view*

A dream of liberals in the 1920s, especially of Senator George Norris of Nebraska, had been the scheme to use the federally owned dams at Muscle Shoals on the Tennessee River to generate cheap electrical power for the people of the Tennessee Valley. This project had been bitterly opposed by private electrical companies and conservatives in Congress had tried to sell off the dams (which had been built to generate power for explosives factories in the First World War). Norris prevented that and now his dream came true. The Tennessee Valley Act set up the Tennessee Valley Authority (TVA) as the first publicly owned electricity organisation in the USA. The TVA created thousands of jobs as it built more dams and constructed power lines. It taught farmers about conservation. Its electricity began to reach hundreds of thousands of poor homes which would otherwise have had to do without fridges, electric stoves and electric light. It also tempted industrialists to set up factories in what, until then, had been one of the most under-industrialised regions of the USA.

Extract from 'History of the United States' by Hugh Brogan, 1985

QUESTIONS

1. Using the information in this section, explain what is meant by the term 'New Deal'.
2. Why was the TVA set up and what was it expected to achieve? Use Sources A, C and E in your answer.
3. Judging from Sources B-E why do you think the TVA has been seen as a showcase for the New Deal?
4. What were the benefits and drawbacks of the scheme developed by the TVA? Use Sources C-E in your answer.

Who opposed the New Deal in the 1930s?

The New Deal faced opposition throughout the 1930s, both from those who thought it did not go far enough and from those who thought it went too far. Amongst those who thought that the New Deal did not go far enough were three individuals who devised their own schemes for reviving the economy. These individuals (Huey Long, Father Coughlin and Dr Townsend) claimed to have substantial support for their ideas. But, Roosevelt's overwhelming victory in the 1936 presidential election ensured that their ideas remained in the political wilderness. Roosevelt was also able to contain opposition from trade unionists who hoped to quicken the pace of change. By making concessions to trade unionists, however, Roosevelt increased the hostility of those who thought the New Deal went too far. Throughout the 1930s, there were strong conservative forces, both politicians and businesspeople who denounced the New Deal as too radical and who hated Roosevelt personally. The New Deal also ran into opposition from the Supreme Court which ruled that key measures were not constitutional.

The New Deal does not go far enough

a. Huey Long's 'Share our Wealth' scheme

In 1928, Huey Long became governor of Louisiana. Two years later he was elected to the Senate. In Louisiana, he ruled very much as he pleased. When people protested that he was breaking the state constitution, he replied: 'I'm the constitution around here now'. Whilst some people disliked Long's dictatorial manner, many others benefited from it. He improved public schools, built new roads and bridges and abolished taxes on the poor. At first, Long (known as the 'Kingfish') supported the New Deal, but in 1934 he announced a nationwide **Share Our Wealth** movement. His aim was to redistribute wealth from the rich to the poor. He guaranteed every American a home worth $5,000, an annual income of $2,500, a car, a radio and better education. To finance the plan, Long wanted to confiscate all fortunes of more than $5 million and to charge 100% tax on incomes over $1 million. By 1935, Long claimed to have over 7 million supporters. He hoped to stand in the 1936 presidential election, but was assassinated in September 1935. In 1936, Long's successor, Gerald Smith, joined forces with Dr Townsend and Father Coughlin (see (c) below) in the new Union Party set up by Coughlin to fight the 1936 presidential election. The cartoon (left) was published on 5 May 1932. It suggested that Huey Long was a Communist and therefore a dangerous threat to the USA.

b. The trade unions

	Days lost through strikes (1,000s)	No. of union members (1,000s)
1930	3,320	3,632
1932	10,500	3,226
1934	19,600	3,249
1936	13,900	4,164
1938	9,150	8,265

c. Father Coughlin and Dr Townsend

Father Coughlin was a radio priest from Michigan who built up a regular Sunday audience of around 40 million people in the mid-1930s. At first, he supported the New Deal. But he broke with it in late 1934 and set up his own National League for Social Justice. He attacked bankers and Jews and made personal attacks on FDR. His aims were reform of the monetary system, a 'just and living wage' for all workers and heavy taxes on the wealthy, but his message was confused. Dr Townsend, on the other hand, had a clear message, focused on the elderly. Many elderly people had lost their savings when the banks failed. Of the 7.5 million Americans over the age of 65 in 1935, half could not support themselves. In 20 states, no pensions of any kind existed. Townsend's solution was to set up a fund, financed by a sales tax, to provide an old age pension of $200 per month. The pension would be provided on condition that the pensioner gave up employment and spent the whole amount each month. This would pump money into the economy and open jobs for younger people. Despite the criticism that this would transfer over 50% of the national income to less than 10% of the population, 7,000 Townsend clubs with over 1.5 million members had sprung up by 1936.

The NIRA (see p.109) allowed workers to join unions, but many employers simply ignored the new regulations. Some union leaders argued that the New Deal should do more to protect workers. Although pressure from the unions led to the Wagner Act 1935 (see p.110), it remained common practice for companies to go to great lengths to prevent unions organising the workers (many used violence against pro-union workers). In 1935, some unions formed the Committee for Industrial Organization (CIO). Its aim was to organise workers in mass production industries and to bring in unskilled workers who had no union. The CIO organised sit-down strikes and used other tactics to increase the pace of change. In 1937, there were 477 sit down strikes involving 400,000 workers. The table above shows the total number of days lost through strikes (if 20 workers go on strike for one day, this counts as 20 days) and the number of union members in the 1930s.

② The New Deal goes too far

Although Hoover was well beaten in the 1932 presidential election, the Republicans still received 15.7 million votes. As a result, there was a large minority of Americans who supported Hoover's 'hands off' approach to government. In 1934, the American Liberty League was set up. Wealthy businesspeople joined conservative politicians in attacking the New Deal in general and Roosevelt in particular. They argued that the New Deal's relief and welfare measures were the first steps towards Communism (see the book cover, right) and undermined traditional American values such as self-reliance. The League went to extremes in its criticisms and it was easy for New Dealers to claim that the League was a group of rich people looking after their own selfish interests. In the 1936 presidential election, Roosevelt found the Liberty League an easier target for attack (see Box 5.17) than the moderate Republican candidate, Alfred Landon.

> ### Box 5.17 FDR on the rich
>
> Businessmen, financiers, speculators, bankers - never before in our history have these forces been so united against one candidate as they stand today. They hate me - and I welcome their hatred. I should like to have it said of my first administration that these forces of selfishness met their match. I should like to have it said of my second administration that these forces met their master.
>
> **Part of a speech made during the 1936 election campaign**

In her book (see above), Elizabeth Dilling claimed that Roosevelt was a secret supporter of Communism and that the New Deal was an attempt to turn the USA into a Communist state.

③ Opposition from the Supreme Court

In 1935 and 1936, the Supreme Court judged that a number of New Deal Acts (notably the NIRA and AAA) were unconstitutional. The judges argued that, according to the American constitution, the federal government was responsible only for national matters which affected all the states. Since Acts like the NIRA and AAA did not affect all states, they were unconstitutional. This was most annoying to New Dealers who argued that the Depression affected the whole nation and the Acts were designed to deal with a national emergency. As a result, Roosevelt, armed with his overwhelming victory in the 1936 presidential election, decided to reform the Supreme Court before it did more damage to the New Deal. In 1936, there were nine judges, six of whom were aged over 70. The only way to change the court was to wait until judges died or retired. Roosevelt surprised Congress by calling for a law which would allow him to appoint one new judge for each of the current judges who was over 70 but refused to retire (up to a maximum of six). But, Democrats as well as Republicans opposed what they saw as an attempt to increase presidential power (see Box 5.18). As a result, the 'court packing' scheme failed. Roosevelt argued that the fight against the Supreme Court was worthwhile because the Court upheld a number of controversial New Deal measures (such as the Wagner Act). But, he lost support in Congress.

The cartoon (right) suggests that FDR wanted to steer the ship of state in his own direction, against the wishes of Congress and the Supreme Court.

> ### Box 5.18 FDR and the Supreme Court
>
> The court defended itself well. Chief Justice Charles Evans Hughes pointed out to the Senate Judiciary Committee that the Court was up to date and not behind schedule as Roosevelt charged. The Court then surprised observers with a series of rulings approving controversial New Deal measures like the Wagner Act and Social Security Act. Then a Supreme Court judge resigned, allowing FDR to make his first appointment since taking office. Feeling he had proved his point, the President then allowed his court packing scheme to die in the Senate. During the next few years, four more vacancies occurred and so a majority in the Court were FDR supporters. But the price was high. The fight badly weakened the President's relations with Congress, opening deep splits within his own party. Many members of Congress who had voted reluctantly for Roosevelt's measures during the depths of the Depression now felt free to oppose any further New Deal reforms.
>
> ***Adapted from 'America Past and Present' by R. Divine, T. Breen, G. Fredrickson & R. Williams, 1995***

Activity
FDR and the opposition

Source C Election results

1. Presidential election 1936

	No votes million	%	Electoral votes
Roosevelt (Dem)	27.7	60.7	523
Landon (Repub)	16.6	36.4	8
Lemke (Unity)	0.89	2.9	0

FDR won 46 states, Landon won just two (Maine and Vermont)

2. Congressional elections

	SENATE		HOUSE OF REPRESENTATIVES	
	Dem	Repub	Dem	Repub
1932	60	35	310	117
1934	69	25	319	103
1936	76	16	331	89
1938	69	23	261	164

Source E Cartoon from the 1930s

A caption below this cartoon said: 'Mother, Wilfred wrote a bad word.'

Source A Cartoon produced after the 1936 election

Vermont and Maine, the only two states with a Republican majority, are in the 'dog house'. They look suitably ashamed.

Source D A historian's view on the 1936 election

Roosevelt's re-election was the most certain thing since George Washington's. To be sure, he had been under attack from the Left for not doing enough and from the Right for doing too much. The *Literary Digest*, a distinguished magazine, conducted a poll by telephone and predicted that Roosevelt would lose. It had not noticed that 67% of American households still lacked telephones, though their members had votes. In reality, nothing could weaken the President's hold on the American people. He had accustomed them to look to him for ideas, leadership and help; and, although the Depression still continued, it was much less severe. 'Your work saved our humble little home. Life is 1,000% better since you took charge of the USA', a former life-long Republican supporter wrote to the President. The blacks turned away from the Republicans to Roosevelt since he was helping them too. With such friends, there was no need to count the enemy.

From 'History of the United States' by Hugh Brogan, 1985

Source B An imaginary conversation

A: Have you heard there's only six dwarfs now?

Q: Only six?

A: Yeah. Dopey's in the White House.

Q: Mr Arbuthnot, you slay me. Well, go on. Tell us more. Why don't you like Mr. Roosevelt? What's the matter with him?

A: Well the trouble with Roosevelt is he's an idealist.

Q: Yes?

A: And the trouble with Roosevelt is he's destroyed individual initiative.

Q: Do tell.

A: And the trouble with Roosevelt is he's a Communist.

Q: I see. Go on.

A: The trouble with Roosevelt is he's a Fascist.

Q: A Fascist too?

A: Certainly, he wants to be dictator. Don't tell me he hasn't got his eye on a third term.

Q: Snakes alive, has he?

A: And the trouble with Roosevelt is his vanity. That's what makes him so stubborn. He just won't listen to reason. And the trouble with Roosevelt is he's got no right to spend the taxpayers' money to build up his personal political machine.

Written by F. Sullivan in 'A Pearl in Every Oyster', 1938

QUESTIONS

1. Using the information in this section, write an account explaining who opposed FDR and the New Deal. Why do you think this opposition developed?

2. 'The opposition to FDR and the New Deal failed to make an impact.' What is the evidence in Sources A, C and D to support this statement? Why do you think this was the case?

3. Look at Sources B and E. What does each Source tell us about the opposition to the New Deal?

How successful was the New Deal?

The sweeping electoral victories of Roosevelt and the Democrats indicate the popularity of the New Deal among the majority of Americans in the 1930s. But critics (both at the time and later) have attacked the New Deal for failing to solve problems brought about by the Depression, especially the problem of unemployment. Some critics complain about too much government interference and waste. Others have suggested that Roosevelt's government did not do enough for those who suffered from the Depression. Defenders of Roosevelt, on the other hand, have argued that the New Deal helped groups of Americans who, until then, had been neglected or ignored by government. Among these groups were farmers, labour organisations, black Americans, women and the poorest people in society. There were limits to this help, defenders of Roosevelt claim, because there were limits to what any government could achieve. Whether or not the New Deal should be judged a success depends on the answer given to questions such as the following. First, did the New Deal achieve its aims? Second, if the New Deal did not completely achieve its aims, did it do enough for it still to be judged a success? Third, did the majority of American people approve of New Deal policies and programmes? Fourth, what about those people who opposed or did not benefit from the New Deal - how much notice should be taken of their viewpoint? And fifth, looking back, did the New Deal improve life in the USA?

1 The New Deal and the economy

One of the main aims of the New Deal was to bring about economic recovery. Most historians would agree that the New Deal was not completely successful in achieving this. The number of unemployed people did not fall below 10% of the workforce before the USA joined the war, for example, and National Income only returned to its 1929 level in 1940 (see right). Most historians, however, agree that some progress was made (see Box 5.19). Although the New Deal failed to solve the problem of unemployment completely, the number of jobless fell steadily between 1933 and 1937. Millions found work in the public works programmes set up by the government and the despair of 1929-32 was lifted. It was noticeable that when Roosevelt cut public spending in 1937-38, unemployment shot up again. In the end, however, it was the approach of war and the need for the production of war materials that led to full employment.

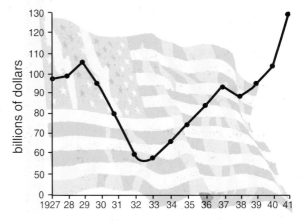

USA National Income 1927-41

(billions of dollars, 1927–41)

Box 5.19 — The New Deal and the economy

Because recovery was incomplete, the size of what was achieved should not be underestimated. The recovery in 1933-37 was almost as great as the expansion in 1922-29. If it is argued that the expansion of the 1920s was remarkable, then a standard has been set against which to measure the achievement of the 1930s.

From 'The American Economy between the World Wars' by J. Potter, 1974

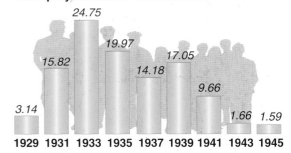

Unemployment as % of workforce

1929	1931	1933	1935	1937	1939	1941	1943	1945
3.14	15.82	24.75	19.97	14.18	17.05	9.66	1.66	1.59

2 The New Deal and poverty

Another important aim of the New Deal was to provide emergency relief for those suffering from the Depression. In addition to the unemployed, there was a hard core of around 40 million Americans who were very poor in the early 1930s. They included groups such as the old, single parent families, black Americans and native Americans. Roosevelt spoke of helping 'the forgotten man at the bottom of the economic pyramid'. For many people, the alphabet relief agencies provided at least a basic standard of living. Also, minimum wage laws helped the very low paid. But none of these programmes was given enough funds to cure the problem of poverty.

3 The New Deal and workers' rights

The New Deal brought demands for better working conditions and workers' rights. Although a number of key measures were passed (notably the Wagner Act 1935), relations between workers and some employers remained difficult. In the Republic Steel strike of 1937, for example (see painting, right), ten strikers were killed in a fight with the police.

115

④ The New Deal and black Americans

Mary McLeod Bethune and Eleanor Roosevelt in 1937.

Some groups, such as farmers and the white unemployed, had obvious reasons for supporting the New Deal. But it is more difficult to say why black Americans began to vote Democrat in such large numbers for the first time since the American Civil War of 1861-65 (see Box 5.20). Many New Deal agencies, especially in the South, discriminated against blacks. Black sharecroppers (poor tenant farmers who paid part of their crops as rent) were driven off the land because of crop reductions ordered by the white-dominated AAA agencies. The NRA became known as the 'Negro Removal Agency' because black industrial workers were pushed out when wage levels were controlled. Roosevelt refused to take steps to help blacks gain equal rights (though he did support an anti-lynching Bill). He feared losing the solid Democrat support of whites in the South. But there were people around the President who cared about the plight of black Americans (including his wife Eleanor) and some black people were appointed to posts in New Deal agencies - such as Mary McLeod Bethune (see above) who headed the National Youth Administration. Most important was the fact that blacks received at least some help from the relief programmes.

Box 5.20

A New Deal for blacks?

a) Most of all, blacks swung to Roosevelt because they had been granted relief. In many areas, they were hit harder than any group by the Depression and survived largely on relief cheques. Unlike the CCC, the WPA imposed no quotas according to race. Also, the National Youth Authority, through the noted black leader, Mary McLeod Bethune, funnelled funds to thousands of young blacks. In 1936, Roosevelt ran better than twice as well among black voters in Chicago than he had done four years previously. By mid-1938, an opinion poll showed 84.7% of blacks as pro-Roosevelt.

From 'FDR and the New Deal' by W.E. Leuchtenburg, 1963

b) Southern states and local officials discriminated against blacks in their administration of relief programmes. In Atlanta, Georgia, for example, blacks received $13 less per month than whites. In Jacksonville, Florida, the city provided 5,000 whites with 45% of all relief funds while 15,000 blacks received only 55%. When blacks complained of inequalities, they faced even greater difficulties securing relief. By the mid-1930s, however, a variety of forces helped to transform the 'raw deal' into a 'New Deal'. By 1939, income for blacks from New Deal work and relief programmes nearly matched income from private employment.

From 'A History of the African American People' by J.O. Horton & L.E. Horton, 1995

⑤ The New Deal and women

By 1930, women made up nearly 25% of the workforce and many suffered from the effects of the Depression. Eleanor Roosevelt and others helped to set up public works programmes for women. Women still faced discrimination, but the 1930s did see some progress. For example, the first woman to become a member of the President's Cabinet was Frances Perkins (she is pictured, right, stitching the first 'Blue Eagle' label into a dress during a ceremony to mark the adoption of the NRA code by clothing firms in New York in 1933. She was appointed Secretary of Labor in 1933). Also, many women became administrators in the alphabet agencies. Molly Dewson, the first full-time director of the Women's Division of the Democrats claimed: 'Roosevelt set a new trend. At last women had their foot inside the door. We had the opportunity to show our ability to see what was needed and to get the job done while working harmoniously with men.'

Frances Perkins

⑥ The New Deal and the arts

The painting above was produced in 1935 by Moses Soyer and entitled 'Artists on WPA'. As well as being given a chance to do their own work, unemployed artists funded by the WPA transformed the look of public buildings by painting murals and exhibiting work. The WPA did not only fund painters. It also employed 6,000 writers (who, for example, produced guide books for each of the 48 states) and set up projects such as the Federal Theatre Project (which employed an average of 10,000 people per year between 1935 and 1939). Critics said the government was wasting its money or that it was funding propaganda.

Source A *WPA report on programmes in Iowa*

Subject: the Donner family. Mr Donner owned a printing business. Savings were lost after the Wall Street Crash and business failed. Had to move to wife's parents' home in 1934. Worked as a labourer and then on a WPA project.

Mr Donner says that WPA workers feel that the work is worthwhile. Not only have men been given work, but also cities have had, at only a small proportion of the total cost, improvements which they might not have had for years. Dubuque in Iowa, for example, now has a municipal swimming pool built as a WPA project, a recreation pavilion and the largest man-made rock garden in the world - a good advert for Dubuque. The chief drawback is that the money poured into the WPA has not created jobs in private industry, partly because WPA wages have been too low and most WPA workers can only buy the bare necessities.

Extract from WPA Division of Research Report on programmes in Iowa, 1937-39

Source B *New Deal cartoon (1)*

Source C *Historians' verdict on the New Deal (1)*

a) The main achievement of the New Deal was the guaranteeing of a minimum standard of welfare. The WPA and the whole series of relief agencies, wages and hours legislation, AAA and social security - each illustrates this new view of the federal government. The ordeal of the Depression changed the American people's belief in the limited powers of the federal government.

From 'Out of Our Past' by C. Degler, 1959

b) The New Deal was a holding operation for American society. It was a series of measures which enabled people to survive the Depression and to hold on until the Second World War opened up new opportunities. Industrial recovery programmes brought modest recovery. Relief and welfare measures allowed the unemployed to struggle through until the war brought them jobs. The plight of the poorest one third of the nation largely remained the New Deal's unfinished business.

From 'The New Deal' by A.J. Badger, 1989

Source D *Historians' verdict on the New Deal (2)*

The least impressive achievement of the New Deal was the economic record. The moderate nature of Roosevelt's reforms led to slow and halting industrial recovery. The nation had barely reached the 1929 level of production a decade later and over 10 million were still unemployed. More significant change occurred in American society. With the adoption of social security, the government acknowledged for the first time its responsibility to provide for the welfare of those unable to provide for themselves. But the New Deal tended to help only the more vocal and organised groups such as union members and farmers. Those with little political clout (such as blacks and women) received little help. The most lasting impact came in politics. FDR proved to be a genius at forging a new coalition. He united the Democratic Party and attracted new groups to it. Since he was able to appeal directly to the people, he gave them a sense of purpose. He was the leader the American people needed in the 1930s.

From 'America Past and Present' by R. Divine, T. Breen, G. Fredrickson & R. Williams, 1995

Source E *New Deal cartoon (2)*

QUESTIONS

1. **Was the New Deal a success? Using the information in this section, explain your answer.**
2. **Using Sources A, C and D make a list of the successes and failures of the New Deal. Which successes/failures were most important? Explain why.**
3. **Mr Donner (Source A) was just one of the three million workers employed by the WPA in the 1930s. How valuable are his comments for historians?**
4. **What points are being made by each of the cartoons in Sources B and E?**

Themes

The Communist leader Lenin fell ill in 1922. In March 1923, he suffered a stroke which paralysed his right side and deprived him of speech. In January 1924, he died. After Lenin's death, the history of the Soviet Union was dominated by the personality and actions of one man - Joseph Stalin (Stalin was not his real name. It means 'man of steel'). By the 1930s, Stalin had built up a personal dictatorship as autocratic and cruel as anything experienced under the Tsars. For this reason, Stalin has often been described as the 'Red Tsar'. This chapter explores three key themes in the development of Stalin's control over the Soviet Union. It starts by looking at why Stalin (who was not very well known in 1922) was able to outmanoeuvre his more famous rivals in the power struggle which followed Lenin's death. By examining Stalin's personality and position in the Communist Party, it is possible to explain how he successfully schemed his way to the leadership of his party and country.

Second, the chapter examines the ruthless policies Stalin used to modernise the Soviet economy. Stalin believed that the West wanted to destroy Communism. Unless Soviet industry and agriculture rapidly caught up with the West, he argued, the country would be crushed in a future war. The human costs of this 'second revolution' were enormous. And third, the chapter considers how Stalin built up his own personal power and kept control. Propaganda produced by the Soviet government presented an image of Stalin as a god-like figure. But, in reality, he used brutal means to remove anybody whom he regarded as a political threat. The chapter focuses on the following questions.

* Why did Stalin and not Trotsky emerge as Lenin's successor?
* What were the aims and effects of the collectivisation of agriculture?
* What were the aims and effects of the Five Year Plans?
* How did Stalin control the Soviet Union?
* What was it like to live in Stalin's Russia?

Key Events

1924 ---------------- **Power Struggle** ---------------- ▶ 1929

Joseph Stalin
(real name: Joseph Djugashvili)

Stalin uses his influential position as General Secretary of the Communist Party to build up his own support and play off other rivals against each other. Stalin successfully isolates Trotsky as his main competitor. Stalin had Trotsky exiled to Siberia in 1928. In 1929 he expelled him from the Soviet Union.

Leon Trotsky
Many thought he would take over from Lenin

1928: Launch of the First Five Year Plan to build up heavy industry. Stalin aims to modernise rapidly and to strengthen the economy. This policy is sometimes called 'socialism in one country'. Industrialisation continues until 1941.

1929-37 ------------- **Collectivisation** ------------- ▶ 1937

1934 ◀--------- **Purges and show trials** --------- ▶ 1938

УДАРИМ ПО КУЛАКУ

АГИТИРУЮЩЕМУ ЗА СОКРАЩЕНИЕ ПОСЕВА

Stalin forces small peasant farms to merge into large 'collectives'. The aim is to make agriculture more efficient in order to support the programme of rapid industrial growth in the Five Year Plans. Opponents of this policy (known as 'kulaks') were arrested or shot.

1934: Murder of Kirov, leader of the Leningrad Communist Party, who was starting to emerge as a possible rival to Stalin. The murder was planned by Stalin but also used by him as an excuse to purge ('clean out') the whole Party of rivals and possible opponents. In 1940 Trotsky was assassinated in Mexico City.

VISITEZ L.U.R.S.S. SES PYRAMIDES!...

The caption of this French cartoon reads 'Visit the Soviet Union's pyramids'.

1941

Stalin: the 'Red Tsar'

Source 1 — A historian's view of Stalin

In 1929, five years after Lenin's death, Soviet Russia embarked upon its second revolution - a revolution engineered and run by Stalin alone. In its scope and immediate impact upon the life of some 160 million people, the second revolution was even more sweeping than the first. It resulted in Russia's rapid industrialisation. It forced more than 100 million peasants to abandon their small, primitive farms and to set up collective farms. It ruthlessly tore the wooden plough from the hands of farmers and forced them to grasp the wheel of modern tractors. It drove tens of millions of illiterate people to school and made them learn to read and write. The rewards of the revolution were outstanding. But so was its cost - the complete loss, by a whole generation, of spiritual and political freedom. The changes introduced by Stalin seem to dwarf anything else in Russia's history. But Stalin was no giant. He was a very different leader from the leaders of the October revolution. Lenin and Trotsky predicted their revolution and their ideas fertilised the soil of Russia, making it ready for the harvest of 1917. Not so with Stalin. He was forced into revolution by immediate dangers. But, once he had started, he continued his journey almost without resting. Behind him were tramping millions of weary and bleeding Russian feet, a whole generation in search of socialism in one country.

Adapted from 'Stalin' by Isaac Deutscher, 1966

Source 2 — Lenin and Stalin

Photographs like this one taken in 1922 were later published to give the impression that Lenin and Stalin had worked closely together (some people have even argued that photographic experts added Stalin to this photo later). In fact, Stalin had only played a minor role in the planning of the October revolution and, afterwards, Lenin had grown suspicious of him. Before his final illness, Lenin wrote: 'Stalin has concentrated an enormous power in his hands; but I am not sure that he always knows how to use that power with sufficient caution.' Stalin managed to prevent Lenin's views becoming widely known and he began to create the myth that he had been Lenin's close companion and was his 'natural heir'.

Source 3 — A portrait of Stalin

A socialist realist portrait of Stalin painted in 1949. All the arts were forced to follow this official style. Stalin was usually painted as a father-like figure whose only concern was the wellbeing of the Russian people. The painter of this portrait was A.P. Bubnov.

QUESTIONS

1. What, according to Source 1, were the main features of Stalin's 'second revolution'?

2. What do Sources 2 and 3 tell us about Stalin's character and way of ruling?

3. Judging from Sources 1-3 and your knowledge of Russia before the revolutions of 1917, would you agree with the view that Stalin was a 'Red Tsar'? Explain your answer.

Why did Stalin and not Trotsky emerge as Lenin's successor?

When Lenin died in January 1924, few people imagined that Stalin would emerge as his successor. Trotsky was the obvious favourite in a field which also included Kamenev, Zinoviev and Bukharin. Between 1924 and 1929 there was a power struggle between these rivals. By 1929, however, a clear victor had emerged - Stalin. Stalin was able to defeat his rivals for a number of reasons. First, there was his personality. Stalin was cunning and ruthless in his handling of the opposition. Trotsky and the other rivals, on the other hand, made tactical mistakes and did much to isolate themselves from potential supporters. Second, there was a battle of ideas. Stalin cleverly outmanoeuvred his rivals by arguing that his idea of 'socialism in one country' naturally followed on from the policies of Lenin. And third (and probably most important), Stalin was General Secretary of the Communist Party. The Communist Party was the most powerful force in Russian politics. As General Secretary of the Party, Stalin could appoint supporters to key posts and therefore block his rivals' paths to power.

Stalin's personality and tactics

Stalin quickly capitalised on the opportunity provided by Lenin's death. Once he had managed to prevent the publication of Lenin's testament (see Box 6.1), he began a series of double-dealings, designed to clear his own path to power. His aim was to play the leading rivals off against each other. At first, he identified Trotsky as his main rival (see Box 6.2) and allied himself with Kamenev and Zinoviev. Their support enabled him to sack Trotsky as War Commissar in 1925. He then turned against Kamenev and Zinoviev. Allying himself with Bukharin and Rykov, he attacked them for supporting Trotsky's idea of 'permanent revolution' (see paragraph 2, top of p.121). These attacks forced Kamenev and Zinoviev closer to Trotsky and this made it seem that Stalin had been right to criticise them. In 1927, Trotsky, Kamenev and Zinoviev were all expelled from the Politburo (Cabinet) and Communist Party. In a final twist, Stalin then turned against Bukharin and Rykov. He claimed that they were opposed to his plans for economic modernisation and sacked them.

This photograph was taken in 1926 at the funeral of Dzerzhinsky, founder of the Cheka (secret police). All those carrying the coffin except Stalin (1) were later eliminated. Key victims were Rykov (2), Trotsky (3), Kamenev (4) and Bukharin (5). Zinoviev (6) was also a victim.

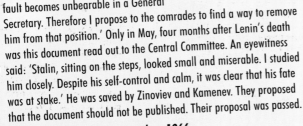

Box 6.1

Lenin's testament, 1922

On 25 December 1922, already seriously ill, Lenin made his last will and testament, criticising a number of leading Communists, including Stalin and Trotsky. On 4 January 1924, Lenin added the following:

Lenin in 1923

'Stalin is too rude and this fault becomes unbearable in a General Secretary. Therefore I propose to the comrades to find a way to remove him from that position.' Only in May, four months after Lenin's death was this document read out to the Central Committee. An eyewitness said: 'Stalin, sitting on the steps, looked small and miserable. I studied him closely. Despite his self-control and calm, it was clear that his fate was at stake.' He was saved by Zinoviev and Kamenev. They proposed that the document should not be published. Their proposal was passed.

From 'Stalin' by Isaac Deutscher, 1966

Box 6.2 Stalin and Trotsky compared

Real name: Joseph Djugashvili

Early life: Born 1879 into a poor peasant family in the remote region of Georgia. Very tough childhood under alcoholic father. Narrow, religious education at training college for priests. Expelled.

Early political activity: 1899 joins revolutionary movement in Georgia.

Role in the party: Follows Lenin into Bolshevik Party in 1903. 1903-17 continues terrorist activity for Bolsheviks. Repeated periods of imprisonment and exile. In 1917 becomes editor of *Pravda* (Party newspaper). Loyalty to Lenin rewarded with post of Commissar for Nationalities in first Bolshevik government. Major role in the civil war. Promoted to General Secretary of Party in 1922.

Real name: Lev Bronstein

Early life: Born 1879 into a moderately prosperous Jewish farming and landowning family. Broad and largely successful modern education in Odessa.

Early political activity: 1897 involved in secret Marxist organisations. Imprisoned.

Role in the party: Broke with Lenin to join rival Menshevik Party in 1903. Leading member until 1917 when he returned from exile to join the Bolsheviks. Became President of Petrograd Soviet and played key role in planning October revolution. Given post of Military Commissar in 1918 and commanded Red Army during civil war. Appointed Commissar of War in 1922.

② A battle of ideas

The power struggle was also a battle of ideas. At first, the battle was between Trotsky's idea of 'permanent revolution' and Stalin's idea of 'socialism in one country'. Trotsky argued that capitalist governments would try to destroy Soviet Communism. Communism could only survive at home if resources were used to promote revolution abroad. Stalin, on the other hand, argued that the priority should be to build up the strength of the Soviet Union. If the Soviet Union was strong, Communism would survive. Resources should be used to strengthen the Soviet economy rather than to promote revolution abroad. When Stalin's view was accepted by the Politburo (Cabinet), the battle turned to how best to run the Soviet economy. Stalin argued in favour of ending the New Economic Policy (NEP - see p.40) and of expanding industry rapidly. Those who supported the NEP (notably, Bukharin and Rykov) lost the battle and were forced to resign.

③ Stalin's position within the Party

In reality, the Soviet Union was a one-party state controlled by the Communists (all members of the government were senior members of the Communist Party - see Source B below). Between 1917 and 1924, the Politburo (Cabinet) appointed Stalin to a series of important jobs in both the Communist Party and the government. As a result, he was able to build up a solid base of Party workers loyal to him. In April 1922, the Politburo appointed Stalin to the new post of General Secretary. This gave him the power to appoint people to carry out the decisions made by the Politburo. Since the people he appointed owed their jobs to him, they tended to support him on the major issues which divided the rivals for the leadership. By 1924, Stalin was the most powerful person in the Communist Party.

Activity
Why did Stalin emerge as Lenin's successor?

Source A *Lenin's testament*

Comrade Stalin, having become General Secretary, has concentrated an enormous power in his hands and I am not sure that he always knows how to use that power with sufficient caution. On the other hand, Comrade Trotsky not only has exceptional abilities (personally, he is, to be sure, the most able man in the present Central Committee), but also is too self-confident and concentrates on the purely administrative side of affairs too much. These qualities of the two most able leaders of the present Central Committee might, quite innocently, lead to a split. As for the others, I will only remind you that Kamenev's and Zinoviev's episode in October 1917 was not accidental [Lenin wanted to launch the revolution immediately, but they argued the time was wrong]. It should not, however, be used against them personally. Nor should Trotsky's non-Bolshevism before 1917 be used against him. Bukharin is not only the Party's best theorist, he is also the Party's favourite. But his theoretical views can only with the very greatest doubt be regarded as fully Marxist.

Lenin's testament, dictated to his secretary on 25 December 1922

Source B *The organisation of the Communist Party in the 1920s*

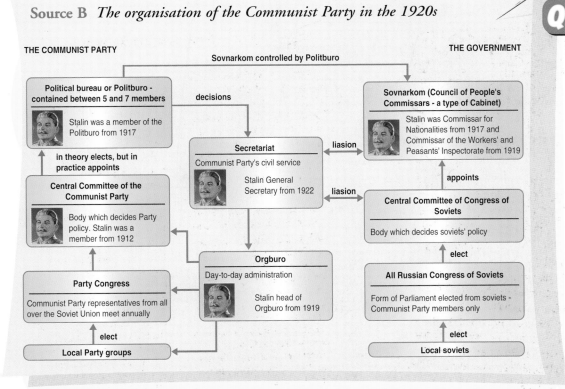

QUESTIONS

1. Why did Stalin and not Trotsky emerge as Lenin's successor? Use the information in this section in your answer.

2. a) Why is Lenin's testament (Source A) an important historical document?
   b) Why did it matter whether Lenin's testament was published or not?
   c) Why do you think leading Communists chose not to publish Lenin's testament?

3. 'Stalin's position in the Communist Party was the most important reason for his victory in the power struggle.' Do you agree? Use Source B in your answer.

What were the aims and effects of the collectivisation of agriculture?

By 1929, Stalin had won the power struggle and cemented his position as Lenin's successor. His personal victory was also a victory for the idea of 'socialism in one country'. As a result, the Soviet government's overriding aim was to modernise and strengthen the Soviet economy. If Soviet Communism was to survive, Stalin argued, Soviet industry must become much more efficient and productive. But this could only be achieved if the long-term problems of agriculture were tackled first. In 1927-28, there was a severe grain shortage in Russian towns. Peasant farmers were either only producing enough for themselves or they were hoarding their produce, waiting for prices to go up. This crisis led to a drastic solution. In 1929, Stalin announced a new programme of 'collectivisation'. All the small pieces of land currently farmed by individual peasants would be taken over by the state and farmed in bigger units. The peasants would live and work together collectively for the good of the state. These big, collective farms ('kolkhoz' and 'sovkhoz') would be mechanised and more efficient. The result would be greater production, better distribution and a surplus which could be exported to pay for the raw materials necessary for industrialisation. The changes planned by Stalin and his colleagues amounted to nothing short of a revolution in the countryside. As a result, historians often describe collectivisation as the 'second revolution'. Since collectivisation was undertaken without taking into account the desires and needs of the peasants, it has also been described as the 'revolution from above'.

1 The economic aims of collectivisation

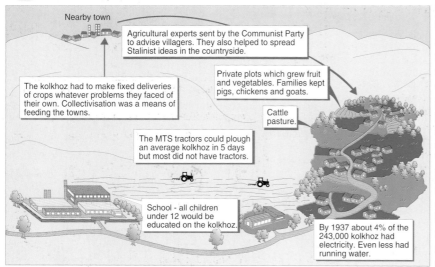

This diagram shows how collective farms (kolkhoz) were organised. From 1929, groups of up to 100 families were forced to pool their land, animals and tools. They would then receive free housing and seed. They were trained and provided with modern equipment (such as tractors) by the local Motor Tractor Station (MTS). They were allowed to cultivate a small plot of their own and to keep a few animals. The government encouraged them to grow cash crops like cotton as well as grain.

In the 1920s, the Soviet Union remained agriculturally backward. Gwyneth Hughes & Simon Welfare point out that: 'Before the October revolution, the great estates and the richest peasants had produced more than two thirds of the grain which went to market. Now the great estates and the rich peasants were no more. The bulk of the grain was produced by ordinary peasants who ate most of what they grew.' (*Red Empire*, 1990). The programme of collectivisation was designed to improve efficiency and output. Small peasant farms were merged into much larger 'kolkhoz' (collective farms) and 'sovkhoz' (state farms). In the kolkhoz, peasants pooled their resources and shared the work and profits. In the sovkhoz, the peasants worked directly for the state. In practice, there was little difference between the two. Both were large enough to make use of tractors (whereas before collectivisation most farms were not) and both had to sell most of their produce to the state at a fixed price.

2 The political aims of collectivisation

Collectivisation had political as well as economic aims. In theory, collectivisation was voluntary. In practice, it met with massive opposition from the peasants. Those with most to lose were the 'kulaks' - better off farmers who had profited from the NEP. In 1929, the government launched an attack against the kulaks. Kulaks were said to be greedy, selfish enemies of modernisation who hoarded their produce to make bigger profits for themselves. A group of 25,000 party workers was sent into the countryside to force the kulaks into submission. Anybody who resisted collectivisation was branded a kulak and punished. Some were sent to labour camps, their land and possessions confiscated. Others were executed on the spot. Historians argue that Stalin created the myth of kulak opposition once it became clear that many peasants would not join collective farms voluntarily. Certainly, the government used collectivisation as a means of extending Communist control over Russian society.

The poster (right) reads: 'We will smash the kulak who tries to reduce the cultivated area'. In a speech made in 1929, Stalin said: 'We must smash the kulaks. We must wipe them out as a class.' Propaganda posters like this encouraged peasants to attack the kulaks. The images played on traditional hatred of Tsarist landlords and many ordinary peasants joined in the violence organised by the 'twenty five thousanders'.

③ The effects of collectivisation

At first, collectivisation was an economic disaster. The pace of change was far too fast. Between December 1929 and March 1930, the government tried to collectivise 60% of all farms. The result was chaos. Peasants resisted by killing their livestock and eating their produce rather than handing it over to the kolkhoz. In addition, by attacking the kulaks, the government destroyed not only the most efficient farmers, but also those most capable of adapting to technological change. In March 1930, Stalin diverted criticism by blaming over-enthusiastic officials. The programme was slowed down and by the end of 1930 official figures suggest that around 20% of all farms had been collectivised. But the damage had already been done. The fall in production and livestock due to peasant resistance or ignorance of new techniques coincided with bad weather and poor harvests. This led to serious famine. In the worst years, 1932-33, historians estimate that 3 million people died (see Box 6.3). They also argue that the disaster was made worse because Stalin refused to take emergency measures (since that would have reflected badly on his planning). Although people were dying of hunger, grain continued to be exported.

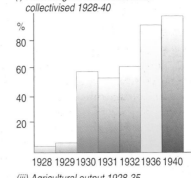

(i) Percentage of farm households collectivised 1928-40

(ii) Number of dead

R I P
Collectivisation 1929-37
Deaths from famine - at least 3 million
Deaths resulting from dekulakisation around 6.5 million

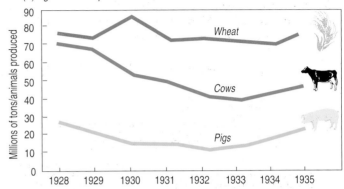

(iii) Agricultural output 1928-35

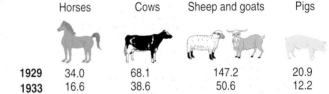

(iv) Number of farm animals 1929 and 1933 (all figures in millions)

	Horses	Cows	Sheep and goats	Pigs
1929	34.0	68.1	147.2	20.9
1933	16.6	38.6	50.6	12.2

Box 6.3   The famine of 1932-33

We arrived at the large village of Petrovo towards evening. There was an unearthly silence. A peasant spoke. 'All the dogs have been eaten, that's why it's so quiet', he said. 'There are hundreds of people here dying of hunger. I don't know how many die each day. Many are too weak to come out of their houses. We've eaten cats, dogs, mice, birds. Tomorrow you will see that the trees have no bark - we've eaten that. And, we've even eaten horse manure. We fight over it. Sometimes there are whole grains in it.'

From 'I Choose Freedom' by V. Kravchencko, 1932

Activity
Collectivisation

Source A   *Stalin's view*

We are advancing full steam along the path of industrialisation to socialism, leaving behind the age-long Russian backwardness. We are becoming a country of metal, a country of cars, a country of tractors. And when we have put the Russian people in cars and the peasants on tractors, let the worthy capitalists who boast so loudly of their 'civilisation' try to overtake us. We shall see then which countries can be classified as backward and which as advanced.

Part of a speech made by Stalin in November 1929

Source B   *A historian's view*

The overwhelming majority of peasants opposed collectivisation. Villages were surrounded by machine guns and forced to collectivise. Masses of peasants were transported to Siberia. Others slaughtered cattle, smashed tools and burned crops rather than bring them into the collective farms. Famine stalked the land.

From J.P. Nettl, 'The Soviet Achievement', 1967

Source C   *A Soviet poster*

A propoganda poster produced in 1930 showing the supposed benefits of collectivisation. The caption reads : 'Day of harvest and collectivisation'.

QUESTIONS

1. Judging from the information in this section, what were the aims and effects of collectivisation?
2. Using Source A explain why Stalin launched a policy of collectivisation.
3. How do Sources A-C differ in their assessment of the impact of collectivisation? Explain your answer.

What were the aims and effects of the Five Year Plans?

Rapid industrialisation was the second part of Stalin's plan to modernise the Soviet Union. The aim was to catch up with the West. Rapid growth in heavy industries (such as coal, iron, steel and oil production) was seen as essential if the Soviet Union was to survive the invasion which Stalin predicted would come from the Soviet Union's capitalist enemies in the West (see Box 6.4). Starting in 1928, Five Year Plans were drawn up. These set targets for the expansion of the economy. In purely economic terms, these plans were successful in achieving self-sufficiency and industrial strength. Indeed, the Soviet Union was transformed into one of the world's major industrial powers. And by the time invasion did come from the West (in 1941), the Soviet Union was able to resist it. However, there was also a considerable human cost involved in attempting to meet the targets set by the Five Year Plans. The emphasis of the Plans was on producing essentials not luxuries. For most workers, living conditions and labour discipline were very harsh.

1 The Five Year Plans

The poster above was produced in 1930. The caption reads: 'Capitalists cannot stop the triumphal march of the Five Year Plan'. German, French and Polish army officers and the Pope are urged on by a capitalist to attack the Soviet Union.

The Five Year Plans, strictly speaking, were not plans at all. Rather, they were a series of ideal targets for output and production set by Gosplan, the central government planning department which had been set up in 1921. Under Stalin's orders, Gosplan drew up a list of targets to be reached by all parts of the Soviet economy. There was very little detailed planning about how the targets were to be met. Rather, it was left to each industry to devise ways of improving production. The plans, started in 1928 and interrupted only by the Second World War, lasted until Stalin's death in 1953. As a result, there were five separate plans, each with a slightly different emphasis (the first focused on iron and steel and electricity whilst the second focused on transport). The historian Alan Bullock points out that, although Stalin demanded the impossible with these plans, 'the magic worked'. The plans captured people's imagination and, even if the targets were not achieved, in every case output went up (see table on p.125).

Box 6.4 — Stalin on industrialisation

No, comrades, the pace must not be slackened. On the contrary, we must quicken it. To slow down means to lag behind. And those who lag behind are beaten. The history of old Russia shows that, because of its backwardness, it was constantly being defeated. If you are backward and weak, then you are in the wrong and may be beaten and enslaved. But if you are powerful, then you are right and people must be wary of you. We are 50 to 100 years behind the advanced countries. We must make good this distance in ten years. Either we do it, or they crush us.

Part of a speech Stalin made to industrial managers in February 1931

2 Propaganda and the stakhanovites

Workers were encouraged to meet the targets set in the Five Year Plans by a propaganda campaign which created an image of a wartime struggle. They were often organised into 'shock troops' and 'brigades' to win various battles for greater production. This produced a genuine commitment, especially in younger workers, which is often overlooked by Western historians. There was even talk of the creation of a new type of individual - the 'homo Sovieticus' (Soviet man). Huge publicity was given to one Ukrainian miner, Alexei Stakhanov, who in 1935 broke all records for coal production. Whilst a team of miners could normally produce seven tons of coal in a six hour shift, Stakhanov (by reorganising the way his team worked) was able to cut

The magazine above shows Alexei Stakhanov in a typical pose, holding his miner's drill.

102 tons. Stakhanov was given superstar status and 'stakhanovite' became the new term to describe workers who achieved similarly heroic feats of production. These stakhanovites quickly developed into a new elite, receiving better housing, health care and wages than other workers.

3 The human cost

As a contrast to the propaganda of the stakhanovite movement, industrialisation also depended on hardship and strict labour discipline. Workers were forced to work long hours, often for very low pay. Pay was further reduced if production targets were not met. Absenteeism was severely punished. By 1940, workers could be dismissed and lose their house and ration card if they were late for work without good reason. Criticism of the system was dangerous because of secret police informers. The fear of stepping out of line was increased by the treatment of so-called 'saboteurs'. Trials were held in which a number of workers were found guilty of deliberately trying to sabotage the Five Year Plans (by breaking machinery, for example). Some were executed. Others were sent to the forced labour camps (gulags). Prisoners from the gulags were themselves an important source of cheap labour for the Five Year Plans.

4 The results of the Five Year Plans

In purely economic terms, the Five Year Plans were a remarkable achievement (see table below). Although the official Soviet figures may be unreliable, it is clear that in just over ten years the Soviet Union became a major world industrial power. Historians are divided about whether this growth could have been achieved without relying on fear and force (see p.132). Many historians, however, point out that the Soviet Union's impressive industrial growth occurred at the same time that the Great Depression hit the capitalist world. Whatever the sacrifices and hardships suffered by Soviet workers, most were better off than the millions of unemployed in Germany, Britain and the USA.

An analysis of the results of the Five Year Plans

Product	Output in 1928	Output in first Five Year Plan 1928-33			Output in second Five Year Plan 1933-37			Output in third Five Year Plan 1937-41		
		A	B	C	A	B	C	A	B	C
Coal (million tons)	36.0	76.2	65.3	64.0	155	130	128	168.6	-	150
Steel (million tons)	4.0	10.6	6.0	6.0	17.3	18	18	18.6	-	18
Oil (million tons)	1.7	22.4	21.1	21.0	47.5	29	26	31.6	-	26
Electricity (million kilowatts)	18	-	-	20	-	-	80	-	-	90

Column A = target   B = Official Soviet figures   C = Western estimate

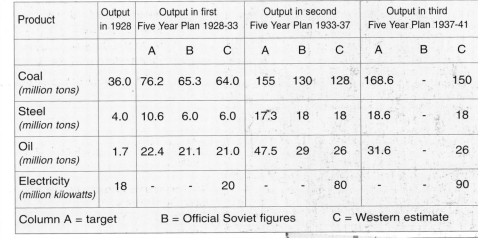

These two pictures show the development of Sverdlosk in the Ural Mountains. The top photo was taken in 1928 and the bottom in 1933.

This photo shows how prisoners from the gulag prison camps played a vital role in the drive for industrialisation. Many major projects relied on workers working by hand. For prisoners, working and living conditions were very hard and many died.

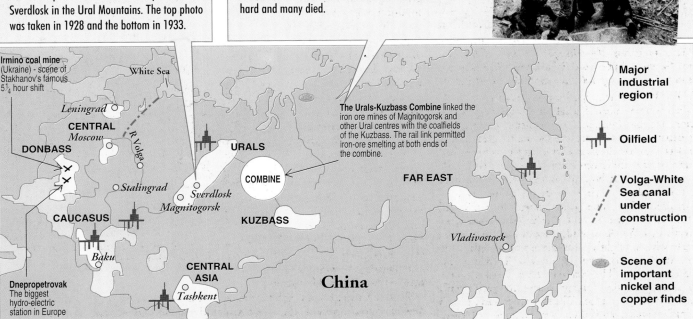

Irmino coal mine (Ukraine) - scene of Stakhanov's famous 5¼ hour shift

White Sea

Leningrad

CENTRAL
Moscow

DONBASS

R. Volga

Stalingrad

URALS

COMBINE

Sverdlosk
Magnitogorsk

KUZBASS

CAUCASUS

Baku

CENTRAL ASIA

Tashkent

China

FAR EAST

Vladivostock

The Urals-Kuzbass Combine linked the iron ore mines of Magnitogorsk and other Ural centres with the coalfields of the Kuzbass. The rail link permitted iron-ore smelting at both ends of the combine.

Dnepropetrovak
The biggest hydro-electric station in Europe

Major industrial region

Oilfield

Volga-White Sea canal under construction

Scene of important nickel and copper finds

Activity
The achievements of the Five Year Plans

Source A *A historian's view (1)*

Waste and inefficiency were often as great as on the collective farms. There were constant breakdowns and valuable machinery was left to rust or was ruined by unskilled operators, many of them peasants who had hardly seen a machine before. Many thousands lost their lives because of lack of safety precautions or froze to death in the cold. Food was short, conditions primitive, life cheap. But the difference from collectivisation is clear. With all its shortcomings and failures, Soviet industry under the Five Year Plans achieved a quantum leap. It was only during the second Five Year Plan that the worst mistakes began to be corrected and the hardships began to be relieved. But it was during the first plan that the foundations were laid. The historian Roy Medvedev says that 1,500 big enterprises were built, including the largest power station in Europe. New sectors of industry were established which had not existed in Tsarist Russia (such as car and tractor manufacture) and new centres were built.

From 'Hitler & Stalin: Parallel Lives' by A. Bullock, 1991

Source B *A Soviet poster*

Source C *An eyewitness account*

Tatiana Fedorova led a team of stakhanovites who helped to build the Moscow Metro. 'No one forced you to do it,' she says, 'everyone wanted to be a stakhanovite. It is very hard to explain, but it was a time of enthusiasts. Everyone was trying to do their best for the motherland. It was such a good time. There wasn't much to eat, we weren't well dressed, we were simply very happy.' They felt they were making an important contribution.

From 'People's Century' by G. Hodgson, 1995

Source D *Industrial growth compared*

1913

	Russia	USA	Britain	Germany	France
Pig iron	4.8	30.9	10.3	19.3	5.2
Steel	5.2	31.3	7.7	18.3	4.7
Coal	36	509.9	287	190	40.8

1940

	Soviet Union	USA	Britain	Germany	France
Pig iron	14.9	31.9	6.7	18.3	6.0
Steel	18.4	47.2	10.3	22.7	6.1
Coal	164.6	359	227	186.6	45.5

All figures in millions of tons
Pig iron   Steel   Coal

Source E *A historian's view (2)*

As a result of the collectivisation programme many peasants left the land, hoping to find jobs in industry. Despite emergency measures, it was impossible to train them properly. The result was a great deal of inefficiency as well as accidents to people and machinery. Peasants were not used to factory discipline. By tradition, they tended to slacken their efforts once their earnings covered their necessities. After a certain point, they preferred leisure to money. They were also used to working hard and long at certain seasons and taking things easy at other times. This attitude was transferred to industry. New workers did not always realise that work could go on when it rained or that punctuality was essential.

From 'Endurance and Endeavour' by J.N. Westwood, 1973

QUESTIONS

1. a) Judging from the information in this section, what were the aims of the Five Year Plans?
    b) To what extent did the Five Year Plans achieve their aims? Use Sources A-E in your answer.

2. Using Sources A and E describe the problems that had to be overcome if the Five Year Plans were to be a success.

3. Write a caption to go with the poster in Source B.

4. Tatiana Fedorova (Source C) was just one of many thousands of workers who built the Moscow Metro. How useful are her comments for historians studying the Soviet Union in the 1930s?

Stalin's manipulation of the past

Stalin's victory in the power struggle and his economic programme of the 1930s required an ability to control political opposition and to generate uncritical support. Central to his project was the need to be seen as Lenin's 'natural' successor. Such an image would increase his status and power. To achieve this image, Stalin encouraged the creation of myths (for example, the myth that he had worked closely with Lenin at the time of the October revolution). He also manipulated historical records and works of art. In 1927, for example, the film director Sergei Eisenstein was instructed by Stalin to re-edit his film 'October' (see p.37) so that scenes showing the importance of Trotsky in the October revolution were cut. Similarly, Trotsky's picture was removed from photographs and he was portrayed as a villain in official texts. This manipulation of the past is one symptom of the 'totalitarian' nature of the state which Stalin created. A totalitarian state is a state which lacks many of the civil rights which are taken for granted in democracies (for example, freedom of speech) and which relies heavily on the police and spies to keep control.

Two versions of a famous photograph taken in 1920. Both versions show Lenin speaking from a podium. The original (left) includes Trotsky and Kamenev standing to the right. But, after Trotsky and Kamenev fell from favour, the photo was retouched by photographic experts so that the two men had disappeared (right). The doctored photograph then appeared in the History textbooks used in schools in the Soviet Union.

This painting shows Lenin meeting Stalin in Finland in December 1905. There is, however, no evidence that this meeting actually took place. The painting was painted by I. Vepkhvadze in the late 1930s. It is one of many examples of paintings produced to reinforce the myth that Stalin worked closely with Lenin before and during the October revolution. This particular meeting is supposed to have taken place during a Bolshevik Party Conference.

3 An extract from a Soviet textbook

Trotsky, enemy of the people, and his disgusting friends organised gangs of murderers and spies in the Soviet Union. They caused train collisions in the Soviet Union and blew up and set fire to mines and factories. They poisoned workers and did all the damage they could.

Extract from an official textbook issued to all Soviet schools in 1938

QUESTIONS

1. What do the sources on this page tell us about Stalin's methods of government?

2. Explain how the purpose behind all three sources is linked.

3. What do these sources tell us about the difficulties historians face when writing about the Soviet Union under Stalin?

4. Using the sources on this page write an account of Stalin's rise to power (a) as Stalin would have wanted it and (b) as it really was.

How did Stalin control the Soviet Union?

By defeating his political rivals and gathering power into his own hands, Stalin was able to set up a totalitarian state (a state which lacks many of the civil rights which are taken for granted in democracies, such as freedom of speech, and which relies heavily on the police and spies to keep control). Indeed, by 1930, Stalin was, in effect, a dictator - what he said was treated as law and he himself made all the important decisions. But, although Western historians have tended to emphasise the brutality of Stalin's regime, it is important to recognise that he did not rely on terror alone to stay in power. For many people, both inside the Soviet Union and abroad, Stalin was seen as a heroic figure who could do no wrong. Throughout his years in power (he remained in power until his death in 1953), he was a genuinely popular leader. It was only after his death that the full extent of the suffering he caused became widely known. This section examines how Stalin managed to persuade people to admire him while, at the same time, using force and brutality against many Soviet citizens.

1 Propaganda and the cult of personality

After the October revolution, many artists, writers and musicians began to experiment with new ways of painting, writing or composing. But Stalin soon put a stop to these developments. From the late 1920s, Soviet artists, writers and musicians were forced to follow the official cultural policy known as 'socialist realism' (see Box 6.5). This policy was designed to ensure that all works of art supported the aims and values of the state. The idea was that works of art (whether paintings, sculptures, novels, poems or performances of music) would inspire people to work together for Communism. But the result was that the freedom of artists, writers and musicians to choose their own style or subject matter was lost. They were forced to produce propaganda or to face unemployment, imprisonment or even execution. The result was that, in the 1930s, propaganda became the main form of Soviet culture. At first, socialist realism concentrated on the model Soviet citizen. But, increasingly, it was Stalin himself who became the main subject of writers and artists. This led to the deliberate development of a 'cult of the personality' (Stalin was portrayed as a god-like figure and people were encouraged to believe that he was some kind of superhuman). This cult of the personality kept people in their place and encouraged them not to be critical (see Box 6.6).

Box 6.5   Socialist realism

(i) Socialist realism defined

The main aim of socialist realism was a realistic description of life. But because the Communist Party had its own view of life, socialist realism turned into crude and lifeless propaganda. Writers had to write about the achievements of the Five Year Plans and other 'significant' subjects or at least write realistic historical novels. More important, black was to be made black and white white with no shades in between. The Soviet hero was to be a paragon of virtue with no inner conflicts. Instead of the grim world around them, authors were urged to see things as they should appear and will appear. Pessimism was banned.

From 'A History of Russia' by N.V. Riasanovsky, 1993

(ii) Socialist realism in art

An example of socialist realist art. This painting was produced in 1937 by V.N. Yakovlev. It shows gold-diggers writing a letter to Stalin to thank him for the new constitution of 1936.

(iii) Socialist realism in poetry

After 1932, all writers had to be members of the government-controlled Writers' Union in order to get their work published. This poem from Avdienko appeared in *Pravda*, the government-controlled newspaper, in 1936.

> O great Stalin. O leader of the peoples
> Thou who broughtest men to birth
> Thou who makes fruitful the earth
> Thou who restorest the centuries
> Thou who makest bloom the spring
> Thou who makest vibrate the musical chords
> Thou splendour of my spring, O thou
> Sun reflected by millions of hearts.

Box 6.6

The cult of personality

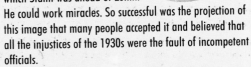

The way Stalin projected himself is instructive. During the 1920s he was the only true apostle of Lenin. Gradually, Stalin became the equal of Lenin. The slogan 'Stalin is the Lenin of today' marked the next stage in which Stalin was ahead of Lenin. He could work miracles. So successful was the projection of this image that many people accepted it and believed that all the injustices of the 1930s were the fault of incompetent officials.

From 'Stalin and Stalinism' by M. McCauley, 1994

2 The Party and the 1936 constitution

Control of the Communist Party was the key to controlling Soviet society. Party workers volunteered to carry out government programmes - for example, collectivisation (see p.122). The Young Communist League (Komsomol) educated and entertained those aged 14 to 28. And, the Party remained the body through which Stalin governed the Soviet Union. The power of the Party was strengthened in 1936 by a new constitution, described by Stalin as 'the most democratic in the world'. In theory, it guaranteed rights. In practice, it was a sham. Although everyone over 18 could vote, only Communist Party candidates could stand for election to the new two tier Parliament (the 'Supreme Soviet'). Besides, the Supreme Soviet only met for two weeks a year. Day-to-day decisions continued to be made by the Sovnarkom which was controlled by the Politburo. In fact, people lost power at local level since local soviets were no longer able to pass laws themselves. They were bound by the decisions of the Supreme Soviet.

A cartoon drawn by a Russian who fled from the Soviet Union to Paris in the 1930s.

3 The control of education

Under the Tsars, over half the Russian population had been illiterate and there was no state system of schooling. In 1922, schools began to be built and a campaign to end adult illiteracy began. The census of 1926 showed 49% of people over the age of 10 were illiterate. By 1939, this figure had fallen to 19%. Also by 1939, a network of elementary schools covered the country. The system was shaped to further Stalin's aims. Teaching was closely monitored and the curriculum was designed to encourage pride in and loyalty to the Soviet Union's achievements. There was strict censorship. Former pupils have recalled how they were ordered to paste cardboard over the photographs of disgraced Communist leaders in their History textbooks. Sometimes people were instructed to burn books. In 1938, the main official textbook became *A Short History of the Communist Party* written by Stalin himself and providing his version of events.

4 The attack on religion

Religious belief was a potential obstacle to Stalin's control of the Soviet Union. The Russian Orthodox Church was very popular and therefore a rival to the new 'faith' of Communism. Stalin accelerated the attack on the Church which had begun immediately after the October revolution. Priests were blamed for the peasants' opposition to collectivisation. Many churches were destroyed or put to new uses (one was even turned into a Museum of Atheism - atheists are people who do not believe in any god). Attacks on church-goers were organised by the 'Godless League' - an official Communist Party group. Priests were given a hard time, losing many of their rights and being forced to pay higher taxes. This religious persecution was later extended to Muslims in central Asia. The caption on the poster above from 1930 reads: 'Religion is a poison. Protect the children.'

This poster was produced in 1923. The main caption reads 'Help the school'. It celebrates the building of new schools. The school in the poster has a metal shop and wood shop on either side of the classroom. The children criticise older people who refuse to join in.

5 Russification

The sheer size of the Soviet Union meant that it included many different ethnic groups and many areas which could make claims to be independent nations. This was a threat to Stalin whose aim was to centralise control into his own hands in Moscow. During the 1930s, therefore, Stalin attempted to destroy the cultures of the separate republics which made up the Soviet Union. This policy was known as 'Russification' and had several features. First, the study of the Russian language was made compulsory in all schools. Second, army recruits were stationed far away from their homeland. Third, leading nationalist politicians, writers and artists were imprisoned or executed during the Purges (see below). The politicians were simply replaced by officials from Moscow. And fourth, Stalin also ordered the deportation of thousands of people to different regions of the country.

6 The Purges

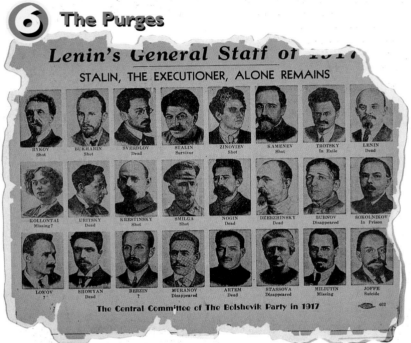

This picture was published by supporters of Trotsky in 1938. It shows how the Purges affected the Bolshevik 'old guard'. By 1938, the only member of the Bolshevik Central Committee of 1917 to retain a position of power was Stalin himself. Whilst fear of rivals might explain why Stalin took measures against former colleagues, it does not explain why the Purges affected so many ordinary people. Historians have put forward a number of theories to explain why the Purges took place (see Box 6.7).

Although Stalin did not rely only on terror to keep control, there was a distinct move in that direction after the murder of Sergei Kirov, leader of the Leningrad Communist Party, in December 1934. Kirov was an excellent speaker known to be critical of the pace of economic change. He was a popular figure who was starting to emerge as a possible challenger to Stalin. Many historians are now convinced that Stalin himself was responsible for organising his murder. Certainly, the murder was a turning point. Beginning in 1935, Stalin began to 'purge' (clean out) Soviet society by eliminating opponents and potential opponents. He began by attacking the 'old guard'. Old rivals like Kamenev and Zinoviev were arrested, put on trial and forced to confess in public to crimes against the state (these trials became known as 'show trials'). They were then executed. Once the Purges started, they gained a momentum of their own. Soon every local Communist Party was weeding out members who had opposed Stalin. Those accused were arrested and either imprisoned in the 'gulags' (labour camps) or executed. The historian Nicholas Riasanovsky writes: 'The purges spread and spread, affecting virtually all Party organisations and government branches, the army (where Marshal Tukhachevsky and seven other top commanders perished at the same time) and almost every other prominent institution including the political police itself.'

Victims of the Purges

The historian Alan Bullock notes that on a single day, 12 December 1938, Stalin approved the execution of 3,167 prisoners. The purge of the army was particularly severe - 228 out of 272 commanding officers and 41,000 out of 43,000 junior officers were arrested and either shot or sent to the camps.

Box 6.7 Explanations of the Purges

1. Stalin felt increasingly insecure because of the problems of collectivisation and the popularity of Kirov. He decided, therefore, to remove all real and imaginary threats.

2. Far from being insecure, Stalin was actually showing just how complete his control was over both the Party and the country. He used the Purges to prove to everybody how powerful he was.

3. The Purges went too far and continued for too long for them to be explained as a carefully worked out policy of control. They suggest that Stalin was paranoid to the point of mental illness and had become unbalanced.

4. Although Stalin started the process, it gathered a momentum of its own as over-enthusiastic officials became carried away. Stalin himself was not, therefore, wholly responsible for the extent of the Purges.

5. Stalin needed cheap labour to complete the great industrial projects which would ensure that the Soviet Union became a major world power. By filling the gulags, he made sure that there was a plentiful supply of cheap labour.

6. Stalin calculated that the Purges would encourage people to be obedient and to work hard to achieve the aims he had decided were in their best interest.

Activity
The show trials

Source B The trial of Zinoviev and Kamenev

This photograph shows the state prosecutor, Andrei Vyshinsky, summing up at the first major show trial - that of Zinoviev, Kamenev and other party officials. They were charged with terrorist crimes, including the murder of Kirov, and of being Trotskyists. Much of the evidence in the show trials was invented and the defendants made public confessions of their guilt. Kamenev, in a final appeal, addressed his sons, saying: 'No matter what my sentence will be, I in advance consider it just. Don't look back. Go forward. Together with the Soviet people, follow Stalin.' All the defendants were sentenced to death and executed within 24 hours.

Source A The mad dog of Fascism

This cartoon was drawn by Boris Yefimov. It shows a dog whose two heads are Trotsky and Bukharin. Trotsky, living in exile in the 1930s, was portrayed as the great enemy of the Soviet Union. Many victims of the Purges, including Bukharin, were accused of being Trotskyists (Bukharin was tried in the last great show trial in 1938 and then executed). The cartoonist Boris Yefimov, whose brother had been shot in the Purges, was the official cartoonist at Bukharin's trial. Stalin himself dictated the subject for each cartoon. Boris Yefimov's feelings about Stalin, like many others who experienced first the revolution and then the dictatorship, were mixed. 'We lived in a kind of nightmare. We saw his brutality. And at the same time you had to lower your head because Stalin must know best. It was like a terrible god who ruled us. We had to obey. We didn't judge. We didn't argue.'

From 'People's Century' by G. Hodgson, 1995

Source C An American cartoon

This cartoon shows the 'old guard' confessing to Stalin that they were guilty of the crimes read out by Vyshinsky (right).

Source D A historian's view

Of the endless trials, public and secret, four were of the greatest importance (the trial of Kamenev, Zinoviev and 14 others in August 1936, the trial of 17 Party officials in January 1937, the secret trial of army commanders in June 1937 and the trial of Rykov, Bukharin and others in March 1938). Among the men in the dock were all the members of Lenin's Politburo (except Stalin and Trotsky), one ex-premier, several vice-premiers, the chief of the trade unions, the chief and top commanders of the army, most Soviet ambassadors and two chiefs of the secret police. All were charged with attempting to assassinate Stalin, to restore capitalism, to wreck the country's economic and military power and with having entered into secret agreements with the Nazis. If these charges had been true, it would have been impossible to account for the survival of the Soviet state.

Adapted from 'Stalin' by Isaac Deutscher, 1966

Source E Bukharin's confessions

Prosecutor: Do you admit that the anti-Soviet organisation of which you are a member engaged in counter-revolutionary activity with the aim of overthrowing the leadership?
Bukharin: Yes. I admit it.
Prosecutor: Do you admit that this organisation engaged in terrorist activities and encouraged kulak uprisings against the leadership?
Bukharin: It is true.

Extract from the show trial which involved Nikolai Bukharin in March 1938. Two years earlier Bukharin had been responsible for drafting the new constitution.

QUESTIONS

1. Judging from the information in this section, how did Stalin control the Soviet Union?
2. a) What were the 'show trials'? Use Sources A-E in your answer.
   b) Why do you think the show trials took place?
3. Judging from Sources A and B why do you think there was so little resistance to the Purges?

What was it like to live in Stalin's Russia?

The impact of Stalin's rule on the everyday life of ordinary Russians may not be quite as clear-cut as it first seems. The most obvious image is that of an increasingly terrorised and controlled society, living in almost constant fear of arrest. As was indicated in the previous section, brutality reached horrifying proportions during the Purges of the late 1930s. Most families were either caught up in the Purges directly or had friends or relatives who were arrested. As a result, some historians have argued, the people of the Soviet Union lived in a constant state of fear and there was little resistance to Stalin's demands because people were terrified. Other historians, however, have modified this picture in the belief that the economic changes of the 1930s were not achieved by terror alone. They argue that, for at least part of the population, living standards improved during the 1930s and there were positive benefits. To say that terror alone explains what it was like to live in Stalin's Russia, these historians argue, is too simplistic. This section explores both these viewpoints.

1 A terrorised and controlled society

This poster says: 'For your holiday, visit the Soviet Union, land of freedom'.

Some historians argue that, in the late 1930s, the Soviet Union became a police state. The whole population was terrified of the secret police and their informers (see Box 6.8). The main feature of ordinary people's lives was fear. One author points out that: 'The only purpose of terror is to make people afraid. To plunge the country into a state of fear the number of victims must be huge. On every floor of every building there must be several apartments from which the tenants have suddenly been taken away. The remaining inhabitants will then be model citizens for the rest of their lives.' (*Hope Against Hope* by N. Mandelstam, 1971).

2 Stalinism - a necessary force for modernisation?

Few Western historians (and few Soviet historians after Stalin's death) have tried to defend Stalin's brutal methods of political control. But some do argue that Stalin's programme of modernisation was both necessary and genuinely popular where it led to long-term benefits (see Box 6.9). They also point to the situation in the rest of the world in the 1930s where, due to the Great Depression, there was mass unemployment and poverty (see Box 6.10).

Box 6.8   Living in terror

They came in the middle of the night. They might be brutal, they might be polite. They searched the flat and bundled the suspect away to the local jail. Prisoners were crowded into filthy cells. In one case in November 1937, 140 men squeezed into a cell designed for 24. People went down with dysentery, scurvy, pneumonia. Then came the interrogation. The usual method was 'the conveyor belt'. A team of officers took it in turns to interrogate a suspect around the clock. They could break almost anyone in a few days. But this was expensive in terms of manpower. It was replaced on 17 August 1937. From now on, people were simply beaten up. Everyone had to confess something and everyone had to denounce someone. One Armenian priest denounced all the parishioners he had buried in the last three years.

Adapted from 'Red Empire' by G. Hughes & S. Welfare, 1990

Box 6.9

Stalin's achievements

In the Soviet Union of the early 1920s hunger was everywhere. Industrial production was extremely low. There were serious rebellions in the army and in the countryside. There was almost no electricity outside large cities. Agriculture was based on tiny plots and medium-sized farms seized by kulaks who forced peasants back into wage labour. Health care was non-existent. The majority of people were illiterate. When Stalin died in 1953, the Soviet Union was the second greatest industrial, scientific and military power in the world and showed signs of overtaking the USA. This was despite the huge losses suffered defeating the Fascist powers. The various peoples of the Soviet Union were united. Starvation and illiteracy were unknown. Agriculture was productive. Medical care of the highest quality was available, free, to all citizens. Education was free. There was no unemployment.

From 'Essential Stalin' by B. Franklin (an American historian and member of the Communist Party of the USA), 1973

Box 6.10

Stalinism in perspective

This photo shows a hunger march in Britain in 1936. Mass unemployment in the 1930s caused widespread poverty throughout the capitalist world. The Soviet Union's economic success in the 1930s, on the other hand, was seen abroad either as a threat or as a reason to support the spread of Communism.

3 A changing society

These two photos show how much life had changed in the Soviet Union by the 1930s. The photo on the left shows a Communist 'christening' where a Party official replaces the priest and the ceremony takes place under the Communist Party flag. The photo on the right shows a group of 'Young Pioneers' (part of the Young Communist League). As well as organising activities and entertainment, this organisation educated young people in the values of the Communist Party.

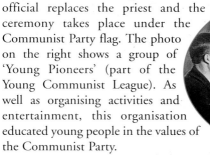

Activity
Women in Stalin's Russia

Source B *Poster produced in 1931*

The caption on this poster reads: 'Working woman in the struggle for socialism and the struggle against religion'. The poster divides the past from the future. The past was a dark age where priests kept women in their place and drunken men beat them. The future is bright. Women make an important contribution, like the architect pictured here.

Source A *An eyewitness account*

The 1920s was a particularly exhilarating time for women, as new laws were passed to give them equality with men. Ella Shistyer taught Muslim women in Uzbekistan, one of the southern republics which became part of the Soviet Union. 'At the same time as teaching them to sew, we told them about equality', she explains. 'They were real slaves. The revolution provided the opportunity for education and culture.' It also brought Ella new opportunities. 'The revolution gave me the right to feel equal with any man. It gave me the right to work, to study as I wanted.' She decided to become an electrical engineer. 'I didn't want just to draw up plans. I wanted to build an electric power station. That was my mission and I achieved it.' She achieved it during the 1930s. 'I loved Stalin from my whole heart', she said, 'I would work enormously long hours and I gave all my strength, all my soul into this.' But, like many others who had worked so hard for Stalin, Ella was sent to prison in Siberia. 'I remember how I used to lick the ice off the metal screws and bolts inside the wooden cattle truck, fearing only that my tongue would stick to them. That's how we travelled for nearly a month.'

From 'People's Century' by G. Hodgson, 1995

Source C *A historian's view*

The first decade or more after the October revolution was full of promise for Soviet feminists (supporters of equality for women). There were new opportunities for Soviet women, perhaps most notably and permanently among Islamic women. In employment and education, it is true, progress towards equality continued into the 1930s. The total number of women workers rose from 24% in 1928 to 39% in 1940. The number of women in higher education rose from 28% in 1927 to 43% in 1937. But these changes mainly resulted from a labour shortage. Most women were channelled into the least skilled and lowest paid jobs with the poorest promotion prospects. Any profession which became dominated by women (such as medicine) became low paid and had low status. There were few women in managerial or skilled positions. Also, paid employment did not ease the burden at home. Soviet men rarely did domestic chores.

From 'Depression and Dictatorship' edited by A. Briggs, 1993

QUESTIONS

1. Using the information in this section, write an account of life in Stalin's Russia.

2. Judging from Sources A and C, what were the positive and negative aspects of women's lives in Stalin's Russia?

3. What does Source B tell us about the official attitude towards women in the early 1930s? Would you say that the poster's message is accurate? Explain your answer.

Themes

The turning point in the interwar years was the Wall Street Crash of October 1929 (see p.100). This led to a worldwide economic slump (the 'Great Depression'). In Germany, this provided the conditions for the Nazis' rise to power (see chapter 4). As soon as they had won power, the Nazis pursued an aggressive foreign policy designed to destroy the postwar settlement (as laid down in the Treaty of Versailles) and to make Germany a major world power again. By the mid-1930s, hopes that the League of Nations would be able to prevent conflict had been dashed. Instead of working through the League, the other Great Powers in Europe, Britain and France, responded to German aggression by adopting a policy of 'appeasement'. The idea was that, by making concessions (giving in to demands), this would satisfy the party making the demands and prevent a major

conflict breaking out. The trouble with this policy was that Hitler interpreted it as a sign of weakness. He took advantage of British and French reluctance to go to war by occupying more and more territory. In September 1938, the British Prime Minister, Neville Chamberlain, persuaded Hitler to sign an agreement to keep the peace. When Hitler broke this agreement in March 1939, appeasement was seen to have failed. British and French policy hardened and war soon followed. This chapter examines the following questions.

* What was the policy of appeasement?
* Why did the League of Nations fail in the 1930s?
* Was Hitler's foreign policy to blame for the Second World War?
* Was the policy of appeasement justified during the Czechoslovakian crisis of 1938-39?
* Why did the Second World War break out in 1939?

Key Events

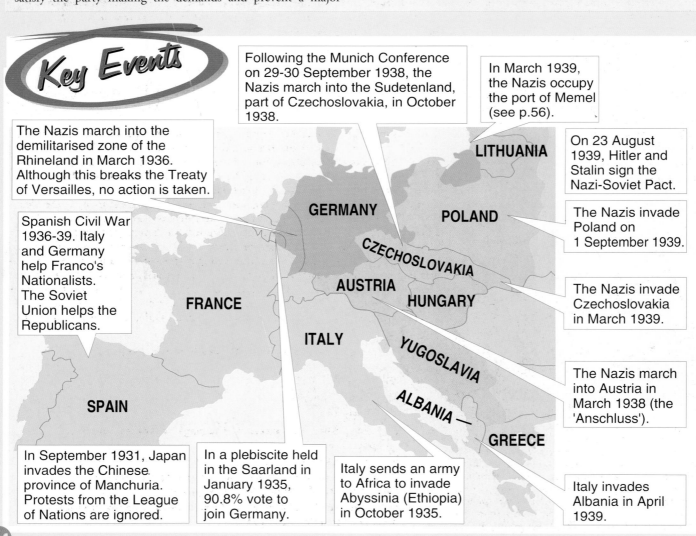

Following the Munich Conference on 29-30 September 1938, the Nazis march into the Sudetenland, part of Czechoslovakia, in October 1938.

In March 1939, the Nazis occupy the port of Memel (see p.56).

The Nazis march into the demilitarised zone of the Rhineland in March 1936. Although this breaks the Treaty of Versailles, no action is taken.

On 23 August 1939, Hitler and Stalin sign the Nazi-Soviet Pact.

Spanish Civil War 1936-39. Italy and Germany help Franco's Nationalists. The Soviet Union helps the Republicans.

The Nazis invade Poland on 1 September 1939.

The Nazis invade Czechoslovakia in March 1939.

The Nazis march into Austria in March 1938 (the 'Anschluss').

In September 1931, Japan invades the Chinese province of Manchuria. Protests from the League of Nations are ignored.

In a plebiscite held in the Saarland in January 1935, 90.8% vote to join Germany.

Italy sends an army to Africa to invade Abyssinia (Ethiopia) in October 1935.

Italy invades Albania in April 1939.

LITHUANIA
GERMANY
POLAND
CZECHOSLOVAKIA
AUSTRIA
HUNGARY
FRANCE
ITALY
YUGOSLAVIA
ALBANIA
GREECE
SPAIN

What was the policy of appeasement?

OVERVIEW

Source 1 — British cartoon from 1938

The cartoon (right) was published on 25 September 1938, at the height of the Czechoslovakian crisis (see pp.144-45). The cartoon sums up the difficulties produced by the policy of appeasement. The British Prime Minister, Neville Chamberlain, strongly believed in appeasement. Here, he is trying to steer the world from 'chaos' to 'peace' along a plank (marked 'Czech crisis'). The plank looks as if it is about to break. The rocks below are marked 'war'. The cartoonist suggests that hopes of peace hung in the balance.

Source 2 — A historian's view (1)

Since 1945, the term 'appeasement' has come to mean any policy that is weak. But this was not the case in the 1930s. Standard dictionaries before the Second World War defined appeasement as 'a way of keeping the peace by soothing, quieting, calming'. The aim in international politics was to reduce tension and to promote harmony. In the 1930s, this meant giving in to those demands from Nazi Germany which seemed reasonable. Postwar dictionaries, however, added new meanings. Appeasement came to mean 'gaining peace by buying off other countries' and 'the giving up of principles to avoid war'. The changed view resulted from Neville Chamberlain's failure to keep the peace. Appeasement had begun as a policy where concessions were offered from a position of strength. But at the Munich Conference in September 1938 (see pp.144-45), Chamberlain gave in to Hitler's demands from a position of weakness. In return for a promise of peace, Czechoslovakia was broken up and non-Nazis were transferred to Nazi rule.

From 'British Appeasement in the 1930s' by W.R. Rock, 1977

Source 3 — A historian's view (2)

Why was the British government not prepared to take stronger action against Hitler in 1936 when he invaded the Rhineland and showed so clearly he intended to destroy the Treaty of Versailles by force? One reason was that the British government had been unhappy about the Treaty of Versailles from the beginning. Many people believed it was too harsh and, in some parts, unjust. They worked to revise the Treaty throughout the 1920s. Also, the memory of the devastation of the First World War remained strong. Governments were determined to do all they could to avoid being dragged into a conflict again. Support for disarmament and the League of Nations came from the churches, members of all political parties and from many newspapers. Unfortunately, the League failed to stop Japan's invasion of Manchuria and Italy's invasion of Abyssinia (see pp.136-37). By working to revise the Treaty of Versailles, British governments had followed a policy of appeasement towards Germany since 1919. Before 1930, Britain had been in control. By the mid-1930s, however, Britain was in a weaker position and, under Hitler, Germany went on the offensive.

From 'The Origins of the Second World War' by R. Henig, 1985

Source 4 — Peace in our time

This photo was taken on 30 September 1938, just after Neville Chamberlain had arrived in Britain following the Munich Conference. He is holding up an agreement made between himself and Hitler which, he claimed, meant 'peace in our time' (see Source A on p.145). At the Munich Conference, Chamberlain agreed to let the Nazis occupy part of Czechoslovakia. Six months later, Hitler broke his promises and invaded the remaining part of Czechoslovakia.

QUESTIONS

1. a) Judging from the sources on this page, what was the policy appeasement?
   b) Why has the meaning of the word 'appeasement' changed?

2. What problems arose as a result of pursuing a policy of appeasement? Use Sources 1-3 in your answer.

3. Using Sources 3 and 4 explain why the policy of appeasement was popular in Britain in the 1930s.

Why did the League of Nations fail in the 1930s?

The League of Nations had been successful in a number of ways in the 1920s (see pp.54-56). Many people in the early 1930s still believed that the League was the best hope for maintaining peace through 'collective security' (nations acting together within the framework of the League). But the rise of dictators like Mussolini and Hitler and of governments dominated by the army like that of Japan threatened the League. If these governments did not get their own way, they either ignored the League or walked out of it. The first major crisis for the League came with the Japanese invasion of Manchuria (a part of China) in 1931. Condemned as an aggressor, Japan left the League in 1933, successfully keeping control of Manchuria. The most serious crisis, however, came in 1935 when Mussolini ordered the invasion of Abyssinia (modern Ethiopia). Although the League applied economic sanctions against Italy, the Italian army continued with the conquest of Abyssinia and Italy then walked out of the League. It now seemed clear that the League was powerless to stop aggression. This was underlined by the failure of the League to take any effective action in the Spanish Civil War (1936-39). Indeed, in the crises which led to the Second World War between 1936 and 1939, the League was more or less ignored.

 ## The Manchurian crisis, 1931-33

Manchuria is a province in north China (see map on p.217). In the 1920s, Japan had built up a strong influence in the area, including ownership of the South Manchurian railway. In 1931, young Japanese army officers guarding the railway caused an explosion along its line and blamed 'Chinese terrorists'. Using this as an excuse, the Japanese army began the conquest of Manchuria. This was complete by December. The Japanese then set up as a puppet ruler the last Emperor of China (who had been overthrown in 1911 - see p.219). The area was renamed 'Manchukuo'. The Chinese government accused the Japanese of aggression and took the matter to the League of Nations. The League set up the **Lytton Commission** to investigate the complaint. In the Lytton Report, published in October 1932, this Commission found that the Japanese were indeed guilty of aggression. The League accepted the Lytton Report (only Japan voted against) and agreed to refuse to recognise the new Manchurian government. Japan was asked to hand the area back to China, but it refused and withdrew from the League. No further action was taken. The League was in a weak position. The Great Powers in the area, apart from Japan, were the USA and the Soviet Union, but neither were in the League (the Soviet Union joined in 1934). Also, most of the world was suffering from the effects of the Great Depression. To many Europeans especially, Manchuria seemed a remote and unimportant area. Refusal to act, however, was a serious blow to the prestige of the League. It gave the impression that force could succeed.

This cartoon, published in Germany on 22 January 1933, comments on the Manchurian crisis. The League is shown as an old woman. A child representing Japan is about to stab a child representing China whilst other states (the Soviet Union and Italy) look on, waiting to see what happens. The caption shows that the old woman is weak and feeble. All she can do is say: 'Tut, tut, Japan, you should warn Auntie next time you want to start a little war.' The cartoon suggests that the League has lost control and lacks strength.

Box 7.1 — The Manchurian crisis

a) Japan had ignored the covenant of the League of Nations. If nobody was prepared to use force to uphold this covenant, the League counted for nothing. Of course, the issue was confused, but the covenant bound League members not to go to war until the League had examined their claim. Japan had simply ignored this. The lesson was not lost on Germany and Italy. Smaller European states felt alarmed by the League's failure in its first confrontation with a major power.

From 'Europe 1880-1945' by J.M. Roberts, 1970

b) Britain showed no desire to risk making an enemy of Japan by trying to remove it from an area of no great importance to Britain. Some officials in London even welcomed Japan's interest in northern China as it kept them away from the area which stretched from Hong Kong to Singapore, a region of great commercial and military importance to Britain. The tame condemnation of Japanese aggression by the Lytton Commission reflected Britain's wish to appease Japan. The League's actions were confined to gestures of disapproval - such as the refusal to recognise the passports and postage stamps of the puppet state of Manchukuo.

From 'The Twentieth Century World' by W.R. Keylor, 1992

2 The Abyssinian crisis and the League

In October 1935, Mussolini ordered the invasion of Abyssinia (modern Ethiopia). Italy had an interest in one of the few areas of Africa which remained uncolonised. Indeed, in 1896 Italian troops had been defeated by Abyssinian forces at the Battle of Adowa. This was a humiliation which Mussolini hoped to avenge. Italy held the neighbouring colonies of Eritrea and Somaliland (see map, right) where their forces could be built up and a victory against the ill-equipped Abyssinians seemed an easy way for Mussolini's Fascist government to win prestige. The invasion was, however, a clear case of aggression by one member of the League of Nations against another. Following the Italian invasion, the ruler of Abyssinia, Emperor Haile Selassie, appealed to the League for help. In October 1935, the League condemned Italy as an aggressor and decided to impose economic sanctions (penalties). The aim was to force Italy to agree to the League's request to stop the invasion. Imports from Italy into League countries were banned and loans to and the export of some raw materials to Italy were forbidden. But it was difficult to make the sanctions bite because, first, some raw materials essential for Italy (such as oil) were not included. Second, countries outside the League (such as the USA and, by then, Germany) continued to trade with Italy. Third, the British government did not close the Suez Canal to Italian ships. And fourth, the British and French governments supported the sanctions in public, but, in private, the two Foreign Ministers drew up a plan for the division of Abyssinia, giving Italy two thirds of the country. This plan, the **Hoare-Laval Pact** (named after the two ministers), was leaked and had to be dropped after a public outcry. Nevertheless, it showed that the two Great Powers in the League were anxious to appease Mussolini, hoping to keep his support against the greater danger of Germany. Mussolini continued the invasion and by May 1936 the conquest was complete. In June 1936, despite Haile Selassie's appeal (see Box 7.2), the League voted to end sanctions against Italy. The next year, Italy left the League.

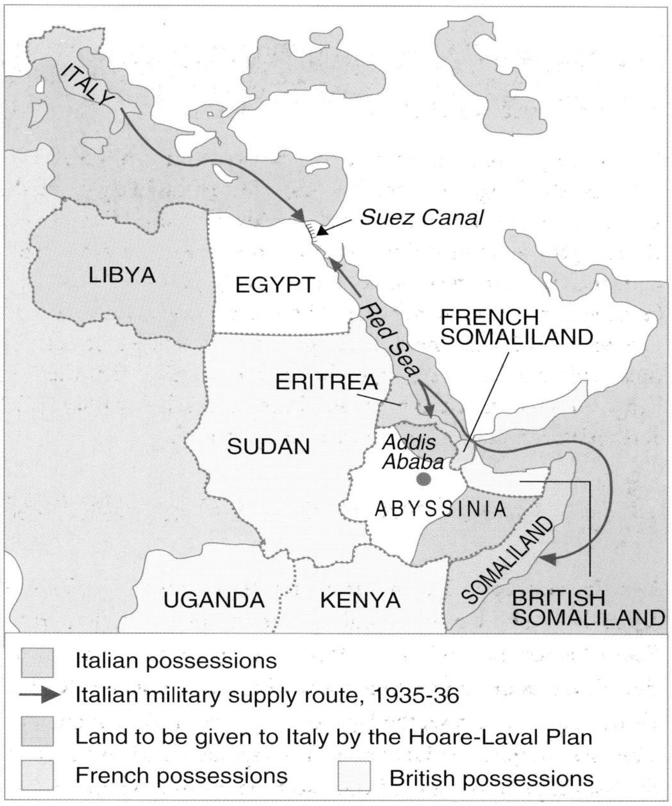
ITALY
Suez Canal
LIBYA
EGYPT
Red Sea
FRENCH SOMALILAND
ERITREA
SUDAN
Addis Ababa
ABYSSINIA
SOMALILAND
UGANDA
KENYA
BRITISH SOMALILAND
Italian possessions
Italian military supply route, 1935-36
Land to be given to Italy by the Hoare-Laval Plan
French possessions
British possessions

The Abyssinian crisis, 1935.

Box 7.2 Haile Selassie's appeal to the League

The issue before the Assembly today is a much wider one than the removal of sanctions. It is not merely a settlement of Italian aggression. It is a question of collective security, of the very existence of the League. It is a question of trust in international treaties and of the value of promises to small states that their independence be respected. In a word, international morality is at stake. I ask the Great Powers who have promised the guarantee of collective security to small states - what measures do they intend to take?

Part of Haile Selassie's speech to the Assembly of the League of Nations, 30 June 1936

3 The Spanish Civil War and the fading of the League

The failure of the League over Abyssinia came at a time when a new threat to peace appeared in Europe itself. The Spanish Civil War began in 1936. Strictly speaking, a civil war was outside the powers of the League, but several European states sent arms and even troops to support either Franco's Nationalists or the Republicans. When the Republicans complained to the League about the aid Italy and Germany were giving to Franco, the complaint was publicised through the League, but the League failed to take any action. It was now little more than a 'talking shop'. By 1937, Japan, Germany and Italy had all left the League. The idea of collective security through membership of the League had disappeared. In Europe, the League could do nothing as Hitler tore up the Treaty of Versailles. In Asia, the League was a bystander as the Japanese invaded northern China in 1937. Between 1937 and 1939, membership of the League declined in Europe as the dictators became more successful. Austria, Czechoslovakia and Albania disappeared after being conquered. Hungary withdrew in 1939, followed closely by Spain (now ruled by Franco). Ten of the 20 Latin American states had withdrawn by 1939. When the Second World War began in September 1939, the League was ignored. It continued a shadowy existence during the war until it was replaced by the United Nations in 1945 (see pp.178-79).

Activity
Why did the League fail?

DOORMAT

This cartoon shows Japan trampling over the League (whose headquarters was in Geneva). Britain's Foreign Secretary, Sir John Simon, is applying 'face-saving' powder. Britain strongly opposed the use of sanctions against Japan.

Source B *Contemporary comment*

There are, inside and outside the League, two ideas about how best to preserve peace. There is the idea that, when a state announces a policy based on aggression, the League has not only the right but the duty to declare loudly and clearly that it will fight such a policy with every means at its disposal. There should be brought into play the collective action provided by Article 16 [which allowed the use of both economic and military sanctions]. There is, however, another idea. This says the aggressor should be treated with consideration and recommends that conversations and negotiations should be carried on. Also, no collective action should be taken and no questions should be raised at the League - because the aggressor does not like that, takes offence, sulks. Unfortunately, this is just the policy that so far has been pursued towards the aggressors. It has had as its consequence three wars [Manchuria, Abyssinia and Spain] and threatens to bring a fourth.

Part of a speech made at the League of Nations Assembly by M. Litvinov, Soviet Foreign Minister, in September 1938 (the Soviet Union joined the League in 1934)

Source C *Cartoon produced in October 1935*

"THE STRENGTH OF A CHAIN IS THAT OF ITS WEAKEST LINK"

This cartoon was drawn shortly after it was announced that sanctions were to be imposed against Italy in an attempt to stop Mussolini's invasion of Abyssinia. The French Foreign Minister, Laval (centre), did not really support sanctions and he is drawn as the weak link in the chain. His arm is attached to Anthony Eden, Minister for League of Nations Affairs (he succeeded Hoare as Foreign Secretary in December 1935) and his legs are linked to the Soviet Foreign Minister, M. Litvinov.

Source D *A historian's view*

From the beginning, the League placed too much reliance on verbal protest and it overestimated the importance of economic sanctions. It operated on the unrealistic assumption that all nations were equal and should have an equal say in world problems. The League was only as strong as its members. But membership of the League was never more than partial. The League looked more like an Anglo-French alliance than a genuine world body. But the real reason for the failure of the League goes deeper. Governments existed for the purpose of safeguarding what they saw as their national interests. They were willing to support the League's ideals only for as long as these appeared to be in their interest. In practice, the old methods of diplomacy and the old state system continued, little altered. The League seemed no more than a kind of moral window-dressing to disguise the lack of a true world spirit.

From 'International Affairs' by E.G. Rayner, 1983

QUESTIONS

1. **Judging from the information in this section, why did the League of Nations fail in the 1930s?**

2. **Using Sources A-D describe the League's main weaknesses.**

3. **What do the cartoons in Sources A and C tell us about the problems faced by the League and how they were being dealt with?**

4. **What evidence is there in Source B to support the views expressed in Source D?**

The cartoons of David Low

Throughout the 20th century, political cartoons have been published in newspapers and magazines which have a mass circulation. Although these cartoons are published to provide humour and light relief, they often also have a serious point to make. Today, cartoons from the past can be of particular use to historians because they provide a view of events which is contemporary (produced at the time) and which, on many occasions, is very different from that found in official sources. In the 1930s, one of the best known political cartoonists in the world was David Low. Low was born in New Zealand in 1891 and moved to Britain after the First World War. He worked for the London *Evening Standard* from 1927-50 and later for the *Daily Herald* and *Manchester Guardian*. During his career he produced over 14,000 cartoons, many of which were circulated in newspapers all round the world. He died in 1963. In the 1930s, Low had a very clear point of view. He believed in freedom and democracy and he hated dictatorship. He was also convinced that the policy of appeasement was weak and unlikely to succeed. In interviews, Low said that he thought that cartoonists should not just set out to amuse their audience. They should try to educate public opinion. He hoped that, by making Hitler and Mussolini look ridiculous, he could encourage opposition to them.

This cartoon was published on 18 October 1933, just eight months after the Nazis had gained power in Germany (see pp.72-74). On 14 October 1933, Germany announced that it had decided to leave the League of Nations. Mussolini, Daladier (French Prime Minister) and John Simon (British Foreign Secretary) look out of the windows. An unused water hydrant is marked 'economic sanctions'.

Extract from a biography of David Low

The period up to the Second World War was Low's heyday. The clear issues of the time suited his style. The *Evening Standard* was an excellent base from which to work. In 1934, a survey showed that the *Standard* was very definitely the favourite paper of the wealthier classes of London and the South East. It was the right paper for Low, the thinking man's cartoonist. Soon after Hitler came to power, Low drew a cartoon of a bonfire outside the League of Nations building [see left]. Beaverbrook newspapers [which owned the *Evening Standard*] were immediately banned from Germany. The cartoon, of course, was then printed around the world. In 1935, the *Evening Standard* and *Manchester Guardian* were banned in Italy too because of a Low cartoon about Hitler's attitude to Mussolini's policy in Abyssinia [see below]. In 1937, the question of Low was taken up with the Foreign Secretary, Lord Halifax, when he visited Germany for talks. Hitler was furious about Low's attacks. On his return, Halifax explained the position to Low and Low 'played it in a less personal key' for a few weeks. Nazi troops then marched into Austria. Low felt his restraint had been pointless. Shortly afterwards, the German government made a formal protest to the Foreign Office about Low's cartoons.

From 'David Low' by C. Seymour-Ure & J. Schoff, 1985

This cartoon was published on 10 May 1935. The 'girls' are Goebbels (Nazi Propaganda Minister), Hitler and Goering (Nazi Minister of Aviation). They are happy because Mussolini has gone off to Africa, leaving Europe to them.

QUESTIONS

1. Look at the Low cartoons on this page and on pages 138 and 143. What conclusions can you draw about Low's political views?
2. Why do you think newspapers containing Low cartoons were banned from Germany and Italy?
3. Using the cartoons on this page describe the skills that a political cartoonist needs.
4. Look at today's newspaper and find a political cartoon. What are the similarities and differences between the modern cartoon and the Low cartoons?
5. What difficulties do historians face when using cartoons as a source of historical information?

Hitler's rise to power in 1933 was a turning point in terms of foreign policy as well as in terms of domestic policy. Hitler was a nationalist (he wanted Germany to be a strong nation again) and he made no secret of his hatred of the Treaty of Versailles. As a result, when the Nazis took control, they abandoned the attempts made by governments in the Weimar era to improve Germany's image abroad. Instead, a new, hardline approach was adopted. Looking back at the period 1933 to 1939, it is possible to find a pattern. Nazi foreign policy developed in stages, becoming more and more adventurous as it chalked up more and more successes. This has led historians to ask two important questions. First, did Hitler have a set plan in 1933 which he then proceeded to carry out or is it more likely that he responded to events, adjusting his aims according to the particular circumstances in which he found himself? And second, who should be held responsible for the outbreak of the Second World War in 1939 - Hitler for his aggressive foreign policy or the other European leaders for their failure to take measures against him? As in most discussions about the origins of the Second World War, the issue of appeasement is central.

Hitler's foreign policy objectives

Hitler began to develop his ideas on foreign policy well before he came to power in 1933. He shared the view of many Germans that the Treaty of Versailles was unjust and must be revised. He also argued that all Germans should be united in one country and that German power, including its armed forces, should be restored. In his autobiography *Mein Kampf*, he said that Germany needed 'lebensraum' (living space) which could only come from expansion in the east, especially at the expense of the Soviet Union (see Box 7.3). This fitted with the Nazis' hatred of Communism - an important feature in their rise to power. Some historians argue that when the Nazis came to power, Hitler had a set plan for achieving these goals which he began to put into practice. Other historians argue that these goals remained long-term objectives which Hitler hoped to achieve if the right circumstances came along.

Box 7.3

Hitler's foreign policy goals, 1924

Germany has an annual increase of population of 900,000. The difficulty of feeding these new citizens must increase year by year and end in catastrophe unless ways are found to avoid the danger of starvation and misery. Only a sufficiently large space on this earth can ensure the independent existence of a nation. The geographical size of a nation is of importance not only as a source of the nation's foodstuffs and raw materials, but also from political and military standpoints. The gaining of land and soil is the objective of our foreign policy. We National Socialists are taking off where we left off 600 years ago. We are putting an end to the perpetual German march to the south and west of Europe and turning our eyes towards the land in the east. However, when we talk of new land in Europe today, we must mainly bear in mind Russia and the border states next to it. Destiny itself seems to wish to point the way for us here by delivering Russia over to Communism. For centuries, Russia drew its strength from the Germanic element of its ruling class. It has now been replaced by the Jew. The end of that Jewish domination will be the end of Russia as a state.

From 'Mein Kampf' by A. Hitler, 1924

Rearmament

LAST POST OR REVEILLE ?

The British cartoon (above), published in September 1935, suggests that it might have been a mistake to allow the Germans to rearm. It shows the League of Nations surrounded by German guns. The League is not sure whether German rearmament is the end of the matter (the 'last post') or the beginning of a new conflict (the 'reveille').

In October 1933, just six months after gaining power, the Nazi government announced that Germany was to withdraw both from a Disarmament Conference organised by the League of Nations and from the League itself. At the same time, rearmament began secretly in Germany (the Treaty of Versailles had limited the size of the army and navy and banned an air force). By March 1935, Hitler was confident enough to announce in public that conscription (compulsory military service) was to be reintroduced in Germany, the army was to grow to 600,000 troops and an air force was to be set up. This was a blatant attack on the Treaty of Versailles, but Hitler judged that there was a general mood in Europe that the Treaty had been harsh on Germany and that concessions should be made. When leaders from Britain, France and Italy met in Stresa in April 1935, the only action they took was to agree to act together if any other clauses in the Treaty were broken (the **Stresa Front**). Hitler's gamble on rearmament had paid off. This was confirmed in June 1935 when Britain signed a Naval Agreement with Germany. Germany agreed to limit its navy to 35% of the size of the British navy. But this was a far bigger navy than that set by the Treaty. This gave other countries the impression that Britain was happy to allow Germany to break the Treaty.

3 The invasion of the Rhineland in 1936

In January 1935, a plebiscite (referendum) was held in the Saarland and 90% of people voted to rejoin Germany. This was a step allowed by the Treaty of Versailles. But then, in March 1936, the German army marched into the demilitarised zone of the Rhineland (see map on p.46). This broke the terms both of the Treaty of Versailles and of the Locarno Treaty (see p.67). The demilitarised zone had been created to reassure the French whose constant worry after the First World War was the revival of German military power. For the Germans, therefore, the reoccupation of the Rhineland was a risky policy. The German army was unprepared if the action led to war. But Hitler took a gamble that there would be no military opposition. The timing was important - Britain, France and Italy were all distracted by the dispute over Abyssinia and the League of Nations was in crisis. Also, France was facing a general election. Besides, the French army was stationed

German troops march across the Hohenzollen Bridge in Cologne into the Rhineland zone on 8 March 1936.

along the Maginot Line (a series of fortifications along the French border) and there were no plans for a rapid counter-attack in the Rhineland. Equally, Britain was not prepared for action. The British government felt that Germany had a case for the revision of the Treaty of Versailles and that the Rhineland was Germany's 'backyard'. Public opinion in both Britain and France was still strongly opposed to war. As a result, no action was taken and Hitler scored an easy triumph. Since 1936, historians have debated whether decisive action then might have stopped further German expansion and even prevented the Second World War breaking out (see Box 7.4).

Box 7.4 — Historians and the invasion of the Rhineland in 1936

a) The remilitarisation of the Rhineland presented the British and French with their first real opportunity to check Hitler's ambitions, but they chose not to do so. In their view, German occupation of German territory was not a significant threat to the balance of power. Britain and France still believed they had enough power to protect themselves and believed that the existence of that power was enough to deter Hitler from aggression. They guessed wrong. Hitler was only impressed by the use of military power, not by the mere existence of arms and manpower.

From 'Twentieth Century European History' by W.L. Kleine-Ahlbrandt, 1993

b) The historian Cameron Watt regards it as a myth to think that the Rhineland crisis was the last great opportunity to overthrow or stop Hitler without a second world war. Watt and his supporters do not believe Hitler would have withdrawn without a fight. Their view is that, in the event of French resistance, the Germans would have carried out a 'fighting retreat'. The French invasion would have been treated as a declaration of war and would have led to a Franco-German war - unless Hitler's nerve had failed him.

From 'Hitler and the Rhineland, 1936' by N. Hederson in 'History Today', October 1992

4 Hitler and the Spanish Civil War

Germany and Italy both provided aid to Franco at crucial points in the Spanish Civil War. For example, German aircraft were used to take Franco's forces from North Africa to Spain right at the start of the war and, later, the Condor Legion provided Franco with 15,000 German troops and air superiority. German military advisers and money also helped Franco to win. Unlike Mussolini, however, Hitler carefully limited the resources given to Spain. He used the war as a trial ground to test out his armed forces, especially the air force (Luftwaffe). The war was also used for propaganda purposes. A victory for the Republicans would have meant an enemy for Fascism and, probably, a close ally with France. In Germany, therefore, the war was portrayed as a battle against a Communist Republic supported by the Soviet Union. The feebleness of the non-intervention policy backed by Britain and France also encouraged Hitler to believe that Western democracies would do little to resist further Fascist advances. The Soviet cartoon, right, shows Mussolini and Hitler shovelling soldiers and military equipment into Franco's mouth. Mussolini says: 'The Devil! The less success he has, the more his appetite grows.' The cartoon was produced in September 1938. A year later, the war was over and Franco was in power.

The Hossbach Memorandum

The Hossbach Memorandum is a very important historical document. It is the account of a meeting held between Hitler, senior ministers and military commanders on 5 November 1937 (the account was written down by Hitler's military adviser, Friedrich Hossbach, five days later). The meeting was held to discuss problems about the pace of rearmament. Hitler, however, spoke for over two hours about the circumstances in which he would go to war against Austria and Czechoslovakia and the probable attitudes of other states to German military aggression (see Box 7.5). The document was used at the Nuremberg trials in 1945 as proof that the Nazis had carefully planned the steps which led to the Second World War. More recently, however, some historians have questioned whether the document really is a blueprint for action. They suggest that Hitler's main aim was to persuade the people at the meeting that they should act with greater urgency or Germany would lose its military advantage.

 **The Hossbach Memorandum**

Actually, the Fuhrer believed that almost certainly Britain and probably France as well had already written off Czechoslovakia and had accepted that this question would be cleared up in due course by Germany. It would, of course, be necessary to maintain a strong defence on our western frontier during the carrying out of our attack on the Czechs and the Austrians. And, it had to be remembered that the defences of the Czechs were growing stronger and the quality of the Austrian army was increasing. Germany simply had to act before 1945. Otherwise, it would lose its military advantage, owing to rearmament elsewhere. The takeover of Czechoslovakia and Austria would mean the gain of foodstuffs for 5-6 million people. The incorporation of these two states within Germany would mean shorter and better frontiers, the freeing of forces for other purposes and the possibility of creating 12 new divisions in the army. The Fuhrer saw this all coming nearer and he would take advantage of it even as early as 1938.

From the 'Hossbach Memorandum', 10 November 1937

 The Anschluss

One of the clauses in the Versailles Treaty which was much resented in Germany was the clause forbidding a union (Anschluss) between Germany and Austria. In 1934, the Austrian Nazi Party was encouraged by the German Nazis to overthrow the Austrian government and the Austrian Chancellor, Dolfuss, was assassinated. But, Mussolini, who wanted to keep his Austrian neighbour independent, moved troops to the Austrian border and Hitler decided to take no further action. During the Spanish Civil War, Germany and Italy moved closer together and in October 1936 they signed an agreement known as the **Rome-Berlin Axis**. Italy was to look for expansion southwards. Germany's area of interest would be central and eastern Europe. This paved the way for union between Germany and Austria. At first, the German government worked towards voluntary union by encouraging Austrian Nazis to put pressure on the Austrian government. When this failed, the Austrian Chancellor, Schuschnigg, was summoned to Germany and bullied by Hitler into taking two leading Nazis into his government - one as Minister of the Interior and therefore in charge of the police and the other as Foreign Minister. When Schuschnigg returned home he decided to hold a plebiscite (referendum) so that the people could decide whether Austria should remain independent. Hitler was furious. A few days later (in March 1938), German troops invaded Austria and the Anschluss was announced (see photo below, left). The only response from Britain and France was a formal protest at this latest breach of the Treaty of Versailles. Hitler was now encouraged to look for further 'living space' at the expense of Czechoslovakia and Poland (see map, below).

Nazi troops march through Vienna after the Anschluss.

A map from a German atlas, 1936. Hitler's aim was to unite all German-speaking people and those who had a German culture (way of life).

Activity
Did Hitler plan World War II?

Source B *A historian's view (1)*

It is necessary to distinguish between Hitler's role in carrying out German foreign policy and his personal responsibility for the goals of the policy itself. As far as carrying out the policy is concerned, Hitler's leading role is clear. When conscription was introduced in 1935 and when the Rhineland was invaded in 1936, it was Hitler who decided the timing and it was Hitler who used his propaganda skills to ease the fears of the other powers. It is over the goals of foreign policy that doubts arise. Because Hitler played a leading role in foreign affairs, it does not necessarily mean that he followed some master plan of his own invention. Hitler wanted to prepare the way for eastward expansion one day. But against that, it could be argued that, in practice, Hitler acted within the same framework as Stresemann in the 1920s. Like Stresemann, for example, Hitler's first objective was to secure revision of the Treaty of Versailles and the restoration of German territory. It is true that, after 1937-38, there was an acceleration of the pace of German foreign policy. This was forced on the Nazi leadership by economic, military and diplomatic factors.

From 'Hitler' by W. Carr, 1978

Source C *German expansion 1933-39*

The Nazis march into the demilitarised zone of the Rhineland in March 1936. Although this breaks the Treaty of Versailles, no action is taken.

Following the Munich Conference on 29-30 September 1938, the Nazis march into the Sudetenland, part of Czechoslovakia, in October 1938.

In March 1939, the Nazis occupy the port of Memel (see p.56).

On 23 August 1939, Hitler and Stalin sign the Nazi-Soviet Pact.

The Nazis invade Poland on 1 September 1939.

The Nazis invade Czechoslovakia in March 1939.

The Nazis march into Austria in March 1938 (the 'Anschluss').

Spanish civil war 1936-39. Italy and Germany help Franco's Nationalists. The Soviet Union helps the Republicans.

In a plebiscite held in the Saarland in January 1935, 90.8% vote to join Germany.

Source D *A historian's view (2)*

Hitler never wavered from his view that the 'living space' Germany required was to be found in eastern Europe and western Russia. This region could supply the food and raw materials Germany needed. It was also inhabited by two 'racial' groups that Hitler detested and was determined to destroy - the majority of Slavs and the minority of Jews. Hitler's policy towards the other Great Powers of Europe can be understood in terms of this single-minded goal of extending Germany's living space eastwards. With Britain, Hitler had no quarrel so long as it remained outside continental affairs. Hitler's policy was therefore different from that pursued in the Weimar Republic. Some historians have seen continuity in foreign policy throughout the interwar period. But this overlooks Hitler's numerous unofficial references to his expansionist policies. The revision of the Treaty of Versailles was just the first step in Hitler's grand design. It was the prelude to conquering and exploiting the vast expanses of the territories to the east.

From 'The Twentieth Century World' by W.R. Keylor, 1992

QUESTIONS

1. Judging from the information in this section, do you agree that Hitler's foreign policy was to blame for the outbreak of the Second World War? Give reasons for your answer.

2. Does it matter whether Hitler had a master plan? Use Sources A- D in your answer.

3. Write a caption which explains what is happening in Source A.

4. On what points do Sources B and D (a) agree and (b) disagree? Which do you think is a better interpretation? Use evidence in this section to support your view.

5. Using Source D, describe Hitler's foreign policy 1933-39.

Neville Chamberlain, Britain's Prime Minister from 1937, was a strong believer in the policy of appeasement. He was confident that he could clear up outstanding problems with Hitler and so achieve his major aim which was to avoid, at all costs, another world war. The great test for this policy was the crisis over Czechoslovakia which arose in September 1938. In that month there seemed a very real likelihood that the whole of Europe would be caught up in a major war. This remained a distinct possibility until the Munich Conference was held on 29-30 September. At this meeting, the fate of Czechoslovakia was decided, though, significantly, no Czechoslovakian representative was invited to attend. When the Conference was over, the Germans were able to occupy part of Czechoslovakia without using force and Chamberlain was able to return to Britain in triumph, boasting that he had negotiated 'peace in our time'. But what appeared to be the triumph of appeasement turned out to be its greatest failure. Within months, Hitler had broken the promises he made at Munich and a major war once more seemed likely.

1 Czechoslovakia in 1938

The Czechoslovakian crisis was sparked by Germany's union with Austria. German-speaking people in Czechoslovakia (who mainly lived in the **Sudetenland** and were therefore known as the 'Sudetendeutsch') began to demand union with Germany and the German government made sure that their campaign was organised by Nazi sympathisers. Hitler, however, had to act more carefully over Czechoslovakia than he had done in Austria. Czechoslovakia was the most democratic and,

Czechoslovakia in 1938

Legend:
- Territory given to Germany at Munich
- Land seized by Poland, September 1938
- Territory given to Hungary at Munich

economically, the most successful of the new states set up at the Paris Peace Conference. The Czechoslovakian army and defences were well organised and well equipped by the Skoda arms works. The Czechoslovakian government had negotiated a treaty with France in 1925 which committed each country to helping the other if either was invaded by Germany. It had also, more recently (in 1936), negotiated a treaty with the Soviet Union. This treaty committed the Soviet Union to helping Czechoslovakia if France became involved in a war against Germany in support of its treaty with Czechoslovakia. As the Hossbach Memorandum (see p.142) suggests, however, once union with Austria had been achieved, Hitler's next target was Czechoslovakia. The crisis came in September 1938 when Hitler promised to support the Sudetendeutsch in their struggle against the Czechoslovakian government. War between Germany and Czechoslovakia seemed a distinct possibility and, if it broke out, the chances were that the whole of Europe would be dragged into war. For the Czechoslovakians, everything depended on the actions of Britain, France and the Soviet Union.

2 British and French foreign policy, 1938

In September 1938, Chamberlain was determined to avoid war. Three times he flew to Germany to meet Hitler. At the first meeting, Hitler demanded self-determination for the Sudetendeutsch at once. Chamberlain agreed to discuss this with the French. When he returned to Germany with agreement to Hitler's demands, Hitler made new demands. He wanted more parts of Czechoslovakia to have self-rule, including those areas with Polish and Hungarian minority populations. This meant, in effect, the destruction of the authority of the Czechoslovakian government. Chamberlain rejected these demands and war seemed near. A statement made by Chamberlain at the time, however, shows how reluctant he was to go to war (and it reveals his attitude towards Czechoslovakia): 'How horrible, fantastic, incredible it is that we should be digging trenches and trying on gas masks here because of a quarrel in a far away country between people of whom we know nothing.' He decided to make one more effort and Hitler agreed to a meeting in Munich. Throughout the crisis, Chamberlain took the lead and the French government followed. The French also wished to avoid war at all costs. If they did not go to war, then neither would the Soviet Union.

The cartoon (above) was published on 24 September 1938. It shows Neville Chamberlain leaving his second meeting with Hitler. He and his colleagues - 'peace' and 'reason' - have been roughed up by Hitler, but they are still alive. The title of the cartoon was 'Mein Kampf' (my struggle). This refers both to Hitler's autobiography (see p.69) and to Chamberlain's struggle to make peace. The 'concessions' marked on Chamberlain's briefcase were those made after the first meeting with Hitler.

❸ The Munich Conference and its aftermath

The Munich Conference was attended by Chamberlain, Hitler, Daladier (the French Prime Minister) and Mussolini. The Czechoslovakian government was not represented. It was simply informed of the terms agreed, after the meeting. The Soviet government, too, was excluded. The terms were harsher than those proposed at Chamberlain's previous meeting with Hitler - Germany was to occupy the Sudetenland within ten days and other parts of Czechoslovakia were to be handed over to Poland and Hungary. The British and French governments agreed to these new borders. The Czechoslovakians were then handed the terms and told that if they rejected them, they would have to fight the Germans alone. They therefore had no choice but to accept them. As a result, Czechoslovakia was completely demoralised and there was no resistance when the Nazis marched in. This would have been a difficult military obstacle for Germany to overcome, if Britain and France had been prepared to risk war. But neither country had fully

The strain shows at the Munich Conference. From the left, Mussolini, Hitler, Hitler's intepreter and Chamberlain deep in negotiations.

rearmed and Chamberlain genuinely believed that it was possible to secure lasting promises from Hitler. After Munich, people in Britain and France were naturally relieved that war had been avoided, but the relief was short-lived. In early 1939, Hitler ordered his armed forces to prepare to 'smash the remainder of the Czech state'. On 15 March 1939, German troops invaded the remaining part of Czechoslovakia.

Activity
Contemporary views on Munich

Source B *British cartoon*

This cartoon shows John Bull (Britain) waking up as his nightmare - the 'war scare' - disappears out of the window. A caption below says: 'Thank goodness that's over!' It was published on 15 March 1939, the very day that the Nazis invaded the remaining part of Czechoslovakia.

Source A *Neville Chamberlain's view*

The real triumph is that the Munich agreement has shown that four Great Powers can agree on a way of carrying out a difficult operation by discussion rather than force of arms. They have prevented a catastrophe which would have ended civilisation as we have known it. Relief at our escape from this great peril of war has, I think, everywhere been mingled with a deep feeling of sympathy for a small and gallant nation. But, ever since I took up my present office, my main purpose has been to work for the peace of Europe. The path which leads to appeasement is long and full of obstacles. The question of Czechoslovakia is the latest and perhaps most dangerous. Now that we have got past it, I feel it may be possible to make further progress along the road to sanity.

From a speech made by N. Chamberlain, 3 October 1938

Source C *Winston Churchill's view*

All is over. Silent, mournful, abandoned, broken, Czechoslovakia disappears into darkness. This block of land, this mass of humans has never expressed the desire to go into Nazi rule. I think you will find that in a period of time that may be measured by years, but which may be only measured in months, Czechoslovakia will be engulfed in the Nazi regime. This is the result of what we have left undone in the last five years - five years of useless good intentions, five years of retreat of British power, five years of neglect of our air defences. We have been reduced from a position of safety and power to where we now stand.

From a speech made by W. Churchill, 5 October 1938

QUESTIONS

1. Judging from the information in this section, was the policy of appeasement justified during the Czechoslovakian crisis?

2. What is the difference between the two views expressed in Sources A and C? What do these sources tell us about the arguments for and against appeasement?

3. Why do you think the cartoon in Source B has been described as a 'misjudgement'?

When Hitler invaded what remained of Czechoslovakia in March 1939, all the hopes for peace briefly raised by the Munich Conference collapsed. A few politicians still hoped that appeasement could still work, but most had run out of patience. As a result, the British and French governments rapidly increased the pace of rearmament in a desperate attempt to catch up with Germany. Once the Nazis had occupied Czechoslovakia, their next obvious target was Poland. Since Poland bordered on the Soviet Union, the Soviet government's position became crucial. Although the British and French governments began to negotiate with the Soviet government in the spring of 1939, in August 1939 Stalin made a pact with Hitler. The two countries agreed not to attack each other and to divide Poland between them. This was the greatest diplomatic shock of the whole interwar period since, previously, the two countries had seemed to be the greatest of enemies. But the Pact provided benefits for both sides. The Soviet Union gained territory and a breathing space. Germany was free to invade Poland without fear of being attacked by the Soviet Union. On 1 September, nine days after the Pact was signed, Nazi troops marched into Poland. This was the final straw. France and Britain issued an ultimatum. When, two days later, Germany had failed to respond, the two countries declared war on Germany. The Second World War had begun.

The lessons of Munich

When, in March 1939, German troops occupied the remaining parts of Czechoslovakia, Britain and France issued a verbal protest and nothing more. Other countries drew the same lesson as Hitler from this. Britain and France, it seemed, would do anything to avoid war with Germany. As a result, Stalin, who had not been asked to take part in the Munich Conference, turned against the idea that collective security (a system of alliances) would keep the Soviet Union safe. The smaller countries of eastern Europe, all militarily weaker than Czechoslovakia, also feared the future. A week after invading the remainder of Czechoslovakia, Nazi troops seized the port of Memel, threatening Lithuania with invasion if it was not handed over. These events turned public opinion in Britain and France strongly against Hitler whose word, it seemed, could not be trusted. Chamberlain still hoped that Hitler could be satisfied without war. But the British and French

This British cartoon was published on 3 July 1939 with the caption: 'Just in case there's any mistake'. The British Prime Minister, Chamberlain and Foreign Secretary, Lord Halifax, stand on the left and a group of leading Nazis on the right. The cartoon suggests that British foreign policy has become much tougher. The British agreement with Poland meant that there would be war if Germany invaded Poland.

governments responded to public opinion by signing an agreement with Poland on 31 March, promising to support it in the event of attack. This was followed by similar guarantees to Greece, Romania and Turkey.

2 Steps towards the Nazi-Soviet Pact

One reason for Hitler's haste was that the German economy was in difficulties in 1939. Plundering the military and industrial resources of countries in the east would help. After Czechoslovakia, therefore, Hitler put pressure on Poland. He demanded the return to Germany of the port of Danzig which was under League of Nations control. He also called for a road and rail link across the Polish Corridor. In May, he further strengthened his position by forming the **Pact of Steel** with Italy (each country agreed to help the other if war broke out). But one problem remained unsolved - the position of the Soviet Union if Germany attacked Poland. In the Summer of 1939, Stalin found himself in the unusual position of being approached by both the Western Allies and by Germany. The British and French governments were still very suspicious about the Communist system and about Stalin's aims in eastern Europe. But, if they were to help Poland, an alliance with the Soviet Union was essential. Equally, it was necessary for the Nazis to remove the danger of war on two fronts. But hatred of Communism had always been central to Nazi propaganda and it did not seem possible for these sworn enemies to suddenly form an alliance.

This British cartoon was published on 29 July 1939 after news reached Britain that Nazi Germany was seeking a deal with the Soviet Union. It shows a group of Nazis queueing outside the office of M. Molotov, the Soviet Foreign Minister. Molotov is busy negotiating with the British.

❸ The Nazi-Soviet Pact

Although the announcement of the Nazi-Soviet Pact (see Box 7.6) shocked the world, in the short term at least the Pact suited both sides. Stalin had three main reasons for signing. First, he had been convinced since the Munich Conference that Britain and France could not be trusted to oppose Hitler. When they approached him for an alliance in the Spring of 1939, they seemed half-hearted. He knew that many people in Britain and France were anti-Communist and would be happy to see Germany attack the Soviet Union. Second, Stalin realised that the Pact provided an opportunity to restore Russian power in eastern Europe. And, third, the Pact gave the Soviet Union a breathing space which it could use to prepare its defences against the Nazi invasion which was bound to come soon. At the same time, the Pact suited Hitler. It removed the fear of having to fight a war on two fronts. He was therefore free to invade Poland and then to turn his attention to western Europe. He could always deal with the Soviet Union in the future, once his position was more secure.

Box 7.6

The Nazi-Soviet Pact, 23 August 1939

(a) Terms of the Treaty

1. Germany and the Soviet Union agree not to attack one another, whether individually or jointly with other powers.
2. If either is attacked by a third power, the other will not support that third party.
3. The Treaty is concluded for a period of ten years.
4. Secret terms were also agreed. These specified how Poland and the Baltic states (Finland, Estonia, Latvia and Lithuania) were to be divided between Germany and the Soviet Union.

(b) Everything I undertake is directed against the Russians. If the West is too stupid or blind to grasp this, then I shall be forced to come to an agreement with the Russians, beat the West and then turn against the Soviet Union with all my forces. I need the Ukraine from the Soviet Union so they can't starve us out like in the last war.

Comment made by Hitler in August 1939 in 'Nazism 1919-45', vol.3, by J. Noakes & G. Pridham, 1988

Activity

The Nazi-Soviet Pact and the outbreak of war

Source A *A historian's view*

By means of the Nazi-Soviet Pact, Hitler secured the Soviet Union's acceptance of Germany's forthcoming invasion of Poland. He also gained relief from the threat of a war on two fronts once he had turned his forces westwards against Britain and France. Stalin, on the other hand, obtained the postponement of a war with Germany which the Soviet Union was unprepared to fight. The Pact gave the Soviet Union time to upgrade their armaments the best they could. The motive for the expansion of Russian territory under the secret terms of the Pact can be summed up in a single phrase - the search for security. Soviet domination of Finland and the Baltic states would help the defence of Leningrad. The recovery of territory lost to Poland in 1920 would restore the historic buffer between the Germanic and Russian populations of eastern Europe.

From 'The Twentieth Century World' by W.R. Keylor, 1992

Source B *Cartoon produced in August 1939*

This cartoon was drawn by Kem, an Egyptian cartoonist who worked for the British Foreign Office during the Second World War.

Source C *Cartoon published on 6 September 1939*

This cartoon was published three days after Britain and France had declared war on Germany. To Hitler's surprise, Mars himself (the god of war) has turned up in his office. Hitler had been expecting Mars' smaller brother. The cartoon, therefore, suggests that Hitler had expected a small war when he invaded Poland on 1 September 1939 and had been surprised when a major war had broken out.

'There's some mistake, it was your small brother I sent for'.

QUESTIONS

1. Judging from the information in this section, why did the Second World War break out in 1939?
2. Using Sources A and B explain why the Nazi-Soviet Pact made the outbreak of a major war more likely.
3. Write a caption for the cartoon in Source B.
4. Look at Source C. Do you think Hitler really was surprised when the Nazi invasion of Poland resulted in a major war? Give reasons for your answer.

Themes

When the First World War was over, it was described as the 'Great War' and the 'war to end all wars'. But, just 21 years later, war broke out on an even greater scale than that experienced in 1914-18. By 1939, the military lessons of the First World War had been well learned. At the same time, technological advances in the interwar years had been immense. These two factors combined to ensure that the Second World War was fought with a new generation of weapons and with new tactics. No longer was warfare a matter of set piece battles between armed forces. In the Second World War, civilians were just as much in the front line as the troops. For example, both sides organised campaigns of mass bombing with the deliberate aim of destroying civilian life and property. In a sense, this was an extension of the sporadic bombing raids of the First World War. But the scale of bombing in the Second World War was immense and, consequently, the damage was more severe than that ever experienced in any war before. In addition, both sides were prepared to experiment with new weapons developed in the war. When the Americans exploded two atom bombs on Japanese cities in August 1945, this did not just bring the unconditional surrender of Japan, it brought the world into the nuclear age. The history of the world since 1945 has been dominated by the knowledge that certain countries have the capability of using weapons of mass destruction. This chapter looks at the impact of World War II by examining the following key questions.

* What happened in World War II?
* Did the nature of warfare change in World War II?
* Why did the USA drop atom bombs on Japan in August 1945?
* How did the war affect the lives of civilians in Britain?

OVERVIEW

What happened in World War II?

Source 1

The war in Europe 1939-41

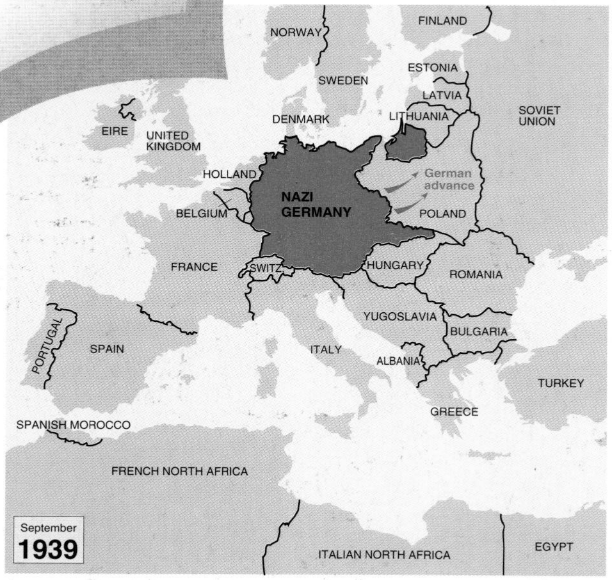

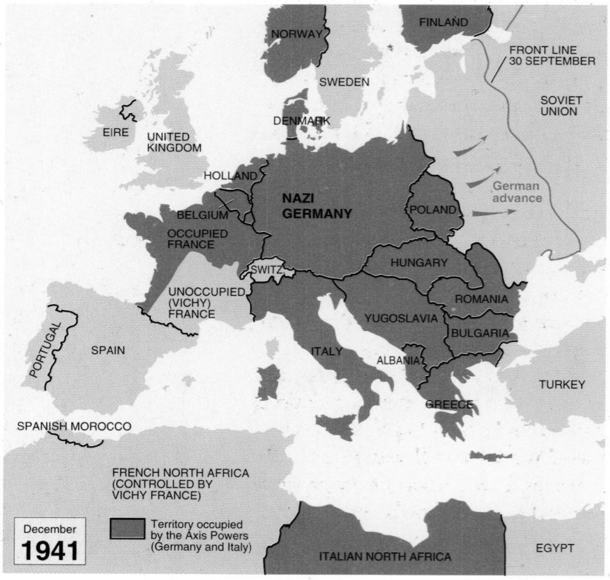

September 1939

December 1941

Territory occupied by the Axis Powers (Germany and Italy)

On 1 September 1939, Germany invaded Poland. Two days later, Britain and France declared war on Germany. For nine months there was little military action outside Poland - the period known as the 'Phoney War'. This ended on 10 May 1940 when the Nazis invaded Holland and Belgium and quickly swept into France. British and French troops were beaten back and between 24 May and 3 June over 300,000 were evacuated from the beaches of Dunkirk. A week later, Italy joined the war on the German side. On 22 June, France surrendered and the Nazis made preparations to invade Britain. In the Battle of Britain (10 July to 31 October), British planes managed to beat back the German air force and thereby prevent an invasion. From 7 September, Nazi tactics changed. German planes began to bomb towns and cities (the 'Blitz'). The Blitz lasted until mid-May 1941. In June 1941, the Nazis invaded the Soviet Union. On 7 December 1941, Japanese aircraft bombed Pearl Harbour, an American naval base in Hawaii. The next day, the USA declared war on Japan. Three days later, Germany and Italy declared war on the USA. This brought the USA into the war in Europe.

Source 2
The war in Europe and North Africa 1942-45

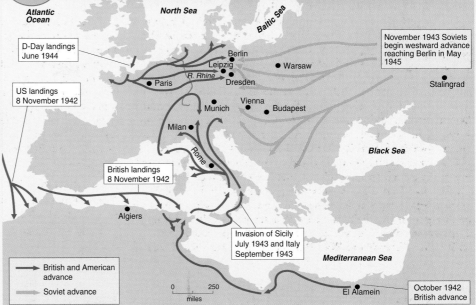

Atlantic Ocean

North Sea

Baltic Sea

D-Day landings June 1944

November 1943 Soviets begin westward advance reaching Berlin in May 1945

Berlin
Leipzig
Warsaw
R. Rhine
Dresden
Paris
Stalingrad

US landings 8 November 1942

Vienna
Munich
Budapest
Milan

Black Sea

British landings 8 November 1942

Rome

Algiers

Invasion of Sicily July 1943 and Italy September 1943

Mediterranean Sea

→ British and American advance

→ Soviet advance

0   250
miles

El Alamein

October 1942 British advance

Source 3
A historian's view

World War II was a 'total' war to an extent that no previous war - not even World War I - came close to matching. By whatever measurement we use - geographic extent, the scale of military and economic mobilisation, the direct impact on civilians, the toll of casualties, the disruption of civilian lives or the dislocation of the world economy - the war of 1939-45 affected more people around the world more directly than any other war before or since. For all those who lived through it, it was the overwhelming experience of the 20th century. But the impact of the war was not all bad. War shook up societies and gave many people - especially women - opportunities of independence and self-discovery which they would not have had in peacetime. The human experience of the war, mixing excitement with tragedy and heroism with cruelty, was infinitely varied but, one way or another, universal. The war was characterised too by new levels of mass communication - both between governments and their own people whose morale they were concerned to keep up and between governments and enemy populations whose morale they hoped to break down. World War II was a war of the air waves. It was a war of propaganda, true and false, of words and images.

From 'World War II' edited by J. Campbell, 1992

Source 4
The war in the Pacific 1941-45

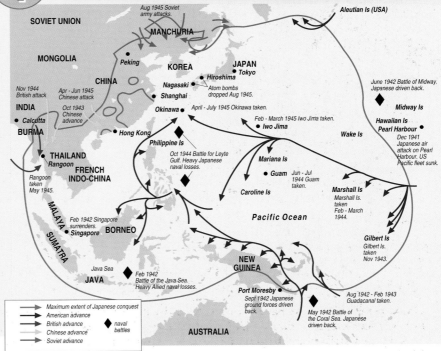

SOVIET UNION

Aug 1945 Soviet army attacks.

Aleutian Is (USA)

MANCHURIA

MONGOLIA

Peking

KOREA

JAPAN
Tokyo

Nov 1944 British attack

Apr - Jun 1945 Chinese attack

CHINA

Nagasaki
Hiroshima

Atom bombs dropped Aug 1945.

June 1942 Battle of Midway. Japanese driven back.

Oct 1943 Chinese advance

Shanghai

Okinawa

April - July 1945 Okinawa taken.

Midway Is

INDIA

Calcutta

Hong Kong

Feb - March 1945 Iwo Jima taken.

Iwo Jima

Hawaiian Is
Pearl Harbour

BURMA

Philippine Is

Wake Is

Dec 1941 Japanese air attack on Pearl Harbour. US Pacific fleet sunk.

THAILAND
Rangoon

Oct 1944 Battle for Leyte Gulf. Heavy Japanese naval losses.

Mariana Is

FRENCH INDO-CHINA

Guam

Jun - Jul 1944 Guam taken.

Rangoon taken May 1945.

Caroline Is

Marshall Is

Pacific Ocean

Marshall Is. taken Feb - March 1944.

MALAYA

Feb 1942 Singapore surrenders.

Singapore   BORNEO

Gilbert Is

SUMATRA

Gilbert Is. taken Nov 1943.

Java Sea

NEW GUINEA

JAVA

Feb 1942 Battle of the Java Sea. Heavy Allied naval losses.

Port Moresby

Sept 1942 Japanese ground forces driven back.

Aug 1942 - Feb 1943 Guadacanal taken.

→ Maximum extent of Japanese conquest
→ American advance
→ British advance
→ Chinese advance
→ Soviet advance
◆ naval battles

May 1942 Battle of the Coral Sea. Japanese driven back.

AUSTRALIA

QUESTIONS

1. Using Sources 1 and 2 draw a time line showing the key events in the war in Europe. Use this time line as the basis of a short piece of writing which describes what happened in the war.

2. Judging from Source 3, why was World War II such an important event in the 20th century? What impact did the war make in (a) the short term and (b) the long term?

3. Using Source 4 write a short piece describing what happened in the Pacific in the war.

4. What do Sources 1-4 tell us about the scope of the war?

Did the nature of warfare change in World War II?

There are a number of ways in which the First World War differed from the Second World War. First, on the whole, there was little movement in the First World War. Along the Western Front, for example, trench warfare brought month after month of stalemate. It was only when the Germans overreached themselves that the Allies, reinforced by American soldiers and equipment, were finally able to push them back. The Second World War, by contrast, was much more a war of movement. Second, the First World War was hellish for those who fought in the trenches. But, on the whole, the war did not result in civilian deaths. It is true that there were isolated air attacks on civilian targets. Nevertheless, very few civilians on both sides were killed. This was not the case in the Second World War. Between 1939 and 1945, civilians were just as much in the firing line as professional soldiers. Third, although the First World War was an international conflict, its scope was by no means as vast as that of the Second World War. The Second World War had more theatres of war, involved more people and resulted in considerably more deaths. And fourth, technological development meant that new or improved weapons and tactics were available by the time the Second World War broke out. So, although, for example, tanks were used to a limited extent in the First World War, by 1939 they were much more reliable and useful.

1 The scope of the war

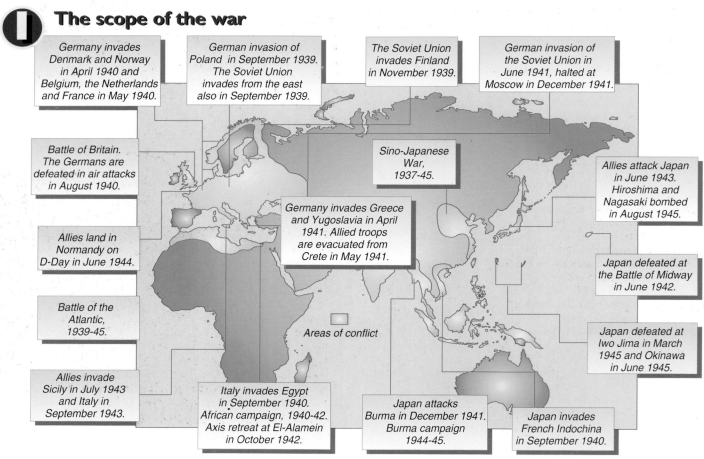

Germany invades Denmark and Norway in April 1940 and Belgium, the Netherlands and France in May 1940.

German invasion of Poland in September 1939. The Soviet Union invades from the east also in September 1939.

The Soviet Union invades Finland in November 1939.

German invasion of the Soviet Union in June 1941, halted at Moscow in December 1941.

Battle of Britain. The Germans are defeated in air attacks in August 1940.

Sino-Japanese War, 1937-45.

Allies attack Japan in June 1943. Hiroshima and Nagasaki bombed in August 1945.

Germany invades Greece and Yugoslavia in April 1941. Allied troops are evacuated from Crete in May 1941.

Allies land in Normandy on D-Day in June 1944.

Japan defeated at the Battle of Midway in June 1942.

Battle of the Atlantic, 1939-45.

Areas of conflict

Japan defeated at Iwo Jima in March 1945 and Okinawa in June 1945.

Allies invade Sicily in July 1943 and Italy in September 1943.

Italy invades Egypt in September 1940. African campaign, 1940-42. Axis retreat at El-Alamein in October 1942.

Japan attacks Burma in December 1941. Burma campaign 1944-45.

Japan invades French Indochina in September 1940.

The map above shows that the war was fought in Europe, Africa and Asia. It was fought on land, at sea and in the air. Although much of the fighting took place between military personnel, it was not just a military affair. Civilians were involved in the war to an extent that had never before been experienced. The phrase 'total war' has been used to describe this type of warfare. Governments on both sides did not just rely on their armies or navies to win military victories. They attempted to destroy the enemy's industries and to damage the enemy's morale by making frequent long-range bombing raids. They also attempted to starve the enemy by preventing supplies reaching their country. This developed from what had happened in 1914-18. There were bombing raids during the First World War, for example, but these were infrequent because the technology at the time was limited (see p.20). Similarly, the British navy had tried to prevent goods reaching German ports in the hope that this would starve the Germans into submission. In the Second World War, the willingness of military leaders to target civilians (and the greater scale of the war) meant much higher casualty figures (see Box 8.1).

Box 8.1 Casualties in World War II

Total deaths (estimated)

World War I	7 - 12 million
World War II	30 - 55 million

It is estimated that about two thirds of those who died in World War II were civilians. It should be noted, however, that estimates vary widely. A survey of the accounts of five historians revealed a variation as follows.

Soviet Union	13.50 - 27.00 million
Germany	4.20 - 7.80 million
Britain	0.39 - 0.45 million
USA	0.29 - 0.41 million

② The war on land

'World War II on land is usually presented as an entirely different kind of conflict from World War I. It is seen as a war of movement rather than a war of static positions and as a war of tanks, aircraft and motorised columns rather than a war of trenches, barbed wire and machine guns. These images are not entirely misleading. Technology did transform the face of war. Most obviously it allowed generals to move troops and guns quickly across large distances. World War II saw the course of whole campaigns change in a matter of days as a result of rapid outflanking moves or armoured breakthroughs. But there was much that did not change. The vast majority of soldiers were infantrymen who covered most of the ground they crossed on foot. Most German soldiers, for example, marched into Russia in 1941 just as Napoleon's army had in 1812. In most places, rapid movement was the exception rather than the rule and much time was taken up with static or near-static warfare.'

From 'World War II' edited by J. Campbell, 1992. Boxes 8.2-8.6 on this page explore these themes.

Box 8.2 — Blitzkreig

Blitzkreig (German for 'lightning war') was the name of the tactic used by the Germans at the beginning of the war. Relying on speed and surprise rather than numbers or better equipment, the Germans swept through enemy territory in armoured vehicles (like those above) and tanks, supported by aircraft. The tactic was a success at first. But it failed in the Soviet Union because the distances were too great, the weather was too cold and the Russian resistance was too fierce.

Box 8.3 — New weapons

Mass production and new technology meant that a greater variety and greater quantities of weapons were available. In addition, both sides set up extensive research programmes. From 1942, the Germans concentrated on improving their rocket technology. In 1944, they launched the first 'V1' flying bombs (small pilotless planes packed with explosives which exploded in Britain after running out of fuel). Later in 1944, V2s (missiles with rocket motors and a longer range and greater impact) were launched (right).

A V2 rocket.

Box 8.4 — Jungle warfare

The Japanese not only out-fought us in Malaya, they out-thought us too. Dress and equipment were as light as possible and their speed at crossing country was remarkable. They had light weapons ideal for jungle fighting - tommy guns or light automatic weapons and hand grenades which were often lobbed from trees. They made great use of bicycles to move quickly.

From 'Malayan Postscript' by I. Morrison, 1942

Box 8.5 — The Battle of El Alamein, October 1942

The British had spent the whole night attacking our front under cover of their artillery [long range guns] which in some places had fired 500 rounds for every one of ours. Load after load of bombs cascaded down among my troops. I gave orders to the artillery to break up the British movement, but we had too little ammunition to do it successfully. Late in the afternoon, German and Italian dive bombers made an attempt to break up the British lorry columns. Some 60 British fighters pounced on these slow machines and forced the Italians to jettison [dump] their bombs over their own lines. Finally a thrust by 160 British tanks wiped out the 164th Infantry Division. Violent fighting followed. Tank casualties that day were 61 German and 56 Italian, all totally destroyed. The supply situation was now approaching disaster. A tanker which we hoped would bring relief to the petrol situation had been bombed and sunk. There was only enough petrol for another two or three days.

Account of the Battle of El Alamein by General Rommel (German commander), published in 1953

Box 8.6 — Tanks

In 1918, the top speed of tanks was just 6 km per hour. By 1939, tanks could travel at speeds over 40 km per hour and they were more comfortable and better equipped. Tanks played a crucial role in Blitzkreig and in the war in North Africa.

A German tank in World War II.

3 The war at sea

In the Second World War, as in the First, vital supplies were transported by sea. It was particularly important for Britain (since it was an island) that these supplies reached their destination. As in the First World War, however, German submarines (U-boats) patrolled the seas and the Allies used a convoy system to protect the merchant fleet. Although the design of U-boats had been improved since 1918, they were still far from perfect (see Box 8.7). Nevertheless, they were able to inflict much damage on Allied shipping (see map, right, and the table below). The war at sea differed from that in the First World War in the following ways. First, the scale of activity was much greater in the Second World War. Second, air power played an important part. In particular, American aircraft carriers were largely responsible for American successes in the Pacific. Aircraft were also used both to defend and to attack convoys. Third, ships were equipped with radar and other tracking devices. And fourth, ships were equipped with bigger weapons and more effective explosives.

The war at sea 1939-45

	1939	1940	1941	1942	1943	1944	1945
U - boat * losses	9	22	35	85	287	241	153
Allied ships lost (1,000 tons)	810	4,407	4,398	8,245	3,611	1,422	458
Ships built USA (1,000 tons)	101	439	1,169	5,339	12,384	11,639	3,551
Ships built, Britain (1,000 tons)	231	780	815	1,843	2,201	1,710	283
Total new ships (1,000 tons)	332	1,219	1,984	7,182	14,585	13,349	3,834

* U-boats are German submarines.

4 The war in the air

"NEVER WAS SO MUCH OWED BY SO MANY TO SO FEW" THE PRIME MINISTER

Although aircraft did play a part in the First World War, the war in the air was a sideshow. This was not the case in the Second World War. By 1939, air power had become central to modern warfare. For example, the German Luftwaffe (air force) played an important part in the Blitzkrieg tactic used in 1939-41. Aircraft supported the ground troops by going ahead and destroying enemy bases, thus preventing the enemy from organising defence. In June 1940, the German army swept through France, forcing its surrender. Hitler then ordered his commanders to prepare for the invasion of Britain. The first phase was an attempt to gain air control. But Britain put up stiff opposition in what became known as the **Battle of Britain** (see poster, left). By September 1940, it was clear that the Luftwaffe would not be able to destroy the British air force and the invasion was called off. Between September 1940 and May 1941, however, German bombers were sent on raids to bomb British cities in what became known as the **Blitz**. Despite heavy civilian casualties, this failed to damage British morale and, later in the war, the British retaliated by the mass bombing of German cities. Before and during the war, great advances were made in aircraft technology. Most important, perhaps, were the invention of the radar and radio-control and the development of planes like the **Spitfire** (a light and fast fighter) and the **Lancaster** (a four-engined long-range bomber).

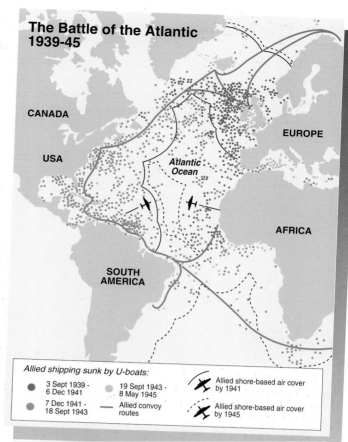

The Battle of the Atlantic 1939-45

Allied shipping sunk by U-boats:
- 3 Sept 1939 - 6 Dec 1941
- 7 Dec 1941 - 18 Sept 1943
- 19 Sept 1943 - 8 May 1945
- Allied convoy routes
- Allied shore-based air cover by 1941
- Allied shore-based air cover by 1945

Box 8.7   U-boats in World War II

People have the wrong idea about submarines. They see them as excellent fighting machines, sitting under water, chasing and sinking surface ships. This was the hope when they were invented, but it was only achieved with nuclear subs. The subs in the Second World War were propelled by diesel engines and under water by electric motors. On the surface they could travel at 15 knots (merchant ships had a speed of 8 knots). The problem was working the electric motors. We had huge lead batteries - the subs had a displacement of 500 tons of which 120 tons was taken up by the batteries. But even then, the top speed was 2 knots - a speed below walking pace. Subs could only hold the maximum speed under water for 30 minutes. They could stay under for three days, but only in special circumstances. So, they were not great hunters. Their success was due to their weapons system and to tactics.

Memories of Lieutenant Werner Schuneman who in 1942 was aged 22 and was an engineer on a U-boat. The account was published in 1994.

Activity
The war in the air

Source B *Mass bombing - Dresden*

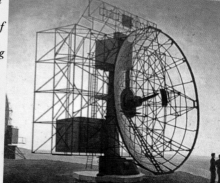

On the night of 13-14 February 1945, 805 British bombers dropped 2,600 tons of bombs on the German town of Dresden, a town of little military significance. Over 50,000 people died in a horrific firestorm.

Source A *Mass bombing*

a) Number of bombs dropped

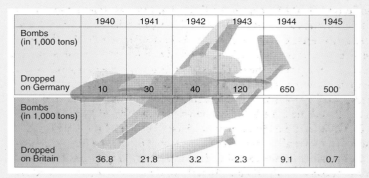

	1940	1941	1942	1943	1944	1945
Bombs (in 1,000 tons) Dropped on Germany	10	30	40	120	650	500
Bombs (in 1,000 tons) Dropped on Britain	36.8	21.8	3.2	2.3	9.1	0.7

b) By 1943, the RAF had adopted a new bombing strategy. No longer were bombers sent on daylight raids to bomb military targets (so-called 'precision bombing'). Rather, they were sent on night raids to bomb German cities (so-called 'mass' bombing). Mass bombing was the modern way of trying to destroy both the morale and the economy of the enemy at the same time. New and improved aircraft, more efficient radar aids to navigation and bomb aiming, and a special 'pathfinder' force (which went ahead to locate the targets) made Bomber Command a formidable force. Yet morale did not break. Bombing failed to bring German industry to a halt and German defences pushed bomber losses up beyond 5% and, early in 1944, to 10%.

From 'Total War', vol.I, edited by P. Calvocoressi, 1989

Source C *'Precision' bombing*

At first, bombers on both sides were ordered to attack specific targets. But they had severe problems achieving accuracy. One reason was that both sides intended to bomb by day since it was easier to find the target. But they soon suffered heavy losses and switched to night raids. Aerial navigation at night relied on airspeed, compass and an estimate of wind speed and direction. Bombsights, too, were little different from those used in 1918. So, since many military targets were close to urban areas, it was inevitable civilians would suffer.

From 'The Century of Warfare' by C. Messenger, 1995

Source D *A British pilot's account*

The worst part of the operation was the need to fly the aircraft straight and level on the bombing run so that the bombs could be aimed accurately and the automatic camera could record the explosions. While this happened, it was not possible to change course to avoid enemy fire. The Germans had started to use ultraviolet searchlights. Within a couple of seconds of the ultraviolet beam shining on a bomber, all the white lights in the area converged, forming a cone from which it was difficult to escape. Crews were dazzled and unable to see fighters emerging from the dark. Just as we released our bombs, we were caught in the cone, but we had to keep flying straight until the camera had taken the vital picture (there was great rivalry amongst crews to bring back a clear picture proving they had hit the target). It seemed like hours, not seconds, that I had to hold our course. Just as the shutter on the camera clicked, fighters attacked. I put the Lancaster into a deep dive - and suddenly we were in blessed darkness. The port outer engine was hit and we were 5,000 feet below normal height, but we were able to make our way home.

Pilot Officer Tony Bird's memories of his first operation to Berlin on 3 September 1942. The account was published in 1994.

Source E *Radar*

After the First World War, the problem of how to stop bombers flying over Britain was of great concern. All sorts of ideas were considered including a death ray which would kill enemy air crews as they flew over. No death ray was invented, but an early warning system 'radar' was developed in the 1930s. By 1939, a network of 51 radar stations had been set up like the one above. Enemy planes could be spotted before they reached Britain, allowing British fighter planes to intercept them. This system was of vital importance during the Battle of Britain.

QUESTIONS

1. Judging from the information in this section, did the nature of warfare change during the Second World War?

2. a) Suppose you worked for Bomber Command in 1944. Using Sources A-D, write a press release justifying mass bombing.

   b) Why might mass bombing be more difficult to justify today?

3. a) What do Sources A-E tell us about the nature of warfare in the Second World War?

   b) How did the nature of warfare differ from that in the First World War?

Why did the USA drop atom bombs on Japan in August 1945?

On 6 August 1945, a new kind of weapon, an atom bomb, was dropped onto the Japanese town of Hiroshima. A single bomb devastated the town, killing 80,000 people instantly and injuring a further 40,000 (many of whom died later from their wounds or from radiation sickness). On 9 August 1945, a second atom bomb was dropped on the Japanese port of Nagasaki. This time 40,000 people were killed instantly. Six days later, Japan surrendered and the Second World War ended. But the explosion of these two atom bombs meant the beginning of a new era - the nuclear age. With the invention of the atom bomb, warfare would never be the same again. For the first time in history, people had invented a weapon that had the potential not just to destroy the enemy, but to destroy the human race. Since August 1945, people have looked back and questioned whether the Americans were right to use the atom bomb against the Japanese. In particular, they have questioned whether it was right to drop two bombs. This section considers why the bomb was used and how its use was justified.

 ## The arms race in World War II

The theory behind the development of atom bombs had been worked out before the Second World War began, but nobody had been able to translate the theory into practice. At first, when war broke out, the development of atom bombs was a priority for both sides. Money was poured into research and teams of scientists conducted experiments. Most notably, the **Manhattan Project** (a top secret $2 billion nuclear research project in the USA) was launched in December 1941. By February 1942, however, the German army had made the decision to abandon research on the atom bomb and to concentrate instead on rockets (see p.151). Members of the Manhattan Project were unaware of this and continued with their research (see Box 8.8). In December 1942, the first chain reaction was achieved. But, it was not until the war in Europe was over that an atom bomb was successfully exploded in a test in the Nevada desert. This test took place in July 1945.

 ## Japan and the war

Japan entered the Second World War when it attacked the American naval base at Pearl Harbour (Hawaii) on 7 December 1941. Its goal was to gain control of South East Asia and, initially, this goal was achieved. But the USA had superior weapons and equipment and, in the long term, this gave them the advantage. By 1944, it was clear that the USA (and allies) would win the war in the Pacific. But the Japanese, under their Emperor Hirohito, had developed a culture in which capture or surrender was considered dishonourable. This, in part, explains the practice of using **kamikaze** (suicide) pilots. These pilots would fly planes packed with explosives into American ships in the hope of destroying them. Although kamikaze attacks did cause some damage (on one day 24 American ships were sunk by kamikaze planes), they did not cause enough damage to threaten the USA's eventual victory. Nevertheless, kamikaze raids did much to suggest that it would not be easy to get the Japanese to surrender. In addition, Allied troops were impressed by the bravery of the Japanese troops they fought against. The account of one ex-soldier writing in 1961 is typical: 'The Japanese are the bravest people I have ever met. In attack, they simply came on, using all their skill and rage, until they were stopped by death. In defence, they held their ground with furious determination. They had to be killed company by company, squad by squad, man by man to the last.'

This painting by Dwight Shepler shows a kamikaze attack on the American aircraft carrier 'Okinawa' in April 1945. Although the ship has been damaged, it has not been destroyed.

③ The USA and the war in the Pacific

Although it was soon clear that the USA would win the war in the Pacific, it was also clear that it would not be an easy victory. Japanese troops had occupied many of the islands dotted across the West Pacific and each one had to be recaptured. American military leaders therefore used the tactic known as **island hopping** - capturing one island and then moving on to the next. This was costly in terms both of equipment and of casualties and it was slow. On many occasions, American troops met fierce resistance. For example, when American troops arrived on Okinawa, their commander said: 'It's going to be really tough. There are 65,000 Japs holed up in the south end of the island and I see no way to get them out except by blasting them out yard by yard'. He was right. It was really tough. Over 7,000 American soldiers were killed. Loss of life on this scale was of great concern to the American government and, without doubt, one reason why the atom bomb was dropped was to avoid further American casualties. A second reason for using the atom bomb was to prevent the Soviet Union gaining influence in South East Asia. By August 1945, the war in Europe was over and the Red Army was preparing to invade Japan via Manchuria (see map on p.217). The Soviet invasion of Manchuria began on 8 August, two days after the first atom bomb was dropped.

The use of the atom bomb must be considered in context. Throughout 1945 the American air force attempted to bomb the Japanese into submission. In March 1945, for example, over 330 B29 bombers dropped fire bombs on Japan's capital Tokyo. The result was utter devastation (see above). So many bombs were dropped that there was a firestorm - gusts of flames at 1000°C travelling at 100 miles an hour or more. Although no records were kept, it is estimated that nearly 100,000 people were killed, 100,000 injured and over 100,000 made homeless.

④ What options were available to the USA?

Once the atom bomb had been successfully tested, the American government had three main options. First, it could simply continue with its existing policy and wait for the Japanese to surrender (in 1946, the American Strategic Bombing Survey concluded that a surrender would have been forced by December 1945 even if the atom bombs had not been dropped and even if no invasion of Japan had been planned). Second, it could explode an atom bomb on an uninhabited island to show the Japanese government how powerful it was - in the hope that this would scare it into immediate surrender (this idea was proposed by American scientists in 1945). Or third, it could drop an atom bomb on a Japanese town without warning - as revenge for the attack on Pearl Harbour and to shock the Japanese government into surrender.

Suppose that 2,000 B29 bombers had dropped all of their bombs on Nagasaki at the same time. That would have been roughly equivalent to the explosive power of the single atom bomb that was actually dropped on 9 August (see Box 8.9). The photo above was taken from an American observation plane just after the bomb exploded. Around 40,000 people died instantly and around 60,000 were seriously injured (around 80,000 died instantly in Hiroshima). Unlike 'conventional' bombs, the explosion of the atom bombs produced radiation which caused sickness and death for many years afterwards. According to the writer John Cox, the eventual death toll in Hiroshima was around 200,000.

Box 8.9 — Nagasaki - an eyewitness account

On 9 August 1945, I was working at the prison camp. It was about 11 am when they dropped the bomb and I actually saw it coming down on a parachute. I saw the plane flying over, then the bomb dropping. Then a blinding flash. There were other people working around me and they were burned to a cinder - I was saved by a pile of rubble. The horrifying thing was to see that people were just shadows. You didn't find the body, but you found the shadow. It was also horrible to see the torn limbs and flesh hanging on so many of the Japanese. We helped them and they were grateful - but it was a horrifying sight to see the horrible burns and the way the flesh hung off them. The biggest horror in the after effects was the utter silence. I had been used to bombing of all kinds and after it you heard cries for help and noise - things happening. The eerie thing was the silence.

Memories of Sidney Lawrence who was a prisoner of war in Nagasaki at the time when the second atom bomb was dropped. This account was published in 1994.

Activity

Why did the USA decide to drop the atom bombs?

Source B The ruins of Hiroshima, August 1945

Source D President Truman's view

a) Having found the bomb, we have used it. We have used it against those who attacked us without warning at Pearl Harbour. We have used it in order to shorten the agony of the war, in order to save thousands of Americans. We shall continue to use it until we completely destroy Japan's capacity to make war. Only a Japanese surrender will stop us.

Part of a speech made by President Truman on 7 August 1945

b) The atom bomb was no 'great decision'. For your information, there were more people killed by the fire bombs in Tokyo than the dropping of the atom bombs accounted for. It was merely another powerful weapon. The dropping of two bombs stopped the war and saved millions of lives. It was just the same as getting a bigger gun than the other fellow had to win the war and that's what it was used for.'

Part of a speech made by ex-President Truman in 1959

QUESTIONS

1. Judging from the information in this section, why do you think the USA dropped atom bombs on Japan?

2. 'In the context of the war, the decision to use the bomb is not hard to understand.' Using Sources A-D give the arguments for and against this statement.

3. a) What do you think President Truman's main aim was when he ordered the two bombs to be dropped? Use Source D in your answer.

   b) Do you think he was right to drop the bombs?

4. What point is being made by the cartoon in Source E?

Source A Historians' views

a) By August 1945, an American victory was absolutely certain. As a result, the dropping of the atom bomb was not essential for victory. Rather, it was justified as being a means for saving American soldiers' lives. But perhaps the thought that it would prevent the Soviet Union from establishing a claim to Japan was not absent from the minds of the American government either.

From 'Age of Extremes' by E. Hobsbawm, 1994

b) The first atom bombs cost $2 billion to develop. This put pressure on the American government to use them. The bomb dropped on Hiroshima was a uranium bomb. The bomb dropped on Nagasaki was a plutonium bomb. The fact that the second bomb was dropped suggests that the American military wanted to compare the effects of the two bombs. The decision to use these bombs, therefore, was nothing less than a grotesque experiment.

From 'The Arms Race: Opposing Viewpoints' by D. Bender, 1982

Source C A British sailor's view

Hiroshima looked like a hurricane had gone through, followed by a fire. I thought 'how could one bomb do that?' We didn't discuss it because we were so glad the war was over. But when I saw Tokyo, it was just as bad - and that had only been fire-bombed and not touched by nuclear weapons. You know, nobody had warned us or spoken about radiation. It was just an atomic bomb that had ended the war. People say it was a dreadful thing to do, but you can only die once - it doesn't matter how and of course war is total war. Women and children are involved. This is what some people don't seem to recognise. The bomb saved many many lives. Can you imagine what would have happened if we had invaded Japan?

Memories of Bill White, a British sailor who was in Japan in August 1945. The account was published in 1994.

Source E Cartoon from 1945

This cartoon shows President Truman as the Statue of Liberty. The other people are (from the left) Attlee (British Prime Minister), Stalin, De Gaulle (French President) and Jiang Jieshi (Chinese leader - see p.222). It is not clear whether they are hugging Truman or reaching for the bomb.

Government censorship and propaganda in World War II

In wartime, people expect and accept greater government control than in peacetime. It is generally agreed that everybody should play their part in working for victory and if that means a loss of individual freedom, then this should be tolerated at least until the war is over. Control of information is always important, but in wartime it can be a matter of life and death. It is no good planning a surprise attack, for example, if a newspaper is then allowed to publish an article which gives the location away. To prevent this happening (and to make sure that only the information they wanted to be released was released), to a greater or lesser extent all the countries which took part in the Second World War practised censorship (the restricting of information). In Britain, for example, there were strict rules about what could or could not be broadcast, published or even written in letters home. Censorship goes hand in hand with propaganda (the promotion of a particular viewpoint regardless of the truth of that viewpoint). In Britain, as in other countries, the government produced propaganda (a Ministry of Information was set up). This attacked the enemy with both truth and lies and promoted all that the government considered praiseworthy and in the interests of the country. For historians, censorship and propaganda make it difficult to find out what was really happening since they cannot always be sure that the 'official view' was a view shared by ordinary people.

These posters show that, during the war, the government was careful to promote an 'official view'. The poster on the left was used as part of a campaign to encourage people to save money in the National Savings scheme (so that the money could be used for the war effort). The poster above was never used. It was banned by the government censor on the grounds that it did not promote a suitable view of Britain. Anne Valery (who lived through the war and was writing in 1991) suggests that, on the whole, censorship was regarded as a necessary nuisance: 'Getting round the censoring of letters became an art form. For instance, the mention of 'yellow' meant North Africa, 'grey' meant Iceland and so on. A letter to a girlfriend suggesting that she painted the ceiling meant that the boyfriend was coming home on leave and "I'm so sorry Granny's so ill' when she wasn't, was asking for a telegram stating that Granny had died so that the writer could be granted compassionate leave.' (from *Talking About the War*, 1991).

QUESTIONS

1. What image of Britain is being promoted by each poster above? Why do you think the government censor banned one, but not the other?

2. It is the historian's job to reveal the truth behind the propaganda. What difficulties might historians face when attempting to do this? How might they be overcome?

3. 'The type of censorship used and propaganda produced during the war can tell us a great deal about what it was like to live through the war.' Explain this statement using the posters above.

4. Can censorship ever be justified? Give reasons for your answer.

Poster captions:

Worth Fighting for...

Worth Saving for

For ways of Saving... ask the officer who pays you

YOUR BRITAIN

SOURCE WORK

How did the war affect the lives of civilians in Britain?

The Second World War made more of a direct impact on the lives of civilians in Britain than the First World War. Admittedly, this was not the case at first. Between September 1939 and May 1940 (the period known as the 'Phoney War'), there was little military activity. But between May and August 1940, there was a very real threat of invasion. And then, between 7 September 1940 and mid-May 1941, civilians in many towns and cities suffered nightly bombing raids (the Blitz). The damage and loss of life in the Blitz was many times greater than the damage caused by the isolated air raids of the First World War. The lives of civilians, however, were not just affected by the fear of invasion or bombing. The whole of British society was mobilised to help the war effort. In May 1940, when the British army was forced to retreat from Dunkirk and there was a real threat of invasion, the **Emergency Powers Act** was passed. This gave a desperate government almost unlimited power over people and property. From then on, civilians could be required to do anything and to be sent anywhere. But the government did not only rely on power. Everybody was encouraged to do their bit. For example, looking after evacuees (children sent away from the cities to protect them from bombing), volunteering to work as an Air Warden or 'digging for victory' (planting vegetables to help in the struggle against food shortages) were all promoted as valuable activities. As in the First World War, women played an important part in the civilian war effort. This time, however, their contribution was taken for granted and there was no special reward at the end of the war.

 ## Conscription

In Britain, conscription (compulsory military service) for men was introduced in May 1939. This was the first time it had ever been introduced in peacetime. At first, men were to serve for six months, but most were then kept on for the remainder of the war (like the author of Box 8.10). Between May 1939 and Autumn 1941, all men aged between 18 and 52 were conscripted. Since military service was compulsory, there was no need for an advertising campaign like that in the First World War. The conscription of women was introduced in December 1941. At first, it only applied to unmarried women aged between 20 and 30. In 1942, the lower age was lowered to 19 and in 1943 the upper age was raised to 51. These women had a choice of working for the WRNS (Women's Royal Navy Service), ATS (Auxiliary Territorial Service), WAAF (Women's Auxiliary Air Force), civil defence or industry. About 25% (460,000) chose the WRNS, ATS or WAAF.

Box 8.10 The call up - an eyewitness account

It was with mixed feelings that I sat down on the platform bench waiting for the train. Dad and my girlfriend Muriel had come along with me and both looked terribly upset. I felt both excitement and anxiety. I knew that I would not like being in the army, yet I felt a little pleased at being one of the first to go. In a way, I was looking forward to the experience. It was only for six months, so the papers said, and I would be home before Christmas. The train puffed to the platform and we walked through the turnstile. The moment of departure was here. Dad was very emotional and upset. I know that he was thinking of another occasion, 20-odd years ago, when he had stepped on such a train. Muriel was in tears and clung to my arm and Dad turned away when she kissed me. It was all so dramatic and a lump in my throat prevented me from saying much.

Memories of James Palmer who was called up and joined the Royal Tank Regiment at the age of 18 in July 1939. The account was published in 1994.

 ## Evacuation

These children are waiting to be evacuated. They had to leave their parents and go to live with families in safer areas. In addition to their belongings, they are holding gas masks. When war broke out, the government expected the Germans to attack with poison gas and people were told to carry gas masks with them at all times.

The government expected bombing raids as soon as war broke out and so plans were made to evacuate (to move) people from cities to areas that were unlikely to be bombed. When the Germans invaded Poland on 1 September 1939, evacuation began. In all, around 1.5 million people were evacuated. Most were children (left) who were sent to live with families in the country or abroad. Many came from poor backgrounds and went to stay with well-off families. These children experienced the comfort of wealth for the first time (Box 8.11) whilst the families looking after them were shocked by their bad health, habits and dirty clothes.

Box 8.11 Evacuation - an eyewitness account

One really good thing about being evacuated to the countryside was the fact that my health improved so much. Although my parents had fed me well, I suffered from pneumonia every winter because of the crowded living conditions at home. From the time I was evacuated I never suffered from it again. The abundance of locally produced fresh fruit and vegetables kept me very healthy.

Memories of Rita Wright who was aged 9 when evacuated from the East End of London. The account was published in 1989.

③ The Blitz

Although the prime target during the Blitz was London (4/5 of bombs were dropped on it), many other towns and cities were bombed. For example, on 14 November 1940, a force of 437 bombers dropped 600 tons of bombs on Coventry, killing 554 people and injuring 865. The bombing failed to damage morale, but it did disrupt everyday life. For example, many homes and offices were destroyed. Fire fighters were busy every night and after each raid there was a great deal of clearing up to do (see below).

Official figures reveal that 27% of people used their own private shelters (see Box 8.12). Others used public shelters or 'self chosen' shelters such as Tube stations (see above). Although, in 1939, the government rejected their use as shelters, many people simply bought a ticket and stayed down there. In September 1940, the government gave in to public demand and opened 80 stations for shelter. Surprisingly, a survey conducted in November 1940 showed that only 40% of Londoners regularly took shelter during a bombing raid. This partly explains the large number of casualties. By June 1941, 43,000 civilians had been killed and 1.5 million had lost their houses.

④ Rationing

Food rationing was introduced in January 1940 (see Box 8.13). Families were given books of ration stamps which they used to buy a fixed amount of certain products. At first, only butter, sugar and bacon were rationed. Eventually, little except seasonal fruit and vegetables was not rationed. To keep up morale, the Minister of Food, Lord Woolton, launched 'Food Facts', a newspaper column explaining why goods were in short supply. He gave helpful tips and recipes - for example, a recipe for marmalade using carrots as oranges were unavailable. The picture above shows the weekly ration for two people in 1941 (excluding bread and other food not rationed). Rationing encouraged people to eat healthily. Many (especially the poor) had never had such a balanced diet. Other goods, such as petrol and clothing, were also rationed.

Box 8.12   The Blitz - an eyewitness account

I spent a particularly bad raid crammed in a neighbour's shelter in Barking. We felt safe and insulated from all that was going on outside, except the noise! But the cramped conditions and discomfort often led to a dash back into the house to fetch a drink or an extra blanket. At the height of the raid it was best to stay put. On this occasion the big bus depot just around the corner took a direct hit and was completely destroyed. When the all-clear sounded we emerged from the shelter to find the garden littered with ugly hunks of concrete which had been hurled over the rooftops when the bus depot went up. Had I been making a dash for it at that moment, I would have been crushed under the weight of falling masonry.

Memories of the singer Vera Lynn who was in London during the Blitz. The account was published in 1989.

Box 8.13   Rationing - a historian's account

The British had to feed themselves. U-boats prowled the Atlantic and in the worst year (1943) the UK lost 833 merchant ships. Bread and potatoes increasingly dominated the diet. Food rationing, introduced early in the war, intensified. At a peak in August 1942, one adult could hope for roughly half a kilo of meat a week. Children got less. Eggs were in especially short supply - the average person might get 30 a year. But the government was careful to ensure that pregnant women and children received more eggs (maybe three a week) and half a litre of milk a day. Rationing was seen by the public as both necessary and fair.

From 'World War II' edited by J. Campbell, 1992

The role played by Winston Churchill

Winston Churchill took over from Neville Chamberlain as Prime Minister at a time of crisis. Chamberlain resigned on 10 May 1940 when news came that Germany had invaded Holland, Belgium and France. Within weeks, all three countries had surrendered to the Germans, the British army had been evacuated from Dunkirk and an invasion of Britain seemed a distinct possibility. During this time of crisis and afterwards, Churchill promoted the public image of a calm and confident leader who put the needs of the nation first. He never wavered in his determination to keep on fighting (even when Hitler tried to negotiate a separate peace in 1941) and he was an expert at raising morale. His speeches to the public on the radio were of great importance. They were often passionate (see Box 8.14) and most people agreed that they were just what was needed to boost morale at the time. Although Churchill was a strong and energetic leader, critics argue that he found it difficult to listen to advice and sometimes made mistakes because of this. Most historians agree, however, that he was the right sort of leader to guide Britain to victory.

Box 8.14 — Speech by Winston Churchill, broadcast on 18 June 1940

Upon this battle depends the survival of Christian civilisation. Upon it depends our own British life and the long continuity of our institutions and our Empire. The whole fury and might of the enemy must very soon be turned on us. Hitler knows that he will have to break us in this Island or lose the war. If we can stand up to him, all Europe may be freed and the life of the world may move forward into the broad and sunlit uplands. But if we fail then the whole world, including the United States, and all that we have known and cared for will sink into the abyss of a new Dark Age made more sinister and perhaps more prolonged by the lights of perverted science. Let us therefore brace ourselves to do our duty and so bear ourselves that if the British Empire and Commonwealth lasts for a thousand years, men will still say 'This was their finest hour'.

Part of a speech made by Prime Minister Churchill and broadcast on the radio on 18 June 1940

This poster was produced in 1942. By then, Churchill was seen as a national hero. The poster emphasises national unity, an important theme of Churchill's. As soon as he became Prime Minister, he was careful to include MPs from the Labour Party and Liberal Party in his War Cabinet so that it represented the nation as a whole.

Women and the war

Although women (over the age of 30) had won the right to vote in 1918, they had not won equality. In 1939, it was still generally accepted that a woman's proper role was as a wife and mother. The majority of married women did not work. Indeed, married women were banned from teaching and from working in government departments and hospitals. Girls were not expected to gain a higher education (it was generally thought that men did not like well educated women). Some colleges refused to take girls or to award degrees to them (giving them instead a certificate which said they had been educated to degree standard). Most girls left school at 14 and were expected to take a job only until they were married. The jobs available to these women were low paid and limited - mainly factory work, nursing, office work or domestic work (as servants). According to Anne Valery: 'We lived in a world where girls were brought up to please, kept in ignorance of sex and advised not to win when competing with boys. When we grew up, birth control was difficult to come by, abortion was a criminal offence, respectable restaurants refused to serve us in the evening if we were unaccompanied, it was shameful to enter a pub and no one, including the police, must ever interfere between a husband and wife, even if she were being beaten. We were the homemakers, the little women and the weaker sex. And then came the war.' (from *Talking About the War*, 1991).

During the war, Britain called on the services of women to a greater extent than any other country. Conscription made sure that all women except those with heavy family responsibilities played a part in the war effort (and many of those with families did voluntary work as well). By 1943, 90% of single women and 80% of married women were doing work of national importance. The photo above shows a woman worker inspecting an aircraft engine. Women mechanics were unheard of in the interwar period. Significantly, however, women in jobs like this were paid less than men.

Activity
Women in the war

Source B *Government poster (1)*

PART-TIME WAR WORKER

JUST A GOOD AFTERNOON'S WORK

Source D *Government poster (2)*

'We could do with thousands more like you..'

JOIN THE WOMEN'S LAND ARMY

Apply to nearest W.L.A County Office or to W.L.A HEADQUARTERS 6, CHESHAM STREET, LONDON S.W.1
Issued by the Ministry of Labour and National Service in conjunction with the Ministry of Agriculture

Source A *An eyewitness account*

The factory was vast and I was told to report for the night shift. Most of the girls were real rough-tough die-hards, loud-voiced and hard-faced. They eyed all newcomers suspiciously and were very unfriendly. I was sent with a group of them to report to a foreman. He surveyed us all and gave each one a job with the exception of yours truly. No doubt I looked nervous and scared. As he turned away I said, 'What shall I do?' He turned and sneered, 'Oh yes! We've forgotten sunshine here! What shall you do? - Here, take this' (he pointed at a broom) 'And sod off!' The day foreman was much nicer and more polite and, in time, I found my place. Once they discovered I could work a certain machine with good results, I was transferred to another department. The girls by now accepted me. Even the foul language flowed over my head. More new girls arrived on war work - models, secretaries, housewives, shop assistants, even a solicitor's wife and a doctor's daughter. I made many friends.

Account of Rosemary Moonen, a former hairdresser, recorded in 'We'll Meet Again' by Vera Lynn, 1989

Source C *A historian's view*

When the Second World War broke out, women were summoned back into the world of work by the pressing needs of wartime production. In the armed services and in the civilian labour force women once again demonstrated what they had clearly shown in the First World War - that they could do any man's job. They drove trucks and buses, operated cranes and heavy machinery, learned to be welders, radar operators, electrical engineers and anti-aircraft gunners. Many women already in the labour force as unskilled workers received training for new and more satisfying jobs. The idea that 'a woman's place is in the home' was temporarily shelved as yesterday's housewives became today's heroic war workers. The most significant change, however, was in the number of married women working for the first time. Between 1939 and 1945, the proportion of married women earning a wage rose from one in seven to one in four in both the USA and Britain.

From 'The Feminist Challenge' by David Bouchier, 1983

Source E *Women after the war*

a) Immediately after the war there was panic over jobs for returning soldiers and a wave of propaganda urged women to go back to their homes. Many did and many were forced out of work. As one woman put it: 'We were no longer comrades with the returning men, but competitors for what little there was.'

From 'The Feminist Challenge' by David Bouchier, 1983

b) Above all the housewife - the wife and mother - should be acknowledged as a full and responsible member of the community. Her home is the factory, her husband and children a worthwhile job. Let women make the most of their hard won freedom, not to build an independent women's world, not to escape from their family responsibilities, but to aim at building a family in which men and women act together for the sake of the children - a world built on partnership.

From an article in a Current Affairs Pamphlet, 1946

QUESTIONS

1. Judging from the information in this section, how did the war affect the lives of civilians in Britain?

2. What contribution to the war effort was made by women? Use Sources A-D in your answer?

3. Judging from Sources A-E how did the role of women change after 1939 (a) in the short term and (b) in the long term?

4. 'The war opened many women's eyes'. Explain this statement using Source A.

5. Would you describe Sources B and D as 'good examples of government propaganda'? Explain your answer.

Themes

World War II broke Europe's domination of world affairs and saw the USA and the Soviet Union emerge as 'superpowers'. Between 1941 and 1945, the Americans and Russians had worked together to defeat Hitler. But even during the war, they saw each other as rivals. Once the war was over, the wartime alliance began to break down. By 1950, much of the world was divided into two competing areas of influence or blocs - the American-dominated West which supported capitalism and the Russian-dominated East which supported Communism. These blocs remained at odds with each other for over 40 years, until the collapse of the Soviet Union in 1991. This period of conflict is known as the 'Cold War' because, although there was a massive build-up of arms, actual war did

not break out between the superpowers. The fact that both sides had nuclear weapons made each side stop short of a direct attack. That does not mean that the Cold War was a time of peace, however. Both superpowers backed and fought wars in other countries with millions of people dying as a result. This chapter looks at the following questions.

* Why did the wartime alliance begin to break down in 1945?
* What were the aims of the Soviet Union in Eastern Europe?
* How did the USA respond to events in Europe 1945-48?
* What were the causes and consequences of the Berlin Airlift?
* What part did nuclear weapons play in the Cold War?
* What were the aims of the United Nations Organisation (UNO)?
* Who was to blame for Cold War?

Key Events

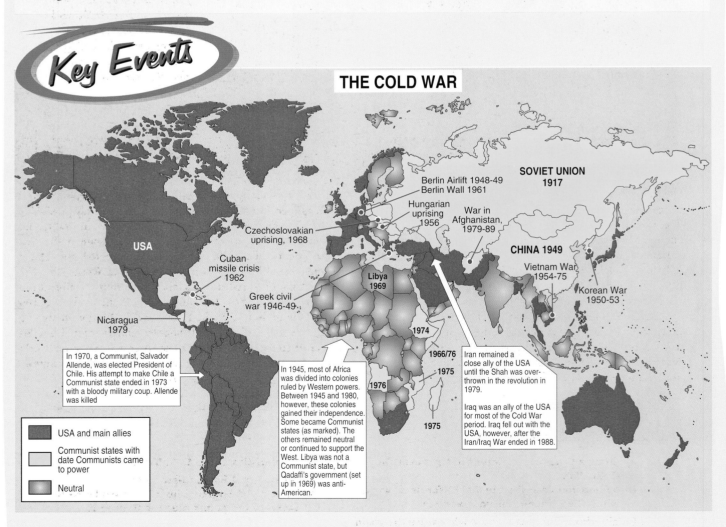

THE COLD WAR

Berlin Airlift 1948-49
Berlin Wall 1961

SOVIET UNION 1917

Hungarian uprising 1956

War in Afghanistan, 1979-89

Czechoslovakian uprising, 1968

USA

CHINA 1949

Cuban missile crisis 1962

Vietnam War 1954-75

Libya 1969

Korean War 1950-53

Greek civil war 1946-49

Nicaragua 1979

1974

1966/76

In 1970, a Communist, Salvador Allende, was elected President of Chile. His attempt to make Chile a Communist state ended in 1973 with a bloody military coup. Allende was killed

1975

Iran remained a close ally of the USA until the Shah was over-thrown in the revolution in 1979.

1976

In 1945, most of Africa was divided into colonies ruled by Western powers. Between 1945 and 1980, however, these colonies gained their independence. Some became Communist states (as marked). The others remained neutral or continued to support the West. Libya was not a Communist state, but Qadaffi's government (set up in 1969) was anti-American.

1975

Iraq was an ally of the USA for most of the Cold War period. Iraq fell out with the USA, however, after the Iran/Iraq War ended in 1988.

- USA and main allies
- Communist states with date Communists came to power
- Neutral

What was the Cold War?

1   A cartoonist's view of the Cold War

This cartoon was produced by an American cartoonist in the 1970s. By the 1970s, both the USA and the Soviet Union had produced enough nuclear weapons to destroy the world many times over. Each side, however, was worried that the other side was developing new and better weapons which would give them the advantage in an all-out war. At the same time, the Cold War was a war of words. Each side tried to persuade its people that the other side was evil.

2   A historian's view of the Cold War

The Second World War had barely ended when humanity plunged into what can be reasonably be regarded as a Third World War, though a very peculiar one. The philosopher Thomas Hobbes pointed out that wars do not only consist of battles or fighting. They also consist of periods when the will to do battle is well known. The Cold War between the two camps of the USA and the Soviet Union, which utterly dominated the international scene in the second half of the 20th century, was unquestionably one of those periods. Entire generations grew up under the shadow of global nuclear battles which, it was widely believed, could break out at any moment and destroy the world. Even those who did not believe that either side intended to attack found it hard not to be pessimistic since they feared that if it could go wrong, sooner or later it would. Nuclear war did not happpen, but for some 40 years it looked a daily possibility. The peculiarity of the Cold War was that, in reality, no imminent danger of world war existed. Despite what their governments said, both superpowers accepted the global distribution of force at the end of the Second World War. The Soviet Union controlled or exercised predominant influence in one part of the globe - the zone occupied by the Red Army and other Communist forces in 1945 - and it did not attempt to extend its range of influence further by military force. The USA exercised control and predominance over the rest of the world and it did not intervene in the zone of accepted Soviet control.

Adapted from 'Age of Extremes' by E. Hobsbawm, 1994

QUESTIONS

1. a) Draw a time line showing the key events in the Cold War.
   b) Would you describe the Cold War as a 'world war'? Give reasons for your answer.

2. Judging from Sources 1 and 2 what were the main characteristics of the Cold War?

3. a) What is the joke in Source 1?
   b) How could Source 1 be used as evidence to support the points made in Source 2?

Why did the wartime alliance begin to break down in 1945?

After the Nazi invasion of the Soviet Union in June 1941 and the Japanese attack on Pearl Harbour in December 1941, the Soviet Union and the USA joined Britain in a wartime alliance. But this alliance was never easy. Historians have identified five main reasons why the alliance began to break down in 1945 (see Box 9.1). These five reasons are examined in this section. Together, the three Allied leaders became known as the 'Big Three'.

 ## Memory of what had happened before 1941

There was a long history of distrust between the Soviet Union and other members of the wartime alliance. American and British governments, for example, had opposed the Bolshevik revolution in 1917 and had even sent troops to support the Bolsheviks' opponents during the civil war which began in 1918 (see p.39). Similarly, the American and British governments did not forget the Bolsheviks' appeal for a 'worldwide Communist revolution' in 1917. Even though Stalin later claimed that he only wanted 'socialism in one country', the American and British governments continued to fear the spread of Communism. Also, they did not forget that the Soviet Union had made a pact with Nazi Germany in 1939 (see p.147) and had been allied to the Nazis for the first two years of the war.

 ## The course of the war

With the USA, Soviet Union and Britain in alliance in 1942, there were immediate arguments about how best to fight. Stalin pointed out that two thirds of German forces were attacking the Soviet Union and demanded the opening of a 'second front' in the west. When the USA and Britain waited until 1944 before invading France, some Russians suspected that this was a deliberate policy to exhaust the Soviet Union (during the war the Soviet Union suffered at least 10 million casualties and great economic damage). Once the Western Front was opened, however, the Nazis were forced back to Germany by the British and Americans in the west and the Red Army in the east. By the end of the war, therefore, the Red Army occupied much of Eastern Europe, whilst British and American troops occupied much of Western Europe.

Box 9.1

Why did the wartime alliance break down?

1. The Allies were suspicious of each other because of what had happened before 1941.
2. Distrust grew because of what happened during the war itself.
3. Meetings of the Big Three resulted in misunderstandings and further distrust.
4. The key players changed.
5. The USA's development of the atom bomb changed the balance of power.

---

③ Meetings of the Big Three

Box 9.2

The Polish question

The future of Poland was of particular importance to the Big Three. Churchill argued that Britain had gone to war so that Poland could be free and independent, whilst Stalin argued that the Soviet Union's future security depended on a friendly Polish government. Churchill and Roosevelt wanted there to be democratic elections in Poland, but Stalin wanted to move the Polish border so that part of Poland was swallowed up in the Soviet Union. He also wanted there to be a Communist government in Poland. Stalin said: 'For Russia, it is not only a question of honour, but security – not only because we are on Poland's frontier, but also because throughout history Poland has always been a corridor for attack on Russia.'

The Allied leaders met three times – at Teheran in 1943 and at Yalta and Potsdam in February and July 1945. These meetings were used to discuss war strategy and arrangements for the postwar world. At Teheran, Stalin was in a weak position (much of the Soviet Union remained under Nazi control), but, by the time of the Potsdam Conference, his position was much stronger (the Red Army had advanced into eastern Germany). Although the Allied leaders remained outwardly friendly, differences of opinion developed at these meetings, especially over the boundaries of postwar Europe (see Box 9.2). The photo above shows Churchill, Roosevelt and Stalin at Yalta in February 1945.

4 Changing personnel

President Roosevelt died in April 1945 and was replaced by his deputy, Harry Truman. Truman was more hostile towards Stalin than Roosevelt had been. For example, after the Potsdam meeting, Truman told an adviser: 'Force is the only thing the Russians understand'. During the Potsdam Conference, the results of the British general election were announced. Labour won and so Churchill was replaced by the new Prime Minister, Clement Attlee. By the end of the Potsdam Conference, therefore, the old ties between Stalin, Churchill and Roosevelt had been broken and new relations began to develop.

5 The impact of the atom bomb

It was at the Potsdam Conference that President Truman was informed that the new atom bomb had been successfully tested and was even more powerful than had been hoped. According to Churchill, this news greatly affected Truman: 'He was a changed man. He told the Russians just where they got on and off and generally bossed the whole meeting.' Once the Americans had dropped the atom bombs on Hiroshima and Nagasaki, it was clear to the world that they would have a military advantage in any war they chose to fight. This undoubtedly affected Soviet-American relations.

Activity
A fading alliance

Source B *A historian's view*

As President Truman put it, looking back at the Potsdam Conference: 'On 24 July I casually mentioned to Stalin that we had a new weapon of special destructive force. Stalin showed no unusual interest. All he said was that he was glad to hear it and hoped we would make good use of it against the Japanese.' Although his reaction has been interpreted as a failure to grasp the importance of Truman's communication, it is more likely that Stalin was playing his cards close to his chest.

From 'Stalin and the Shaping of the Soviet Union' by A. de Jonge, 1987

Source D *Stalin's private views*

Perhaps you think that because we are allies of the English we have forgotten who they are and who Churchill is. They find nothing sweeter than to trick their allies. Churchill is the kind who, if you don't watch him, will slip a kopek [a small coin] out of your pocket. And Roosevelt? Roosevelt is not like that. He dips his hand only for bigger coins.

The above comments were made by Stalin in private at Yalta in February 1945.

From 'Conversations With Stalin' by M. Djilas, 1962

Source A *The Potsdam Conference, July 1945*

This photo shows Attlee, Truman and Stalin at the Potsdam Conference in July 1945.

Source C
American cartoon from February 1945

This cartoon shows Stalin, dressed as a policeman, helping Russia to steal territory. When a second policeman comes over from the 'World League Police Station', Stalin assures him there is nothing to worry about.

QUESTIONS

1. Using the information in this section, write a paragraph explaining why the wartime alliance began to break down in 1945.

2. Which of the reasons for the breakdown of the wartime alliance is illustrated by each of Sources A-D? Explain your answers?

3. a) What do Sources C and D tell us about relations between the Allies in February 1945?

   b) How had relations changed by September 1945? Use Sources A and B in your answer.

What were the aims of the Soviet Union in Eastern Europe?

Although no shots were fired, Eastern Europe was the first battlefield upon which the Cold War was fought. Before the Second World War, the Soviet Union had been the only Communist country in the world. It was surrounded by hostile neighbours and, as a result, had good reason to feel vulnerable and open to attack. When the Second World War was over, Stalin was determined to make sure that the Soviet Union was surrounded by at least some friendly governments. Between 1945 and 1948, Hungary, Poland, Romania, Bulgaria and Czechoslovakia all produced Communist governments which were supported by the Soviet Union. This finished off the wartime alliance. To those in the West (especially in the USA), events in Eastern Europe were very alarming. Communism, it seemed, was spreading in just the way that Lenin and others at the time of the October revolution had said it would. Some people even began to argue that the Soviet Union was aiming to take over the whole world. This section considers what sort of aims the Soviet Union had once the war was over. In particular, it considers whether events in Eastern Europe were the first steps on the path to world Communism or whether they had more limited objectives.

1 The strategic importance of Eastern Europe

After the First World War, the Western Allies had seen the countries of Eastern Europe as a barrier against newly created Bolshevik Russia. In the interwar period, most Eastern European countries were hostile to the Soviet Union and some (for example, Hungary and Romania) fought with Germany in the Second World War. It has already been noted (Box 9.2) that Poland was of particular strategic importance to the Soviet Union since Russia had frequently been attacked via Poland. Control of other Eastern European countries would also provide protection for the Soviet Union's flank. There were, therefore, military reasons why the Soviet Union might want to control the governments of countries in Eastern Europe. There were also economic reasons. Before the war, the Soviet Union had been isolated. If it was surrounded by friendly countries, it would have a ready-made market for its goods. In 1945, the Soviet Union was in a particularly good position to gain control of Eastern Europe since the Red Army had liberated the area, driving the Nazis back into Germany.

2 Soviet aims at the end of the war

By the end of the war, little concerning the future shape of Europe had been decided in any sort of detail. Behind the scenes, however, Churchill and Stalin had reached an understanding now known as the **percentages deal** (see Box 9.3). Although Churchill later complained about Soviet expansion in Eastern Europe, it seems that Stalin saw the percentages deal as a recognition of the power of the Soviet Union in Eastern Europe. Certainly, what was agreed was a pretty accurate guide as to what actually happened. It should be recognised, however, that the war had taken its toll on the Soviet Union and it simply could not afford to be too ambitious (Box 9.4).

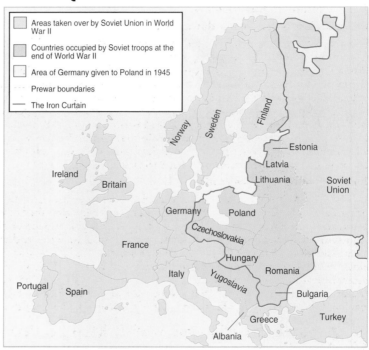

	Areas taken over by Soviet Union in World War II
	Countries occupied by Soviet troops at the end of World War II
	Area of Germany given to Poland in 1945
····	Prewar boundaries
—	The Iron Curtain

Europe in 1949.

3 Events in Eastern Europe after the war

Between 1945 and 1948, the Soviet Union tightened its grip on Eastern Europe. At first, it was sensitive to Western demands for free elections. Later, 'puppet' governments were put in place and all important decisions were made from Moscow. There were three phases leading to Soviet control.

Phase 1 - Gaining a foothold

In 1945, few of the countries in Eastern Europe had strong Communist parties which could be relied on to win elections (see Box 9.5 and chart, right). At first, the Soviet government encouraged the creation of coalition governments in which Communists held at least a few key ministries. Many of these Communists had been trained in Moscow. This ensured that they obeyed the instructions given to them by the Soviet government. At the same time, the Red Army remained in these countries.

Phase 2 - The Soviet clamp-down 1946-48

Later, the Soviet government used its Communist allies to drive out non-Communists from the coalition governments. By 1949, Hungary, Romania, Bulgaria, Poland and Czechoslovakia had all become one-party states. Opposition parties were banned and policies controlled by the Soviet Union. When Czechoslovakia, Poland and Hungary showed an interest in joining the Marshall Plan programme (see pp.170-71), for example, Communist leaders from these countries were summoned to Moscow and told they could not join. In 1947, COMINFORM (Communist Information Bureau) was set up to bring all European Communist parties more firmly under Soviet control. The only country to defy Stalin successfully was Yugoslavia.

Phase 3 - Building a Soviet bloc

In 1949, COMECON (Council for Mutual Economic Assistance) was set up to bring the economies of the East European countries in line with the Soviet model. Industries were owned and run by the state, with rigid systems of planning. Agriculture was also brought under state control and state farms and collectives set up. Much of Eastern Europe had been agricultural before the war and so the Soviet Union put an emphasis on developing industry. Results were quite impressive at first. In Czechoslovakia, industrial production in 1955 was double the prewar level. But, by the 1960s, progress had slowed. Plans were often too rigid and the economy run for the benefit of the Soviet Union, not the locals.

4 How far did the Soviet Union aim to go?

This cartoon appeared in a British newspaper, the 'Evening Standard', on 2 March 1948. Stalin's Foreign Minister, Molotov, is spinning the globe. In a caption, he asks Stalin: 'Who's next to be liberated from freedom, Comrade?' On the desk, the American Secretary of State, George Marshall, looks on helplessly. The cartoon illustrates the negative view of the Soviet Union in the West in the late 1940s - a time when the 'domino theory' first became popular (see Box 9.6). Although many historians now believe that the Soviet Union's objectives were limited (to provide a defensive ring around the Soviet Union), this was not how it appeared to many people in the West at the time. Western governments (especially the USA) argued that the Soviet Union's aim was world domination.

Box 9.5 — Communists in Eastern Europe

The basic problem remained. The Communists were a small minority in most East European countries right after the war. In all parts of the region, non-Communist political parties wanted to play a role in government. The outcome of elections held shortly after the war showed the problems. Although held under the watchful eye of Russian authorities, the Communist Party only received 17% of votes in the Hungarian election of 1945. In Czechoslovakia which was the one East European country where a large Communist movement had existed before the war, the Party won 38% of the vote in May 1946.

From 'The World Since 1945' by T.E. Vadney, 1987

☐ Votes for Communists before clampdown
☐ Votes for Communists after clampdown

HUNGARY
1945 — 17%
1947 — 61%

POLAND
1946 — Election postponed
1947 — 80%

ROMANIA
1946 — 90%

BULGARIA
1945 — 90%
1946 — 79%

CZECHOSLOVAKIA
1946 — 38%
1948 — 79%

Box 9.6 — The domino theory

According to the domino theory, when one state falls to the Communists, this knocks down another which knocks down a third and so on. As with dominoes, the process continues and speeds up unless action is taken to stop it. The model assumes that the Soviet Union's aims were unlimited.

Activity
Poland after the war

Source A Poland before and after World War II

Legend:
- – – – Prewar boundary
- ···· Postwar boundary
- ☐ Land given to Poland in 1945
- ☐ Land lost to Soviet Union in 1945

Soviet Union
Danzig
East Prussia
East Germany
Stettin
Warsaw
POLAND
R. Oder
R. Neisse
Czechoslovakia

The postwar borders of Poland were agreed at Yalta. At Yalta, Stalin also agreed that free elections should be held in Poland and that Polish political exiles in London should join the government. Neither promise was kept.

Source B Letter from Stalin to Truman

It must be borne in mind that Poland borders on the Soviet Union - which cannot be said about Great Britain or the USA. Poland is to the security of the Soviet Union what Belgium or Greece is to the security of Great Britain. You evidently do not agree that the Soviet Union is entitled to seek in Poland a government that would be friendly to it. But you should understand that the Soviet government cannot agree to the existence in Poland of a government hostile to it. In World War II, the Soviet people freely shed their blood on the fields of Poland, fighting for the liberation of that country. That makes a friendly Polish government a necessity.

Part of a letter written by Stalin to President Truman in April 1945 (in reply to a letter from Truman in which Truman had called for 'genuine democratic elements' in the Polish government)

Source C A historian's view (1)

First, contrary to what was thought in Western countries at the time, there was no free competition between Communist and non-Communist parties in Poland. Power passed directly from the Germans to the Soviet army and from the Soviet army to the Soviet-controlled Communist provisional government. The Polish Communists were handed power on a plate by the Soviet army and successfully stopped all attempts to share power. Second, there was never any need to impose Communism on Poland by brute force. All possible opposition groups had already been destroyed. They had been discredited by prewar or wartime failures, deserted by the Allies or destroyed in the Warsaw uprising against the Germans in 1944. Third, there was no conspiracy between Russian and Polish Communists. Indeed, the Polish Communist movement differed from the Russian on many issues and was deeply divided. Both Polish and Russian Communists felt their way forward in a very uncertain and confusing situation.

From 'Communist Power in Europe 1944-49' edited by M. McCauley, 1979

Source D A historian's view (2)

Roosevelt came away from Yalta with a feeling of triumph. Stalin quickly began to shatter the American illusion. He refused to reorganise the Polish government in any significant way. He suppressed freedom of speech, assembly, religion and the press in Poland and made no move to hold free elections. To a greater or lesser extent, the Russians followed this pattern in the rest of Eastern Europe, making it perfectly clear that now that they held the region, they would not give it up. They shut the West out completely. By any standards, the Soviet actions were high handed.

From 'Rise to Globalism' by S. Ambrose, 1980

Source E An American cartoon

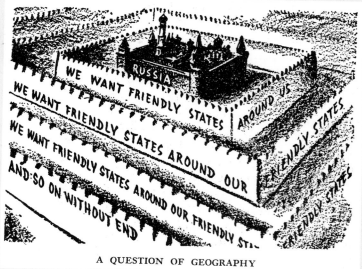

A QUESTION OF GEOGRAPHY

QUESTIONS

1. Judging from the information in this section, what were the aims of the Soviet Union in Eastern Europe?

2. Can Stalin's attitude towards and actions in Poland be justified? Give reasons for your answer using Sources A-D.

3. 'Poland was a pawn in the superpowers' game. There was little concern for the Polish people.' What is the evidence in Sources A-D to support this view?

4. What point is being made by the cartoon in Source E? How fair is it? Give reasons for your answer.

Winston Churchill's Fulton speech, March 1946

Within months of being cheered as the hero who had led Britain to victory against the Nazis, Churchill was forced to stand down as Prime Minister. The general election of July 1945 was won convincingly by Labour. This was a bitter blow for Churchill and it is clear from his memoirs that he was depressed for many months afterwards. At the beginning of 1946, Churchill travelled to the USA. It was while he was there that he made a speech which most historians agree was a landmark in the history of the Cold War. It was in this speech, for example, that the phrase 'the iron curtain' was used for the first time.

Churchill and Communism

Churchill's opposition to Communism was deep rooted. In 1924, for example, he said: 'From the earliest moment of its birth the Russian Bolshevik government has declared its intention of using all the power of the Russian Empire to promote a world revolution. Their agents have penetrated into every country. Everywhere they have endeavoured to bring into being "germ cells" from which the cancer of Communism should grow.' Although he was committed to the wartime alliance, Churchill's memoirs make it clear that he remained suspicious of Stalin. By 1946, Churchill was also worried that the American government was not being tough enough in its dealings with the Soviet Union.

" Churchill's speech

A shadow has fallen upon the scenes so lately lighted by the Allied victory. Nobody knows what Soviet Russia and its Communist International organisation intends to do in the immediate future, or what the limits, if any, to their expansive tendencies. We understand the Russians' need to be secure on their western frontiers from all renewal of German aggression. We welcome Russia to her rightful place among the leading nations of the world. It is my duty, however, to place before you certain facts about the present situation in Europe. From Stettin in the Baltic to Trieste in the Adriatic, an iron curtain has descended across the continent. Behind that line lie all the capitals of the ancient states of central and eastern Europe - Warsaw, Berlin, Prague, Vienna, Budapest, Belgrade, Bucharest and Sofia. All these famous cities are subject to a very high and increasing measure of control from Moscow. This is certainly not the liberated Europe we fought to build up. Nor is it one which contains the essentials of permanent peace. "

From a speech made by Winston Churchill at Westminster College, Fulton, Missouri in the USA on 5 March 1946

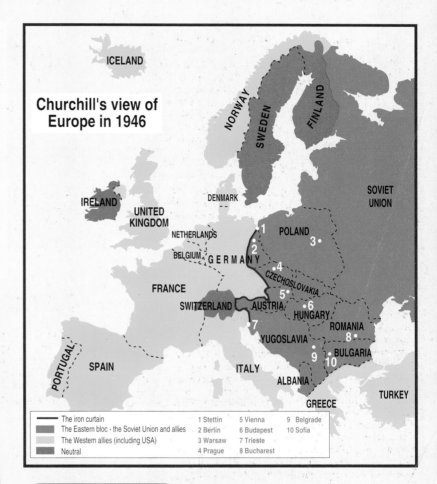

Churchill's view of Europe in 1946

─── The iron curtain	1 Stettin	5 Vienna	9 Belgrade
The Eastern bloc - the Soviet Union and allies	2 Berlin	6 Budapest	10 Sofia
The Western allies (including USA)	3 Warsaw	7 Trieste	
Neutral	4 Prague	8 Bucharest	

QUESTIONS

1. **What do you think Churchill was trying to achieve by making the Fulton speech?**

2. a) **What does this speech tell us about Churchill's attitude towards the Soviet Union?**

   b) **Do you agree with Churchill's interpretation of Russian actions since 1945? Give reasons for your answer.**

3. **Why do you think Churchill's speech is an important source for historians studying the origins of the Cold War?**

How did the USA respond to events in Europe 1945- 48?

Since 1917, Americans had seen Communism, with its aim of 'world revolution', as a threat to their capitalist system. The cooperation during the war had only been temporary, brought about by the need to defeat Fascism. When the Russians showed no sign of pulling back from the areas occupied by the Red Army, the old American suspicions resurfaced. The USA believed that the Soviet Union was trying to spread Communism first through Eastern Europe and then to the West and beyond. Truman, who became President in April 1945, was less used to dealing with Stalin and less diplomatic than Roosevelt. Besides, the American economy was in a very healthy state after the war and, from July 1945, the Americans had the atom bomb. As a result, they hoped that they could put pressure on the Soviet Union through their superior military and economic strength.

 The policy of 'containment'

From 1946, President Truman's government gave up any attempt to continue the wartime cooperation with the Soviet Union. Believing that Stalin intended to build an empire which extended from Eastern to Western Europe and beyond, Truman's government decided to **contain** the Soviet Union, preventing its expansion beyond the iron curtain (as defined in Churchill's Fulton speech - see p.169). The first important test of this policy in Europe came in March 1947 when the American government announced aid to Greece and Turkey. Since 1944, there had been a civil war in Greece, with Britain helping the government to fight left wing forces which included the Greek Communist Party. When Britain announced in 1947 that it could no longer afford to help the Greek government, the USA stepped in, fearing that Greece (along with its neighbour Turkey) would come under Soviet control (see Box 9.7a). In fact, Greek Communists received no help from Stalin who was anxious to avoid further problems with the USA. President Truman announced the aid to Greece and Turkey in an important speech in March 1947. It was the first public announcement of the policy of containment and became known as the **Truman Doctrine** (see Box 9.7b).

 The battle of ideas

The Cold War started as a war of words. In his speech (Box 9.7b), President Truman argued that the world was becoming divided into two camps - the capitalist camp and the Communist camp. The capitalist world, he claimed, was free whilst the Communist world was not. To protect the free world, the USA would use its economic and military strength. Once Truman had delivered this speech, it was clear that every country had a choice to make. The British cartoon (above) from *Punch* (18 June 1947) illustrates that choice. It portrays Truman and Stalin as rival bus drivers. Stalin offers Communism whilst Truman offers capitalism to the countries of Europe. It is significant that Stalin is pushing countries onto his bus whilst Truman politely raises his cap.

Box 9.7 — The Truman Doctrine

a) There isn't any doubt in my mind that Russia intends an invasion of Turkey. Unless Russia is faced with an iron fist and strong language, another war is in the making. We should maintain complete control over Japan. We should create a strong government in China and Korea. I'm tired of babying the Soviets.

Part of a letter from President Truman to James Byrnes, Secretary of State, 5 January 1946

b) At the present moment in world history, nearly every nation must choose between alternative ways of life. The choice is often not a free one. One way of life is based upon the will of the majority, free elections, individual liberty, freedom of speech and religion and freedom from political tyranny. The second way of life is based upon the will of a minority forcibly imposed upon the majority. It relies upon terror, a controlled press and radio, fixed elections and a lack of personal freedom. I believe it must be the policy of the United States to support peoples who resist being enslaved by armed minorities or by outside pressures. I believe that we must help free peoples to work out their own destiny in their own way.

Part of President Truman's speech to the American Congress, 12 March 1947

 **The Marshall Plan**

By the time that Truman made his speech (Box 9.7b), it had become clear that the desperately needed economic recovery of Europe was not taking place. If containment was to work, then countries outside Soviet influence had to be strengthened. As a result, to encourage economic recovery, the European Recovery Plan was launched in 1947 by General George Marshall, the American Secretary of State. The **Marshall Plan** or **Marshall Aid** as it became known was financial aid to European countries to help them to rebuild their war-damaged economies. The aid was offered to all European countries, but the Soviet Union and the countries it dominated in Eastern Europe turned the offer down. This had been expected by the Americans who saw the plan as a strong weapon in the developing struggle against the Soviet Union. It was argued that Communism (which was strong in Western European countries such as France and Italy) gained support when economic conditions were bad. Economic aid would help to prevent this. Under the Marshall Plan, aid began to flow into Europe from 1948.

Activity
The impact of the Marshall Plan

Source B *Marshall announces his plan*

Europe's requirements for the next three or four years of foreign foods and other essential products - principally from the USA - are so much greater than its present ability to pay that it must have substantial additional help or face economic and political disaster. It is logical that the USA should do whatever it can to restore normal economic health to the world, without which there can be no political stability and no peace. Our policy is directed not against any country or doctrine, but against hunger, poverty, desperation and chaos. Its purpose should be the revival of a working economy so as to produce the conditions in which free institutions can exist.

Speech made by George Marshall at Harvard University, 5 June 1947

Source C *Reaction from the Soviet Union*

It is becoming more and more evident to everyone that the Marshall Plan will mean placing European countries under the economic and political control of the USA. It will mean direct interference by the USA in the internal affairs of those countries. The Plan is an attempt to split Europe into two camps and to complete the formation of a bloc of countries hostile to the interests of the Soviet Union.

Part of a speech made by A. Vyshinsky, deputy Soviet Foreign Minister, to the United Nations General Assembly, 18 September 1947

Source E *A poster promoting the Marshall Plan*

Source A *The distribution of Marshall Aid*

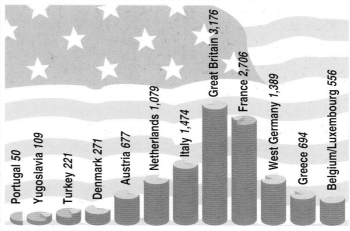

All figures in $ million

The total amount of Marshall Aid allocated by the American Congress was $13.15 billion. The above graph shows how this total was divided between the various countries.

Source D *A historian's view*

In the USA, support for the Marshall Plan was widespread. This was because of the Cold War and the increasingly anti-Soviet attitude of both the Truman government and Congress. It was also because the Plan benefited the USA directly. Most of the money for the goods needed to rebuild Europe was spent in the USA itself. The Marshall Plan represented a huge government subsidy to American business, workers and agriculture and it played a vital part in fuelling the postwar boom in the USA. In Europe, the results seemed equally impressive. By the time the Plan came to an end in 1952, about $13 billion had been spent. With goods supplied by the USA, industrial output rose to 35% above prewar levels. Agricultural output rose to 10% above prewar levels.

From 'The World Since 1945' by T.E. Vadney, 1987

Source F *The views of Churchill and Truman*

Churchill was convinced that the Marshall Plan was 'the most unselfish act in history'. The USA was offering to finance, from its ample resources, the reconstruction of the war-racked continent of Europe. Truman had a somewhat different view. His objective was economic reconstruction with a political purpose: 'to save Europe from economic disaster and lift from it the shadow of enslavement by Russian Communism'. 'I think', said Truman in his memoirs (published in 1956), 'the world now realises that without the Marshall Plan it would have been difficult for Western Europe to remain free from the tyranny of Communism.'

From 'The Cold War' by H. Higgins, 1993

QUESTIONS

1. a) **Judging from the information in this section, how did the USA respond to events in Europe between 1945 and 1948?**
   b) **Why do you think the USA responded in this way?**
2. **Judging from Sources A, B, D and F what were the aims of the Marshall Plan and how effective was it?**
3. **Explain the comments made by Vyshinsky (Source C). What do they tell us about the Cold War in its early years?**
4. a) **Write a caption for the poster (Source E), supporting the Marshall Plan.**
   b) **How might your caption differ if you were a Russian?**

At the Yalta Conference it was agreed that, immediately after the war, Germany should be divided into four zones. Each zone was to be controlled by one of the four Allies (the USA, Britain, France and the Soviet Union). Berlin, the German capital which lay deep in the zone controlled by the Soviet Union, would also be divided into four zones (see map below). This arrangement was seen as a temporary measure, but the coming of the Cold War meant that it lasted much longer than expected. In fact, Germany became the focus in the struggle between the Western Allies and the Soviet Union. When, in 1948, the Soviet Union tried to push its former allies out of Berlin by cutting off all land routes to the city, the Western Allies responded by carrying in supplies by air. The Berlin Airlift was the biggest operation of its kind ever mounted. By refusing to yield to Soviet pressure, the Western Allies managed to keep control of their part of Berlin. The conflict over Berlin, however, led to greater division and greater tension between the two blocs.

1 The German 'problem'

After Hitler was defeated, the Allies were uncertain about the future of Germany. It was expected that the military occupation of Germany, organised through the division of the country into four zones (see map, right), would be temporary. The idea was that a German state would re-emerge once the political system was rid of Nazis. It was also agreed that Germany would pay reparations (compensation) for the damage caused by the war. The amount to be paid was not decided. As cooperation between the Western Allies and the Soviet Union broke down in 1945 and 1946, agreement over Germany became more difficult. The Western Allies believed that the Soviet Union was aiming to set up a central German government which would be Communist controlled. The Soviet government, on the other hand, believed that the Western Allies intended to set up a separate capitalist state in West Germany (the American, British and French zones).

2 The immediate causes of the Berlin Airlift

The first years after the war were particularly hard for the Germans. The whole of Germany suffered from inflation and food shortages and there was widespread poverty. By the end of 1946, however, the American government had come to the conclusion that the recovery of the German economy was essential for the recovery of non-Communist Western Europe (Box 9.8a). In December 1946, the British and American governments merged their zones to make a single economic unit (known as **Bizonia**). In 1948, the French agreed to join and **Trizonia** was created. Once the three Western zones had merged, American aid (through the Marshall Plan) was used to stimulate economic recovery. Then, in June 1948, a plan was put forward by the Americans to reform the German currency. A new Deutschmark was to replace the now worthless Reichsmark (in 1948, a pound of coffee cost 1,500 marks whilst the average income was 300-400 marks per month). For the Soviet Union, this was the last straw (see Box 9.8b). Trizonia was bigger than the Soviet zone and it contained more German industry. Worried that the Western Allies were planning to set up a new separate West German state which would be absorbed into the Western capitalist system, the Soviet government used its one remaining weapon - control of land access to Berlin. The new currency was introduced into Trizonia on 20 June and into West Berlin on 23 June. A day later, the Berlin Blockade began (see paragraph 3 below).

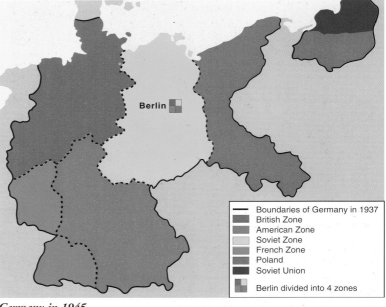

Germany in 1945.

Boundaries of Germany in 1937
British Zone
American Zone
Soviet Zone
French Zone
Poland
Soviet Union

Berlin divided into 4 zones

Box 9.8 American policy and the Soviet response

a) The USA is firmly of the belief that Germany should be administered as a single economic unit and that zonal barriers should be completely destroyed so far as economic life in Germany is concerned. The American government has formally announced that it is its intention to unify the economy of its own zone with any or all of the other zones. So far, only the British government has agreed. If complete economic unification cannot be secured, we shall do everything in our power to secure maximum unification.

Part of a speech made by American Secretary of State, James Byrnes, in Stuttgart, September 1946

b) Western currency reform is against the wishes and interests of the German people. The separate currency reform completes the splitting of Germany. It is a breach of the agreement made at Potsdam that Germany would be treated as an economic whole. The Western Powers claim it is impossible to agree on a four-power currency reform for the whole of Germany. But this is just an excuse. The introduction of two currencies in Germany will mean that trade relations will be destroyed. Interzonal trade will in practice become trade between two separate states since two different currencies will be used.

Part of a speech made by Marshal Sokolovsky, Soviet Military Governor of Berlin, 18 June 1948

③ The Berlin Blockade

This photo shows West Berliners waving as a plane carrying supplies comes in to land in West Berlin during the Airlift.

In 1948, the Soviet government gradually tightened control over road and rail links between the Western zones and Berlin. When the new currency was adopted in West Berlin on 23 June, the Russians then began a blockade. All land links with Berlin were blocked and power and coal supplies to West Berlin were cut off. The Western Allies had three choices. They could pull out of West Berlin. They could try to open up the land routes by force (which would mean risking a full-scale war). Or, they could bring supplies into West Berlin by air. President Truman decided that an airlift was the solution. Between 28 June 1948 and May 1949, an Anglo-American airlift kept West Berlin supplied with up to 12,000 tons of food and fuel per day (see Box 9.9). The Russians, aware of American superiority in the air, did not interfere with the Airlift. The threat of an atomic attack also existed. As a warning to the Soviet Union, Truman ordered B-29 bombers, capable of carrying atom bombs, to be sent to Britain. Eventually, however, the Soviet Union gave up the Blockade and in May 1949 began re-opening land routes to Berlin. The Berlin Airlift, however, was the first major confrontation of the Cold War.

Box 9.9   A report on the Berlin Airlift, 1949

In the 318 days since the Airlift began, British and American aircraft have made 195,530 flights to Berlin, carrying 1,583,686 tons of supplies. British aircraft have made 63,612 flights carrying 369,347 tons - made up of around 185,000 tons of food, 97,000 tons of coal, 50,000 tons of fuel, 21,000 tons of miscellaneous goods and 15,000 tons of supplies for the British services in Berlin. In the reverse direction, British aircraft have carried out from Berlin about 30,000 tons of freight and over 65,000 passengers. Although the British contribution to the Airlift (in terms of flights and tonnage) was only about a quarter of the total, the RAF was responsible for the bulk of the organisation on the ground (six of the eight airfields were in the British zone).

Report made by Arthur Henderson, British Secretary for Air, 11 May 1949

This well known cartoon appeared in 'Punch' in July 1948. The man in the chimney is Stalin. The storks (birds which are often pictured carrying babies) represent the planes flying to West Berlin during the Airlift. By drawing storks, the cartoonist suggests that the planes are bringing new life to West Berlin. Stalin wants to shoot the birds down (he has a gun), but has not quite plucked up courage to do so.

④ The consequences of the Berlin Airlift

The Berlin Airlift confirmed the division of Germany (and Berlin) for the duration of the Cold War. The Federal Republic of Germany (West Germany) was established by the Western allies in May 1949. The Russians set up a separate state, the German Democratic Republic (East Germany), in their zone in October 1949. The Blockade certainly alarmed the people and governments in Western Europe and North America. This alarm resulted in the formation of a military alliance whose aim was to counter what was seen as the Soviet threat. In April 1949, the **North Atlantic Treaty Organisation** (NATO) was set up. This showed that the containment of the Soviet Union was to take an increasingly military form. The failure of the Blockade also led the Russians to strengthen their position. In 1949, the Soviet government set up the Council for Mutual Economic Assistance (COMECON) - an organisation whose aim was to improve trade between East European countries. In 1955, the **Warsaw Pact** was set up. This was the Soviet Union's military response to NATO.

Activity
The consequences of the Berlin Airlift

Source B The North Atlantic Treaty, Article 5

The members of NATO agree that an armed attack against one or more of them in Europe or North America shall be considered an attack against them all. As a result, they agree that, if such an armed attack occurs, each of them, in exercise of the right of individual or collective self-defence recognised by Article 51 of the Charter of the United Nations, will take such action as is necessary (including the use of armed force) to restore and maintain the security of the North Atlantic area.

Part of the North Atlantic Treaty signed by the 12 founding members in April 1949

Source C The Warsaw Pact Treaty

Article 111. The members of the Warsaw Pact shall consult with one another on all important international issues affecting their common interests. They shall immediately consult with one another whenever, in the opinion of any one of them, a threat of armed attack on one or more of the parties to the Treaty has arisen, in order to ensure joint defence and the maintenance of peace and security.

Part of the Warsaw Pact Treaty signed by the 8 founding members in May 1955

Source E An American diplomat on NATO

I recommended that it should be our policy not to allow any country to join NATO unless it was properly part of the North Atlantic area. This principle, if followed, would have excluded Greece and Turkey and probably Italy as well. My aim was to avoid anything that could appear to the Soviet leaders as an aggressive encirclement of their country. To this day I can see no reason for the admission of Greece and Turkey other than the desire on our part to have military bases there.

An extract from the memoirs of George Kennan, published in 1968. Kennan was a senior American diplomat and policy advisor who had been one of the architects of the policy of containment.

Source A Map showing members of NATO and the Warsaw Pact

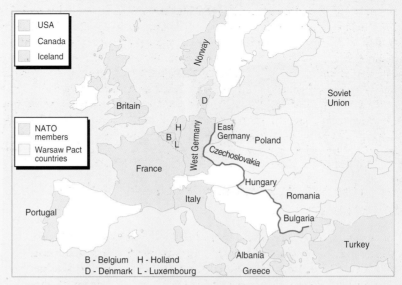

USA
Canada
Iceland

NATO members
Warsaw Pact countries

Norway
Britain
D
East Germany
H
B L
West Germany
Poland
Czechoslovakia
France
Hungary
Italy
Romania
Portugal
Bulgaria
Albania
Greece
Turkey
Soviet Union

B - Belgium H - Holland
D - Denmark L - Luxembourg

At first, NATO contained 12 member states. Membership was extended to Greece and Turkey in 1952 and to West Germany in 1954. West Germany's membership was controversial since it meant allowing German rearmament. The Soviet Union reacted by setting up the Warsaw Pact - a military alliance like NATO for Communist countries. Albania signed the Treaty of Warsaw, but left the Warsaw Pact in 1968.

Source D A Soviet cartoon

This cartoon was produced in the Soviet Union in 1952. The men are NATO generals. Note the nuclear bomb attached to the American general on the far right.

QUESTIONS

1. Judging from the information in this section, what were the causes and consequences of the Berlin Airlift?
2. a) Why do you think **NATO** and the Warsaw Pact were set up?
   b) What does the creation of these organisations tell us about the development of the Cold War? Use Sources A-C in your answer.
3. What point is being made by the cartoon in Source D?
4. Judging from Source E would you say that **NATO** was purely a defensive organisation? Give reasons for your answer.

What part did nuclear weapons play in the Cold War?

The first atom bomb was exploded in a test in the USA on 17 July 1945. Less than a month later, the USA dropped two atom bombs on the Japanese towns of Hiroshima and Nagasaki (see pp.154-56). The terrifying power of this new superbomb shocked the world. For four years, the USA remained the only nuclear power. But other countries were desperate to make their own atom bombs. Despite American efforts to protect their secret, an atom bomb was exploded at a test site in the Soviet Union in July 1949. This led to an arms race. Now that both superpowers had the atom bomb, they began to pour money into projects to build more and bigger bombs and new delivery systems. Each side suspected that the other aimed to build up enough weapons to be able to make a 'first strike' which would prevent the other side firing back. The USA made most of the technological breakthroughs, but it never took the Soviet Union long to catch up. As a result, the danger of nuclear war overshadowed every conflict in the Cold War. Historians have debated fiercely about the effects of the arms race. Some think it increased tension, wasted resources and created instability around the world. Others argue that the fear of what would happen if nuclear weapons were used acted as a 'deterrent' and kept the peace.

① The USA, nuclear weapons and the Baruch Plan

The successful development of the atom bomb in 1945 gave a military advantage to the USA which thoroughly alarmed the Soviet government (see Box 9.10a). The Americans refused to share their atomic knowledge with the Soviet Union - an important factor in the breakdown of the wartime alliance (see pp.164-65). Some Americans hoped that having the atom bomb would give the USA the power to settle disputes and to play the role of 'world police officer' (see Box 9.10b). In 1946, the Americans proposed a plan for the control of atomic energy, known as the **Baruch Plan** (named after the official who presented it). An International Atomic Development Authority was to be set up to oversee and control the use of atomic energy. It would have the power to inspect all atomic energy activities. The USA agreed to stop manufacturing atom bombs and to destroy its existing bombs as soon as the system of inspection was in place and the punishments for those breaking the rules had been agreed. The Soviet Union, however, wanted the USA to destroy its stock of bombs immediately. The historian T.E. Vadney points out that: 'The American refusal to destroy its nuclear weapons meant that, while the Soviet Union would have to stop work on the development of nuclear weapons, the USA would keep its existing arsenal. This was no small point as it would take time to set up the international agency and to conduct inspections. A period of years might pass in which the USA had nuclear weapons but the Soviet Union did not.' The Baruch Plan was eventually dropped.

② The Soviet atom bomb, 1949

The Soviet atomic research programme was transformed in 1945. Scientists' pay was trebled. By 1949, the director, Igor Kurchatov, led a team of half a million scientists. In August 1949, an American plane carrying scientific instruments picked up clear evidence of the first successful Soviet atomic test. This was a great shock to the American public. Most people expected it to be ten or more years before the Soviet Union developed an atom bomb. Immediately, Truman ordered a new, more powerful weapon to be built - the hydrogen bomb (**H-bomb**). News of the Communists' victory in China in late 1949 further alarmed the American government. As a result, defence spending was massively increased (see right).

Box 9.10 — The power of the atom bomb

a) At the final defeat of Germany, there was great joy. Russia could be made safe at last. She could put her house in order, protected by the 300 divisions of her army. Then plump came the atom bomb. At a blow, the balance which had seemed set and steady was suddenly shaken. The 300 divisions had lost much of their value. It was clear that the West did not trust the Russians and it aroused all their old suspicions.

Part of a letter written to the British government by Clark Kerr, British Ambassador to the Soviet Union, December 1945

b) We can drop, at a moment's notice, atomic bombs on any spot on the world's surface and return to our base. With vision and guts and plenty of atom bombs, modern planes and strategically-located airbases, the USA can prevent wars of aggression. The atom bomb in American hands is like keeping a stick behind the door. It is to be used only when a bandit nation goes berserk.

Part of a speech made to the American Senate by Senator Edwin Johnson, 28 November 1945

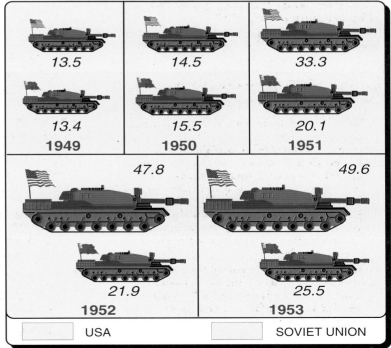

13.5	14.5	33.3
13.4	15.5	20.1
1949	**1950**	**1951**
47.8	49.6	
21.9	25.5	
1952	**1953**	

USA   SOVIET UNION

American and Soviet defence spending, 1949-53. All figures are in $ billions.

❸ The arms race

Once the Soviet Union knew how to make nuclear weapons, the USA was in danger of losing its military advantage. As a result, it poured more money into defence. But this only encouraged the Soviet Union to try to catch up. The result was an arms race with both sides trying to gain or regain an advantage. The development of nuclear weapons was the most dangerous element of the arms race. Both sides built huge numbers of missiles (see right) and it was difficult for either side to keep a lead for any length of time. In 1953, for example, the Soviet Union tested an H-bomb only a few months after the first American test. By the 1960s, the two sides had enough missiles to destroy the world many times over (see Box 9.11). Although Britain and France built their own nuclear weapons, these were insignificant compared to those built by the USA and Soviet Union. The cartoon above illustrates the arms race. The American President, Eisenhower, and the Russian leader, Khrushchev, are fighting for first place whilst the British Prime Minister, Macmillan, and the French President, de Gaulle, are some way behind.

❹ Key phases in the arms race

For the USA, nuclear weapons came to be seen as a cheap alternative to matching the huge conventional (non-nuclear) armies of the Eastern bloc. American defence policy went through three main stages from 1950.

Phase 1 - Massive Retaliation (1950-62) The USA threatened to cause huge damage if the Soviet Union attacked with conventional forces.

Phase 2 - Mutual Assured Destruction or 'MAD' (1962-67).
When the Soviet Union caught up with the USA, both sides knew that they could not destroy all the other side's nuclear weapons. As a result, neither side could afford to attack first.

Phase 3 - Flexible Response.
From 1967, the USA began to produce a greater variety of weapons and delivery systems. By producing weapons which were smaller, more accurate and easier to move, the USA knew that the Soviet Union could never be sure of destroying all the USA's weapons and therefore would still not risk making a first strike.

The arms race in the 1960s

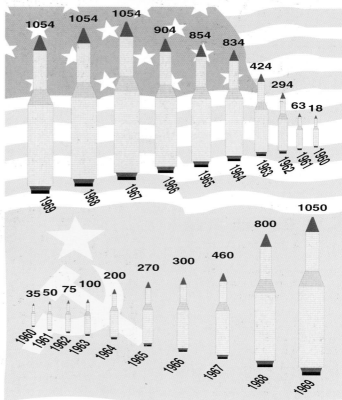

This diagram shows the number of nuclear missiles produced by the USA (top) and the Soviet Union, 1960-69.

Box 9.11 Khrushchev remembers

I remember President Kennedy once stated that the USA had the nuclear missile capacity to wipe out the Soviet Union twice over, whilst the Soviet Union had enough atomic weapons to wipe out the USA only once. When journalists asked me to comment, I said jokingly: 'Yes, I know what Kennedy claims and he's quite right. But I'm not complaining. We're satisfied to be able to finish off the USA first time round. Once is quite enough. What good does it do to destroy a country twice? We're not a bloodthirsty people.'

Nikita Khrushchev took over as Soviet leader after the death of Stalin in 1953 and remained in power until 1964. This extract comes from 'Khrushchev Remembers' edited by E. Crankshaw, 1971

❺ Attempts at disarmament

At certain times in the Cold War, the tension between the superpowers relaxed. Between 1953 and 1956, for example, relations improved after the death of Stalin in the Soviet Union and election of President Eisenhower in the USA. A summit meeting in Geneva in 1955 was friendly. But relations worsened again eight months later when Soviet tanks crushed an uprising in Hungary. After the Cuban missile crisis in 1962 (see pp.190-93) there was a second period when relations between the superpowers improved - the period of **detente** (the French for 'relaxation'). This lasted until 1979. Although, during these periods, both sides made efforts to reduce or to limit the number of nuclear weapons they held, neither side was prepared to let the other get the upper hand. As a result, no real progress was made towards nuclear disarmament (see Activity on p.177).

Activity
Living in a nuclear world

I THINK WE'VE TURNED THE CORNER

DISARMAMENT TALKS

Source B Historians' views

(a) The role of nuclear weapons in preserving peace during the Cold War has been widely recognised. One crisis or another would have turned into real war were the two superpowers not aware of the horrendous potential costs.

From 'The End of History and the Last Man' by F. Fukuyama, 1992

(b) Although nuclear weapons have not been used since 1945, their existence has been very important. Whilst the superpowers and their allies have not risked direct confrontation, lesser powers have fought numerous 'small' non-nuclear wars. More people have been killed in these 'small' wars since 1945 than during any comparable period of 'peace'. The danger of nuclear war may be one reason for this increase. In practice, nuclear weapons are unusable for virtually all present-day conflicts. If used on the battlefield, the troops on both sides would be destroyed.

From 'Overkill' by J. Cox, 1981

Source C The balance of the forces in 1963

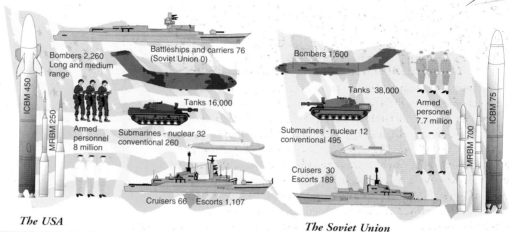

ICBM 450
MRBM 250
Bombers 2,260 Long and medium range
Battleships and carriers 76 (Soviet Union 0)
Tanks 16,000
Armed personnel 8 million
Submarines - nuclear 32 conventional 260
Cruisers 66   Escorts 1,107

The USA

Bombers 1,600
Tanks 38,000
Armed personnel 7.7 million
ICBM 75
MRBM 700
Submarines - nuclear 12 conventional 495
Cruisers 30 Escorts 189

The Soviet Union

Source D Attempts at disarmament, 1963-79

ICBM 75

1963   1968   1972   1979

Partial Test Ban Treaty
Banned all nuclear test explosions except those underground. Over 100 countries signed, but not France or China.

Non-Proliferation Treaty
Nations without nuclear weapons agreed not to make them. Nuclear powers agreed not to help them. Over 100 countries signed, but not France or China.

SALT 1
After several summit meetings, the USA and Soviet Union agreed to limit some types of missile. But no limits on delivery systems, so the arms race continued.

SALT 2
As in SALT 1, the USA and Soviet Union agreed to limit some types of missile. But other missiles and delivery systems not limited, so the arms race continued.

QUESTIONS

1. Judging from the information in this section, what part did nuclear weapons play in the Cold War?

2. Would you say that nuclear weapons made the world a safer place in the 1960s and 1970s? Discuss the points made by Source B in your answer.

3. Using Source C assess the strengths and weaknesses of each superpower in 1963. How might each superpower use your assessment to justify the development of new weapons?

4. Use Source D to explain the point being made in Source A.

What were the aims of the United Nations Organisation (UNO)?

The League of Nations was set up after the First World War to keep the peace. It failed. The League was powerless against the aggression of dictators like Hitler and Mussolini. By the time the Second World War began, it was thoroughly discredited (see pp.136-38). Despite this, the Big Three (Britain, the USA and the Soviet Union) agreed at the Teheran Conference in 1943 to set up a new international organisation to guarantee world peace. This was to be the UN - the United Nations Organisation. Detailed plans were drawn up by Britain, the USA, the Soviet Union and China at the Dumbarton Oaks conference in Washington in 1944 and further changes made at Yalta in February 1945. The new organisation was created by allies fighting a common enemy with victory in sight. The mood was one of hope. There was the hope that the mistakes made by the League of Nations could be avoided and that a just and lasting peace could be made. Some people even hoped that, one day, the UN might become a world government. But this mood of optimism was quickly disappointed. There has rarely been a day since the end of the Second World War when there has not been an armed conflict going on somewhere in the world. In addition, the UN soon found itself caught between two sides battling for supremacy in the Cold War.

1 Avoiding the problems of the League of Nations

'History doesn't repeat itself'
Several major powers either never joined or soon left the League of Nations. Also, it lacked fire power (see pp.54-56 and Box 9.12). The cartoon above suggests that these lessons had been learned. President Truman leads forward an armed woman representing the UN. Unlike the League, the UN had the power to raise an army.

Box 9.12 — The League of Nations - a historian's view

The League was never a truly international organisation. The USA's refusal to join crippled it from the beginning. Germany and the Soviet Union were only members for seven years, Japan only until 1933. The League had no military or even police forces and had to rely on individual members' loyalty in carrying out economic or military action. It was, essentially, a talking shop because no major power allowed the League to shape its policy. When faced with real tests, as in 1931 when Japan seized Manchuria and in 1935 when Italy attacked Ethiopia, the League failed.

From 'A History of the World in the 20th Century' by F. Spencer, 1970

2 Building the peace

OURS...to fight for

Freedom of Speech

Freedom of Worship

Freedom from Want

Freedom from Fear

In August 1941, Churchill and Roosevelt drew up the 'Atlantic Charter'- a list of war aims. The 'four freedoms' on the poster above are the four reasons they gave for fighting the Nazis. They later became the basis for the UN Charter (see Box 9.13).

Box 9.13 — The UN Charter

a) We the people of the United Nations are determined to save succeeding generations from the scourge of war which twice in our lifetime has brought untold sorrow to mankind. We believe in fundamental human rights, in the dignity and worth of the human person and in the equal rights of nations large and small. We aim to promote social progress and better standards of life, to practice tolerance and to live together in peace with one another as good neighbours. To accomplish these aims we have agreed to combine our efforts.

Introduction to the United Nations Charter, June 1945

b) You have created an instrument for peace and security and for human progress. The world must now use it. If we fail to use it, we shall betray those who have died in order that we might meet here in freedom and safety to create it. If we seek to use it selfishly - for the advantage of any one nation or any group of nations - we shall be equally guilty of betrayal.

Part of a speech made by President Truman after the signing of the UN Charter in San Francisco, June 1945

Activity

How the UN is organised

Source A   *The veto*

a) At Yalta, the Russians (remembering their difficulties with the League which ended in their expulsion) were worried they would be isolated in the UN. Therefore they accepted an American proposal. Permanent members were to have a veto (the power to block decisions).

From 'Shattered Peace' by D. Yergin, 1977

b) In 1945, the veto was as important to the Americans as to the Russians. The United States Senate would probably not have agreed to membership of the UN without it. American opponents of the League of Nations had argued that the League had the power to commit the USA to wars it did not want to fight. The veto would prevent this.

From 'The World Since 1945' by T.E. Vadney, 1987

Source B   *How the UN works*

The permanent members of the Security Council are Britain, the USA, the Soviet Union (now Russia), France and China.

Security Council
Contains 5 permanent members and 10 other members elected every two years by the General Assembly. It can order ceasefires, economic sanctions and the use of force. Members must obey Security Council decisions.

SECRETARIAT

Secretary - General
International civil service headed by Secretary General. Over 25,000 members who are loyal to UN, not their home countries.

International Court of Justice
The 15 judges are appointed by the General Assembly and Security Council. The Court settles disputes between members, but only if they agree to bring the dispute to the Court.

General Assembly
Each member of UN has one vote. The General Assembly meets to discuss all matters relating to the UN Charter and agrees budget. On most important questions, a two thirds majority is needed.

Specialised Agencies
IMF International Monetary Fund
World Bank
UNESCO UN Educational, Scientific and Cultural Organisation
WHO World Health Organisation
IAEA International Atomic Energy Agency
FAO Food and Agriculture Organisation
ILO International Labour Organisation

UN Agencies
UNHCR UN High Commission for refugees
UNICEF UN Children's fund
UNFPA UN Fund for population Activities
UNRWA UN Relief and Works Agency for Palestinian refugees

Economic and Social Council
The General Assembly selects 54 members. The Council coordinates the work done by the various UN Agencies.

Source C

A historian's view

In the 1970s, we must record regrettably that the UN has not fulfilled the high hopes invested in it in 1945. As the founders had foreseen, the UN could not work effectively without Great Power agreement. The Soviet Union came to feel that the UN was just another vehicle of American policy and in the early years the Russian contribution was just one word - 'Niet' (no). The USA could always round up a majority because so many states depended on American aid and goodwill.

From 'World Powers in the Twentieth Century' by H. Ward, 1978

Source D   *UN membership*

Year	Number of member states
1945	51
1960	100
1970	127
1980	154
1996	184

Today, UN membership covers most of the world. It expanded in the 1960s and 1970s when former colonies gained their independence and in the 1990s due to the break-up of the Soviet Union. The historian Eric Hobsbawm argues that the main reason why the UN has survived is that membership proves that a state's existence is recognised by the international community.

QUESTIONS

1. Judging from the information in this section, what were the aims of the UN? Why were they so difficult to achieve?

2. Using Sources A-D explain why it was so important that permanent members of the Security Council had a veto.

3. 'The General Assembly is the key decision making body in the UN.' Judging from Source B do you agree with this statement?

4. How did the Cold War affect the way in which the UN worked? Use Source C in your answer.

179

Who was to blame for the Cold War?

The Cold War finally ended when Soviet Communism collapsed in 1991. But many historians wrote books about the origins of the Cold War before 1991. Since the Cold War was actually developing at the time when they were writing, what they wrote was influenced by what was happening around them. Looking back at the work of Western historians, it is possible to find three distinct groups (see Box 9.14). First, there were the **traditionalists** who blamed the Soviet Union for the Cold War. Second, there were the **revisionists** who argued that the USA was mainly to blame for the Cold War. And third, there were the **post-revisionists** who argued that there were misunderstandings on both sides and that both sides were to blame. Soviet historians mainly followed their government's line and blamed the West for the Cold War (though some Soviet historians saw faults on both sides). This section concentrates on the views of Western historians.

1 The traditionalists

According to the traditionalists, the Soviet Union abandoned the wartime alliance and adopted a policy of expansion based on the old Bolshevik idea of 'world revolution'. The evidence for this, they claim, was the expansion of Soviet power in Eastern Europe after 1945. Traditionalists also argue that Communist parties all over the world were working under Stalin's orders, trying to bring Communists to power. They suggest that the USA had tried to keep on friendly terms with the Soviet Union, but found Stalin impossible to deal with.

The USA was then forced to take a tough line towards the Russians. The result was the policy of containing Communism announced in the Truman Doctrine (see p.170). It was the Russian refusal to accept the Marshall Plan which led to the division of Europe into two blocs. The division became a military one after the Berlin Airlift and the setting up of NATO. Traditionalists also argue that the personality of Stalin and the secretive nature of Soviet government made it impossible to negotiate with the Russians.

Box 9.14

1. The traditionalists   **2. The revisionists**   **3. The post-revisionists**

In cartoons, the Soviet Union is often represented as a bear. The USA is often represented as an eagle or as Uncle Sam (see Source F on p.181).

2 The revisionists

Revisionist historians argue that, at the end of the Second World War, the Soviet Union was interested in security, not expansion. At the end of the war, they point out, the Red Army occupied countries which, before the war, had mainly been hostile to the Soviet Union. It was to protect the Soviet Union from invasion that Communist governments were set up in these countries. Revisionists also point out that the USA had become richer and more powerful during the war whereas the Soviet Union had suffered immense damage and therefore presented no real danger to the USA. In addition, the USA had a monopoly of the atom bomb, a factor which added to Soviet insecurity. In reality, revisionists argue, the USA was aware of its economic and atomic superiority over the Russians. Its aim was to make sure that as much of the world as possible remained within the capitalist system and open to American trade. The USA, therefore, was not forced into action against the Soviet Union. Rather, it took the initiative to further American aims.

3 The post-revisionists

Traditionalists and revisionists mainly argued with one another in the 1960s and 1970s. Since then, post-revisionists have agreed that the blame for the Cold War must be shared to some extent by both sides. In particular, it has been argued that there was a great deal of misunderstanding on each side about what the other was trying to achieve. Both sides felt threatened and yet both probably wanted peace. One problem was the lack of information. The Americans thought the Red Army was larger and better equipped than in fact it was. The Russians were afraid of the atom bomb and could not feel safe while only the USA had this weapon. There were also very real problems that were bound to cause tension in postwar Europe - such as what to do about Germany. Post-revisionists have tried to examine events in the Cold War from the point of view of both sides.

Activity

A variety of verdicts on the Cold War

Source A *A historian's view (1)*

American leaders were determined that in 1945, unlike after the First World War, the USA would seize its chances. The postwar period seemed an ideal opportunity to put into practice America's idea of 'peace and prosperity'. There was another factor of great importance - the vital needs of the American economy. The USA had to export American goods and had to import strategic raw materials. Many Americans, remembering the Great Depression, warned of disaster unless American trade expanded.

From 'American Foreign Policy' by T.G.Paterson, J.G. Clifford and K.J. Hagan, 1977

Source B *A cartoon (1)*

Source C *A historian's view (2)*

Stalin preferred to concentrate on his own sphere. His most provocative actions, like the Berlin Blockade, were reactions to the Truman Doctrine, the Marshall Plan and Western policy in Germany. There is, then, reason to give as much of the responsibility for the origins of the Cold War to the USA as to the Soviet Union. But the causes of the Cold War were more complicated. The USA was responding to a range of what it saw as dangers. American policies were an attempt to cope with the results of the Second World War as much as a response to the Soviet system.

From 'A Preponderance of Power' by M. Leffler, 1992

Source D *A historian's view (3)*

The Cold War was the brave and essential response of free men to Communist aggression. The West was faced at the end of the Second World War with a relentless drive for domination by the Soviet Union. In the end, nothing could satisfy Stalin's paranoia [suspicion]. His own advisers failed to do so. Why does anyone suppose that any American policy could have done so?

From 'The Origins of the Cold War' by A.M. Schlesinger, 1967

Source E *A historian's view (4)*

Moscow argued that the Soviet Union had to have friendly states on its borders. But where does defence end and aggression begin? If one must have a 'friendly state' (say Poland) on one's border, one must also have a 'friendly state' (say Germany) on Poland's border and one must have a 'friendly state' (say France) on Germany's border. If this went on, there would only be Communist states and the Communist dream of 'world revolution' would have come true. By 1947, Soviet tactics had so alarmed the American people that strong popular support could confidently be expected for a get-tough-with-Russia policy.

From 'America faces Russia' by T.A. Bailey, 1964

Source F *A cartoon (2)*

QUESTIONS

1. Judging from the information in this section, who was to blame for the outbreak of the Cold War? Give reasons for your answer.

2. Look at Sources A-F and say whether each supports the traditionalist, revisionist or post-revisionist view? Give reasons for your answers.

3. Take Sources A, C, D and E and, looking back through this chapter, find evidence to support the view given in each source.

4. Write a caption to go with the cartoons in Sources B and F.

Themes

As the Cold War developed, fear and hatred of Communism returned in the USA. After the First World War, there had been a Red Scare (see p.89). Similarly, in the 1950s, the USA experienced a second Red Scare. As well as concern about the spread of Communism abroad, fears grew about the dangers of Communism within the USA itself. Politicians used the issue to gain easy popularity. The most notorious was Senator Joe McCarthy who from 1950 to 1954 led a vicious anti-Communist campaign. This created an atmosphere of hysteria and ruined the lives and careers of many people. In foreign policy during this period, only tough anti-Soviet policies could protect Presidents and other politicians from accusations of being 'soft on Communism'. The first major crisis of the Cold War outside Europe came in 1950 when the Korean War broke out. It was argued that if the USA did not act, then Communism would spread. In the 1950s, the USA began a massive build-up of nuclear arms (including the development of the hydrogen bomb). The next major battle in the Cold War - the Cuban missile crisis of 1962 - was the most dangerous of all. It almost led to all-out nuclear war. It was around the time of the Cuban missile crisis that the USA's involvement in Vietnam began to escalate rapidly. The Vietnam War dragged through the 1960s and only ended (in defeat for the Americans) in 1975. It was during the Vietnam War that, for the first time in the Cold War, many Americans openly criticised their government's policies. This chapter looks at the response of the USA to the Communist threat by examining the following key questions.

* How did the Communist threat affect life in the USA?
* Why was the Korean War a significant event in the development of the Cold War?
* What were the causes and consequences of the Cuban missile crisis?
* What were the causes and consequences of the Vietnam War?

Key Events

1. Between 1950 and 1954, Senator Joe McCarthy's anti-Communist crusade (see right) dominated American politics. This second Red Scare ruined many Americans, though little proof was produced to back up the accusations.

2. In the Korean War (1950-53), a UN force, dominated by the USA, fought against troops from Communist North Korea and China.

KOREA MUST BE REUNIFIED!

3.

The two superpowers came face to face during the Cuban missile crisis of October 1962. In the first direct confrontation of the Cold War, nuclear war seemed increasingly likely until Soviet ships were ordered back.

VICTORY'S JUST around THE corner.

4. The Vietnam War lasted from 1954 to 1975. The USA's involvement escalated after Kennedy was elected President. Despite its technological superiority, the USA was unable to win the war and was forced to withdraw in 1975.

1950	Eisenhower elected President. Korean War begins. Senator Joe McCarthy launches his anti-Communist crusade.
1952	USA explodes first hydrogen bomb (H-bomb).
1953	Korean War ends.
1954	Vietnam divided into two at Geneva Conference.
1959	Cuban revolution. Fidel Castro overthrows Bastista and seizes power.
1960	Kennedy elected President.
1961	American-backed Cuban exiles invade Cuba at Bay of Pigs. Invasion is a disaster. Berlin Wall is built.
1962	Cuban missile crisis.
1963	Kennedy assassinated. Johnson becomes President.
1969	Peak number of US troops in Vietnam. Nixon becomes President.
1973	Ceasefire in Vietnam.
1974	Ford becomes President after Nixon resigns.
1975	USA withdraws from Vietnam.

The 'Red threat'

Source 1

An anti-Communist textbook

The Communists do not care about peace. They hope that the man in the street will think that Communists could not possibly be preparing for war when they talk so much about peace. People who say one thing and believe another are hypocrites. Communists are among the greatest hypocrites in history. The years since World War II have given more than enough evidence of the determination of the Soviet Union to destroy the USA and all it stands for. It should be recognised, of course, that the great danger from Communists in the USA does not come from those who openly belong to the United States Communist Party. Rather, the most dangerous Communists are those who long ago dropped out of sight or perhaps were never in the Party's record. These and others sent to this country by the Soviet Union are awaiting the day when they will be given orders to destroy the dams and bridges and factories and military bases of the USA. In the meantime, they will try to live as quietly as possible. They do not want to attract attention - which they will certainly get if they join the Party. The Chinese Communists are willing to take the risk of atomic war because China is a backward nation of almost 700 million people. Of course, tens of million of the Chinese people would be killed in such a war - but this does not particularly bother the Chinese Communist leaders.

An extract from an American High School textbook published in 1963, quoted in 'The Anti-Communist Impulse' by M. Parenti, 1969

Source 2 — Anti-Communist films (1)

Source 3 — A politician's view

Now the great harsh fact in today's troubled world is that Communism is at war and it's at war against us, at war against all non-Communist nations. The great harsh fact is that Communism is the only major threat to the peace of the world anywhere in this world today, and the sooner we realise this the better. The great harsh fact is that Communism wants the whole world. In Cuba, in the Congo, at the Berlin Wall, in Indonesia, in Vietnam - wherever the flames of conflict are being fanned, Communism is the cause. Now, the methods it uses in its drive to conquer the world are based solely on what will work. If they can bury us, as they've promised to do - if they can win the world, as they've said they will - if they can do this without nuclear war, then they will try to avoid nuclear war. But remember this, it is not compassion or decency which prevents their attacking us. They respect our power. This is why we must maintain the peace through being prepared through military spending.

Part of a speech made by Barry Goldwater, the Republican presidential candidate, in 1964

Source 4 — Anti-Communist films (2)

Between 1948 and 1954, Hollywood film makers produced more than 40 anti-Communist films. They can be divided into three groups - spy thrillers, films dealing with the Communist Party in the USA and those about worldwide events in the Cold War. The films were made quickly and followed a formula. Evil clearly came from outside the USA and stemmed from an easily identifiable source. Non-Communist Americans were portrayed as being pure whilst Communists fit a pattern of evil. Those actors portraying Russians represented the Russian elite - the deadliest of secret agents. As a result, the impression was that all Communists, whether domestic or foreign, were spies. Communist activities were portrayed as a constant round of intrigue, brutality and suffocating discipline. American Communists were shown as regretting having joined the Communist Party. Their attempts to escape usually ended in suicide or murder.

From 'Hollywood and the Cold War' by L.K. Adler in 'The Spectre' edited by R. Griffith & A. Theoharis, 1974

QUESTIONS

1. **What do Sources 1-4 tell us about attitudes in the USA after World War II?**
2. **How balanced is the textbook in Source 1? Give reasons for your answer.**
3. **Judging from Sources 1-4 how did fear of Communism affect American society in the Cold War?**
4. **Why do you think films like that advertised in Source 2 were made? Using Source 4, describe the sort of scene you might find in the film.**

How did the Communist threat affect life in the USA?

During the Second World War, the Americans' fear of Communism had temporarily been put aside. After all, the USA and the Soviet Union were allies in the struggle against Fascism. Once the war was over and the Cold War began, however, fear of Communism returned in the USA and, just like after the First World War, a Red Scare swept the country. Although the United States Communist Party had very few members, many Americans believed that even small numbers of Communists working within the government were capable of damaging the American system. Politicians won easy popularity by playing on the fears of Communism. A number of sensational spy cases, most connected with the development of nuclear weapons, seemed to confirm suspicions that Communists were operating secretly in government (see Box 10.1). The Republican Party accused the Democratic President, Harry Truman, of being 'soft on Communism' and gained a majority in Congress in 1946. Truman responded by setting up a **Loyalty Programme** to investigate all government employees and dismiss any who had any links with the Communist Party. Suspicions remained, however, that there was an 'enemy within' - a Communist conspiracy to weaken the USA. Any Communist activity abroad added to these suspicions and in 1950 anti-Communism began in its most extreme form in a campaign led by Senator Joe McCarthy. His influence declined in 1954, but anti-Communism remained a powerful force throughout the Cold War.

The growth of anti-Communism after 1945

After 1945, the Soviet Union and Communism quickly took the place of Germany and Fascism in the minds of many Americans. In 1946, a Soviet spy ring was uncovered in Canada. It was responsible for handing over atomic secrets to the Soviet Union. Worried by this, **HUAC** (the House of Representatives Un-American Activities Committee) started a search for Communists in government, trade unions and the Hollywood film industry. Then, in 1947, Truman's government set up a Loyalty Programme to investigate government employees. People were called before HUAC or Loyalty Boards and quizzed about possible past membership of the Communist Party or other organisations which were supposed to be Communist- influenced. These investigations often ignored people's civil liberties. A principle of 'guilt by association' was introduced. People who had joined the Communist Party in the Depression in the 1930s and since left it found themselves treated as 'security risks' and lost their jobs. In 1948, a direct attempt was made to destroy the United States Communist Party - 12 of its members were charged and found guilty of conspiring to teach and support the overthrow of the American government by force. Evidence was given by undercover FBI agents. The action was out of all proportion to the threat from a tiny minor party and it encouraged action against anyone in public life who was or was thought to have Communist sympathies.

Some Hollywood film makers and actors, such as Ronald Reagan and Gary Cooper, cooperated with HUAC and provided the names of people in the film industry thought to be Communists. Others were not Communists but opposed what they regarded as a 'witch-hunt'. The photo above shows members of this group (including Humphrey Bogart and Lauren Bacall) in Washington. They went there in October 1947 to protest about the work of HUAC. A third group, which included Communists, refused to answer questions, using their rights under the American constitution. A blacklist was drawn up by Hollywood producers who were anxious to show their patriotism. Those on the blacklist were refused work. They included famous actors like Charlie Chaplin and Paul Robeson.

Box 10.1

The Hiss trial

In 1948, came the most sensational spy case. It involved Alger Hiss, a high-ranking official in the State Department. He was accused of passing secrets to the Soviet Union in the 1930s. The accuser was Whittaker Chambers, a self-confessed former Soviet agent now giving evidence against former 'colleagues'. Hiss denied all charges and unsuccessfully sued Chambers for libel. Hiss was then found guilty of perjury and sent to prison for five years. He could not be tried for treason because of the number of years since the alleged spying. The evidence against Hiss was a set of documents typed on his typewriter. At one point in the trial, Chambers took FBI agents to a farm owned by Hiss where they discovered microfilm hidden in a pumpkin. Hiss has always denied the charges and claimed he was set up. The case still divides historians.

Alger Hiss at his trial (left)

2 The rise and fall of Senator McCarthy

The Hiss case (see Box 10.1) seemed to confirm treason in high places. This treason, it was argued, could explain some notable successes for Communism in 1949. First, the victory of the Chinese Communists who beat the American-backed Nationalists. And second, the news that the Soviet Union had successfully tested an atom bomb. In 1950, Republican Senator Joe McCarthy was looking for an issue that would help his re-election in 1952. He took up the suggestion that he should use the growing fears of Communism as his theme and launched his campaign with a sensational speech. He claimed to have the names of 205 Communists employed by the State Department. This was the Department responsible for the USA's foreign policy. McCarthy's attack struck a chord, not least because the outbreak of the Korean War in June 1950 seemed to confirm his fears about Communist expansion. And, for the next five years, McCarthy waged a wild campaign using a committee in the Senate to conduct his hearings. He was always hinting about treason in high places, but was never able to prove it. In fact, he did not uncover a single fresh case. But he cleverly used press deadlines and peak time television to promote his cause. People hauled before his committee were smeared as Communists. Public figures who opposed him were accused of disloyalty and Communist sympathies. At first, Republicans saw McCarthy as a weapon against the Democrats in the 1952 Presidential election. But after Eisenhower (a Republican) was elected, McCarthy continued his attacks. It was only when he attacked the loyalty of the army in 1954 that he lost popularity and the support of the Republican leadership. He died, an alcoholic, in 1957, but the effects of his campaign were lasting.

Activity
McCarthyism

Source B Speech made by McCarthy

In 1944, 180 million people were under Soviet domination and 1,625 million on our side. Today, 800 million are under Soviet domination and 500 million on our side. The odds have changed from 9-1 in our favour to 8-5 against. This is the result of the traitorous actions of people who have been treated so well by this nation - those with the finest homes, the best education and the best jobs. This is glaringly true in the State Department which, in my opinion, is thoroughly infested with Communists. I have here 57 cases* of individuals who appear to be card carrying members or certainly loyal to the Communist Party, but who, nevertheless, are still helping to shape our foreign policy.

Part of a speech made to the Senate on 20 February 1950
* Note the reduction from the 205 members mentioned in his first speech on 9 February.

QUESTIONS

1. Judging from the information in this section, how did the Communist threat affect life in the USA?
2. What was McCarthyism? Use Sources A-D in your answer.
3. 'McCarthyism helped to ensure that the Cold War became colder.' Explain this statement using Sources A-D
4. What point is being made by the cartoon in Source C? Why do you think it is typical of cartoons produced in the McCarthy era?

Source A Senator McCarthy - a photo

McCarthy often used photos, charts and documents to support his arguments. But, on close examination, they usually proved far less than he claimed. McCarthy's first major speech was made on 9 February 1950. In this speech, he held up a list which, he said, contained the names of 205 Communists employed by the State Department. Some historians claim this was in fact a laundry list.

Source C Cartoon produced in 1950

This cartoon was entitled 'Red Fascism'. It is typical of the sort of images produced during the McCarthy era in the USA

Source D Historians' views

a) Loyalty Boards often grilled federal employees about their views on foreign policy, trade unions, HUAC and race relations. A person's reading became another topic. Did he own any books concerning the government of the Soviet Union? Taste in music - the records of Russian composers - might trigger concern. Accusers were often anonymous. The possibilities for malice were numerous. A rival at work or a jilted lover might talk to the FBI.
From 'Nightmare in Red' by R.M. Fried, 1990

b) For four frenzied years McCarthy rode high. His witch-hunting encouraged states and cities to set up their own security programmes and to demand loyalty oaths from their employees. Local groups hounded suspected Communists. Several thousand people lost their jobs and hundreds were imprisoned. Communists were denied passports. Worse still, McCarthyism poisoned American public life, demoralised and made less efficient the State Department and damaged the reputation of the USA abroad.
From 'The Limits of Liberty' by M.A. Jones, 1983

Why was the Korean War a significant event in the development of the Cold War?

The Korean War began when, on 24 June 1950, troops from Communist North Korea invaded American-backed South Korea. On the next day, President Truman declared that the USA would go to the aid of South Korea. The USA took the matter to the Security Council of the UN (United Nations - see p.178-79) with the result that a UN force (made up of troops from 16 nations, but dominated by American troops) was sent to South Korea under the command of an American - General MacArthur. This was the first time in the Cold War that one of the two superpowers had become directly involved in a military conflict and it set a pattern. Throughout the Cold War, when one superpower became directly involved in a military conflict, the other superpower only became indirectly involved (by providing weapons and supplies). Soviet and American troops never actually fought each other. In Korea, the fortunes of each side swung violently in 1950 before military stalemate was reached. Altogether, the war lasted for three years and cost the lives of around two million people. The war marked the spreading of the Cold War from Europe on to a world stage.

1 Origins of the Korean War

The Allies had agreed at the end of the Second World War that Korea should be occupied by Soviet troops in the north and American troops in the south. The dividing line was the 38th parallel of latitude (see map, right). Korea, which had been under Japanese control since 1910, was to be an independent country after elections had been held. These elections were to be organised by the UN. In the meantime, however, the American and Soviet governments worked to ensure that power went to Korean politicians whose views suited their own. The result was that elections were never held. Instead, a Communist government came to power in the north and an American-backed anti-Communist government came to power in the south. In effect, both parts of Korea were ruled by dictators - Kim Il Sung in North Korea and Syngman Rhee in South Korea. The problem was that both North Korea and South Korea claimed to have authority over the whole of Korea. Although Russian and American troops were eventually withdrawn, the two superpowers continued to support the rival Korean governments. Disputes occurred frequently and finally, in June 1950, North Korean troops invaded South Korea - the outbreak of the war. The North Korean government presented the war as a struggle to unite Korea under a truly national government (see Box 10.2a). But President Truman immediately declared support for South Korea (see Box 10.2b) and took the issue to the United Nations. The Security Council condemned the invasion by North Korea and called on members of the UN to assist South Korea. The USA had already ordered naval and air strikes and General MacArthur was placed in charge of the 16 nation UN force sent to Korea. The force arrived just in time to save the South Korean troops who had been driven into a small corner around Pusan (see map on p.187).

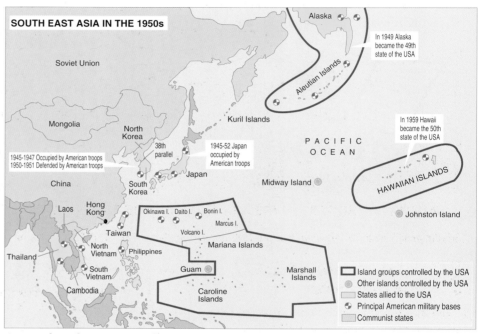

A map of South East Asia in the 1950s.

② The United Nations and the Korean War

The United Nations acted quickly in support of the USA because, by a stroke of good luck for the Americans, the Soviet Union was boycotting the Security Council and was therefore unable to use its veto. The Soviet government was protesting at the exclusion of Communist China from the Security Council. Although Chinese Communists had won power in 1949, their place on the Security Council was still taken by the Chinese Nationalists (whom the Communists had defeated). As a result of the Soviet Union's absence, the American resolution that an armed force should be raised was accepted unanimously by the Security Council. This was the first time (and the only occasion in the period 1945 to 1990) that the Security Council ordered armed intervention to be used to solve a problem. In August 1950, the Soviet Union ended its boycott of the Security Council and used its veto to block further action. When the UN's General Assembly (supported by the USA) passed the 'uniting for peace' resolution which gave it the power to raise forces against an aggressor if Security Council action was blocked, the Soviet Union declared this illegal. In fact, the new power was only used rarely by the General Assembly - for example, during the Suez crisis of 1956 when British and French troops invaded Egypt (a UN force was sent to restore peace in the area). While the Cold War lasted, it remained difficult for the UN to act decisively (since measures proposed by one superpower were vetoed by the other). The Korean War was an exception.

Countries which provided troops for the UN force in Korea

USA   FRANCE   HOLLAND   GREECE   TURKEY   SOUTH AFRICA   PHILIPPINES   AUSTRALIA

CANADA   BRITAIN   BELGIUM   LUXEMBOURG   ETHIOPIA   THAILAND   NEW ZEALAND   COLUMBIA

The USA provided 50% of the ground forces, 85% of the naval forces and 90% of the air forces

③ The course of the Korean War

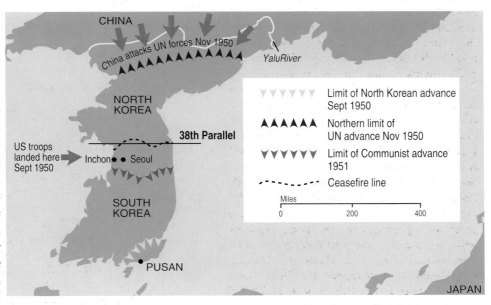

When war broke out, South Korean troops were driven right back (see map, right). General MacArthur's first aim, therefore, was to prevent the total collapse of South Korea's resistance by sending American forces to the Pusan peninsular. In September, a successful counter-attack was launched. The North Korean troops were outflanked by an amphibious attack on Inchon. They then retreated in some disorder as the Americans and their UN allies reached the South Korean capital, Seoul, and then the 38th parallel. At this point, the aims of the war changed. The USA received the approval of the UN's General Assembly to push into North Korea in attempt to unite the country. As UN troops drove the North Koreans back towards the Yalu River on the border of China, General MacArthur confidently told President Truman that the Chinese Communists would not enter the war. He was wrong. In November 1950, the Chinese sent across around 250,000 volunteers to reinforce the North Korean army. It was now the turn of the UN force to retreat. By March 1951, the two sides were roughly back where they had started. With the entry of China into the war, the Americans had a choice. MacArthur called for air attacks on Chinese bases, saying 'there is no substitute for victory'. But if the Soviet Union had then decided to support China, there was a risk of a Third World War. Truman's government, which had considered but rejected the use of nuclear weapons against China, decided to limit the war to Korea. MacArthur was dismissed for promoting his own policy. He went home a war hero, but his dismissal cleared the way for a ceasefire. An armistice was finally agreed in 1953. A demilitarised zone was set up. The boundary was roughly along the 38th parallel.

4 The consequences of the Korean War

The immediate results of the war were great destruction and large numbers of dead and wounded on both sides. The Korean War also increased the general tensions of the Cold War in Europe. Massive American rearmament (see Box 10.3), including the development of the hydrogen bomb, was a direct result of the Korean War. Also, the Korean War ensured that the Cold War spread to Asia. The USA made alliances with friendly countries like the Philippines and in 1951 it signed the ANZUS Pact with Australia and New Zealand (a security treaty providing for mutual defence in the event of armed attack). Japan was rebuilt with American aid and a final peace treaty was signed with Japan in 1951, signalling the end of American occupation. By way of contrast, the USA refused to have any dealings with Communist China. Instead, the USA aided the Nationalist Chinese who had retreated to the island of Taiwan and it recognised the Nationalist government as the 'true' government of China. Perhaps most important for the future, was the American decision to increase the aid which went to opponents of Communism in Vietnam.

Box 10.3

Consequences of the Korean War - historians' views

a) The Truman administration used the Korean War to increase the American Defence Department budget. It shot up to $48 billion in 1951 and to $60 billion by 1952. The American nuclear stockpile grew rapidly in 1950-51, reaching at least 750 warheads, up from about 100-150 in 1948. The American army increased by 50% to 3.5 million troops. Two new divisions were sent to Europe, making a total of six there. The hydrogen bomb was developed by March 1951. A new jet bomber, the B52, made its maiden flight in 1952. This military expansion was awesome. The Cold War rested on a dangerously military footing.

From 'American Foreign Policy' by T. Paterson, J. Clifford & K. Hagan, 1977

b) With McCarthyism on the rise in the USA, the Korean War confirmed the view of a worldwide Communist conspiracy. Serious writers described how Stalin, blocked in Europe, recruited his 'junior partner' Mao Zedong (the Chinese Communist leader) to start a war in Korea. Kim Il Sung was hardly mentioned. The myth of a massive threat served the interests of the leaders of those in charge of American industry and the American military.

From a review of 'Uncertain Partners: Stalin, Mao and the Korean War' by J. Gittings, 1994

Activity
The USA and the Korean War

Source B *General MacArthur*

a) It seems difficult for some to realise that here in Asia is where the Communist conspirators have chosen to make their play for global conquest. Here we fight Europe's war with arms while the diplomats there still fight with words. If we lose the war to Communism in Asia, the fall of Europe is inevitable. There is no substitute for victory.

Speech made by General MacArthur in 1951, explaining why he wanted to make attacks across the Chinese border

b) MacArthur called for the use of atomic weapons. He produced a list of targets for which he needed 26 atomic bombs. He also wanted four more to drop on the Chinese forces.

From 'Korea - the Unknown War' by J. Halliday & B. Cummins, 1988

Source A *A variant on the domino theory*

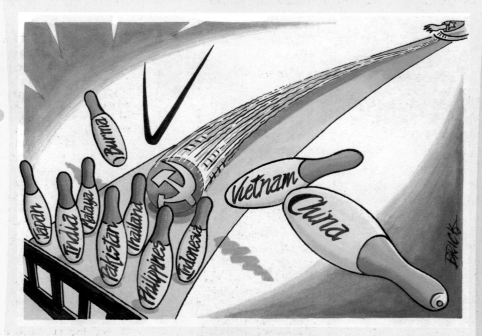

The journalist Stewart Alsop used the comparison of a ten pin bowling game. The Soviet Union was the hard hitting, ambitious bowler. 'We are losing Asia fast', Alsop said, 'The head pin was China. It is down already. The two pins in the second row are Burma and Vietnam. If they go, the three pins in the next row, Thailand, Malaya and Indonesia, are pretty sure to topple in their turn. And, if all the rest of Asia goes, it will almost certainly drag down the four pins of the fourth row - India, Pakistan, Japan and the Philippines.'
Quoted in 'Rise and Fall of the Great Powers' by P. Kennedy, 1988

Source C *Truman's memoirs*

This was not the first time the strong had attacked the weak. I remembered Manchuria, Ethiopia, Austria. I remembered how each time that the democracies failed to act it encouraged the aggressors to keep going ahead. Communism was acting in Korea just as Hitler, Mussolini and the Japanese had acted earlier. I felt certain that if South Korea was allowed to fall, Communist leaders would be encouraged to conquer nations nearer to our shores. No small nations would have the courage to resist threats and aggression by stronger Communist neighbours.

From 'Years of Trial and Hope', the memoirs of Harry Truman, published in 1956

Source D *Republic of Korea army poster*

The caption on this poster reads: 'Drive out Communists to unify our country'.

Source E *A historian's account (1)*

Stalin, checked in Berlin owing to the Airlift, had been casting his eyes around for easy pickings and here, so he thought, was his opportunity. A successful Korean expedition would have produced a number of effects. First, it would have regained the initiative in the Cold War for the Soviet Union. Second, it would have inflicted a damaging blow to American prestige in the Far East. And third, it would have strengthened the Communist military position in Asia. Stalin therefore proceeded with the steady build-up of military forces in North Korea.

From 'Struggle for the World' by British historian Desmond Donnelly, 1965

Source F *A historian's account (2)*

Documents released in Moscow more than 40 years later showed that Stalin was most reluctant to go along with Kim Il Sung of North Korea. The Korean War, contrary to Truman's and most Americans' beliefs, was not triggered by a militarily aggressive Stalin who commanded an undivided Communist Empire. Instead, the Communist bloc was already breaking up and Stalin was deeply worried about the threat that Mao's China posed to the Soviet leadership. Stalin feared that if he did not go along with Kim Il Sung's plans, the North Koreans would turn to Mao for help. Stalin also feared, with good reason, that Truman was pulling Japan into an American military alliance that could threaten the eastern Soviet Union. A Communist Korea could help to meet that threat. Stalin therefore went along with Kim Il Sung, but with no enthusiasm. He carefully protected himself by telling Kim that the North Koreans were on their own. If they ran into trouble, Stalin was not going to bail them out.

From 'The American Age' by W. Lafeber, 1994

Source G *Poster produced in Korean War*

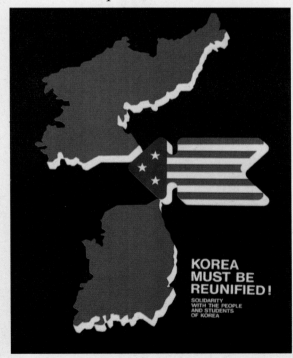

This poster was produced by the International Union of students. The arrow is keeping the two halves of Korea apart.

QUESTIONS

1. **Judging from the information in this section, why was the Korean War a significant event in the Cold War?**

2. **Using Sources A-C explain why the USA became involved in the Korean War.**

3. **What do Sources D and G tell us about who was to blame for the Korean War? What evidence is there in the other sources to support the view expressed in each picture?**

4. **Judging from Source F, how accurate is the historical account in Source E? What does Source E tell us about Western attitudes during the Cold War?**

What were the causes and consequences of the Cuban missile crisis?

Latin America, especially Central America, was considered by the USA to be its 'own backyard'. The USA was by far the strongest power in the Americas and it had great influence over the political life and economies of the Latin American countries. As the Cold War developed, the American government used this influence to keep Communism out of their 'backyard'. At first, any revolutionary movements in Latin America were successfully defeated with the help of the USA. But, in 1959, a revolution in Cuba brought Fidel Castro to power. Whether or not Castro was a Communist when he came to power, the American government decided that he was acting like a Communist and, in 1961, they backed an unsuccessful attempt to overthrow him. The USA's hostility encouraged Castro to turn to the Soviet Union for help. The Soviet government supplied economic aid and military support to Cuba and then, in 1962, a secret agreement was made to station nuclear weapons in Cuba. When the American government found out that nuclear weapons were being stationed so close to the USA, a crisis developed. As Soviet ships carrying the nuclear weapons steamed towards Cuba, the island was surrounded by the American navy. At first, it seemed that neither the Soviet Union nor the USA would back down and there was a very real danger of nuclear war. When the Soviet ships finally stopped and turned back, there was great relief throughout the world.

1 The USA and Latin America

Early in the 19th century, the USA had warned Europeans in the **Monroe Doctrine** (of 1823) that they should keep out of the American hemisphere. By the 20th century, the USA had the power to enforce this policy and it often interfered in the running of Latin American countries - American troops frequently occupied the small countries of Central America and the Caribbean, for example. The USA also tried more peaceful ways of keeping control in the area - President Roosevelt described this as the 'good neighbour policy'. After 1945, the USA tried to win support by providing both economic and military support (see Box 10.4). A number of agreements were made with other American countries. These included the **Rio Military Pact** (set up in 1947 to keep peace in the Americas), the **Organisation of American States** or **OAS** (set up by 31 states in 1948 to promote peace and development in the Americas) and the **Alliance for Progress** (set up by President Kennedy in 1961 to fund projects in Latin American countries).

2 The Cuban revolution and the victory of Fidel Castro

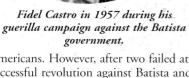
Fidel Castro in 1957 during his guerilla campaign against the Batista government.

Since 1898, when the USA had helped Cuba to gain its independence from Spain, the island of Cuba had been under the influence of the USA. Its economy was largely owned by American firms and depended on a single crop - sugar. The Americans also had an important naval base on Cuba at Guantanamo. Between 1934 and 1959 Cuba was ruled by General Batista, a military dictator, who made sure he did not displease the Americans. However, after two failed attempts, Fidel Castro led a successful revolution against Batista and took control of Cuba in 1959. Most Americans had few regrets about Batista's downfall, but President Eisenhower's government was suspicious of Castro, suspecting him of being a Communist. These suspicions increased when Castro began a thorough programme of reform of Cuba's economy and society. Castro's government nationalised industries and took over land to redistribute to the peasants. It also dealt harshly with former supporters of Batista. Castro was aware of the danger of falling out with the USA, but, at the same time, he was determined to carry through his reforms.

A map of Central and Latin America.

USA
Mexico
Cuba
Bahamas
Haiti
Belize
Puerto Rico
Guatemala
Honduras
Venezuela
El Salvador
Nicaragua
Costa Rica
Guyana
Panama
Surinam
Galapagos Islands
French Guiana
Columbia
Ecuador
Brazil
Peru
Chile
Bolivia
Argentina
Paraguay
Uruguay
Falkland Islands
South Georgia
South Shetland Islands
South Orkney Islands

Box 10.4   The USA in its 'backyard'

To prevent Communism in Latin America, the USA was willing to use force. Guatemala became a test case in 1954. Three years earlier, Arbentz, a left winger, had been elected President. His main aim was land reform. Some uncultivated land was taken from the American-owned United Fruit Company, the largest landowner in Guatemala. Compensation was offered to the company. United Fruit wanted more money as compensation. Exploiting anti-Communism in the USA, the company began a campaign with the message that Communism was threatening Latin America. The USA's Ambassador in Guatemala said: 'Arbentz thought like a Communist, talked like a Communist and, if not actually one, would do until one came along.' The USA then overthrew the Arbentz government. The CIA helped a pro-American Guatemalan army officer into power.

From 'American Foreign Policy' by T. Paterson, J. Clifford & K. Hagan, 1977

3 Castro and the USA

President Eisenhower's government quickly decided that Castro was a danger to American interests and probably a Communist (see Box 10.5). The President refused to meet Castro when he visited the USA in 1959 and he refused Cuba loans and economic aid. When Castro turned to the Soviet Union for help, the USA imposed a trade embargo (ban) on Cuba. In particular, the USA refused to buy Cuban sugar, the basis of the Cuban economy. A vicious circle was created. The more pressure the Americans put on Castro, the closer Castro moved towards the Soviet Union. The American government feared that if Communism was established in Cuba, then it would spread elsewhere in Latin America. In March 1960, Eisenhower secretly ordered the CIA to prepare plans to overthrow Castro.

Box 10.5   Was Castro a Communist?

Castro later claimed that he had been a Communist ever since he read the works of Marx and Lenin years before the Cuban revolution, but the evidence is more complicated. Before the revolution of 1959, Castro had received little help from the Cuban Communist Party though he later used the Party to carry out his programme of reform. When Castro visited the USA in 1959, Vice President Nixon had a long talk with Castro and came away believing the Cuban was not a Communist. Nevertheless, relations soon fell apart. Historian Richard Welch believes: 'Castro only became a Communist some time between 1960 and 1961'. The Soviet leader, Khrushchev, said: 'Castro will have to gravitate towards us like an iron filing to a magnet.'

From 'The American Age' by W. LaFeber, 1994

4 The Bay of Pigs invasion, 1961

In 1960, John Kennedy (a Democrat) was elected President in the USA. He inherited the CIA plan to overthrow Castro. During the election campaign, Kennedy had attacked his Republican rival, Richard Nixon, for allowing a 'Communist satellite' to appear in Latin America. After the election, the CIA plan seemed to offer a quick solution to that problem. Eisenhower had ordered the CIA to prepare anti-Castro Cuban exiles for an invasion of Cuba. The Americans believed that the invasion would trigger a general Cuban uprising against Castro's government (which, the CIA believed, had become unpopular). The invasion force, trained in Guatemala and numbering around 1,500, landed in the **Bay of Pigs** in April 1961. No uprising took place and, within hours, the invaders were rounded up by Castro's troops. The invasion was a disastrous failure (see Box 10.6). Castro scored a great propaganda victory as American involvement in the training of the invaders and their transportation in unmarked American planes became clear. The USA stood accused of trying to overthrow the rightful government of a foreign country by illegal means. The most serious result of the failed invasion was that it led to deeper Soviet involvement in Cuba. The result of that involvement was the Cuban missile crisis of 1962.

Box 10.6   The Bay of Pigs

Kennedy pressed ahead with the Bay of Pigs invasion despite warnings from his military advisers. The leader of the CIA operation, Richard Bissell, knew little about Cuba and its people and, as it turned out, about the Bay of Pigs. The CIA thought photos of sharp coral reefs that wrecked landing craft revealed only seaweed. When Kennedy told former Secretary of State Dean Acheson, even this old Cold War Warrior was astounded. 'You didn't need to consult experts to discover that 1,500 invading Cubans weren't as good as 25,000 pro-Castro Cubans', he told the President.

From 'The American Age' by W. LaFeber, 1994

A Cuban poster from the 1960s commemorating the revolution. The Argentinian-born revolutionary Che Guevara is in the middle of the second row, below Fidel Castro. Che was Castro's chief lieutenant during the Cuban revolution and served as Minister of Industry from 1961-65. He then left Cuba to encourage revolutions in other Latin American countries. He was killed by American-supported troops in Bolivia in 1967.

Apart from sugar, Cuba's best known export was cigars. This American cartoon was drawn just after the Bay of Pigs invasion in 1961 (a 'fiasco' is a disaster). It shows a Havana cigar exploding in the face of Uncle Sam (the USA). The idea of an exploding cigar is particularly suitable. After the failure of the Bay of Pigs invasion, President Kennedy set aside $100 million to wage a secret war against Castro. The CIA was ordered to sabotage the Cuban economy. It also made plans to kill Castro. One plan was to give Castro a box of exploding cigars.

5 The Cuban missile crisis, 1962

In May 1962, the Soviet leader, Khrushchev, persuaded Castro to agree to station Soviet nuclear weapons in Cuba. The first missiles arrived in Cuba on 8 September. On 14 October an American U-2 spy plane took photos revealing that missile sites were being built (see right). The issue was no longer just about Cuba. Instead, it had turned into a clash between the two superpowers. One wrong move by either side and the Third World War might begin. From the outset, Kennedy was determined that the missiles must be removed. He argued that the presence of Soviet missiles just 145 km from the USA was something no President could accept, whatever the consequences. He called together a

An aerial photograph of Cuba in 1962, showing evidence that missile sites were being built.

special Executive Committee (known as the **Ex Comm**) to advise him. This ruled out talking to the Soviet leadership because it could delay decisions. It also ruled out a full-scale military invasion of Cuba. Two options remained. First a 'surgical' airstrike which would destroy the missile bases without killing civilians. But the air force could not guarantee such accuracy. Besides, Soviet technicians might be killed, making a Soviet military response likely. The Ex Comm therefore decided on the second option - a naval blockade of Cuba. This would prevent further missiles and equipment from reaching Cuba. Kennedy made a speech on 22 October and the blockade was set up the next day. Tension was high because Soviet ships, carrying missile parts, were approaching the blockade. This was the first direct military confrontation between the two superpowers in the Cold War. When a U-2 was shot down over Cuba, all-out war seemed a real possibility. The crisis only ended when messages were exchanged between the leaders (see Box 10.7) and Khrushchev called back the Soviet ships.

The Cuban missile crisis - a time line

DISCOVERY OF MISSILES REMAINS A SECRET ➤

14 Oct U-2 spy plane identifies nuclear missile bases in Cuba.

15 Oct Kennedy sets up Ex Comm to deal with crisis.

19 Oct President's press officer denies rumours that missiles found in Cuba.

22 Oct Kennedy makes speech on TV. Announces discovery of missiles and US response - a naval blockade.

AMERICAN ARMED FORCES ON FULL ALERT ➤

23 Oct Naval blockade set up.

26 Oct Khrushchev letter to Kennedy. No mention of American missiles in Turkey.

27 Oct Khrushchev sends tougher message mentioning Turkey. U-2 plane shot down over Cuba. Kennedy replies to first message and secretly agrees to remove missiles in Turkey.

28 Oct Soviet ships turn back. The crisis is over.

6 Results of the crisis

The Cuban missile crisis ended when Khrushchev agreed to remove the nuclear missiles from Cuba in return for a promise from the USA that it would not invade Cuba. There was also a secret deal that the American nuclear missiles based in Turkey would be removed. In the short term, the real threat of nuclear war appeared to shock both sides and there was a thaw in their relations. Kennedy and Khrushchev agreed to set up a telephone **hot line** between the White House and the Kremlin. Then, in July 1963, a treaty was signed banning nuclear tests in the atmosphere (see also p.177). Whilst both leaders could claim to have gained from the crisis, Khrushchev's reputation suffered because he was seen to have been the one to back down. In 1964, he was deposed and replaced by Brezhnev. During the crisis, less powerful states had only been able to stand and watch. Some (for example, France and China) drew the conclusion that they needed their own nuclear forces in order to have any independence.

Box 10.7 Messages exchanged between Khrushchev and Kennedy

a) If promises were given that the President of the USA would not attack Cuba and the blockade were lifted, the question of the missile sites in Cuba would be an entirely different question. We and you ought not to pull on the ends of the rope in which you have tied the knot of war because, the more the two of us pull, the tighter the knot will be tied.

Letter from Khrushchev to Kennedy, 26 October 1962

b) We agree to remove those weapons from Cuba which you regard as offensive weapons. We agree to do this and to state this commitment in the UN. Your representatives will then make a statement to the effect that the USA, on its part, bearing in mind the anxiety and concern of the Soviet state will evacuate its nuclear weapons from Turkey.

Part of a message from Khrushchev to Kennedy, broadcast over Moscow Radio on 27 October (this message also demanded that the USA promise not to invade Cuba)

c) I have read your letter of 26 October with great care and welcomed the statement of your desire to seek a prompt solution to the problem. As I read your letter, the key elements of your proposals are as follows:

1. You would agree to remove these weapons systems from Cuba under UN supervision and to halt further introduction of such systems into Cuba.

2. We would agree (a) to remove promptly the blockade of Cuba and (b) to give assurances against an invasion of Cuba.

Letter from Kennedy to Khrushchev, 27 October 1962 (Kennedy ignored the message demanding that the USA withdraw missiles from Turkey)

Activity
The missile crisis

Source B *Khrushchev's view*

a) Some people present matters as though we installed the missiles for an attack on the USA. This is of course stupid. Why do we have to install missiles in Cuba when, possessing sufficient intercontinental missiles of the necessary range and power, we are able to strike a blow from our own territory? We installed missiles on Cuba specifically for the defence of Cuba and not for an attack on the USA.

Speech made by Khrushchev to the Supreme Soviet, 12 December 1962

b) We were sure that the USA would never accept Castro's Cuba. They feared, as much as we hoped, that Cuba might become a magnet which would attract other Latin American countries to Communism. We had to prevent the USA from interfering in the Caribbean. The logical answer was missiles. I had the idea of installing missiles with nuclear warheads in Cuba without letting the USA find out they were there until it was too late to do anything about them. We had no desire to start a war.

From 'Khrushchev Remembers' by N.S. Khrushchev, 1971

Source A *The range of missiles stationed in Cuba*

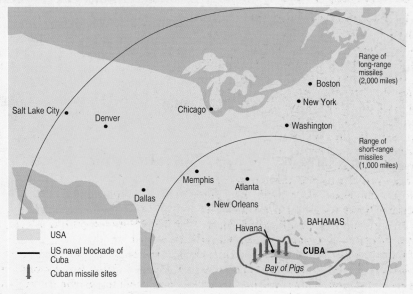

This map shows the area that could have been targeted by the Soviet Union once nuclear weapons were stationed in Cuba. It should be noted, however, that nuclear missiles based in the Soviet Union were capable of reaching the USA. It should also be noted that it was not illegal to station Soviet missiles in Cuba. After all, the USA did the same in Turkey (which bordered the Soviet Union).

Source C *Cartoon produced in 1962*

The cowboy on the left is President Kennedy. Castro rides the donkey. Behind him is Khrushchev.

Source D *A historian's view*

How close the superpowers came to nuclear war only became clear a quarter of a century later when American and Soviet documents became declassified. It was then revealed that, in addition to the long-range nuclear missiles, Khrushchev had placed Luna missiles with nuclear warheads in Cuba. These missiles had a range of just 25 miles. If the American forces had invaded and communications with Moscow had been cut, the Soviet commander in Cuba had the authority to use these missiles against the invading American force. When McNamara, the Defence Secretary in 1962, heard this in 1992, he was deeply shaken. 'No one should believe that American troops could have been attacked by tactical nuclear weapons without the USA responding with nuclear warheads', he said, 'Where would it have ended? In utter disaster.'

From 'The American Age' by W. LaFeber, 1994

Source E *A journalist's view*

In a seminar held in March 1988 which looked back at the Cuban missile crisis, former Defence Secretary McNamara spoke of coming up for air from the White House situation room on Saturday 27 October. 'It was a beautiful Fall evening, the height of the crisis and I went up into the open air to look and to smell it because I thought it was the last Saturday I would ever see', McNamara said. Fyodor Burlatsky, who had been one of Khrushchev's advisers, went pale. 'That was when I phoned my wife and told her to drop everything and to get out of Moscow. I thought your bombers were on the way', he said.

From 'The Cold War' by M. Walker (who has worked as both Moscow correspondent and Washington correspondent for 'The Guardian'), 1993

QUESTIONS

1. Judging from the information in this section, what were the causes and consequences of the Cuban missile crisis?

2. Why was the Cuban missile crisis a significant event in the Cold War? Use Sources A-E in your answer.

3. Judging from Sources A and B what were the aims of the Soviet leadership? Were Soviet actions justified?

4. Why do you think the cartoonist chose the scene drawn in Source C?

5. Martin Walker described the 13 days after 14 October 1962 as 'the most dangerous period of the Cold War'. Explain this statement using Sources D and E.

What were the causes and consequences of the Vietnam War?

When the Cold War spread from Europe to Asia, the USA became determined to prevent the spread of Communism throughout South East Asia. It was for this reason that the USA had participated in the Korean War and for the same reason that the USA became involved in Vietnam. The problem that the USA faced when it became involved in Vietnam, however, was that the leaders of the Vietnamese independence movement (the Nationalists) were also Communists. Since nationalism was very popular, so too was Communism. As a result, the USA faced the hostility of the majority of the Vietnamese population. This, combined with the difficult jungle terrain, made it difficult to fight a successful war and American troops soon became bogged down. The USA's involvement in Vietnam started in 1950 and continued under five different Presidents until 1975. Despite this, the USA failed to prevent the victory of Communism in Vietnam. The Vietnam War caused enormous damage in terms of lives and property and it created deep divisions in the USA and among its allies.

 ## The origins of the Vietnam War

Vietnam had been part of French Indo-China since the 19th century, along with Laos and Cambodia (see map on p.186 for its location in South East Asia). During the Second World War, the area was occupied by the Japanese, but in 1945 French rule was restored. By then, a Vietnamese nationalist movement had grown up. It was opposed to all foreign rule. During the Second World War, Nationalists combined with Communists to form the 'Vietnamese Independence League' or 'Viet Minh', under the leadership of Ho Chi Minh. In 1945, the Viet Minh set up an independent Vietnam with its capital at the northern city of Hanoi. The French refused to accept independence and for nine years French forces fought against Viet Minh troops. The USA began giving aid to the French in 1950 when the Korean War began and, by 1954, the USA was paying 80% of the cost of the war against Ho's forces. In 1954, the French were defeated at the **Battle of Dien Bien Phu**. Following this, the Geneva Conference divided the country into two along the 17th parallel (see map on p.195). Elections for a national government were to be held in 1956. The Democratic Republic of North Vietnam was set up by Ho Chi Minh in the north. The South Vietnamese government was led by the American-backed Ngo Dinh Diem.

Box 10.8 — **The domino theory (see also p.167)**

The loss of any of the countries of South East Asia to Communist aggression would have critical results. The loss of any single country would probably lead to relatively swift surrender to Communism by the remaining countries of this group. In all probability, Communist domination of the rest of South East Asia and India, and in the longer term the Middle East, would follow. This would endanger the security of Europe.

An American foreign policy statement from 'The Pentagon Papers', 1971

 ## The Americans become involved

Date	N° troops	Date	N° troops
1960	900	1968	535 000
1961	2600	1969	542 000 Peak
1962	11000	1970	474 000
1963	16700	1971	139 000
1965	184 000	1973	Ceasefire
1966	385 000	1975	Withdrawal

Number of American troops in Vietnam 1960-75.

American involvement in South East Asia was based on the domino theory (see Box 10.8). After the French army had been defeated in 1954, the USA backed the anti-Communist Ngo Dinh Diem. In 1956, Ngo refused to hold the elections agreed at Geneva. The USA supported him, knowing he would lose a free election. But Ngo was an increasingly embarrassing ally. He used American aid to attack the many enemies he had made during his harsh dictatorship. In 1961, Ngo's opponents in the South set up the National Liberation Front. Its military wing, the **Vietcong**, was supported with troops and weapons supplied by Ho Chi Minh's government. As war within Vietnam escalated, President Kennedy sent more 'advisers' (military personnel) to help Ngo's army. By the time Kennedy was assassinated (November 1963), the number of Americans serving in Vietnam had risen dramatically (see table, left). Ngo was also assassinated in November 1963. His successors, however, were no more successful in gaining support in the South or winning the war. Kennedy's successor, Lyndon Johnson, believed that it was vital to defeat Communism in Vietnam. To this end, Johnson increased the USA's involvement in Vietnam still further.

3 Full-scale war in Vietnam

In August 1964, two American ships were fired on by North Vietnamese gunboats in the Gulf of Tonkin. Without revealing that the ships had been helping South Vietnamese commando raids, President Johnson persuaded the Senate to give him wide powers to expand the war. When an American military base was attacked in early 1965, Johnson used his powers to start bombing raids on North Vietnam. The aim was to cut off supplies from the North to the Vietcong and to demoralise the North (see Box 10.9). But the raids failed to achieve either goal and Ho Chi Minh sent his regular army into the South. Johnson then decided to commit large-scale ground forces to Vietnam. Once American forces had been committed, it was difficult to reverse the process unless victory was gained. The American commander, General Westmoreland, continually called for more troops, claiming that victory was just around the corner. But the Vietcong were experts at guerilla warfare. For all their superior weapons and equipment the Americans made no progress. As a result, opposition to the war began to grow both in the USA and elsewhere as television pictures revealed the horrors of modern warfare.

A map of Vietnam. Supplies and weapons were transported from North Vietnam to the Vietcong in the South via the Ho Chi Minh trail through Laos and Cambodia.

Box 10.9   Bombing raids - a historian's view

Simultaneously with the bombing offensive in the North, American airmen drastically stepped up their activity in the South. The sheer size of the American effort was unbelievable. The statistics boggled the mind. By 1970, more bombs had been dropped on tiny Vietnam than on all the targets in the whole of human history. Napalm [jellied petrol used in bombs] poured into villages while weed killers defoliated the countryside. Yet it did not work. Hanoi did not quit. Men and supplies to the South increased. And, the political situation in Saigon got worse.

From 'Rise to Globalism' by S. Ambrose, 1980

4 Defeat and withdrawal

In January 1968, the Vietcong launched a massive offensive against towns and cities throughout South Vietnam, including an attack on the capital Saigon. American assurances that the war was being won were now shown to be false. President Johnson, after meeting top advisers, announced fresh peace negotiations and the reduction of air strikes in North Vietnam. He also made the decision not to stand for re-election that year. It was the beginning of the long process of American withdrawal from Vietnam. Under Johnson's successor, Richard Nixon, American forces were steadily reduced. Attempts were made to disguise defeat by claiming that the South Vietnamese army was now strong enough to carry on the struggle. Also, heavy bombing raids were made on both North Vietnam and, secretly, on Cambodia (through which supplies reached the Vietcong). In 1973, a peace treaty was signed by North Vietnam and the USA.

This cartoon, produced in 1975, shows the five Presidents involved in the Vietnam war. From the left they are Eisenhower (President 1953-61), Kennedy (President 1961-63), Johnson (President 1963-69), Nixon (President1969-74) and Ford (President 1974-77).

In 1975, the South Vietnamese army was defeated and the North Vietnamese entered Saigon (which was renamed Ho Chi Minh City). Communist governments were also installed in Laos and Cambodia in 1975. The war cost the Americans 57,605 dead and 303,700 wounded. The number of Vietnamese who died was far higher, over a million. Yet the war had achieved nothing. It did great damage to the USA abroad and divided the nation at home.

Activity
The USA in Vietnam

Source B Johnson on the USA's involvement

Why are we in Vietnam? We are there because we have a promise to keep. Every American President since 1954 has offered support for the people of South Vietnam to defend its independence. We are also there to strengthen the world order. Around the globe, from Berlin to Thailand, there are people whose wellbeing rests on the belief that they can count on us if they are attacked. To leave Vietnam would be to shake the confidence of all those people in the value of an American commitment and in the value of America's word. We are also there because there are great stakes in the balance. Let no one think that retreat from Vietnam would bring an end to the conflict. The battle would be renewed in one country and then another. The central lesson of our time is that the appetite for aggression is never satisfied.

Part of a speech made by President Johnson in 1965

Source C A historian's view

Economically, the USA was 50 to 100 times more productive than North Vietnam. Militarily, it had the firepower to bomb the enemy back into the Stone Age - or, with nuclear weapons, it could obliterate South East Asia altogether. But this was not a war in which that superiority could be made effective. Fighting was reduced to a series of small-scale encounters in jungles and paddy fields. But the difficulties of fighting the war hid a larger political problem. The North Vietnamese and the Vietcong were fighting for what they believed in very strongly. The South Vietnamese government, by contrast, appeared corrupt, unpopular and in a distinct minority - opposed by both Buddhist monks and the war-weary peasants.

From 'Rise and Fall of the Great Powers' by P. Kennedy, 1988

Source E Ho Chi Minh's tactics

When fighting in an enemy-occupied area, we must use guerilla tactics. We must absolutely not go in for large-scale battles and big victories unless we are 100% certain of success. The aim of guerilla warfare is to nibble at the enemy, harass him in such a way that he can neither eat nor sleep in peace, to allow him no rest, to wear him out physically and mentally, and finally to annihilate him. Wherever he goes, he should be attacked by our guerilas, stumble on land mines or be greeted by sniper fire. Here is what French soldiers say in their letters: 'In Vietnam, death is lying in wait for us in every cave, every bush, every pond'.

From 'Selected Writings' by Ho Chi Minh, 1977

Source A Nixon and the Vietnam War

The Vietnam War became increasingly unpopular in the USA. In the late 1960s and early 1970s, there were mass protests against it. President Nixon said that his policies were designed to suit the majority of Americans who remained silent during these protests. This cartoon is based on Nixon's idea that there was a 'silent majority'.

Source D Vietcong tunnel system

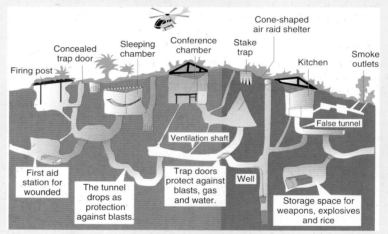

Tunnel systems like this stretched for 200 miles around Saigon. They protected the Vietcong from bombing raids and allowed them to advance undetected. The tunnels were narrow (1 metre high), making it difficult for American troops to attack the enemy.

QUESTIONS

1. Judging from the information in this section, why did the USA become involved in Vietnam? What were the consequences?

2. What point is being made by the cartoon in Source A?

3. Why was the Vietnam War an important event in the Cold War? Use Source B in your answer.

4. Judging from Sources C-E why did the USA fail to win the Vietnam War?

Vietnam - a television war

The Vietnam War has been described as 'the first war to be fought on the television screen'. By the mid-1960s, most American households had a television and the nightly audience for television news shows was often around 60 million people. At first, reports of the Vietnam War generally supported the government's view that the war was necessary to prevent the spread of Communism. But, as the war dragged on, television pictures became more dramatic and critical. In 1965, a CBS reporter, Morley Safer, was invited by an American army officer to accompany his troops on an operation against a Vietnamese village which was supposed to be sheltering Vietcong soldiers. The film (see below) was a turning point. After this, news programmes began to show some of the horrors of the war. Reporting became more doubtful about ultimate victory and more outspoken in its criticism of the way the war was being conducted. This affected the way in which Americans responded to the war. Indeed, many historians agree that negative television coverage helped to create serious divisions over American foreign policy for the first time since 1945. Television newsreels and documentaries, therefore, provide historians with an important source of materials for the study of the Vietnam War.

Morley Safer's film

The American troops walked towards the village in single file, everyone firing with no return fire. The only three marines wounded were shot by their own men. This only added to the troops' anger and they simply tore the village apart. Safer's film showed American marines setting fire to Vietnamese thatched huts. The pictures showed the full force of television - the ability to dramatise, fastening on one incident, one day in the war. Safer's film prepared the way for a different view of the war among Americans at large. There was, from that moment on, a greater acceptance of bad news about Vietnam. Despite all the fine words of the President and the politicians, it was realised that there was something terribly wrong going on out there. Over night, one TV correspondent with one cameraman could become as important as ten or 20 Senators.

A description of CBS journalist Morley Safer's film (broadcast on American TV in 1965) and its impact in 'The Powers That Be' by D. Halbertam, 1979

The summary execution of a Vietcong captive (2)

During the Tet holiday in January 1968, the Vietcong caught American forces completely by surprise by attacking nearly every city in the South. Most embarrassing of all, enemy soldiers actually attacked the American Embassy in Saigon. During the Tet offensive, American television networks concentrated on specific events and showed scenes never before screened. On the evening of 2 February 1968, NBC news broadcast the most sensational report of the war when it presented a film showing the chief of the South Vietnam National Police, General Nguyen Ngoc Loan, holding a pistol to the head of a Vietcong captive and then shooting him. The cameraman who filmed the event described the execution as follows: 'Loan pulls out his pistol, fires at the head of the Vietcong captive, the Vietcong captive falls, zoom on his head, blood spewing out.' Recognising a scoop, the newsmen beamed it to New York by satellite. NBC officials cut the final terrifying 17 seconds so that, as shown and viewed by 20 million people, the film ran for only 6 seconds after the killing. But the effect was devastating.

From 'One Nation Divisible' by R. Polenberg, 1980

The summary execution of a Vietcong captive (1)

This photo shows the chief of South Vietnam's police force executing a Vietcong captive in the street on 2 February 1968. After the shooting he said: 'They killed many Americans and many of my people.' The event was filmed by an American television crew (see below left).

QUESTIONS

1. Judging from the information on this page, what part did television play in the Vietnam War?

2. What use do you think historians can make of television programmes made at the time of the Vietnam War?

3. Suppose you had seen the news broadcast which showed the scene pictured above. Describe how you would have reacted.

4. Watch a news broadcast on television and compare an item on the programme with a report of the same item in a newspaper. How do the two reports differ? Which is of most use for a historian?

5. 'Television shapes events, it does not simply record them'. Use the information on this page to explain this statement.

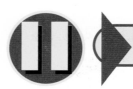

The Soviet Union's domination of Eastern Europe after 1945 was a major factor in the development of the Cold War (see pp.166-68). After Stalin's death in 1953, however, there seemed to be signs that the Soviet Union might relax its grip on Eastern Europe. In February 1956, Nikita Khrushchev (who had emerged as Soviet leader) made his 'secret' speech (see Overview opposite). The speech was highly critical of Stalin and some countries in Eastern Europe believed that it was a sign that they would be allowed greater independence. By the end of the year, however, this was seen to have been a false dawn. The Hungarian uprising of October 1956 was crushed by Soviet troops with great loss of life. If the Cold War had been thawing before the Hungarian uprising, it froze again after it. Indeed, five years later, the division of Europe became a concrete reality when Khrushchev ordered the Berlin Wall to be built. Khrushchev was replaced in 1964 by Leonid Brezhnev. Under Brezhnev, close political, economic and cultural control of Eastern Europe remained a priority. This was most clearly demonstrated by the invasion of Czechoslovakia in 1968. Another 20 years of hardline Soviet rule followed. It was only in the late 1980s that President Gorbachev's policies of openness ('glasnost') and restructuring ('perestroika') within the Soviet Union encouraged the spread of democratic, anti-Soviet movements in Eastern Europe which were able to win independence. By 1991, both the Soviet Union and its empire in Eastern Europe had collapsed. This chapter examines events in Eastern Europe between 1953 and 1991. It considers the following questions.

* What were the causes and consequences of the uprisings in Hungary in 1956 and Czechoslovakia in 1968?

* Why was the Berlin Wall built in 1961?

* Why did the Soviet Union become involved in the war in Afghanistan?

* What role was played by Solidarity in the removal of Soviet power from Poland?

* Was Gorbachev responsible for the collapse of Soviet power in Eastern Europe?

Key Events

East Germany
1953 Popular uprising against Soviet rule is crushed by use of force.
Aug 1961 After the number of people escaping to the West through Berlin rises, the Berlin Wall is built to divide East and West Berlin.
Oct 1989 Gorbachev criticises the East German leader, Honecker. Mass demonstrations lead to the collapse of the Communist government.
Nov 1989 The Berlin Wall is pulled down.
Mar 1990 East and West Germany are reunited and free elections held.

Czechoslovakia
Feb 1968 New Communist leader, Alexander Dubcek, introduces reforms - 'socialism with a human face'. The new, freer atmosphere becomes known as the 'Prague Spring'.
Aug 1968 Brezhnev orders the Soviet invasion of Czechoslovakia. The invasion is met with passive resistance and 72 killed.
1977 New dissident movement called Charter 77 set up by Vaclav Havel.
1989 In January, August, October and November, demonstrations are held which eventually force the Communist government to resign. Havel is joined by Dubcek in these demonstrations. Havel is then elected President.

Poland
1956 Strike at Poznan motor plant leads to riots. At least 53 killed. Soviet Union agrees to new government led by Gomulka.
1970 Shipyard workers go on strike in Gdansk. Over 50 killed.
1980-81 A series of strikes leads to the setting up of Solidarity (a trade union). The Polish army takes control of the government to prevent Soviet invasion.
Aug 1988 Economic problems and strikes force the government to talk to Solidarity. Free elections are agreed.
June 1989 Solidarity wins free elections.

Hungary
July 1956 Hungary tries to break away from Soviet control. Pro-Soviet leader Rakosi is forced to resign.
Oct 1956 New government set up under Imre Nagy. Khrushchev orders Soviet invasion and a month of bitter fighting begins. Around 3,000 dead. Nagy executed.
1988 Government introduces reforms and in late 1988 Gorbachev accepts a multi-party system.
Mar 1989 Mass demonstrations followed by free elections.

Developments in Eastern Europe, 1953-90.

Destalinisation

Source 1 — Stalin's death

This photo shows people in Moscow mourning the death of Stalin in March 1953. The Soviet poet Yevgeni Yevtushenko wrote: 'A sort of paralysis came over the country. People who had been trained to believe that Stalin was taking care of everyone were lost without him. The whole of Russia wept. So did I.'

Source 2 — Khrushchev's 'secret' speech

Nikita Khrushchev

'Stalin was a very distrustful man, sickly suspicious. This created in him a distrust even towards loyal Party workers whom he had known for years. Everywhere and in everything he saw 'enemies', 'two faces' and 'spies'. Lenin's strengths - patient work with people, stubborn and painstaking education of them, the ability to persuade people to follow him without using force - were entirely foreign to Stalin. He discarded Lenin's methods for those of violence, mass repression and torture. He acted on an increasingly larger scale, often breaking laws. Mass arrests and the deportation of thousands of people and execution without trial or without normal investigation created conditions of insecurity, fear and even desperation. False confessions of guilt were obtained by cruel and inhuman tortures. You see to what Stalin's mania for greatness led? He had completely lost touch with reality. He demonstrated his suspicion and arrogance not only to individuals in the Soviet Union, but also to whole parties and nations. Comrades, we must abolish the cult of the personality decisively.'

From the speech made by Nikita Khrushchev at the Twentieth Congress of the Communist Party in February 1956. The speech was supposed to be made in secret, but news of it quickly leaked out and caused a sensation.

Source 3 — A historian's view

By any measure, Khrushchev's 'secret' speech was a remarkable event in Communist history. For a quarter of a century, Stalin had exercised astonishing power. He had become the voice of Communism itself. Therefore, to attack such a legend so soon after Stalin's death raised the very real possibility of disruption within the Soviet Union and in Eastern Europe. At the same time, the people living in the Soviet satellites in Eastern Europe interpreted these developments as signs that the Soviet Union was moving towards tolerance and freedom. They were mistaken. Destalinisation was never intended to be a genuine liberalising of Soviet society. Nor was Khrushchev calling for a change in the way in which Communism worked in the Eastern bloc. Nonetheless, this was how many of the Soviet satellites in Eastern Europe interpreted his words. Khrushchev's heavy hand in Hungary in 1956 was clear proof that destalinisation had in no sense been intended as a softening of the Soviet Union's fundamental attitude to its own security in Eastern Europe. Destalinisation was a false dawn for those who thought it would lead to genuine independence.

From 'Stalin and Khrushchev: the USSR 1924-64' by M. Lynch, 1990

QUESTIONS

1. Using the information on these two pages, draw a time line showing the key events in Eastern Europe between 1953 and 1990.

2. How would you expect the factory workers in Source 1 to react to news of Khrushchev's 'secret' speech (Source 2)? Give reasons for your answer.

3. a) Why do you think Khrushchev's 'secret' speech (Source 2) made an impact in Eastern Europe?
   b) Why do you think Michael Lynch (Source 3) described it as a 'false dawn'?

4. '1956 was a turning point in the history of Eastern Europe.' Explain this statement using the information on these two pages.

What were the causes and consequences of the uprisings in Hungary in 1956 and Czechoslovakia in 1968?

Khrushchev's 'secret' speech of February 1956 encouraged the satellite states in Eastern Europe to press for greater independence from the Soviet Union. By far the most serious challenge to Soviet control came from Hungary. Pressure for reform (see Box 11.1) led to a full-scale uprising against Soviet rule which was only halted by Soviet military intervention. The Soviet response in Hungary clearly demonstrated the limits of destalinisation and showed that the Soviet Union was determined to keep its hold over the satellite states. The invasion also served as a warning to other countries in Eastern Europe and it was not until 1968 that another major challenge to Soviet rule emerged. This time a new breed of reforming Communism in Czechoslovakia threatened to undermine Soviet influence. Again, the result was military intervention. By 1968, the Soviet leader was Leonid Brezhnev. He now stated in no uncertain terms that any further attempts to break away from the Soviet Empire would be similarly punished. This policy became known as the **Brezhnev Doctrine** (the Soviet version of the Truman Doctrine - see p.170)

① The Poznan uprising

Following the death of Stalin, the Soviet grip on Poland appeared to be loosening. Newspapers began to print comments critical of the government and in May 1956 30,000 political prisoners were released. New tax and wage regulations, however, had caused a fall in living standards and in June 1956 workers at a motor plant in Poznan went on strike. The strike rapidly became a major political demonstration. When the government sent in troops and 300 tanks to restore order, at least 53 people were killed (eyewitnesses claimed more). The cartoon above shows a West German cartoonist's reaction to this news. Following the uprising, Khrushchev visited Poland and allowed a new moderate leader, Stanislaw Gomulka, to stay in power. Gomulka declared that he would be independent and pursue 'the Polish path to Communism'.

Box 11.1 Causes of the Hungarian uprising

- Desire for greater democracy and freedom
- Falling living standards
- Popularity of Nagy
- Concessions made in Poland
- Khrushchev's 'secret' speech
- Anti-Soviet feeling
- Hatred of Rakosi's brutal regime

FREE HUNGARY

② Hungary after 1945 - Rakosi and Nagy

After the war, Soviet influence ensured that Matyas Rakosi (who was loyal to Moscow) became Prime Minister in Hungary. When protests broke out against his strict regime, leading opponents were executed and over 200,000 were sent to prisons. When Stalin died, however, Rakosi was replaced by the more moderate Imre Nagy. Although he was a Communist, Nagy wanted greater independence for Hungary (he had been dismissed as Agriculture Minister in 1949 for holding 'incorrect views'). In 1953, he began reforms which allowed peasants to leave the collective farms set up by the Rakosi government. Pressure from Moscow in 1955, however, brought Rakosi back to power. This was very unpopular with the Hungarian people. Encouraged by Khrushchev's 'secret' speech and the concessions made in Poland, there was great popular pressure for reform (see Box 11.1 above).

③ The Hungarian uprising - key events

JULY	23 Oct	24 Oct	28 Oct	31 Oct	4 Nov	14 Nov
Rakosi forced to resign as Prime Minister and replaced by Gero (who was backed by Moscow).	Demonstrations in Budapest. Crowds destroy statue of Stalin and government calls in Soviet tanks to restore order.	Government agrees to the appointment of Nagy as Prime Minister. He invites non-Communists to join his government.	Soviet troops withdrawn from Budapest. Demonstrations turn into a general strike. Strong anti-Soviet feeling.	Nagy announces new programme of reforms including free elections, an end to government control of the media and withdrawal from the Warsaw Pact.	Soviet forces return to Budapest. Bitter street fighting follows and around 3,000 Hungarians killed.	Hungarian resistance finally crushed. Nagy arrested and later shot. New hardline government set up under pro-Soviet Janos Kadar. Over 200,000 refugees flee to the West through Austria.

4 Anti-Soviet feeling in Hungary

This famous photo was taken in October 1956. On 23 October, a huge statue of Stalin was torn down and dragged through the streets of Budapest. Its head was broken off and a road sign was stuck in the nose as an act of defiance.

Box 11.2 — A historian's view

On 23 October, students took to the streets to demand that the Stalinist puppets be replaced by Imre Nagy. Workers joined the students and the riot spread. Khrushchev agreed to give Nagy power, but that was no longer enough. The Hungarians demanded the removal of the Red Army from Hungary and the creation of an anti-Communist political party. By 28 October, the Russians had given in and begun to withdraw their tanks. On 31 October, the day after the Suez crisis began and less than a week before the American presidential elections, Nagy announced that Hungary was leaving the Warsaw Pact. Russian tanks crushed the Hungarian rebels. President Eisenhower did not even consider giving military support to the Hungarians and he would not have done so even if there was no Suez crisis. Under no circumstances would he risk World War III for Eastern Europe. Liberation [the idea that the USA would fight for freedom] was a sham. However deep Eisenhower's hatred of Communism, his fear of nuclear war was deeper.

From 'Rise to Globalism' by S. Ambrose, 1980

6 The results of the uprising

For Hungary, the uprising led to a return to stricter control under the loyal Communist regime of Janos Kadar. This also sent a message to the other satellite states about the limits of destalinisation. In addition, the Hungarian uprising had wider consequences. In the Soviet Union, senior politicians were critical of Khrushchev and this put him under pressure to achieve foreign policy successes elsewhere. In the West, governments condemned the use of force. As a result, Cold War tension increased. There was also a further lesson. The West's failure to send troops to help the Hungarian rebels showed that there was an unspoken agreement that Eastern Europe was within the Soviet Union's sphere of influence. Despite Western propaganda, there was little real chance of Western troops being sent to any country in Eastern Europe.

5 Why did the Soviet Union use force in Hungary?

'I'll be glad to restore peace in the Middle East, too'.

The Soviet Union allowed Gomulka to come to power in Poland because he was acceptable both to the Soviet government and to the Polish people. Also, he made it very clear that his reforms would not threaten Soviet control in Poland. In Hungary, however, the people refused to accept the Soviet government's choice of leader (Rakosi and then Gero). Once Nagy (the people's choice) was in power, it seemed at first that the Soviet government would allow him to introduce reforms (on 28 October, for example, Soviet tanks withdrew from Budapest). But, the anti-Soviet demonstrations gathered momentum. On 31 October, Nagy announced that Hungary intended to leave the Warsaw Pact. This was the turning point. Soviet tanks stormed back to Budapest and used force to end the opposition to Soviet control. Khrushchev later wrote: 'From our viewpoint, a small group, taking advantage of the mistakes of the old regime, had overthrown the legal government of Hungary. If this succeeded and NATO took root in the middle of the Communist countries, it would pose a serious threat to Czechoslovakia, Romania and the Soviet Union itself.' Some historians have argued that the **Suez crisis** distracted the West (on 31 October, Britain and France went to war against Egypt). Others disagree (see Box 11.2).

7 Background to the crisis in Czechoslovakia in 1968

During the 1960s, many Czechs had become increasingly discontented both with their poor living standards and with their lack of political freedom (see Box 11.3). In January 1968, however, the Czechoslovakian Communist Party elected Alexander Dubcek to replace the hardline Stalinist Antonin Novotny as Prime Minister. Dubcek had gradually emerged as the leader of the group in the Communist Party which supported reform. In April 1968, Dubcek announced a series of reforms (see Box 11.4). Czechoslovakia immediately buzzed with a new atmosphere of excited discussion about political change and greater individual freedom. Dubcek called his new brand of Communism 'socialism with a human face'. It was hugely popular. The loosening of state control over the media led to a wave of political discussion and mass meetings during what became known as the **Prague Spring**.

8 The Soviet response

A young Czech, arms raised in protest, faces Soviet tanks in Bratislava in August 1968.

Although Dubcek had assured Moscow that Czechoslovakia would remain a loyal ally of the Soviet Union, Brezhnev (the Soviet leader who had replaced Khrushchev in 1964) was worried that the reforming spirit of the Prague Spring might spread. As in 1956, there was the worry that reform might lead to a collapse of the Warsaw Pact. At first, Brezhnev tried to negotiate with Dubcek. But when this failed, the Soviet leadership decided to use force. The fact that a Congress (party conference) of the Czechoslovakian Communist Party was due to be held in September 1968 helps to explain the timing of the Soviet invasion. The Congress would have been sure to have given official support to Dubcek's reforms. Under the pretence of Warsaw Pact training manoeuvres, an invasion force was assembled in August. On the evening of the 20 August, 400,000 Warsaw Pact troops invaded Czechoslovakia. The Czechoslovakian leadership was taken by surprise. To avoid bloodshed on the scale of Hungary in 1956, Dubcek told people to offer only **passive resistance**. This was organised through radio broadcasts and resulted in far fewer casualties than in 1956 (73 Czechs were killed).

9 The consequences of the uprising in Czechoslovakia

Perhaps the most important consequence of the uprising in Czechoslovakia was the announcement of the **Brezhnev Doctrine**. In a speech made in August 1968, Brezhnev said that if the government in any Communist country attempted to make capitalist reforms, then other Communist states should act together to prevent such a change. This was the Soviet equivalent of the Truman Doctrine (which stated that the USA would send money or arms to support any country which was threatened by Communism). This made it quite clear that further attempts at reform in Eastern Europe would not be tolerated. In Czechoslovakia, following the Soviet invasion, Dubcek and his ministers were replaced by Soviet loyalists under Gustav Husak (unlike Nagy after Hungarian uprising, Dubcek was not executed). Economic reforms were ended, censorship returned and the secret police reappeared. Again, the invasion caused outrage in the West. But again, the West was distracted (the USA was bogged down in the Vietnam War and European leaders were worried that student riots in Paris would turn into revolution). By 1968, therefore, the Soviet leadership knew it would be opposed by no more than angry words.

Activity
The Soviet invasion of Czechoslovakia

Source B *Czechoslovakian radio broadcast*

To the entire people of the Czechoslovakian Socialist Republic. Yesterday, on 20 August at around 11 pm, troops from the Soviet Union and other Warsaw Pact countries crossed the frontiers of the Czechoslovakian Socialist Republic. This happened without the knowledge of the Czechoslovakian leadership. In the evening hours, the leadership of the Czechoslovakian Communist Party had been discussing the preparations for the 14th Party Congress. The Czechoslovakian leadership appeals to all citizens of our Republic to remain calm and not to offer resistance to the troops on the march. Our army, security police and people's militia have not received orders to defend the country. The Czechoslovakian leadership regards this act as against not only the fundamental principles of relations between Communist states, but also as against the principles of international law.

Part of a broadcast made by the Czechoslovakian Communist Party leadership on Prague radio on 21 August 1968

Source C *A Soviet news report*

Party and government leaders in the Czechoslovakian Socialist Republic have asked the Soviet Union and other allied states to give brotherly help with armed forces. This threat was brought about by counter-revolutionary forces. The troops will be withdrawn as soon as the threat to Czechoslovakia and to neighbouring Communist countries has been eliminated. The actions that are being taken do not attack the interests of any country. They serve the purposes of peace. The brotherly countries are firmly resisting any threat from outside. Nobody will ever be allowed to break a single link from the chain of Communist countries.

Part of a statement issued by the official Soviet press agency, Tass, on 21 August 1968

Source D *An American cartoon from 1968*

This cartoon portrays Brezhnev and his deputy, Kosygin, as American gangsters. The man in the middle is the Czechoslovakian leader Alexander Dubcek. American gangsters were rumoured to kill rivals by tying them up, dipping their feet in cement and, when it had dried, dropping them into deep water.

QUESTIONS

1. a) Using the information in this section, explain why there were uprisings in Hungary in 1956 and in Czechoslovakia in 1968.
   b) What were the similarities and what were the differences between these two uprisings?
2. What point is being made by each of the cartoons in Sources A and D. Design your own cartoon to show the opposite view.
3. How and why do Sources B and C differ in their explanation of what happened in Czechoslovakia on 20 August 1968?
4. How does Source E help us to understand why there was little resistance to the Warsaw Pact invasion? Can you think of other reasons why there was little resistance?

Source E *A historian's view*

Change would threaten the power of Communist leaders in Eastern Europe and would probably mean the new rulers taking revenge for what had happened in the past. For ordinary Communist officials, much was at stake. They gained a great deal from holding government jobs. They enjoyed higher salaries than the average working person. They had advantages of many kinds, such as access to better housing and to shops which stocked a wider variety of goods. Most important, they were able to gain the best educational opportunities for their children.

From 'The World Since 1945' by T.E. Vadney, 1987

SOURCE WORK

Historians do not only base their accounts on official documents and reports in the media, they also make use of personal accounts. These can be very useful for historians, but they must be handled with care. For example, the date when the account was written might be important. This page contains a personal account written in June 1996. Since the account was written 40 years after the events it describes, it has inevitably been shaped by the author's later experiences and by hindsight (knowledge of what happened later). Similarly, the account on this page describes just one man's experience of the Hungarian uprising. Other people might give very different accounts. Nevertheless, the account provides a unique insight into the events of 1956 since it is an account written by an eyewitness. The author experienced the events he describes and has formed judgements about them. As a result, his account is a valuable contribution to our understanding of what happened in Hungary in 1956.

An Austrian soldier helps a Hungarian refugee and her children across the border at Nicklesdorf on 6 November 1956. Their luggage is a single suitcase.

Zoltan Sigety's account

In 1956, I was in a labour camp specially built for political prisoners over a coal mine. Conditions were stricter than in camps for common criminals and we were isolated from them because the government was afraid we would 'infect' their minds with anti-Communist ideas. No radios or newspapers were allowed. When the revolution exploded in 1956, the newly formed miners' union forced our prison governor to release us all. During the ten days before the Soviet invasion, I stayed with my father and sister's family in Miskolc [Hungary's second largest town, in the north]. There I saw a huge demonstration, the siege of the AVO (secret police) headquarters, the killing of unarmed civilians by police fire and later the body of an AVO man hung in the main square. At the same time, events in Budapest turned in favour of the demonstrators. Although Stalin died in 1953, my reasons for leaving Hungary in 1956 were the same as in 1952 - namely, I did not wish to live under dictatorship. In addition, my chances to work in my profession were greatly reduced with a prison record. Being single, the only reservation was leaving my ageing father, but luckily he was secure in my married sister's home. Getting out of the country was relatively simple compared to 1952 - no minefields, watchtowers and constant patrols along the border. Once the general strike was over, the trains ran again and one could get near enough to the Austrian border. Starting with five friends, my little group grew to 35. When we got off at the last railway station, none of the others knew which way to go and they left me to find the last 20 miles on foot to safety. The only 'hot' moment was when I had to bluff my way past two Russian guards who aimed their sub-machine guns at me and shouted 'Stop'. From Austria, we left on the first train of 600 refugees to England.

Background information

My name is Zoltan Sigety, Hungarian by birth, but lived and worked in England as a chemical engineer after 1956. History caught up with me first near the end of World War II when, as a teenager, I was thrown out of my home together with my parents by the invading Soviet army in the middle of winter, robbed and held captive by marauding soldiers who were let loose to rape and loot the countryside for three days. In the next seven years, I was to learn to fit into a Communist world where the first loyalty was not to the Party or our national leader, but to Stalin, the 'most wise leader and benefactor of mankind'. When I could not stomach this any longer, I escaped to Austria (in 1952), only to be betrayed by a 'friend' in the Soviet zone and consequently captured and sent to a Hungarian labour camp for four years. The Hungarian national uprising opened my prison gates, to allow me to witness the glorious but tragically unequal fight of the Hungarian 'David' against the Soviet 'Goliath'. When it was all over, I faced again Soviet soldiers near the Austrian border, but managed to lead 35 compatriots to safety, ending up in England where we were granted political asylum.

QUESTIONS

1. What problems might historians face when using personal accounts? How is it possible to overcome these problems?

2. Write a newspaper article on the 1956 uprising in Hungary based on the personal account on this page.

3. What do the passages on this page tell us about Zoltan Sigety's attitudes and beliefs? How typical would you expect his views to be? Give reasons for your answer.

4. Think of an event you and colleague lived through about a year ago. Write your own account of the event and compare it with your colleague's account. What conclusions about personal accounts can you draw?

Why was the Berlin Wall built in 1961?

Berlin was the site of an important superpower confrontation in 1948-49 - the Berlin Airlift (see pp.172-73). Although the blockade was eventually lifted and the Airlift could stop, the basic issue remained - how were the two superpowers to find a suitable arrangement given that the Western Allies remained in control of territory deep within what had become East Germany? For ten years, little changed. The British, American and French zones which had merged to form West Berlin continued to be controlled by the Western Allies. East Berlin remained part of the German Democratic Republic (East Germany). Towards the end of the 1950s, however, the 'German problem' re-emerged. For the Soviet leader, Khrushchev, Berlin was 'a bone which sticks in the throat and needs to be coughed up'. His aim was to push the Western Allies out of Berlin. When this failed, he ordered a wall to be built along the border between East and West Berlin. Not only did this prevent people from moving freely between the two parts of the city, it also provided a solid and permanent reminder of the division between East and West.

1 East Germany after 1949

In June 1953, discontented workers at a construction project, angry at a government order to increase production by 10%, went on strike and marched to the government buildings. They were joined by supporters and an anti-Soviet riot began. Soviet tanks were sent in (see above), killing an undisclosed number of demonstrators before order was restored.

The German Democratic Republic (GDR) was set up in October 1949, five months after the Western Allies had set up the Federal Republic of West Germany. The Soviet Union refused to recognise the existence of the Federal Republic and the Western Allies refused to recognise the existence of the GDR. From this point of separation, the two states took two very different routes. In the GDR, Walter Ulbricht (leader of the East German Communist Party) closely copied the Stalinist model of a planned economy. The emphasis was on the growth of heavy industry at the expense of consumer goods. But this soon led to unrest among East Germans who could see the much higher living standards in West Germany (the West German economy was boosted by Marshall Aid). In June 1953, three months after the death of Stalin, this unrest spilled over into riots and demonstrations on the streets of East Berlin. After this uprising, Ulbricht did change his economic policy and, with Soviet aid, more emphasis was placed on consumer production. However, the GDR as a whole and East Berlin in particular remained much poorer than West Germany.

2 Relations between East and West Germany

In the 1950s, tension was increased by the refusal of each of the two Germanies to recognise the other's existence (tension was especially high in 1954 when West Germany was invited to join NATO). Konrad Adenauer, the first Chancellor of West Germany, was committed to the idea of West European unity as a defence against Soviet expansion and he strongly believed in German reunification (the joining together of the two Germanies). The East German leader, Walter Ulbricht, on the other hand, continued to be a loyal follower of Soviet policies and opposed reunification. The cartoon (right) shows the Soviet attitude to the news in 1954 that the Western Allies had agreed to allow West Germany to rearm and to become a member of NATO. West Germany is portrayed as a fierce, warlike dog. The dog is being held back by a paper chain attached to a hook shaped like a dollar sign. Each link of the chain (which would clearly be useless if the dog pulled at it) has 'security' written on it. Discussing West Germany's membership of NATO, Britain says to France: 'Don't worry, he's on a chain'.

③ Defections to the West

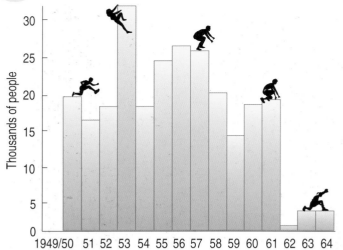

In 1949, the total population of the GDR was 17.5 million. But, between 1949 and 1961, 2.6 million people defected (escaped) to the West. It was not only the numbers that were important. Many of the defectors were just the sort of skilled and talented people that the GDR needed to rebuild its economy. By 1961, over 16,000 engineers, 15,000 teachers, 30,000 students and 5,000 doctors had defected.

④ Khrushchev's German policy

The German problem was at the heart of Khrushchev's foreign policy. He became seriously worried about the economic and political consequences of so many defections to the West. As the historian Roy Medvedev points out: 'When former capitalists, big landowners or rich peasants emigrated to the West, dissatisfied with the changes which were taking place in the GDR, Khrushchev and the East German government were not too concerned. The departure of highly qualified specialists and skilled workers was another matter, however.' (*Khrushchev*, 1982). Besides, Khrushchev needed a foreign policy success to silence his opponents (who had criticised him after the Hungarian uprising). In 1958, he issued his **Berlin Ultimatum**. Since, after the war, no peace treaties had been signed, he suggested that the USA, Britain, France and the Soviet Union all sign with the two Germanies a peace treaty which recognised the current frontiers. Berlin, he suggested, should become a free, self-governing, demilitarised city. But this would mean that land access to West Berlin would pass from control of the Soviet Union to the control of the GDR. Since the Western Allies were committed to German reunification, they could not officially recognise the existence of the GDR. As a result, they refused Khrushchev's proposal. Khrushchev threatened to negotiate a separate peace treaty with the GDR (giving control of land access to Berlin to the GDR), but he backed down when President Eisenhower invited him for talks in the USA in September 1959.

⑤ The U-2 incident and its consequences

In September 1959, Eisenhower and Khrushchev agreed to a summit meeting in Paris in May 1960. But, on 1 May, just weeks away from the summit, an American U-2 spy plane was shot down 1,200 miles inside Soviet territory and its pilot, Gary Powers, was captured. At first, the Americans claimed the plane was studying weather conditions, but Soviet scientists produced evidence that it was spying. When Eisenhower refused to apologise in public, Khrushchev stormed out of the summit meeting. This ended any chance of a thaw in the Cold War. The following June, Khrushchev tried to bully the new American President, John Kennedy, into agreeing to withdraw from Berlin. Again, his demand was refused and Kennedy threatened to use force to defend West Berlin. It was just after this that the decision was made to build the Berlin Wall. On the night of 12 August 1961, the East German government acted on orders from Moscow. That evening police and soldiers put up a barbed wire fence to seal off West Berlin. Four days later, work began on a major defensive barrier (see below). Anybody trying to cross the border without permission would be shot, attacked by dogs or risk treading on mines.

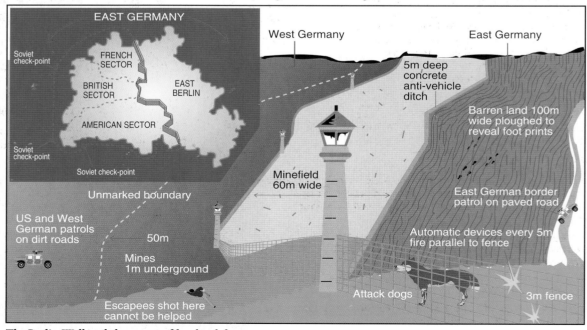

The Berlin Wall and the system of border defences.

Activity
The significance of the Berlin Wall

Source A Escaping from East Berlin

This East German soldier leaps to safety over the barbed wire barrier put up in August 1961. Within weeks, escapes like this were impossible.

Source B A historian's view

West Berlin was a glittering outpost of capitalism - luxurious, prosperous and bustling. The USA poured $600 million into West Berlin to make it a shining example of our way of life. The economic comparison with East Berlin was damaging enough, but the comparison between the individual freedom in West Berlin and the tight police controls around it was still worse. The contrast led 300,000 East Germans each year to disappear into West Berlin. West Berlin also contained the biggest number of spying agencies ever assembled in one place. It was an almost unbelievable bonus to be able to carry out intelligence missions 110 miles deep in the enemy's territory. Western radio stations and other propaganda arms also had this advantage. For all these reasons, West Berlin was a deep running sore to the East.

From 'The Cold War and its Origins', Vol.II, by D.F. Fleming, 1961

Source D Historians' verdicts on the building of the Wall

a) In an odd way, the Berlin Wall created greater international understanding. By stopping the loss of manpower, it saved East Germany from economic collapse. This lessened the likelihood of desperate measures which the Soviet Union would then have had to support and the West would have had to resist.

From 'Stalin and Khrushchev' by M. Lynch, 1990

b) The Berlin crisis was a dreadful moment, but it was followed in Europe by a long period of stability, if not calm. The Soviet Union was not unhappy with the outcome. The Foreign Minister Andrei Gromyko noted that the Wall had done its job. A problem had been solved. For the 190 people who were to die in the attempt to escape across the Wall, their problems were solved with grim finality. For the 17 million people left in the GDR, their citizenship was uncomfortably close to imprisonment.

From 'The Cold War' by M. Walker, 1993

Source C The Wall comes down

In October 1989, mass demonstrations led to the collapse of the East German government. In November, people on both sides of the Berlin Wall helped to tear it down. In this photo (right), East German border guards watch the wall being demolished.

Source E President Kennedy visits Berlin

Two thousand years ago the proudest boast in the world was 'civis Romanus sum' [I am a Roman citizen]. Today, in the world of freedom, the proudest boast is 'Ich bin ein Berliner' [I am a Berliner]. There are many people in the world who do not understand what is the great issue between the free world and Communism. Let them come to Berlin. And there are some who say in Europe and elsewhere that we can work with the Communists. Let them come to Berlin. Freedom has many difficulties and democracy is not perfect, but we never had to put up a wall to keep our people in.

Part of a speech made by President Kennedy on a visit to West Berlin, 26 June 1963

QUESTIONS

1. Why was the Berlin Wall built and why was its construction an important event in the history of the Cold war? Use the information in this section and Sources A and B in your answer.

2. 'A victory for the West'. Is this a fair comment on the construction of the Berlin Wall? Use Sources A, B, D, and E in your answer.

3. Why do you think the tearing down of the Berlin Wall in 1989 (Source C) was an important event?

4. Judging from Sources D and E what were the consequences of the construction of the Berlin Wall?

From the mid-1960s, relations between the superpowers gradually improved, a process known as **detente** (see also p.176). Indeed, the decade 1969 to 1979 was probably the warmest in the Cold War. There were two main long-term reasons for this. First, the Cuban missile crisis in 1962 (see pp.190-93) made leaders on both sides realise how close the world had come to a nuclear holocaust. And second, in the late 1950s a split developed in the Communist world between the Soviet Union and its neighbour China. This split deepened in the 1960s and, as far as the USA was concerned, a divided Communist world was less of a threat. Despite the uprising in Czechoslovakia in 1968, superpower relations warmed. In 1972, the SALT I Treaty was signed (see p.177). Then, in 1975, 35 countries (including the Soviet Union and the USA) signed the **Helsinki Agreement**. This gave official recognition to the postwar frontiers in Europe (which pleased the Soviet Union) and committed those who signed to respect human rights (which pleased the USA). The Helsinki Agreement, however, was the high point of the period of detente. When Soviet troops moved into neighbouring Afghanistan in 1979, the temperature in the Cold War dropped. The American Senate refused to agree to the measures in the SALT II Treaty and, within months, there was talk of a 'New Cold War'. This section examines why the Soviet Union became involved in Afghanistan and what the consequences were.

The 'arc of crisis' in 1979

By the late 1970s, the countries from Afghanistan in the north to Somalia in the south had become a centre of superpower rivalry. The map and notes below explain some of the reasons why the region was described as the 'arc of crisis' by the American government in 1978.

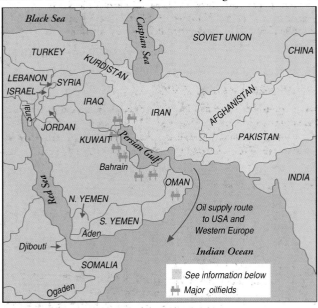

The Middle East in 1979.

Iran
Between 1953 and 1979, Iran supported the USA. In 1979, however, an Islamic revolution brought the Ayatollah Khomeini to power. His Islamic government turned against the USA, holding American citizens hostage in their own embassy. At first, Iran supported a worldwide Islamic revolution. This alarmed Soviet leaders who feared the spread of Islamic fundamentalism to the Soviet Union.

Afghanistan
In 1955, Afghanistan had been a founder member of the group of non-aligned states (those states which supported neither the USA nor the Soviet Union). Increasingly, however, it moved towards the Soviet Union. In 1979, civil war broke out between the pro-Soviet government and Muslim tribespeople called the 'Mujahadeen'. China was also worried by a pro-Soviet government on its borders.

Pakistan
Pakistan gained independence in 1947. From the 1950s, it supported the USA, signing the Mutual Defence Agreement in 1954. In the 1970s, however, Pakistan's political and trade links with China grew.

Background to Soviet involvement in 1979

In 1978, the leader of Afghanistan was overthrown by a pro-Soviet group led by Nur Taraki. Taraki began introducing Communist reforms and signed a **Treaty of Friendship and Cooperation** with the Soviet Union. Although the Afghan government was moving closer towards the Soviet Union, there was a great deal of opposition to the Communist reforms from the Afghan people. In 1978-79, a civil war developed between the government and rebels known as the **Mujahadeen**. The name means 'Fighters for Allah' and their supporters' main concern was that Communism would destroy the traditional Islamic way of life. In 1979, Taraki was replaced by Hafizullah Amin as Afghan leader, but he had even less success against the Mujahadeen. By December 1979, the Communist government seemed about to collapse. It was at this point that the Soviet government decided to act. Soviet aims are outlined in Box 11.5.

Box 11.5 **Soviet aims and the domino theory**

a) The excuse for the Soviet invasion of Afghanistan was the need to support a Communist government with whom the Soviet Union had signed a Treaty of Friendship. The invasion, therefore, followed the Brezhnev Doctrine (see p.202). The pro-Soviet government had provided the Russians with a useful military base within fighter plane reach of the oil states of the Middle East. A secondary consideration was to secure Afghanistan as a reliable buffer state on the Soviet Union's southern borders and to prevent the spread of Islamic fundamentalism.

From 'The Soviet Union from Brezhnev to Gorbachev' by I. Derbyshire, 1989

b) The American domino theory in the Middle East

Activity
The Soviet Union's Vietnam?

Source B A historian's view (1)

The results of the Afghanistan invasion proved in hindsight to be even more far-reaching than Soviet leaders had anticipated. Victory in the military campaign was not as quick and decisive as had been expected. Russian troops were able to gain control of urban centres, but were faced with guerilla resistance in the countryside. By 1988, this guerilla warfare had accounted for more than 50,000 Soviet casualties and was continuing to tie up more than 100,000 Soviet troops. Further, it imposed an economic burden on the Soviet regime which it could not afford. The war lost Russia friends in the Islamic world and Third World and pushed China closer to the USA. It also brought Western sanctions. There was a temporary halt to the export of American grain and high-tech goods to the Soviet Union. There was a partial boycott of the 1980 Moscow Olympics. There was the collapse of the SALT II agreement and the start of a Western arms build-up. American troops were sent to guard the Persian Gulf. In the USA, a new anti-Soviet President, Ronald Reagan, was elected in 1980, determined to build up American strength.

From 'The Soviet Union from Brezhnev to Gorbachev' by I. Derbyshire, 1989

Source D Soviet soldiers return home

This photo shows members of the Red Army returning to the Soviet Union from Afghanistan after the end of the war in February 1989.

Source A Cartoon from 1980

SOVIET 'OLYMPICS'

This cartoon was produced when the USA and some other Western countries announced that, as a protest against the Soviet invasion of Afghanistan, they would not be sending athletes to compete in the 1980 Olympic games which were to be held in Moscow. In 1984, the Soviet Union boycotted the Los Angeles Olympics. USSR stands for 'Union of Soviet Socialist Republics'. It is another name for the Soviet Union.

Source C Brezhnev's view, 1980

Why did Washington fly into global hysterics? What is behind all the lies about a 'Russian war against the Afghan people', the 'Soviet threat to Pakistan' and so on? The main motive is that the USA wants to set up a web of military bases in the Indian Ocean, the Middle East and in African countries.

Part of a speech made by Leonid Brezhnev in 1980

Source E A historian's view (2)

Although the Soviet Union emphasised many reasons for their invasion, the American government view of the Soviet action emphasised only two - that the Soviet Union aimed to add to the territory under its influence and that the Soviet Union hoped to place itself in a position where it could cut off the West's oil imports from the Persian Gulf. The USA condemned Soviet actions in Afghanistan, using many of the same terms that the Soviet Union had used to describe American actions in Vietnam ten years earlier. From the American point of view, the mass bombing of rebel-held territory and the use of chemical weapons proved that the Soviet Union was a brutal power.

From 'Contemporary International Relations' by D. Papp, 1991

QUESTIONS

1. Judging from the information in this section, why did the Soviet Union become involved in the war in Afghanistan?
2. What point is being made by the cartoon in Source A?
3. 'The Soviet Union's Vietnam'. Judging from Sources B, D and E why do you think this label was used to describe the war in Afghanistan?
4. Compare Sources C and E. How did Soviet and Western explanations of the Soviet Union's involvement in Afghanistan differ? What does this tell us about the Cold War?

From 1945, Poland was the most independent of all the Soviet satellite states. This was due in part to its long history of being invaded and of opposing those who invaded it. It was also due to the strength of the Roman Catholic Church in Poland. The Catholic Church is opposed to Communism and this made it difficult for Polish Communists to win the support of the majority of Polish people. In 1956, Poland was the first satellite state to test the Soviet Union after Khrushchev had made his 'secret' speech (see p.200 - the Poznan uprising). The Hungarian uprising followed soon afterwards. Similarly, in the late 1980s, developments in Hungary and Poland started a process which led to the break-up of the Soviet Empire and to independence throughout Eastern Europe. The concessions won in Poland in 1956 were the result of strikes and demonstrations. And again, in 1980 and afterwards, strikes and demonstrations played a key role in Poland. From 1980, however, opposition to the government was organised by a new organisation - **Solidarity**. Although Solidarity started out as a trade union, it soon developed into a political party. In its early years, Solidarity was an illegal organisation whose leaders were frequently imprisoned. By 1990, however, Solidarity had the support of the majority of the Polish people and its leader, Lech Walesa, was elected President of Poland.

 ## Poland in the 20th century

1918	Poland becomes an independent republic.	Poland invaded by Germany and the Soviet Union.
1939		
1944	Soviet forces drive the Germans out of Poland.	
1947	Poland becomes a Communist state, ruled by the Soviet-backed Polish United Workers' Party.	
1956	Poznan uprising (see p.200). Gomulka becomes leader.	
1970	Government announces price rises. Strikes in Gdansk and Gdynia - 45 killed, 1,000 injured. Gomulka replaced by Gierek.	
1979	At a demonstration in Gdansk shipyards, Lech Walesa calls on workers to organise.	
1980	Strike in Gdansk leads to **Gdansk agreement** (see Box 11.6). Solidarity becomes the first independent union in Eastern Europe.	
1981	General Jaruzelski takes over government. Martial law is declared. Solidarity is banned and its leaders imprisoned.	
1982	Widespread unrest. Walesa is released from prison early.	
1983	Walesa is awarded Nobel Peace Prize.	
1989	Solidarity is legalised. First democratic elections in Eastern Europe since 1945. Solidarity wins 162 seats in the lower house and 99 out of 100 seats in the upper house. The Communists give way without violence.	

 ## Unrest in Poland in the 1970s

In the late 1960s, living standards in Poland became steadily worse. Anger at government increases in fuel and food prices just before Christmas 1970 led to a major demonstration in Gdansk. On 16 and 17 December, in what became known as the **December Massacre**, 45 people were killed and over 1,000 injured. In the hope of bringing calm, Gomulka (who as First Secretary of the Communist Party had led Poland since 1956) resigned and was replaced by Gierek. The new government cancelled the price increases, raised wages, imported food (at considerable cost) and dismissed officials at all levels. The press was given greater freedom (until 1974). By 1973, Poland was enjoying an economic boom. But, by 1976, this boom had collapsed. Again, there was unrest and rioting. Again, the government responded by cancelling price increases and raising wages. This worked in the short term, but by 1980 there were severe shortages and soaring prices. In August 1980, a shipyard strike at Gdansk developed into a much broader protest against the Polish government (see Box 11.6). It was after this strike that a new, independent trade union was created - **Solidarity**.

Box 11.6   The Gdansk agreement

By the summer of 1980, Poland had a massive foreign debt. Meat was either unobtainable or hugely expensive. Inflation was rising. There was nobody to blame but the government. But equally there was no constitutional way of blaming the government or of pressurising it into acting (or into explaining its actions). As a result, the strikes in August were immediately political. They could not be settled by negotiation because the workers were not allowed to join organisations which could negotiate on their behalf. After meeting Soviet leaders, Gierek made an agreement with the strikers. The strikers accepted the leading role of the Communist Party, Poland's Communist system and its membership of the Russian bloc. In return, the strikers won astonishing victories - the right to strike, the right to form trade unions independent of the state, wider discussion of the government's economic policies, less censorship, increased wages and pensions, promises on working conditions and regular broadcasts of Catholic Church services. Nobody doubted that something extraordinary had happened.

From 'World Politics Since 1945' by P. Calvocoressi, 1991

③ Lech Walesa and Solidarity

Lech Walesa was a leading figure in the movement which eventually led to the collapse of the Soviet-backed government in Poland. A committed Catholic, he was born in 1943 and trained as an electrician. In 1967, he began work at the Lenin shipyard in Gdansk. He was an organiser in the 1970 strike which led to the December Massacre. In 1976, he was sacked for criticising the government. In 1978, he set up the Baltic Committee for Free and Independent Trade Unions. Two years later, he helped to organise the shipyard strike at Gdansk. As the strike spread, Walesa emerged as the chief negotiator for the opposition to Gierek's government and he showed great skill in keeping the strikes peaceful while the negotiations were going on. After the Gdansk agreement had been signed, Walesa became a national hero (he was also portrayed as a hero in the West since he had stood up to the Communists). He then launched a new (and now legal) independent trade union called **Solidarity**. Solidarity quickly became the focus of opposition to the Communist government and it soon had as many as 10 million members.

④ Jaruzelski and martial law

Zomo riot police imposing martial law in Poland in 1981.

Leading members of Solidarity were careful to argue that they were not interested in party politics. This was not enough to reassure the Soviet government, however. During 1981, a series of unofficial strikes threatened to plunge Poland into civil war. Walesa was criticised by some for his moderate approach. But he was well aware that any attempt to overthrow the government would lead to a Soviet invasion. Against Walesa's advice, other Solidarity leaders began to call for free elections. The government's response was to appoint an army officer, General Jaruzelski, as Prime Minister. On 12 December 1981, the new government took decisive action. All across Poland, Solidarity leaders were arrested. Their buildings were taken over and the movement was banned. Jaruzelski then declared martial law to 'save Poland from the actions of reckless extremists'. Solidarity was not prepared for this and, at first, there was little organised protest. Where workers did attempt to defend mines and factories, they were attacked by the ZOMO riot police. The constant presence of tanks, riot vehicles and military policemen ensured that martial law was enforced (see left).

⑤ Passive resistance

In prison, Walesa appealed for non-violent resistance and refused to cooperate with Jaruzelski's plans to make him a leader of an official trade union which would replace Solidarity. At the same time, Solidarity continued to function as an underground movement. In 1982, Walesa was released to a hero's welcome and returned to a job at the Gdansk shipyard. Although under a 24 hour police guard, he continued to appeal for non-violent resistance through letters and meetings with foreign journalists. In 1983, he was awarded the Nobel Peace Prize and, once again, became the focus of media attention. For the next five years Solidarity continued its campaign of **passive resistance**. In 1989, this tactic paid off. By then, the economic position in Poland had become so bad that the government was forced to legalise Solidarity once more and to appeal to it for help. In return for its help, Solidarity demanded free elections. The government agreed and in June 1989 Solidarity won a stunning success (it won 99 out of 100 seats in the Senate and all 162 seats it was allowed to stand for in the lower house). Jaruzelski resigned as Prime Minister and Parliament immediately elected him President. A leading member of Solidarity, Tadeusz Mazowiecki, took his place as Prime Minister. At this crucial moment, far from threatening a Soviet invasion, the Soviet leader Mikhail Gorbachev sent a message of congratulations. Following Jaruzelski's resignation in October 1990, Lech Walesa was elected President in Poland's first free presidential election.

A French poster supporting Solidarity

Activity
The development of Solidarity

Source B Walesa in prison

Lech Walesa's wife, Danuta, and baby Ania hold a poster demanding Lech Walesa's release from prison in 1982.

Source A A historian's view (1)

The strikes at Poland's Gdansk shipyard and the formation of the Solidarity movement brought the sharpest challenge to the Soviet system in Eastern Europe since the Prague Spring of 1968. The power of Solidarity lay in its threefold aims. The opposition to higher food prices rallied widespread support. The two demands for legalising strikes and allowing the broadcast of the Roman Catholic mass over state radio each Sunday rallied the working class, the Church and its supporters. All three demands were met in the agreement negotiated in August 1980. The readiness of the Polish government to compromise and the unwillingness of the Soviet government to worsen its relations with the West after Afghanistan gave Solidarity room to mobilise. But, to put pressure on the Polish government, the Soviet army held some threatening military manoeuvres and the KGB made it clear it was seriously alarmed. The Soviets were reassured by the appointment of Jaruzelski as Prime Minister, but when Polish leaders visited Moscow in March 1981, the Soviet government issued a plain warning that 'the Communist community is indivisible and its defence is the concern not just of each individual state, but of the Communist coalition as a whole'.

From 'The Cold War' by M. Walker, 1993

Source C A historian's view (2)

Martial law brought a curfew from 6 pm to 6 am. This was violently enforced and those found on the street after 6 pm were likely to be arrested or shot. Telephones were cut off and news broadcasts became a tissue of ridiculous lies. Poles responded to Walesa's appeal for non-violent resistance in various imaginative ways. They stopped buying the official newspaper or watching television. They would go for walks at television news time or put their sets in front of the window, the screens facing outwards. They listened to Radio Free Europe and the BBC to gain a true picture of how things were.

From 'Lech Walesa' by Mary Craig, 1991

Source D A British cartoon from August 1989

This cartoon appeared in the 'Sunday Times' on 20 August 1989.

Source E Lech Walesa in 1980 and 1990

a) Lech Walesa is the 37 year old unemployed electrician whose walrus moustache, shabby suit and shrewd eyes have made him an easily recognisable symbol throughout the world of Poland's revolt against a corrupt and incompetent system. He has struggled for a decade to create genuine, free trade unions - a struggle which has cost him his job and constant police harassment. What will happen in the long term is unknown. But a sort of revolution has occurred, without a drop of blood being spilt.

From an article in the 'Times', 27 December 1980

b) As widely expected, Lech Walesa gained a majority of the vote in the first free presidential elections held in Poland on 25 November 1990. In the first round, Walesa won 39.96% of the vote, Tyminski 23.1% and Mazowiecki 18.08%. Since none of the candidates had an overall majority, a run-off was held between Walesa and Tyminski on 9 December and Walesa won 75% of the vote. The elections were called in early October after President Jaruzelski had agreed to resign and to transfer power to a freely elected head of state.

From an article in the 'Guardian', 10 December 1990

QUESTIONS

1. Judging from the information in this section, what role did Solidarity play in the removal of Soviet power from Poland?

2. Judging from Sources A-C what were the aims and tactics of Solidarity? Why do you think Solidarity used these tactics?

3. What role did Lech Walesa play in the struggle against Communist rule in Poland? Use Sources B, C and E in your answer.

4. Use Source E (b) to explain the point being made by the cartoon in Source D.

Was Gorbachev responsible for the collapse of Soviet power in Eastern Europe?

When the Soviet leader Leonid Brezhnev died in 1982, he was replaced first by Yuri Andropov (who died in 1984) and then by Konstantin Chernenko (who died in 1985). In 1985, a younger man was appointed to the post of General Secretary of the Communist Party - Mikhail Gorbachev (who was 54 years old). When Gorbachev became leader, the so-called 'New Cold War' was at its height. The superpowers were locked into an arms race and there seemed little chance of any major change in the international balance of power which had lasted for the previous 40 years. Yet, by the end of 1991, just six years after Gorbachev came to power, Soviet control of Eastern Europe had collapsed and the Soviet Union itself had broken up into 15 separate states. This rapid collapse of Soviet power was certainly one of the most dramatic developments in the 20th century and it was all the more dramatic because it happened without widespread bloodshed. While there is little doubt that Gorbachev can take some credit for this lack of bloodshed, there is a debate about the extent to which he was responsible for the collapse of Soviet power. Some people argue that he helped to engineer it whilst others argue that a collapse was inevitable anyway and there was little he could do about it. This section examines the issues raised by this debate.

  Perestroika and glasnost

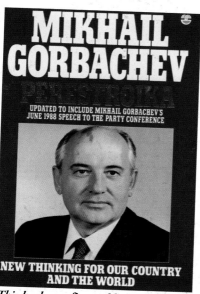

This book was first published in Britain in 1987.

In October 1985 Gorbachev launched a new programme of reforms (see right). Central to this programme were the twin policies of **perestroika** (economic restructuring - see Box 11.7) and **glasnost** (openness and free speech). To improve the Soviet Union's economic position, Gorbachev argued, it was necessary to be more flexible - to allow local as well as central economic planning and to allow some private ownership. Whilst this clearly meant an end to the centrally planned economy of the Stalinist period, it was not far from Lenin's New Economic Policy (see p.40). Hand in hand with perestroika went the policy of glasnost (greater openness). Gorbachev was particularly concerned about the constant falsification of economic figures. Greater openness would mean the publication of more accurate figures which would allow people to gain a realistic picture about the state of the economy. But glasnost did not just apply to economic figures. It was taken to mean that all types of government control should be lifted. As a result, newspapers and TV programmes began to change. Criticism of the government became possible and, for the first time, there were reports on the darker side of Soviet life (a drugs problem was admitted for the first time in 1987, for example).

Box 11.7 — Perestroika

At some stage (this became particularly clear in the late 1970s), the country began to lose momentum. Economic failures became more frequent. Difficulties began to pile up. Elements of what we call 'stagnation' began to appear. A country which was once quickly closing on the world's advanced nations began to lose one position after another. The aim of perestroika is to ensure - within the next two or three years - the transition from an excessively centralised economic system which relies on giving orders to a democratic system based on a combination of centralism and self-management. Perestroika means overcoming stagnation. Perestroika is the development of democracy, socialist self-government, encouragement of initiative and creative endeavour, improved order and discipline, more criticism and self-criticism. Perestroika means aiming at ever better satisfaction of the Soviet people's requirements for good living and working conditions, for good rest and recreation, education and health care. In principle, I can say that the end result of perestroika is clear. It is a thorough renewal of every aspect of Soviet life.

From 'Perestroika' by M. Gorbachev, 1987

2 Gorbachev's foreign policy

Gorbachev's foreign policy had three main elements - to reduce defence spending (see Box 11.8), to avoid the danger of nuclear war and not to interfere in the running of countries outside the Soviet Union. Gorbachev's promotion of glasnost won great support in the West and there were soon signs that the Cold War was thawing. In 1987, Gorbachev and President Reagan signed the Intermediate Nuclear Forces (INF) Treaty (see above) in which both superpowers agreed to withdraw and dismantle large numbers of nuclear weapons. This was followed by the Strategic Arms Reduction Treaty (START) signed in July 1991 which reduced long-range nuclear weapons by one third.

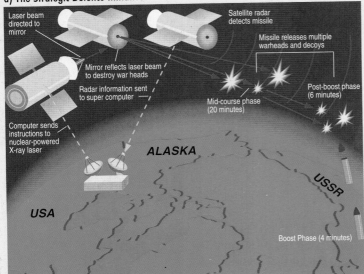

Box 11.8   Gorbachev and 'Star Wars'

a) The Strategic Defence Initiative

Laser beam directed to mirror

Satellite radar detects missile

Missile releases multiple warheads and decoys

Mirror reflects laser beam to destroy war heads

Radar information sent to super computer

Post-boost phase (6 minutes)

Mid-course phase (20 minutes)

Computer sends instructions to nuclear-powered X-ray laser

ALASKA

USSR

USA

Boost Phase (4 minutes)

The Strategic Defence Initiative (SDI), also known as 'Star Wars', was set up in 1983. The aim was to defend the USA against nuclear missiles with laser beams based in space.

b) It is clear from Mikhail Gorbachev's own speeches that one of the main reasons for reforming the Soviet economy was the realisation that the Soviet Union was going to have serious problems remaining competitive economically and militarily. In particular, President Reagan's SDI threatened to make obsolete an entire generation of Soviet nuclear weapons. It shifted superpower competition into areas like microelectronics where the Soviet Union had serious disadvantages.

From 'The End of History & the Last Man' by F. Fukuyama, 1992

3 Continued economic decline

When Gorbachev launched his reform programme in 1985, he called for a doubling of national income in 15 years. Despite his efforts to regenerate the economy through perestroika, however, little changed. One major problem was that the economy failed to respond competitively to the new age of computers and electronics (see Box 11.8). A second was that military spending continued to devour huge amounts of money. Although Gorbachev succeeded in reducing the Soviet Union's nuclear arsenal, his policies failed to pull the Soviet economy out of its rut. A number of blows - such as a slump in oil prices, the nuclear accident at Chernobyl in 1986 and the Armenian earthquake of 1988 - did not help. The main problem, however, was that, although people agreed there needed to be a new economic order, there was no agreement about how it should work. Government campaigns - such as the campaign against drunkenness launched in 1985 - had little effect. And the move towards local decision making backfired since managers used their new independence to concentrate on goods which produced high profits. This led to a shortage of basics (like soap or toothpaste) and further hardship for ordinary people. Also, although Gorbachev hoped that glasnost would restore confidence in the government, it had the opposite effect. Freedom of speech meant the freedom to hold different political views. Glasnost, therefore, encouraged opposition to the one-party system. It also held out the hope of change both at home and abroad. Gorbachev's policies, therefore, can be said to have contributed both to the collapse of Soviet power in Eastern Europe and to the collapse of the Soviet Union which followed it.

4 The domino effect in Eastern Europe

When Gorbachev launched his programme of reforms in the Soviet Union, it had a knock-on effect in Eastern Europe. Once it became clear that the Soviet leadership meant what it said about greater openness, the people of Eastern Europe began to press for change. The spark was a speech delivered to the United Nations on 8 December 1988. In this speech, Gorbachev said: 'The use or threat of force can no longer and must no longer be an instrument of Soviet foreign policy.' This gave out the signal that the Soviet Union would not use force if the people of Eastern Europe decided on change. Within months, the people of Eastern Europe had taken full advantage of this and overthrown their Soviet-backed governments. The process began in Hungary. In March 1989, 100,000 Hungarians marched through Budapest demanding the withdrawal of Soviet troops. The following month, Solidarity was legalised by the Polish government and in June it won an overwhelming electoral victory. This set the dominoe's tumbling. By Spring 1990, mass demonstrations had overthrown the Communist governments in Hungary, Poland, East Germany, Czechoslovakia, Romania and Bulgaria. Whilst this was surprising enough, perhaps more amazing was the lack of bloodshed. With the exception of Romania and Yugoslavia, the Communist governments gave in without a fight.

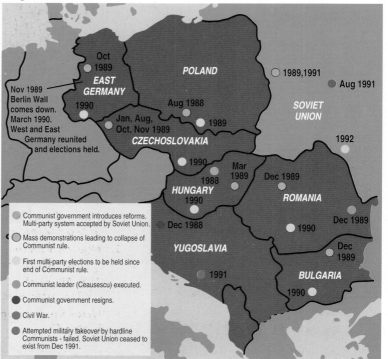

The domino effect in Eastern Europe.

Activity

The end of the Cold War

Source B A historian's view (1)

In August 1991, an attempt was made to remove the Gorbachev regime by force. Though it failed, Soviet politics had taken a step forward towards disintegration. The attempted coup gave Boris Yeltsin, leader of the Russian Republic (the largest state in the Soviet Union), an opportunity to appear as the strong man of the Soviet scene. The army, the only threat to his supporters, did not move against him. Gorbachev lost power and resigned. The demolition of the Communist Party of the Soviet Union began almost immediately. Relatively without bloodshed, the huge creation which had grown out of the Bolshevik victory of October 1917 was coming to an end. There were good grounds for rejoicing over that. But it was far from clear that nothing but good would follow. When on 31 December 1991 the Soviet Union flag over the Kremlin was hauled down, to be replaced by the Russian flag, the Soviet Union disappeared from history to be replaced by a new Commonwealth of Independent States.

From 'History of the World' by J.M. Roberts, 1994

Source D A historian's view (2)

The fall of the East European satellites in 1989 and Moscow's reluctant acceptance of German reunification in 1990 demonstrated the collapse of the Soviet Union as an international power, let alone a superpower. Internationally speaking, the Soviet Union was like a country comprehensively defeated, as after a major war - only without a war. The collapse of the Union itself was due to the breakdown of central authority. This forced every region or sub-unit of the country to look after itself and to save what it could from the ruins of an economy sliding into chaos. Hunger and shortage lie behind everything that happened in the last two years of the Soviet Union.

From 'Age of Extremes' by E. Hobsbawm, 1994

Source A The break-up of the Soviet Union

This map shows the 15 independent states which were created after the collapse of the Soviet Union in 1991.

Source C American cartoon from 1992

QUESTIONS

1. **Judging from the information in this section, was Gorbachev responsible for the collapse of power in Eastern Europe?**

2. **'Nobody won the Cold War. It simply fizzled out'. Do you agree with this statement? Use Sources A-D in your answer.**

3. **Why do you think the Soviet Union collapsed in 1991? Use Sources A, B and D in your answer.**

4. **Write a paragraph explaining the points being made by the cartoon in Source C.**

Themes

The 20th century has seen enormous change in China. First, before 1911, China was ruled by an Emperor. In 1911, however, the Emperor was overthrown and the imperial dynasty (royal family) which had ruled China for centuries collapsed. Second, there was a period of confusion and violence as warlords fought against each other and Nationalists fought against Communists in a series of bloody civil wars (1911-49). And third, the years since 1949 have seen China's emergence as a Communist giant in Asia. The first 27 years of Communist rule were dominated by Mao Zedong, a leader who managed in the 1960s to inspire the same sort of fanatical loyalty that Hitler and Stalin had inspired in the 1930s. Mao had become leader of the Chinese Communist Party (CCP) during the 'Long March' of 1934-35 when, to avoid military defeat, a group of several thousand Communists had marched 9,500 km from Jiangxi province in the south east to Shaanxi province in the west. Having masterminded the Communist victory in 1949, Mao was then responsible for the major policy decisions which were made after 1949. In particular, Mao supported the 'Great Leap Forward' (an attempt to industrialise and reorganise the countryside) and he called for the Cultural Revolution (an attempt to regain the momentum of the Communist revolution). This chapter explores the history of China in the 20th century through the following key questions.

* Why was it difficult to rule China in the early 20th century?
* What was it like to live in China at the start of the 20th century?
* Why did relations between the CCP and GMD deteriorate after 1927?
* How did the CCP manage to win power?
* What impact did Communist rule make on China?
* What were the causes and aims of the Cultural Revolution?

Key Events

Note. There are two ways of writing Chinese names in English. Older books use the Wade-Giles system (**Peking**, **Mao Tse-Tung** or **Chiang Kai Shek**, for example). This chapter uses the Pinyin system (**Beijing**, **Mao Zedong** or **Jiang Jieshi**, for example).

IMPERIAL CHINA ──────▶| ── WARLORD ERA ──────────▶

| 1900 | 1911 | 1916 | 1921 | 1923 | 1927 |

The Boxer Rebellion.

Emperor Puyi (above) is overthrown in the 'Double Tenth' revolution.

Death of Yuan Shikai (above) who ruled China 1911-16.

In 1921, the Chinese Communist Party (CCP) is set up. Mao Zedong attends the first meeting (above).

First United Front
Between 1923 and 1927, the CCP works together with the Nationalist Party (GMD). This uneasy alliance is broken in 1927 when GMD troops massacre Communists in Shanghai.

WARLORD ERA ────────────▶| COMMUNIST CHINA ──────────▶

| 1934 ──▶ 1935 | 1936 ─▶ 1946 | 1949 | 1957 ─▶ 1960 | 1966 ──▶ 1969 |

The Long March 1934-35
Around 100,000 Communists begin the march, but less than 10,000 survive. Nevertheless, the CCP escapes destruction.

Second United Front
Between 1936 and 1946, the CCP and GMD join forces against the Japanese. After the Japanese surrender in August 1945, efforts to keep the peace fail and civil war breaks out again.

CCP Victory
In 1949, the CCP finally defeats the GMD and sets up a new Communist State - the People's Republic of China. Its first head of state is Mao Zedong.

The Great Leap Forward, 1957-60 The reorganisation of collective farms into communes and the attempt to set up small-scale industrial projects leads to widespread famine. Mao admits the policy was mistaken.

The Cultural Revolution, 1966-69
Mao calls on young people to rebel against those in authority and to revive the revolution which is losing momentum. The result is great upheaval and a climate of fear.

Why was it difficult to rule China in the early 20th century?

Source 1 A map of China in 1900

- Border of China
- Border of province
- Province which gained independence after 1900

RUSSIA

River Amur

Manchuria

Outer Mongolia (independent since 1911)

Gobi desert

Inner Mongolia

Xinjiang

Gansu

Hebei
Beijing
Korea

Tianjin

Shanxi

Shandong

Japan

Qinghai

Yellow River

Shaanxi

Henan

Anhui

Jiangsu

Nanjing
Shanghai

Tibet (independent since 1912)

Hubei

Zhejiang

Himalaya mountain range

Nepal

Sichuan

River Yangzi

Hunan

Jiangxi

Fujian

Wuhan

Bhutan

Guizhou

British India

Burma

Yunnan

Guangxi

Guang Dong

Taiwan

French Indo-China

Guangzhou

Source 2 A historian's description of China in the early 20th century

At the end of the 19th century, China was a vast, feeble agrarian empire whose population was concentrated in the eastern half of the country. The main agricultural regions differed from each other in size and wealth, but each contained a central, populous, fertile core located on an important river system. Each was largely self-sufficient in food, although there was a great deal of trade between the regions. Together, they were home to around 397 million people in 1893 (the year of Mao Zedong's birth). This was around one quarter of the earth's population. Most people spent almost all their income just to eat. This poverty reflects one central fact about China - population density. With 25% of the world's population, China only possesses 6% of the earth's arable land. Every village had its landless or nearly landless peasants who scratched out a living (around 60% of the population). Above them were families who owned enough land to keep themselves (around 30% of the population). At the top of the scale were wealthy landlord families who avoided all manual labour and lived on their income. For centuries, the family system had been the bedrock on which Chinese civilisation was built. Everyone was expected to obey parents and elders. Everyone was expected to marry and to produce sons to carry on the family name. Until the late 19th century, the Chinese had generally resisted Western culture which they considered barbarian. But, in 1898, Germany, Russia, England and France forced the Chinese government to grant special **spheres of influence**. Western ideas and culture flooded into Chinese cities (the cities of China only contained a small proportion of the population, but their influence on national life was great). By the early 20th century, some Chinese people admired and copied foreigners, whilst many resented and even hated them.

From 'People's China' by C. Dietrich, 1994

QUESTIONS

1. Judging from Sources 1 and 2, why was it difficult to rule China in the early 20th century?

2. Suppose you had travelled through China in 1900, using Sources 1 and 2 describe what you would have seen.

3. Use Source 2 to make a list of the main characteristics of China in the early 20th century. What similarities and differences are there with Tsarist Russia in 1900 (see p.27)?

What was it like to live in China at the start of the 20th century?

At the start of the 20th century, China, like Tsarist Russia, was a sick and wounded giant. Because of its sheer size and ever-expanding population (around 400 million by 1900), China had always been a difficult country to rule effectively. For 2,000 years it had been governed by a series of dynasties (ruling families). In 1900, the Manchu dynasty was in power. The head of the dynasty at any time was the Emperor who, like the Tsars of Russia (see p.29), ruled as an autocrat. The Chinese Emperor ruled from the 'Forbidden City' in China's capital, Beijing. Also like the Tsars, the Chinese Emperors had become completely out of touch with the daily realities of life for the people they ruled. The vast majority of people in China were peasants, living a life somewhere between starvation and survival on land rented from landlords who also controlled the local courts and taxes. The problems of effective rule were further complicated by the influence exerted by foreign powers (especially Japan, Russia, Germany, Britain and France). Although this creaking imperial political system collapsed in 1911, the problems of government remained. It was not until the Communist victory of 1949 that anything like political stability was achieved. The early 20th century, therefore, was a period of great confusion and upheaval.

The last years of imperial China

Photographs showing the three-year old Puyi and the Empress Dowager Cixi.

In 1898, Emperor Guangxu's powerful and conservative aunt, the Empress-Dowager Cixi (see left), became concerned that her nephew was falling under the influence of reformers who were urging him to introduce dangerous political change. She therefore seized power for herself, executing the reformers and placing the Emperor under house arrest. Cixi began to rule alone, but made a series of mistakes which increased the unpopularity of the dynasty (see Box 12.1). Most seriously, she gave her backing to the unsuccessful **Boxer Rebellion** against foreign influence (see Box 12.2). The defeat of the Boxer Rebellion contributed to a growing sense of national humiliation and to the growth of revolutionary feeling. This resulted in a serious political crisis when, within a day of each other in November 1908, the Emperor and then Cixi herself died. This left a three year old child, Puyi, as the new Emperor (see far left). The power to rule was given to a regent, Puyi's uncle Prince Chun. Chun, however, angered many leading politicians by replacing officials with his own supporters and he angered many landowners by raising taxes. When the harvest failed in 1911, a rebellion broke out in Szechwan province and the Emperor was forced to give up his throne.

Box 12.1
Reasons for the unpopularity of the Emperor in the early 20th century

a) Chinese society was very divided. At the top, there was a small group of highly educated officials, large landowners and wealthy merchants. The bottom 60% of the population scraped a living as poor peasants. Poverty and the corruption of local officials led to frequent uprisings.

b) Since the 1840s, European countries had been exploiting China. They had forced China to open special 'treaty ports' where foreign trade could be carried out. Europeans took control of the local communities around these ports, running them virtually as colonies. Europeans also controlled most of China's industry.

c) In 1895, the Chinese suffered a humiliating defeat at the hands of the Japanese.

d) The Boxer Rebellion (see Box 12.2).

Box 12.2
The Boxer Rebellion

In 1900, a secret society called 'Boxers United in Righteousness' organised a rebellion designed to rid the country of foreign influence. In special rituals, Boxers went into a trance, believing this made them invulnerable to swords or bullets. However, the murder of Chinese Christians and some Westerners and the destruction of foreign-owned property led to Western intervention. An international 'police force' was sent to crush the rebellion. Cixi, who initially supported the Boxers, was forced to pay compensation. This was another humiliating defeat for the Manchu dynasty.

Boxers killing Christians in a Church in 1900.

2 Sun Zhongshan and the 'double tenth' revolution of 1911

By the end of the 19th century, support for revolutionary groups had begun to grow in China. One of these groups was led by Dr Sun Zhongshan (see photo in Box 12.3). Although Sun was a strong nationalist (he believed that China should be independent), he had also been influenced by Western ideas (he had been educated in Hawaii and Hong Kong). Sun's aim was to overthrow the imperial family, set up a republic (a state without a royal family at its head) and to modernise the primitive Chinese economy by rapid industrialisation along Western lines. In 1905, Sun set up a new secret society called the 'Tongmenghui'. This later developed into the **Guomindang** (GMD) or Nationalist Party (see Box 12.3). After six frustrating years working towards revolution, a series of events brought Sun to power. In October 1911, a police raid on a building in Wuhan (see map on p.217) revealed a list of Sun's supporters. Amongst those named were several leading army officers who, rather than face arrest, decided to rebel against the Manchu dynasty. Their rebellion (later known as **Double Tenth** as it started on the tenth day of the tenth month) spread quickly and soon most of southern China was controlled by the rebels. An assembly of rebel leaders was held in Guangzhou (see also map on p.217) and Sun was elected **Provisional President of the Republic of China** (even though northern China was still controlled by the Imperial Court and Sun himself was abroad at the time, collecting funds for his movement in Washington).

3 Yuan Shikai and the warlord era

General Yuan Shikai was in charge of the imperial army in October 1911. The Imperial Council called on him to crush the rebellion in the south. But Yuan double-crossed the imperial family and, instead, made a deal with Sun Zhongshan. Yuan agreed to join forces with the rebels provided that he was allowed to take over as President of the new Republic. As a result of the loss of support of the imperial army, Emperor Puyi abdicated and, after 300 years of imperial rule, the Manchu dynasty collapsed. Once in power, however, Yuan had no intention of governing as a democrat and began to set himself up as a military dictator. In a second act of betrayal, he turned on the GMD, banning it in 1914. By 1916, he was making plans to crown himself Emperor. His death later that year plunged China into a period of chaos and violence usually known as the 'warlord era' (see Box 12.4). Although, in theory, there continued to be a republic with a President and Prime Minister, in practice China was controlled by local gang leaders known as **warlords**.

Yuan Shikai

Box 12.3
Sun Zhongshan's three principles

After the revolution of 1911, Sun turned the Tongmenghui into a new political party called the Guomindang (GMD). The aims of the GMD were based on what Sun called the 'Three Principles' (see below).

1. Democracy
China should have an elected Parliament.

2. Nationalism
Chinese people should work together to expel foreign influence. The Chinese should rule themselves.

3. The people's welfare
Everyone should enjoy a basic standard of living. The government should help by controlling industry.

Box 12.4
The warlord era

For China as a nation, the warlord era was a time of disaster. In the old order, the ruling class had been made up of educated men who gained office only after a long and difficult course of study in history, philosophy and literature. Their education included many reminders that they must care for the welfare of the common people. They had not always behaved in a way which fitted the ideals in the works they studied, but at least they knew that the Emperor would be annoyed with them if they abused the peasants so badly as to cause a revolt. In the warlord era, by contrast, almost all power came from the possession of money or military force. A man could start out as a bandit, expand his force until he controlled a small area and then force the local people to pay him taxes. He would then negotiate deals and alliances with the military forces in neighbouring areas. He could, in short, convert himself from a bandit to a minor warlord. If he were sufficiently competent and lucky, he might someday rule a province. The central government no longer had the will or the ability to protect people. The poor suffered terribly whether they were workers in the growing textile mills of Shanghai or tenant farmers beset by landlords, tax collectors, soldiers and bandits.

From 'Modern China' by E. Moise, 1994

4 The Fourth of May movement

On 4 May 1919, students at Beijing University launched a protest movement against the Chinese government. The protest began because students were disappointed at China's treatment in the Paris Peace Conference (China lost territory to Japan). But the protest soon developed into a broader criticism of China's culture and of its ineffective government. The unrest spread to other universities and a boycott of Japanese goods continued for over a year. The Fourth of May movement was important because it rekindled interest in Western ideas (such as democracy and the freedom of the individual). These ideas had been introduced by Sun Zhongshan in the late 19th century. But there was now a new and revolutionary ingredient to be added. According to the writer Han Suyin (speaking in 1965): 'For China, the watershed between yesterday and today began on 4 May 1919. All my generation date ourselves from the year and the day which means nothing in the Western world but means everything to a quarter of the world's humanity.' It was from the Fourth of May movement that the idea that China might be able to follow Russia and have a Communist revolution came. Certainly, the ideas of Karl Marx were first explored by many students only as a result of the Fourth of May movement.

The photo (right) shows students demonstrating in Tiananmen Square, Beijing, in support of democracy in May 1989. Since the Fourth of May movement was launched in 1919, Tiananmen Square has been the traditional place to hold political rallies and May has been an important month.

5 The birth of the Chinese Communist Party

The Chinese Communist Party (CCP) was set up in 1921. At first, it remained very small (the historian, P. Bailey, estimates that there were just 133 members in 1923). Most members were from the educated upper and middle classes. Following the ideas of Karl Marx to the letter, the early leaders believed that a Communist revolution would be led by workers who lived in the towns and cities. Mao Zedong (see Box 12.5) was one of the few founding members of the CCP to recognise that this was virtually impossible in an agricultural country like China. Only 6% of the population lived in the towns and cities and 250 million of the country's 260 million workers were peasants. Mao's idea that the Communist revolution should be led by the peasants helps to explain why he rose to the leadership of the CCP. In the 1920s, the CCP came under increasing pressure from **Comintern** (the Communist International - an organisation based in Moscow whose aim was to promote Communism around the world). Comintern encouraged the CCP to work closely with the GMD. The aim was to get the two parties to form a joint (and hopefully stronger) revolutionary movement. A Comintern agent, Michael Borodin, helped Sun Zhongshan to improve the GMD's organisation and in 1924 the two parties reluctantly agreed to work together to defeat the warlords. This became known as the **First United Front**.

Box 12.5   **Mao Zedong (1893-1976)**

This painting of the first meeting of the CCP shows Mao (standing) taking a leading role.

Mao was Chinese head of state, revolutionary leader and Marxist thinker. In the 1911 revolution, he fought with Sun Zhongshan's Nationalist forces in the overthrow of the Manchu dynasty and in 1919 became politically active with the Fourth of May movement. In 1921, he was a founding member of the CCP and later its leader. In 1927, he led the Communists in a civil war against the forces of Jiang Jieshi (see p.223) and in the following year set up a Soviet in south east China. In 1934-35, the period of the Communists' Long March and relocation in the north west (see pp.224-25), Mao emerged as leader. After this, he wrote his chief works of political philosophy. He finally achieved victory in 1949 and became chairman of both the CCP and the newly formed People's Republic of China. Maoism differs from Russian Communism in its emphasis on the peasantry as the driving force of revolution.

From 'The Culture of Youth' edited by P. Furtado, 1994

Activity
Mao and the development of the CCP

Source B *Mao's own account (1)*

After the Fourth of May movement, I had devoted most of my time to student political activities. In the winter of 1920, I organised workers politically for the first time and began to be guided by Marx and the history of the Russian revolution. During my second visit to Beijing I had read much about events in Russia and eagerly sought out what little Communist literature was then available in Chinese. By the summer of 1920, I had become in theory and to some extent in action, a Communist. In the May of 1921, I went to Shanghai to attend the first meeting of the CCP. Altogether, there were 12 of us. The following October, the first provincial branch of the Party was organised in Hunan and I became a member of it. In May 1922, the Hunan Party, of which I was then Secretary, had already set up more than 20 trade unions among miners, railway workers and so on. The work of the CCP was then mainly concentrated on students and workers and very little was done among the peasants.

Part of an interview with Mao Zedong given in 1937

Source D *Mao talking to peasants in the early 1930s*

Source E *Mao's own account (2)*

In a very short time, several hundred million peasants in China's central, southern and northern provinces will rise like a tornado or a tempest - a force so extraordinarily swift and violent that no power, however great, will be able to overcome it. They will send all imperialists, warlords, corrupt officials, local bullies and evil gentry to their graves. All revolutionary parties and all revolutionary comrades will stand before them to be tested - to be accepted or rejected by them. To march at their head and lead them? To follow in the rear, criticising them? To face them as opponents? Every Chinese is free to choose among the three, but circumstances demand that a quick choice be made. To give credit where due, if we give ten points to the accomplishments of the revolution, then the achievements of people living in cities and the military rate only three points. The remaining seven points should go to the peasants.

Part of a pamphlet written by Mao in 1927

Source A *Why did Communism grow in China after 1921?*

- Fourth of May movement brought new ideas to Chinese politics
- Lessons learned from Russian revolution
- Part played by Mao Zedong
- CCP well organised
- Breakdown of central government left a political vacuum
- Poverty in China brought discontent with political rulers
- The corruption and violence of warlords made them unpopular
- CCP links with GMD helped it gain credibility
- Political instability in China brought desire for change
- Help from Communist Russia
- Members of CCP prepared to die for their cause

Source C *The CCP and the GMD*

In order to destroy the imperial system, it is necessary to set up a united front. The CCP has therefore decided to join with the National Revolutionary Party, Guomindang. There are two reasons for joining the GMD. In the first place, we want our propaganda to reach the many workers who belong to the GMD and to win them over to us. In the second place, we can only fight the imperial system if we join forces. If we do not join the GMD, we shall remain isolated and we shall preach a Communism which consists of a great and noble ideal, but which the masses do not follow. If we join the GMD, we shall be able to show the masses that we too are for revolutionary democracy. We shall be able to gather the masses round us and then split the GMD. We do have a problem, however. On the one hand, we have to fight local bullies and bad gentry and the middle classes. On the other hand, we have to cooperate with the GMD which represents them.

Part of a speech made by Liu Reng Jing to a Comintern meeting in 1923

QUESTIONS

1. Judging from the information in this section, what was it like to live in China in the early 20th century?

2. Why was the CCP set up in 1921 and what led to its growth? Use Sources A and B in your answer.

3. Judging from Sources B, D and E what was Mao's contribution to the early development of the CCP?

4. What were the advantages and disadvantages of an alliance between the CCP and the GMD? Use Source C in your answer.

Why did relations between the CCP and the GMD deteriorate after 1927?

The chaotic condition of China in the early 1920s pushed the GMD and the CCP into an uneasy marriage of convenience. In 1925, Sun Zhongshan died and was replaced by the anti-Communist Jiang Jieshi (see Box 12.6). Although the First United Front continued during the Northern Expedition of 1926, Jiang brought it to an end in 1927 when, in an attempt to set up a one-party state, he ordered GMD soldiers to execute all the Communists they could find. This was a turning point in Chinese history. The Communists, forced out of the cities, began to regroup in rural areas. Increasingly, the CCP fell under the influence of Mao. He helped to set up the Jiangxi Soviet in southern China (which, by 1934, had over three million members) and he organised workers and peasants into a guerilla army. This **Red Army** resisted wave after wave of GMD attacks until, eventually, it was forced to break out of its base in the south. This marked the beginning of what became known as the **Long March**. For 368 days, members of the Red Army marched westwards and then northwards, aiming to link up with Communists at Yanan. Around 100,000 men and women set out on the march, but less than 10,000 completed it. That anybody managed to survive is remarkable, but whether the Long March should be seen as a victory for the CCP or a defeat is still keenly debated by historians.

Box 12.6   Jiang Jieshi (Chiang Kai-Shek) 1887-1975

Jiang was a politician, leader of the GMD and a soldier. He fought in the overthrow of the Manchu dynasty and then, during 1913-16, against the would-be dictator President Yuan Shikai (see p.219). In 1918, he allied himself with the Nationalists (GMD) and in 1925 took control of the Nationalist army. In collaboration with the CCP in 1926, he undertook a campaign against the Northern warlords, achieving victory in 1928 by taking Beijing. Jiang then headed a new government at Nanjing. Meanwhile, in 1927, he purged the GMD of Communists and began a civil war against the CCP. This was suspended during 1937-46 to make a common cause against the Japanese. By 1946, the GMD was riddled with corruption and the army demoralised and, in 1949, Jiang was finally defeated by the Red Army of China. He fled to Taiwan and formed a government-in-exile. Enjoying American support, he was able to modernise Taiwan's economy, but relations with the USA cooled in the 1970s.

From 'Depression and Dictatorship' edited by P. Furtado, 1993

Jiang Jieshi (middle) with two allies in 1928 - the warlords Yan Xishan (right) who controlled Shanxi province and Feng Yuxiang who controlled the area to the west of Shanxi. Unable to accept Jiang's authority, the two rebelled against him and a war was fought between 1929 and 1930.

The Northern Expedition of 1926

At first, the United Front brought benefits to both the CCP and the GMD. By 1926, Jiang felt strong enough to launch a new attempt to unify the whole of China under a single government. The so-called **Northern Expedition** was carried out by Jiang's National Revolutionary Army. At the same time, Mao and other Communist leaders organised strikes and peasant uprisings designed to loosen the warlords' grip on particular regions or towns. By early 1927, this cooperation had brought success. Jiang's forces controlled most of southern China and as far north as Wuhan and Nanjing whilst the Communists, led by Zhou Enlai, had captured the major industrial city of Shanghai (see map on p.217). A unified and politically stable China seemed a distinct possibility - so long as the alliance held.

The GMD poster (above) celebrates victories in the Northern Expedition. The big portrait at the top shows Sun Zhongshan. Jiang is the man on the horse below.

2 The Shanghai massacre, 1927

Jiang had no intention of sharing the government of a united China with the CCP. As a result, on 12 April 1927, as GMD troops arrived in Shanghai (where members of the CCP had organised strikes and taken control), Jiang ordered them to round up Communists and to execute them. The Communists in Shanghai were taken completely by surprise (the GMD, after all, were supposed to be their allies). It is difficult to know how many were killed - historians estimate between 5,000 and 15,000. Many were decapitated in the street by GMD execution squads - as the CCP poster (right) shows. Jiang then extended the policy to other major industrial centres. In August 1927, the CCP decided on an armed struggle and called on their supporters to rise up against the GMD. But when CCP supporters rose up against the GMD in Guangzhou in December 1927, several thousand were killed by GMD soldiers. Many were identified by the red dye stain that the red sashes they wore during the uprising had left on their necks. According to an American embassy official, the first victims were shot. Then, others were tied together and pushed into a river to drown - to save ammunition.

A CCP poster produced after the Shanghai massacre, showing a member of the CCP being killed by a capitalist and a GMD soldier.

3 The Jiangxi Soviet

The surviving members of the CCP in Shanghai and the other cities fled to the countryside. Many went to Jiangxi province where, under the leadership of Mao, they set up the **Jiangxi Soviet** (in China, the term 'soviet' was used to mean any area under CCP control). In May 1928, Mao was joined by a Communist who had served in the GMD army, Zhu De. Not only did Zhu bring a private army of 2,000 men, he also brought ideas about the best way to defeat an army that was numerically and technically superior. Over the next six years, a new Red Army was created. Most of those serving in it were peasants. They became very skilled at 'hit and run' tactics which were designed to avoid all-out battles (see Box 12.7a). These tactics allowed them to resist the GMD's **extermination campaigns** which started in 1930. The Jianxi Soviet convinced Mao that the best way to convert peasants to Communism was to act in ways which contrasted with the brutality of the warlords and GMD troops. As a result, the Red Army gave to the peasants land seized from landlords and it behaved with care and consideration to the local population (see Box 12.7b). At first, Mao's

A member of the CCP taken prisoner by the GMD during an extermination campaign, just before the Long March began in 1934.

tactics were regarded with suspicion by the CCP leadership in Shanghai. Their success, however, became increasingly clear. By 1932, the Jiangxi Soviet had grown into a community of about 3 million people with its own schools, hospitals, factories and collective farms.

Box 12.7 — Mao and the Red Army in the early 1930s

a) Mao on guerilla tactics

The following was a slogan made up of eight Chinese characters which all Red Army officers knew by heart:

> When the enemy advances, we retreat.
> When the enemy camps, we harass.
> When the enemy tires, we attack.
> When the enemy retreats, we pursue.

From 'The Selected Works of Mao Zedong', 1967

b) The army imposed three simple rules - prompt obedience to orders, no stealing whatever from poor peasants and prompt delivery to the CCP government of all goods confiscated from landlords. Eight other rules were adopted and put to music, to be sung and remembered by all troops.

1. Shut the doors when you leave a house.
2. Return and roll up the straw matting.
3. Be courteous and polite to the people and help them.
4. Return all borrowed articles.
5. Replace all damaged articles.
6. Be honest in all transactions with the peasants.
7. Pay for all articles purchased.
8. Be sanitary. Dig toilets at a safe distance from people's houses.

From 'The Other Side of the River: Red China Today' by E. Snow, 1963

In 1931, the Japanese invaded the north east region of Manchuria and set up a puppet state under the ex-Emperor Puyi (see p.136). Jiang Jieshi decided not to oppose the Japanese invasion because he felt he first needed to remove the internal threat posed by the Jiangxi Soviet. As he put it: 'The Japanese are a disease of the skin, but Communism is a disease of the heart.' So, having agreed a truce with the Japanese (the Jiangxi Soviet declared war on the Japanese in 1932), Jiang concentrated his efforts on crushing the Communists. In October 1933, Jiang launched the fifth extermination campaign against the Jiangxi Soviet. Previous campaigns had been successfully resisted by the CCP's guerilla tactics. But, by October 1933, Jiang was receiving military aid and advice from Nazi Germany. Hitler, seeing Jiang as an ally in the fight against Communism, had sent over General von Seekt, one of Germany's top military advisers. On von Seekt's advice, GMD troops abandoned the tactic of entering CCP controlled territory. Instead, they surrounded the Jiangxi Soviet with a fortified network of trenches which completely cut off the Communists' supply routes. The GMD army then began to push slowly into Communist territory. During 1933, the Jiangxi Soviet lost 60,000 troops and 58% of its territory. Defeat seemed inevitable. As a result, in October 1934 the Communist leadership took a desperate 'all or nothing' decision to break out of the stranglehold. On the night of 15-16 October 1934, around 100,000 Red Army soldiers broke through the weakest link in the GMD fortifications and began marching west to link up with other Communist bases at Yanan (see map below) in the province of Shaanxi. This was the beginning of the **Long March** during which the Red Army travelled around 9,500 km over terrain which included huge mountains and treacherous marshes. The marchers lacked food and supplies and they had to fight numerous battles against the GMD and warlords. Whilst the march was a success in the sense that the survivors reached their goal, it was a very costly success. Less than 10,000 of the marchers survived.

Activity

The Long March

Source A   *Map showing the route of the Long March and comments made by eyewitnesses*

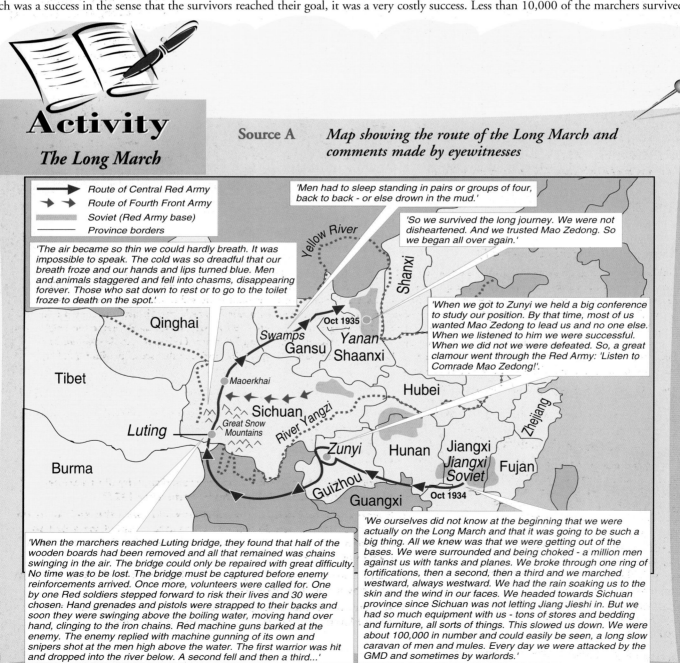

Legend:
- Route of Central Red Army
- Route of Fourth Front Army
- Soviet (Red Army base)
- Province borders

'Men had to sleep standing in pairs or groups of four, back to back - or else drown in the mud.'

'So we survived the long journey. We were not disheartened. And we trusted Mao Zedong. So we began all over again.'

'The air became so thin we could hardly breath. It was impossible to speak. The cold was so dreadful that our breath froze and our hands and lips turned blue. Men and animals staggered and fell into chasms, disappearing forever. Those who sat down to rest or to go to the toilet froze to death on the spot.'

'When we got to Zunyi we held a big conference to study our position. By that time, most of us wanted Mao Zedong to lead us and no one else. When we listened to him we were successful. When we did not we were defeated. So, a great clamour went through the Red Army: 'Listen to Comrade Mao Zedong!'.'

Qinghai

Yellow River

Shanxi

Oct 1935

Swamps   Yanan
Gansu   Shaanxi

Tibet

Maoerkhai

Hubei

Sichuan   River Yangzi

Luting   Great Snow Mountains

Zhejiang

Burma

Zunyi   Hunan   Jiangxi
                        Jiangxi Soviet   Fujan

Guizhou   Oct 1934

Guangxi

'When the marchers reached Luting bridge, they found that half of the wooden boards had been removed and all that remained was chains swinging in the air. The bridge could only be repaired with great difficulty. No time was to be lost. The bridge must be captured before enemy reinforcements arrived. Once more, volunteers were called for. One by one Red soldiers stepped forward to risk their lives and 30 were chosen. Hand grenades and pistols were strapped to their backs and soon they were swinging above the boiling water, moving hand over hand, clinging to the iron chains. Red machine guns barked at the enemy. The enemy replied with machine gunning of its own and snipers shot at the men high above the water. The first warrior was hit and dropped into the river below. A second fell and then a third...'

'We ourselves did not know at the beginning that we were actually on the Long March and that it was going to be such a big thing. All we knew was that we were getting out of the bases. We were surrounded and being choked - a million men against us with tanks and planes. We broke through one ring of fortifications, then a second, then a third and we marched westward, always westward. We had the rain soaking us to the skin and the wind in our faces. We headed towards Sichuan province since Sichuan was not letting Jiang Jieshi in. But we had so much equipment with us - tons of stores and bedding and furniture, all sorts of things. This slowed us down. We were about 100,000 in number and could easily be seen, a long slow caravan of men and mules. Every day we were attacked by the GMD and sometimes by warlords.'

Source B *Painting of the Long March*

The end of the Long March. The survivors reach Yanan.

Source C *Mao's view*

For 12 months, we were under daily reconnaissance and bombing from the skies, whilst on land we were encircled and pursued by a huge force. We encountered untold dangers on the way, yet by using our two legs we marched across 11 provinces. Let us ask, has history ever known a long march to equal ours? No, never. The Long March is a manifesto. It has shown the world that the Red Army is an army of heroes, while Jiang Jieshi and his like are powerless. The Long March also tells the 200 million people in 11 provinces that only the road of the Red Army leads to freedom. Without the Long March, how could the masses have learned so quickly about the existence of the great truth which the Red Army embodies? The Long March has sown many seeds which will sprout and produce a harvest in the future. To sum up, the Long March has ended with victory for us and defeat for the enemy.

Part of a speech made by Mao Zedong in December 1935

Source D *A historian's view (1)*

Unlike many other great themes of history, the story of the Long March is equal to the emotions which it arouses. Beginning with a series of disasters, it ended with a grim struggle against the odds, with feats of heroism, hardship and survival similar to those the British celebrated at Dunkirk. Some incidents seem more like fiction than a reality of history. The soldiers crossed mountain peaks covered with snow. They gained respect from the people by their honest dealing and ready payment for goods. In north west Sichuan the army passed though trackless marsh where they were surrounded by quicksand and bog and many, with one false step, disappeared forever. On only one occasion, did they fight the main GMD force. In May 1935, at the crossing of the Dadu River near Luting, the whole Communist force faced destruction. After a forced march of 80 miles in 24 hours and an assault along a cable bridge in the face of machine gun fire, the crossing was seized and the Red Army escaped the trap.

From 'China This Century' by R. de Crespigny, 1992

Source E *A historian's view (2)*

Of the 90,000 men who broke out of Jiangxi, only one in ten reached the new base in the north. The Long March is often described as an epic victory. An epic it was, but to call it a victory is only wisdom after the event. In itself, it was a disastrous retreat following a devastating defeat. The Jiangxi Soviet had been destroyed. Now nine out of ten of the Red Army were killed or scattered.

From 'Rebellions and Revolutions: China from the 1800s to the 1980s' by J. Gray, 1990

QUESTIONS

1. Judging from the information in this section, why did relations between the CCP and GMD deteriorate after 1927?

2. Suppose you had been a journalist travelling with the Red Army on the Long March. Use Sources A-C to write a report for a British newspaper. How would your account have differed if written for a GMD newspaper?

3. Using Sources A and D explain what happened at the Luting bridge and why it was so important.

4. A 'massive defeat' or a 'great victory'? Which best describes the Long March? Use Sources D and E in your answer.

Between 1937 and 1945, there was a three-way struggle for control of China - between the Japanese invaders, Jiang's Nationalist forces and the Communist Red Army. During this period the CCP and GMD cooperated in a **Second United Front** against their common enemy, the Japanese. In reality, however, the truce between the CCP and GMD was very fragile. The CCP took advantage of the conflict to increase its already powerful support among the peasants (by introducing further land reforms and by continuing to behave with care and consideration to the local population). By contrast, the reputation of the GMD and its leader, Jiang, began to decline as a combination of military defeat and corrupt and incompetent government led many people to question the GMD's ability to govern. Despite hopes that cooperation between the CCP and GMD would continue after Japan had surrendered in August 1945, a civil war broke out in 1946. Although, at first, the Red Army lacked the equipment and numbers of the GMD (which was backed by the USA), its discipline and tactics were superior. In October 1949, the GMD leadership fled to Taiwan and the People's Republic of China was born. This section examines both the long-term and short-term reasons for the CCP's victory (see Box 12.8).

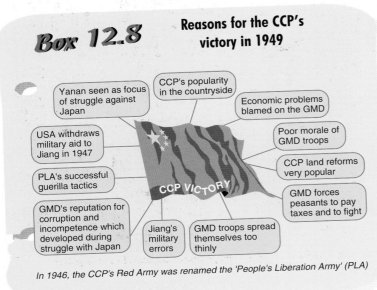

Box 12.8 — **Reasons for the CCP's victory in 1949**

- Yanan seen as focus of struggle against Japan
- CCP's popularity in the countryside
- Economic problems blamed on the GMD
- USA withdraws military aid to Jiang in 1947
- Poor morale of GMD troops
- PLA's successful guerilla tactics
- CCP land reforms very popular
- GMD's reputation for corruption and incompetence which developed during struggle with Japan
- Jiang's military errors
- GMD troops spread themselves too thinly
- GMD forces peasants to pay taxes and to fight

CCP VICTORY

In 1946, the CCP's Red Army was renamed the 'People's Liberation Army' (PLA)

2 World War II

'Although, by 1939, Japanese forces occupied the coast and key urban centres in the north and along the lower Yangzi, they found it impossible to conquer the vast interior. Between 1939 and 1944, there was a virtual stalemate. At first, China stood virtually alone against Japan. The Japanese attack on Pearl Harbour in December 1941, however, was a turning point. With the USA and Britain now at war with Japan, China's resistance to the Japanese was seen as a heroic contribution to the struggle against Fascism. As a result, aid from the USA increased massively. Jiang was made supreme commander of the war in China. Although eyewitnesses often commented on the corruption of Jiang's regime, recent studies have shown that his power was limited. The GMD's political control weakened after 1937 when the Japanese invasion forced the GMD to abandon its headquarters in Nanjing. Also, many army commanders were never completely loyal and committed to Jiang. The weakness of the Nationalist forces was highlighted in 1944 when the Japanese launched a major offensive. Nationalist resistance was swept aside easily. By 1944, however, the war in China was of secondary importance. American troops were concentrating on taking Japanese-held islands in the Pacific.'

From 'China in the Twentieth Century' by P. Bailey, 1988

1 The Second United Front

After the Long March, Jiang continued his attempts to crush the CCP. But the new CCP base at Yanan (the **Yanan Soviet**) was close to the expected point of a full-scale Japanese invasion from Manchukuo (Manchuria). Many GMD military leaders were therefore critical of Jiang, arguing that at this time of national danger 'Chinese must not fight Chinese'. They began a 'go-slow' campaign, making a secret agreement not to fight the CCP forces at Yanan. When, in December 1936, Jiang himself went to Yanan to find out what was happening, he was kidnapped by his own generals and forced to negotiate with the CCP leader Zhou Enlai. The result was the setting up of the **Second United Front**. Under the terms of this truce, Jiang recognised Communist control over the north west border region (though his troops continued to blockade the Yanan Soviet). The Communists, for their part, recognised Jiang as China's official leader.

The war with Japan, 1937-45

National frontiers
Land held by Japan, 1937
Land held by Japan, 1937-39
Land held by Japan, 1944
Land held by CCP in 1945

The Red Army and the peasantry

During the struggle against Japan, the CCP leadership continued the policies which had been successful in the Jiangxi Soviet (see p.223). Red Army officers trained peasants to use guerilla tactics against the Japanese (much of the most serious fighting against Japan took place in CCP controlled areas). In addition, great efforts were made to ensure that relations between the peasants and Red Army were close. These policies had political as well as military goals. The CCP hoped to win over the peasants to Communism. The woodcut (right) illustrates the ideal relationship between peasants and the Red Army. It has the slogan 'support our common people's own army' and shows peasants and soldiers working together. At the top, peasants bring food and horses for the Red Army. They welcome soldiers with music and a banner. In the frame below, peasants carry one wounded soldier and provide another with a drink. In the third frame, peasants give a recruit a send-off. At the bottom, peasants care for a disabled soldier.

The civil war

In 1945, both superpowers tried to prevent the outbreak of civil war in China. The American government did not want either political instability or the spread of Communism in Asia. President Truman sent George Marshall, his Secretary of State, to try and bring about an agreement between Jiang and Mao. At the same time, the USA continued to supply the GMD with weapons. Stalin (much to the annoyance of the CCP) also called for cooperation and refused to provide aid to the Red Army. Many historians believe Stalin saw Mao as a potential rival for leadership of the Communist world. In the event, the wishes of the superpowers were ignored (see Box 12.9). When the Soviet Union withdrew from Manchuria in March 1946, both Communist and Nationalist forces (the Communist forces were now known as the **People's Liberation Army - PLA**) tried to move in. Renewed fighting broke out. To most outsiders, it seemed that the Nationalists were bound to win (they had superior numbers and equipment) and in the first year they took control of many major towns and cities. But a number of factors led to CCP success. First, Jiang's forces became too thinly spread - spread out like a series of islands in the deep of the surrounding Communist-controlled countryside. The result was that the PLA was able to target and pick off pockets of Nationalists, using guerilla tactics. Second, Jiang made the mistake of sending too many troops to the north where they were tied down and isolated. Third, in 1947 American aid to the GMD was cut. And fourth, owing to low morale and anger at the corruption within the Nationalist army, increasingly large numbers of Nationalist troops began to change sides, taking with them their American weapons. In 1948, the PLA was strong enough to abandon guerilla tactics and fight head-on. In the **Battle of Huai-Hai** more than 500,000 GMD troops were killed and the GMD leadership forced to retreat. In January 1949, Jiang retreated to Taiwan and set up a 'Republic of China' which he ruled until his death in 1975.

A woodcut from North China, produced during the war against Japan (1937-45).

Box 12.9 The civil war - a historian's account

Once the Japanese had been defeated, the American General, George Marshall, put much effort into bringing together the CCP and GMD. On 10 October 1946, an agreement was reached. But Jiang's forces attacked within weeks and the civil war began. During the first half of 1947, the Nationalists spread themselves too thinly. In 1948, the PLA counter-attacked and captured vast quantities of weapons. The decisive blow was the Battle of Huai-Hai where an entire Nationalist army surrendered and its commanding officer committed suicide. The CCP was assisted by information from Communist spies. For example, General Fei, Jiang's Assistant Chief of Staff, was actually a Communist spy and all the Nationalist battle plans and movements were known to the CCP in advance. After Huai-Hai, the Nationalist camp was completely demoralised and a delegation sent to try to negotiate a ceasefire. Since General Fei was on the Nationalists' team, Mao was able to outmanoeuvre them at every turn. The final thrust came a few weeks later when the Communists launched an attack across the Yangzi River. Within three days, Nanjing, the GMD capital, had fallen. The PLA swept on south through a region demoralised by inflation and corruption. Even those who had begun as Jiang's most solid supporters were not sorry to hear Mao proclaim the birth of the People's Republic of China on 1 October 1949.

From 'Communism' by G. Stern, 1991

Activity
Why was the CCP successful?

Source A *The PLA and the peasants - an artist's impression*

This painting was produced in 1967. It shows peasants welcoming members of the PLA during the civil war.

Source B *Eyewitness account - the CCP*

The soldiers looked fierce enough with their big fur caps and ear-flaps, their padded cotton uniforms draped around with bullet belts and hung with dangerous looking home-made grenades. All were well armed, with Japanese rifles or automatic weapons of American make. In every group of half a dozen or so there would be one with a scrap of paper in his hand. These, we discovered, contained the addresses of the private houses in which squads were to stay. Several times, I saw a soldier approach a knot of bystanders and, presenting his paper with a polite bow and a wide smile, ask directions to the street and house number his group were seeking. These must have been some of the first occasions in the history of the town of Tianjin [a port just south of Beijing - see map on p.217] when uniformed soldiers had used all the forms of Chinese courtesy to ordinary civilians. The civilians were at first astounded and in the end mightily pleased. It made a great effect on them. As the weeks passed, standards of politeness, modesty, honesty and high discipline showed no signs of falling off. There was no looting or stealing.

Eyewitness account of a German who was in Tianjin in December 1948. It appeared in 'Mao and the Chinese Revolution' by J. Ch'en, 1965.

Source D *Eyewitness account - the GMD*

Nearly everyone in the GMD was on the make. Officers fiddled their accounts, drawing pay for twice the number of men they really commanded and keeping the extra for themselves. Army stores were sold on the black market. The only things the GMD seemed to think about were money, food, drink and women. When soldiers are living like that, they don't want to fight and they don't want to die. In any case, there was no feeling in the GMD that they were fighting for a cause. None of the men in the GMD had any respect for their officers. None of the officers respected their generals and the generals didn't respect Jiang Jieshi. The GMD army often robbed the local people, taxed them and lived off their food. The Communists did none of these things. People knew that, even in the days before Japan's defeat, the Communists had been eager to fight the foreign invaders first and their GMD enemies afterwards. The GMD had done exactly the opposite. The ordinary people had always felt that the Communists were at least fellow Chinese.

Eyewitness account of a Nationalist soldier, Lobsang Thondip, who deserted and joined the PLA in mid-1946. He was interviewed after the war.

Source C *The strength of the armies*

Relative strength PLA/GMD 1945-49			
Russian Estimates	**PLA**	**GMD**	**RATIO**
July 1946	1,200,000	4,300,000	1 : 3.58
June 1947	1,950,000	3,730,000	1 : 1.9
June 1948	2,800,000	3,670,000	1 : 1.3
American Estimates			
July 1946	1,000,000	3,000,000	1 : 3
end of 1946	1,100,000	2,600,000	1 : 2.36
June 1947	1,150,000	2,700,000	1 : 2.35
beginning 1948	1,150,000	2,723,000	1 : 2.37
February 1949	1,622,000	1,500,000	1 : 0.92
CCP Estimates			
September 1945	860,000	3,700,000	1 : 4.3
July 1946	1,278,000	4,300,000	1 : 3.36
June 1947	1,950,000	3,730,000	1 : 1.9
June 1947	2,800,000	3,650,000	1 : 1.3
November 1948	3,000,000	2,900,000	1 : 0.96
June 1949	4,000,000	1,500,000	1 : 0.37

QUESTIONS

1. Judging from the information in this section, how did the CCP manage to win power in 1949?

2. What evidence is there to support the view illustrated in Source A?

3. Why was the CCP successful? Use Sources B, C and D in your answer.

4. a) What does Source C tell us about the development of the civil war?

   b) Why do you think the estimates vary so much?

On 1 October 1949, standing above the Gate of Heavenly Peace in Beijing, Mao announced the birth of the People's Republic of China. But the People's Republic immediately faced a number of difficult problems (see Box 12.10). In the course of trying to solve these problems, China became a one-party totalitarian state. Indeed, there are similarities between the early years of Communist rule in China and the early years of Nazi rule in Germany or Stalin's rule in the Soviet Union (see chapters 4 and 6). In particular, once the CCP had gained power, its policies were designed to eliminate any opposition and to increase the Party's control over almost every level of the country's social, economic and political life. By the time the new constitution confirmed Mao as Chairman of both the CCP and the People's Republic in 1954, Communist Party control already stretched through each layer of Chinese society with groups of Communist Party officials (**cadres**) running courts, schools, the media, town councils and the newly established 'People's Communes' (see p.230 below). 'Thought reform' (control of education), economic planning and new forms of political organisation were all designed to change the nature of Chinese society in a fundamental way. Like Hitler and Stalin, Mao was impatient for change and the CCP pushed the people hard in the early years of Communist rule. Although some successes were achieved in the early years, the **Great Leap Forward** which was launched in 1957 ended in disaster.

Box 12.10 — Mao's problems and solutions

THE PROBLEMS

1. Land reform, collectivisation and communes.
2. Five Year Plans.
3. 'Thought Reform'.
4. Marriage Law 1950.
5. Party control.

1. Wartime damage to industry.
2. Inflation
3. Population growth.
4. Unemployment.
5. Social and political division.

THE SOLUTIONS

2 Industrial change

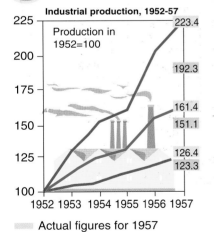

Industrial production, 1952-57

Production in 1952=100

225 — 223.4
200 — 192.3
175 — 161.4 / 151.1
150 —
125 — 126.4 / 123.3
100 —
1952 1953 1954 1955 1956 1957

- Actual figures for 1957
- Five Year target
- Industry — Agriculture
- Total (industry and agriculture)

The economic challenge facing the CCP was similar to that in Russia after the revolution of October 1917. The CCP aimed to turn a backward, largely peasant society into a powerful, industrialised nation. To do this, the CCP took control of what remained of China's badly damaged industry. By 1953, Mao decided there had been sufficient recovery for more ambitious planning and the first Five Year Plan was launched. This followed the Soviet model (see pp.124-26). Indeed, it relied heavily on Soviet technical aid and investment. It was a success. By 1957, nearly 700 major industrial projects had been started and a transport network built. The number of people living in towns rose from 71 to 92 million.

1 Changing attitudes

When the CCP took power, China had suffered nearly 40 years of war. Many people were poor, illiterate and wary of change. Two early reforms illustrate the way in which the new Communist government hoped to change attitudes and to create a new society. First, the Marriage Law of 1950 introduced a new 'democratic' form of marriage. It banned arranged marriages, prevented the marriage of children and made the killing of unwanted babies and bigamy (marrying two people) illegal. Whilst this reform can be seen as an attempt to improve the status of women (who had few rights before 1949), it can also be seen as a subtle method of political control. As the historian P. Bailey points out: 'By insisting that all marriages had to be registered with the Communist authorities, the government hoped to shift the focus of loyalty from the family to the state.' Political control was also the purpose of the second reform - 'thought reform'. Mao's ideas were made the central part of the curriculum at school and college and compulsory study groups (run by the cadres) were set up in every workplace and village. People who did not agree with Mao's ideas were sent either to labour camps or for a period of 're-education' working with the peasants. The aim was that everyone should believe in and obey the instructions of the CCP and its leaders. That attitudes were slow to change is suggested by the **Hundred Flowers campaign** (see Box 12.11).

Box 12.11 — The Hundred Flowers campaign

In 1956, in the middle of a period of rapid social and economic reform, Mao made a speech in which he called on the people to comment on the way his government was tackling China's problems. 'Let a hundred flowers blossom', Mao said, 'let a hundred schools of thought compete.' Soon, however, this traditional Chinese saying (which invited people to enter into a public discussion of the way in which the country was run) backfired. Posters attacking government policy appeared, students demonstrated and newspapers adopted a critical tone. In June 1957, therefore, the Hundred Flowers campaign was halted. Many of those who had criticised the government were arrested and sent to labour camps to have their ideas 'corrected'. Some historians argue that the campaign was a genuine mistake - Mao underestimated the strength of opposition. Others claim that it was a cunning policy to trick the government's opponents into identifying themselves.

3 Land reform and collectivisation

Change in the countryside began with the Land Reform Law of 1950. This extended to the whole country what had been happening in all Communist areas since the 1930s. Local cadres supervised the seizure of land from wealthy landlords and organised its redistribution amongst the poorest classes of peasants (see Box 12.12). At the same time, cadres encouraged local people to put landlords on trial or even to attack them. By encouraging peasants to attack landlords and by legalising the seizure of land, the CCP gained support from poor peasants and destroyed its most dangerous source of opposition. Land reform therefore consolidated Communist power. The second stage of the Communist transformation of the countryside was collectivisation. The aim was partly economic (to increase the efficiency of food production) and partly political (to encourage a Communist way of life). Unlike in Stalin's Russia (see p.122-23), however, peasants were encouraged, not forced, to share land, tools and labour. Between 1952 and 1956, there were three stages.

1. **Mutual Aid Teams**. Groups of 7-10 families shared tools and animals but owned their land privately.
2. **Simple Collectives**. Land was owned privately but up to 30-40 families shared out the total profits.
3. **Advanced Collectives**. These were much larger units (300-400 families). Everyone part-owned the land. All animals, tools and profits were shared.

4 The Great Leap Forward

By 1956, 95% of peasant families had been collectivised without any of the violence of the Soviet experience. But, despite the success of the process, food production had not risen to the rate Mao intended. When the second Five Year Plan was launched in 1957, Mao described it as the 'Great Leap Forward'. His aim was to speed up China's modernisation still further (he talked of making up '20 years in a day'). Central to the Great Leap Forward was the 'industrialisation of the countryside'. Mao argued that the future lay not with large-scale industries based in cities, but with small-scale 'backyard' industries in the countryside. The method of achieving the industrialisation of the countryside was to be the setting up of **People's Communes**. To create a Commune, several collective farms were joined together into a huge unit of up to 30,000 people. These were then split up into smaller 'production brigades' of 1,000-3,000 people who had responsibility for organising the small-scale industries. Even smaller production teams of 200-1,000 people were in charge of fields and animals. Each family received a share of food and wages calculated on the basis of the number of 'work points' earned by their brigade. But the Communes were more than an economic unit. Socially, they were a challenge to the traditional family unit. Peasants no longer lived in their own homes, but in military-style barracks. The sexes were sometimes separated and meals were eaten in large canteens. Communes became a new type of self-supporting community with their own schools and health service. The most successful were held up as models for others to follow (see poster right and caption below).

In the mid-1960s, posters like the one on the right were produced praising the achievements of the people of Dazhai Commune in Shaanxi province. The peasants there transformed unusable hill sides into fertile fields and they lived and worked together on a basis of strict equality. The Dazhai peasants were honoured like the stakhanovites in the Soviet Union (see p.124). But, in the 1980s, the Chinese government admitted that government money had been used to make sure that this Commune was a success.

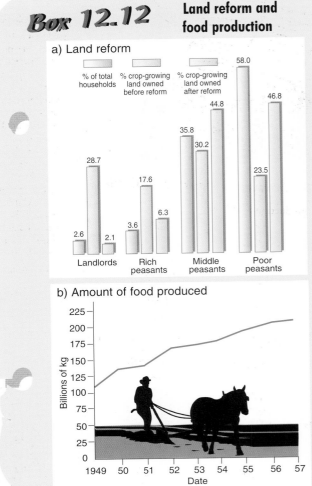

Box 12.12 — **Land reform and food production**

a) Land reform

- % of total households
- % crop-growing land owned before reform
- % crop-growing land owned after reform

	% of total households	% crop-growing land owned before reform	% crop-growing land owned after reform
Landlords	2.6	28.7	2.1
Rich peasants	3.6	17.6	6.3
Middle peasants	35.8	30.2	44.8
Poor peasants	58.0	23.5	46.8

b) Amount of food produced

(y-axis: Billions of kg, 0 to 225; x-axis: Date, 1949 to 57)

Activity
Why did the Great Leap Forward fail?

Source B Production statistics 1957-60

a) Grain production, 1957-60

	Actual	Claimed
1957	185	185
1958	204	250
1959	170	270
1960	160	150

All figures in millions of tons

b) The state statistical bureau claimed that in 1958 production of food, crops and cotton had nearly doubled in one year. On this basis, the government set ambitious targets for 1959, aiming for an increase of a further 50%. The leadership became a captive of its own claims.

From 'China' by J.K. Fairbank, 1992

Source D An eyewitness account

Only production counted. We worked night and day to build seven extra generators. I hardly slept for a week. Then we got a Polish engine to drive the generators. It did not have enough power, but they went ahead. Mao had said we could do anything. In no time, the engine's bearings went. After we went through three engines we had to go back to the city electricity supply, but it could not produce enough. The machines broke down. I was taken off my work and sent to tend the steel ovens.

A factory worker's memories of the Great Leap Forward, recorded in 'Breakfast with Mao' by A. Winnington, 1986

Source A A historian's view

Mao was trying to achieve economic miracles by whipping people into a fever of enthusiasm. Everyone was supposed to work very long hours under difficult conditions to achieve in months economic change that would normally have taken years. The Great Leap began with genuine popular enthusiasm and some genuinely spectacular results. In the first eight months of 1958, agricultural production was well above levels in 1957 and steel production was 50% up. At this point, Mao and other leaders lost all sense of reality and began demanding even higher rates of growth. The situation soon began to deteriorate. Reports of tremendous success became obligatory and soon everyone was making them regardless of reality. These inflated figures were then used as the basis for further planning. In 1959, the Great Leap became a disaster. Sheer fatigue took its toll. Then peasants all over China were urged to plough the land very deeply. The theory was that the soil deep below the surface would be very fertile. But the actual result was often to bury the topsoil and bring to the surface worthless clay and sand. The Party also ordered that seeds be planted more closely together with the result that they died or were stunted due to overcrowding. Bad weather made these problems worse. The 1959 harvest was low. Hunger became widespread. People began to starve and to die from disease. During the 'three bitter years' of 1959-61 the total number of deaths was at least 16 million more than it would have been in three years of normal food supply.

From 'Modern China' by E. Moise, 1994

Source C 'Backyard' furnaces

In July 1958, in an attempt to bring small-scale industry to the countryside, a campaign was launched to produce steel in small 'backyard' furnaces (see above), each only capable of producing a few tons of steel. A million had been set up by October and 100 million people worked them. But the scheme was a failure. People did not know how to operate the furnaces properly and most of the metal produced was worthless. Also, many peasants neglected their farming to work the furnaces.

QUESTIONS

1. Judging from the information in this section, what impact did Communist rule make on China?
2. Why did the Great Leap Forward fail? Use Sources A-D in your answer.
3. What do Sources B-D tell us about the nature of Communist rule in China?

The failure of the Great Leap Forward led to a split in the CCP. In 1960, Mao resigned as President of the People's Republic of China and between 1960 and 1966 he was forced to remain in the background while Liu Shaoqui, Deng Xiaoping and Peng Zhen controlled government. In 1966, however, Mao launched what has become known as the **Cultural Revolution**. Mao argued that the momentum of the Communist revolution was being lost and that it was up to young people to get the revolution going again. As a result, thousands of young people left their schools and colleges to become **Red Guards**. These Red Guards then travelled around China promoting Maoist views and attacking 'counter-revolutionaries' - anyone they suspected of opposing Mao in thought or action. Previously, Mao had discouraged fanatical loyalty to himself and his ideas, but now he actively promoted it. The result was great upheaval. Wherever they went, the Red Guards created a reign of terror, often using violence against those suspected of being counter-revolutionaries. By 1968, the violence was out of control and Mao himself was forced to use troops to break up the gangs of Red Guards. By then, Mao's position was secure and his policies were being pursued. But the price was high. For many people the Cultural Revolution was a time of great suffering.

1 The aftermath of the Great Leap Forward

Between 1960 and 1966, the CCP was split between two main groups. On the one hand, 'moderates' like Liu Shaoqui, Deng Xiaoping and Peng Zhen opposed the policies pursued in the Great Leap Forward. They supported measures which split Communes into smaller units, which allowed peasants to have larger private plots of land and which provided cash rewards for hard work. They also supported an emphasis on large-scale industrial projects run by skilled managers (rather than on small-scale 'backyard' industries run by ordinary people). On the other hand, Mao and his supporters believed that a truly Communist society could only be created if the revolution regained its momentum. In the Soviet Union, Mao argued, the revolution had lost its momentum when a new middle class of Party officials had grown up and destroyed the revolution's earlier drive towards equality. The moderates, Mao claimed, were leading China down a capitalist road which was slowing down the revolution (his opponents therefore became known as the 'capitalist roaders'). He, however, wanted to go down the Communist road. Whilst the policies of the moderates produced steady growth between 1960-66, Mao planned his comeback. In 1963 he published his *Little Red Book* (see p.235) and launched the **Learn from the PLA campaign** - an attempt to spread Maoist ideas through the army. Then, in 1966, he launched the Great Proletarian Cultural Revolution.

On 16 July 1966, accompanied by several hundred young people, Mao (aged 72) swam 14 km down the River Yangzi, proving that he was physically fit. This swim attracted a great deal of media attention and signalled Mao's return to power.

2 The launch of the Great Proletarian Cultural Revolution

In the spring of 1966, Mao called on all young people in China to rebel against the non-Communist behaviour of older people. He appealed to young people because they had no revolutionary experience (they were too young to remember the CCP's struggle to win power) and because he felt they were being brought up to accept inequality and to obey orders far too easily. According to the historian P. Bailey, what Mao wanted was 'nothing less than a total transformation of people's thought and behaviour'. He wanted a clean break with the past and a complete change in attitudes. That is why the term 'Cultural Revolution' is used. Using the slogan 'to rebel is justified', Mao encouraged young people to take to the streets in demonstrations and to criticise anything that was old, traditional or Western. In June 1966, schools and colleges were closed down and students encouraged to join the Red Guards (see p.233). At the same time, buildings and walls were plastered with **big character posters** - posters which promoted Mao's ideas (see right).

In May 1966, a student, Nie Yuanzi, put up a poster criticising Beijing University for banning student demonstrations. Mao had this poster printed in the 'People's Daily' newspaper and encouraged people to put up posters criticising people in positions of power. The photo (right) shows students reading posters criticising Liu Shaoqui in February 1967.

Red Guards

Red Guards were groups of Maoists (mainly students) who organised themselves in military-style units to spread Mao's ideas and to root out opponents. Mao encouraged the growth of the Red Guard movement and provided Red Guards with free travel passes so that they could travel round the country. Between August and November 1966, Red Guards attended huge rallies in Beijing. At these rallies Mao urged them to attack both the 'capitalist roaders' and the **four olds** - old ideas, old culture, old customs and old habits. The result was a campaign of violence. Red Guards took the law into their own hands. They bullied and sometimes tortured and killed people whom, they claimed, were opponents of Mao. They prevented shops from selling Western clothes or music and banned the sale of alcohol, perfume and antiques. By 1967, China seemed on the verge of civil war.

Red Guards force suspected counter-revolutionaries to wear dunce's hats. Bullying of this sort was common in the Cultural Revolution.

The cult of the personality

During the Cultural Revolution no criticism of Mao was tolerated. By 1967, the moderates who had ruled China in the early 1960s were either in prison or in disgrace (Liu Shaoqui died in prison in 1969. Deng Xiaoping survived to take over the leadership of China after Mao's death). As opposition to Mao was removed, worship of him reached new heights. Mao's *Little Red Book* became a bible that people carried with them at all times. It became commonplace to see groups of people sitting in circles, waving the book in the air and chanting slogans from it. Pictures of Mao decorated every street and public building (see right) and, in many houses, the painting of Mao became a holy shrine (many families chanted a morning and evening prayer in front of it, for example). Although, later, Mao claimed that his Defence Minister, Lin Biao, had encouraged Mao worship in order to advance his own position, Mao himself did nothing to discourage it.

Pupils at Beijing middle school during the Cultural Revolution. Note the huge poster of Mao.

 ## The end of the Cultural Revolution

By 1967, Mao's position in power was secure but there was a very real danger that the process was running out of control and could even result in civil war. Indeed, in the Spring of 1967, rival groups of Red Guards had even begun to fight each other in a fanatical effort to prove which group was the most loyal to Maoist thought. Starting in the Summer of 1967, Mao began to take measures to end the disorder. Schools and colleges were reopened and the PLA was ordered to disarm Red Guards. Many thousands of Red Guards were rounded up and sent to the countryside to work amongst the peasants (around 18 million in all). New Revolutionary Committees, dominated by members of the army, were then set up to supervise them. Some disruption and violence continued in 1968, but order had been restored by 1969 and in that year Mao announced that the Cultural Revolution was officially over. Whilst historians agree that the Cultural Revolution was an important episode in Chinese history, Box 12.13 shows that there are many views about why it took place.

Box 12.13 **Different interpretations of the Cultural Revolution**

The Cultural Revolution was a movement like many other movements in Chinese history - for example, the Fourth of May movement (see p.220).

The Cultural Revolution was a power struggle between Mao and his 'moderate' opponents.

The Cultural Revolution was a genuine attempt to regain the momentum of the revolution.

The Cultural Revolution was designed as a warning to both superpowers to keep out of Chinese affairs. It was both anti-Western and anti-Soviet.

Mao knew he was nearing the end of his life and wished to achieve a kind of immortality. Therefore, he used the Cultural Revolution to encourage a cult of personality.

Activity
The impact of the Cultural Revolution

Source A   *A historian's account*

On 18 August, a million Red Guards were brought to a rally at Beijing's huge Tiananmen Square. At dawn, Mao appeared to a tumultuous welcome and mingled with the delirious students for six hours. A middle school girl pinned a Red Guard armband on him, causing the participants to shout: 'Chairman Mao is our supreme commander and we are his little soldiers.' Next day, red ink headlines breathlessly recounted the spectacle to the entire nation. Until cold weather prevented it, millions more were brought to the capital. The last rally in November 1966 reportedly numbered 2.5 million. Never since 1949 had China's youth tasted such excitement. Praised by their government as 'courageous and daring path-breakers', excited by adventure and idealism and delivered from school work, they descended on Beijing. Additional hordes, with government permission and free passage, jammed railways to travel and 'exchange experiences' with youths from other regions. They wore a green PLA uniform, a wide leather belt and, most important, a bright red armband with the words 'Red Guard' sewn in yellow. Some changed their names to more revolutionary ones. They sang 'The Great Helmsman' and danced the Loyalty Dance to Chairman Mao. They always carried their *Little Red Book* and some committed to memory every word of its 270 pages.

From 'People's China' by C. Dietrich, 1994

Source B   *An eyewitness account*

It was a time of terror. Every night we heard loud knocks, things breaking and children crying. We knew the Red Guards would one day come to our house. At 11 pm one night the knocks finally came, loud and sharp. There were seven or eight Red Guards, all men or boys, wearing white cloths over their mouths and noses and dark clothes. Their leader carried a whip. He struck it against the table with a loud crack. 'Liang Shan', he said, 'is there anything capitalist or anti-Communist in your house?' Father stammered 'No, no. I had some pictures of Liu Shaoqui, but I turned them in. Nothing else.' 'Pig!', the man hit the table again. 'What you must understand is that this is a revolutionary action. Right?', he said, 'You welcome it, don't you? Say it.' My father didn't answer. Two Red Guards took him by each arm and grabbed his head, pushing so he was forced to kneel down. They shook him by his hair so his glasses fell off. The others were already starting to go through our things. Then one of them cried out that he had found two Western-style ties and a Western-style jacket. 'What's the meaning of this?' 'Ties', my father mumbled. They kicked him. 'Ties! Do you think we are children? These are capitalist ties.' Father tried to say something. The whip slammed down on his hand. From the other room came two Red Guards with armfuls of books. They dumped them on the floor - old Chinese poetry and history books - and burned them there. Everything we owned was in a mess on the floor. The next day we found they had also taken all of father's money.

Account written by Liang Heng (who later became a famous author). He was 12 years old when the raid on his house took place in 1966.

Source C   *Mao and the Red Guards*

This photo shows Mao surrounded by Red Guards in 1966.

Source D   *Red Guards*

Red Guards exercising during the Cultural Revolution.

QUESTIONS

1. Judging from the information in this section, why did the Cultural Revolution begin and what were its aims?

2. Judging from Sources A-D how did the Cultural Revolution affect life in China?

3. What do Sources B-D tell us about the nature of the Cultural Revolution?

4. 'Government propaganda'. Is this a good description of Source C? Explain your answer.

SOURCE WORK

Chairman Mao's *Little Red Book*

Central to the Cultural Revolution was the publication of *Quotations from Chairman Mao Zedong*, better known as the *Little Red Book*. This is a collection of extracts from Mao's speeches and articles first published in its small red plastic-bound format in 1963. It is important to note that the *Little Red Book* contains very little material written after 1959. Indeed, most of the extracts had been written before the CCP won power in 1949. The book therefore contains the ideas of Mao the revolutionary rather than Mao the ruler. The book was first published for distribution to soldiers during the Learn from the PLA campaign of 1963. This campaign encouraged people to look at the army as a model of good Communist living and to copy their way of life. Every soldier was given a free copy of the *Little Red Book*. Then, as the Cultural Revolution gained momentum, the *Little Red Book* became a kind of bible to the Red Guards. Waving the *Little Red Book* at meetings and rallies became a way of showing approval and loyalty. Quoting from the book became a way of justifying a particular course of political action. Before long, almost every Chinese citizen (and many people abroad) had read the book. Indeed, the book's extraordinary influence on the minds of so many millions of people is probably unparalleled in history.

Chinese soldiers read Mao's 'Little Red Book' in 1971.

The *Little Red Book* in the 1970s

Mao's *Little Red Book* is the number one best seller in the world today. Nobody knows how many million copies have been put into circulation. The book is now available in every country in the world except the Soviet Union. As a result, the thought of Chairman Mao, at the present moment, is influencing more individuals than any other single human document. This alone should be enough to persuade us to read the ideas, philosophy, dreams, ambitions and projects for the future which are contained in this small book. We Americans are not likely to be won over by Mao's philosophy. But, if we value our future in the world and our influence, especially in Asia, it is important to understand the nature of the appeal of Maoism. We should remember that words do move worlds. Most philosophies had their origin in Asia. Most of them have seemed as strange and alien as Mao's. But this has not kept them from spreading from country to country. One observation on the nature of Mao's ideas. They are directed essentially to a primitive peasant people to whom the world of the industrial revolution is only now beginning to unfold. They are rooted in Mao's version of the theory of Karl Marx. Many of the passages are directed towards military questions. This is because, for most of Mao's life, he has faced military problems - first, the problem of how to win power and then the problem of keeping power in a very hostile world.

This passage appeared on the back of a record sleeve produced in 1973. The record contained extracts from the 'Little Red Book' spoken in English by an actor. The passage on the record sleeve was written by the American Harrison E. Salisbury.

QUESTIONS

1. **Why is the 'Little Red Book' such an important source for historians?**

2. **Why do you think the 'Little Red Book' was published?**

3. **'Central to the Cultural Revolution was the publication of the 'Little Red Book'. Explain this statement using the evidence on this page and in the previous section.**

4. **What does the evidence on this page tell us about the nature of Communist rule in China?**

235

Index